Punishment and Modern Society

Studies in Crime and Justice

DAVID GARLAND

PUNISHMENT AND MODERN SOCIETY

A STUDY IN SOCIAL THEORY

THE UNIVERSITY OF CHICAGO PRESS

The University of Chicago Press, Chicago 60637
Oxford University Press, Oxford
© 1990 David Garland
All rights reserved. Published 1990
Paperback edition 1993
Printed in the United States of America
99 98 97 96 95 94 93   5 4 3 2

Library of Congress Cataloging-in-Publication Data

Garland, David.
    Punishment and modern society : a study in social theory / David
    Garland.
        p.   cm. — (Studies in crime and justice)
    Includes bibliographical references.
    ISBN 0-226-28380-1 (cloth)
    ISBN 0-226-28382-8 (paperback)
    1. Punishment.   I. Title.   II. Series.
HV8675.G37   1990
364.6—dc20   90-6987
                                                                CIP

♾ The paper used in this publication meets the minimum requirements of the
American National Standard for Information Sciences—Permanence of Paper
for Printed Library Materials, ANSI Z39.48-1984.

Contents

For Anne

Acknowledgements

I consider myself exceptionally fortunate in having enjoyed the intellectual stimulation and support of three excellent institutions in the space of the last five years, and I am glad to have an opportunity to say so. A fellowship at Princeton University's Davis Center for Historical Studies in 1984–5 provided me with a year in which to develop my ideas, in the company of historians who saw social theory and history as mutually enlivening disciplines and who encouraged me to do the same. A semester's teaching in the spring of 1988 on the Jurisprudence and Social Policy program at the University of California, Berkeley, allowed me to rehearse the book's arguments amidst a community of like-minded scholars and to benefit from their thinking about the social foundations of law. Both these institutions helped enormously in the production of the present book and I am grateful to them for this and much besides. Above all, though, I owe thanks to my friends and colleagues at the Centre for Criminology and the Social and Philosophical Study of Law, here in Edinburgh. Their constant encouragement and criticism, together with the free exchange of ideas and argument which characterizes the Centre, make it one of the liveliest and most rewarding settings in which to do work of this kind.

I would also like to thank a number of individuals who took the trouble to read the entire draft manuscript, and whose extensive criticisms and commentaries have done much to enhance the quality of what is offered here. Beverley Brown, Stanley Cohen, Richard Ericson, James B. Jacobs, Sheldon Messinger, and Peter Young helped in this way, as did two unnamed publisher's readers, and I am grateful to them all. Lydia Lawson also deserves special thanks for the speed and alacrity with which she typed and revised the manuscript.

Finally, and as always, I am grateful to Anne Jowett for her help and encouragement, and it is a particular pleasure to dedicate this book to her.

The editors of the *British Journal of Sociology* and the *ABF Research Journal* have kindly allowed material, first published in these journals, to be reproduced in Chapters 2, 6 and 7 of the present book in a slightly revised form.

D.G.

Introduction

The punishment of offenders is a peculiarly unsettling and dismaying aspect of social life. As a social policy it is a continual disappointment, seeming always to fail in its ambitions and to be undercut by crises and contradictions of one sort or another. As a moral or political issue it provokes intemperate emotions, deeply conflicting interests, and intractable disagreements. This book is written in the belief that punishment puzzles us and disappoints our expectations because we have tried to convert a deeply social issue into a technical task for specialist institutions. It argues that the social meaning of punishment is badly understood and needs to be explored if we are to discover ways of punishing which better accord with our social ideals. To this end it constructs what is, in effect, a sociology of legal punishment, drawing upon the work of social theorists and historians who have tried to explain punishment's historical foundations, its social role, and its cultural significance.

The book is thus an argument *for* the social approach to punishment as well as an exposition of it. It begins by showing how the institutional framework of modern penology tends to narrow our perceptions of the phenomenon and obscure the social ramifications of punishment. By way of a remedy to this, the interpretative approach of the sociology of punishment is introduced and its main principles are described. A major part of the book is a critical exposition of the most important theoretical perspectives in this field and a development of the arguments which they have to offer. It thus serves as a textbook of sorts, and my aim in this respect has been to present these ideas lucidly and forcibly in a form which avoids simplification but is nonetheless accessible to non-specialists. In a field which is becoming rich in individual case-studies but lacks much in the way of sustained general writing, this presentation of other people's work entails a greater than usual duty of care, and I have sought to be faithful to the arguments of the original works even where these views diverge markedly from my own. I have also taken care to separate exposition from critique, so that readers should be able to disagree with me and still learn from the book.

As will quickly become apparent, the present study seeks not just to present the sociology of punishment in a coherent form, but also to develop that discipline by expanding its explanatory range and deepening its interpretative power. To this end I endeavour to open up new lines of enquiry and to explore areas of the subject which have largely been passed over by other writers, particularly regarding the psychological attitudes which underpin punishment and the cultural frameworks in which it exists. This concern with the nature of punishment's social support and its cultural significance is a deliberate attempt to shift the sociology of punishment away from its recent tendency—engendered by Foucault and the Marxists—to view the penal system more or less exclusively as an apparatus of power and control, and to recognise that criminal laws and penal institutions usually encapsulate moral values and sensibilities that are widely shared—even if the older Durkheimian tradition overstates the extent to which this is true. To set out matters in this way is not to deny for one moment the obvious and overwhelming fact that punishment revolves around the exercise of power and control: rather it is to ask just what kind of power is involved, what are its social meanings, the sources of its authority, the basis of its social support?

Running throughout the book there is also a cumulative argument for the necessity of a multidimensional interpretative approach which sees punishment as an overdetermined, multifaceted social institution. This conception is set out fully in the concluding chapter, where its theoretical and practical implications are discussed. To some extent this represents a challenge—or at least a small provocation—to other practitioners in this field of study, since it insists that the frameworks with which they work are often partial and limiting and that a more pluralistic approach is required. This argument for an analytical pluralism will no doubt surprise some readers and strike others as perfectly obvious, but it seems to me that there is a real danger of singular—and hence reductionist—interpretations coming to dominate in this field, and the whole animus of the present work is directed against such an outcome.

One other cumulative argument which runs through this work—this time directed at non-specialists—should perhaps be made explicit here in case I have failed to make it fully apparent in the pages that follow. It seems to me that the analyses and interpretations which are presented in this study go some way towards demonstrating the inherent depth and complexity of punishment as a social institution and ought, therefore, to suggest the value of regarding punishment as a central object of social theory. Such a suggestion, for sociologists at least, inevitably echoes the arguments of Émile Durkheim— who took punishment to be an index of society's invisible moral bonds, and hence a privileged object of social investigation—and will evoke a certain scepticism because of this. But in contrast to Durkheim, my argument will not be that punishment is uniquely expressive or somehow in touch with the heart of things—whatever that might mean. Instead my point is simply that, in common with other social institutions, punishment displays a complexity of function and a richness of meaning sufficient to challenge sociological understanding and to repay social analysis. Studied with sufficient care and attention, it is a form of life which can yield a surprisingly rich crop of insights and illuminations about the society in which it takes place and about the people whom it involves.

If I am right in this, and if this book suggests how such a case might be made out, then punishment should in future be seen not as a specialist topic of interest only to criminologists, but as a complex social institution, worthy of the attention of more mainstream sociology.

1

The Sociology of Punishment and Punishment Today

1. The Problem of Punishment Today

The aim of this book is simple. It sets out to provide a rounded sociological account of punishment in modern society, showing—at least in outline—how penal processes come to exist in their present form and with what kinds of consequences. To this end it employs the interpretative tools of social theory and the information and insights produced by historical studies, together with materials which are more properly penological.[1]

Such a straightforward project inevitably entails some presumptions which are not quite so straightforward. Most importantly, it presumes that juridical punishment is not the transparent and rather self-evident institution of crime control that it is commonly taken to be. Were this the case, a study of this kind would be rather unnecessary, there being little need to restate the obvious. But in fact punishment's role in modern society is not at all obvious or well known. Punishment today is a deeply problematic and barely understood aspect of social life, the rationale for which is by no means clear. That it is not always perceived as such is a consequence of the obscuring and reassuring effect of established institutions, rather than the transparent rationality of penal practices themselves.

Like all habitual patterns of social action, the structures of modern punishment have created a sense of their own inevitability and of the necessary rightness of the status quo. Our taken-for-granted ways of punishing have relieved us of the need for thinking deeply about punishment and what little thinking we are left to do is guided along certain narrowly formulated channels.[2] Thus we are led to discuss penal policy in ways which assume the current institutional framework, rather than question it—as when we consider how best to run prisons, organize probation, or enforce fines, rather than question why these measures are used in the first place. The institutions of punishment conveniently provide us with ready-made answers for the questions which crime in society would otherwise evoke. They tell us what criminality is and how it will be sanctioned, how much punishment is appropriate and what emotions can be expressed, who is entitled to punish and wherein lies their authority to do so. In consequence, these difficult and troublesome questions no longer arise. They are authoritatively settled, at least in principle, and only matters of detail

---

[1] My analyses draw primarily upon materials concerning Britain, the USA, and Canada. I do not, however, mean to imply that specific penal developments can always be explained in the same way in these different places, or that precisely the same penal policies and patterns of deployment are common to all of them.

[2] On the question how institutions guide our thinking, see M. Douglas, *How Institutions Think* (Syracuse, NY, 1986), p. 69.

need to be concluded—details which can be left to experts and administrators in specialist institutions set aside for that purpose.

Once a complex field of problems, needs, and conflicts is built over by an institutional framework in this way, these problematic and often unstable foundations disappear from view. In their place all that is immediately visible are the categories and forms of action which the established institution holds out to us. Through repeated use and respect for their authority, these instituted ways of doing things create their own 'regime of truth' which simultaneously shores up the institutional structure and closes off any fundamental questions which might undermine it. The penal system's very existence helps us to forget that other answers to these problems are possible: that institutions are based upon convention rather than nature. For all these reasons, and for most of the twentieth century, the institutions of punishment have normally been surrounded by a sense of their own appropriateness and transparency. Questions about punishment became a matter for penologists —technical experts whose frame of reference was given by this institutional structure.

But institutions and their regimes are not unshakeable nor beyond challenge, particularly where they fail to serve needs, contain conflicts, or answer troublesome questions in a way that is perceived as satisfactory. And, despite their institutional girding and a historical entrenchment stretching back to the early nineteenth century, a growing sense of doubt, dissatisfaction, and sheer puzzlement has now begun to emerge around our modern penal practices. The contemporary period is one in which penological optimism has given way to a persistent scepticism about the rationality and efficacy of modern penal institutions.[3] This shift of attitude began to emerge towards the end of the 1960s when rising crime rates, growing prison unrest, and a collapse of faith in the rehabilitative ideal combined to undermine confidence in 'penal progress' and the inevitability of 'penal reform'. The new era has been one of continuing crisis and disruption in a penal system which no longer takes seriously the rehabilitative values and ideologies upon which it was originally based. Within this context it is becoming the conventional wisdom of criminologists, penologists, and social scientists that contemporary methods—particularly that of imprisonment—appear increasingly to be 'irrational', 'dysfunctional', and downright counter-productive. Like the crime it is supposed to deal with, punishment is nowadays seen as a chronic social problem. It has become one of the most perplexing and perpetual 'crises' of modern social life, replete with intractable difficulties and disturbing results, and currently lacking any clear programme which could facilitate its reform.

The most celebrated discussion of punishment's 'failure' is to be found in the

---

[3] Perhaps what is most in need of explanation is the persistence, since the Enlightenment, of the belief that punishment can work as a positive force for the good of the offender and for society, despite the recurring disappointments and sobering experiences of practitioners throughout this whole period. I will return to this question in ch. 8.

work of Michel Foucault, who argued that penological failure has been a persistent—and indeed a 'functional'—characteristic of the modern prison ever since its inception. But the same presumption of failure appears in numerous other less avant-garde texts, including the work of the historian Lawrence Stone, one of Foucault's sternest critics. Stone takes it as simply uncontroversial to characterize twentieth-century prisons as 'vestigial institutions' which are 'even less useful for system maintenance than an appendix in an individual'. According to this view, which is shared by many, twentieth-century prisons survive 'simply because they have taken on a quasi-independent life of their own, which enables them to survive the overwhelming evidence of their social dysfunction'.[4] And it is not just the prison that is problematic: the contemporary intuition that 'nothing works' extends with only slightly less force to probation, fines, and community corrections.

As explanations of punishment, Foucault's latent-functions approach and Stone's dead-weight-of-history suggestion raise more problems than they solve—as I will try to show in the chapters which follow. But the point of mentioning them here is to indicate the growing conviction among social scientists that the methods of modern punishment are neither obvious nor self-evidently rational; that, on the contrary, they stand in serious need of explication. Where once penal institutions appeared to offer a self-evident rationale, in the late twentieth century they increasingly come to seem less obviously appropriate. Their 'fit' with the social world and their grounding in the natural order of things begin to appear less and less convincing. It used to be that most criticism of punishment's failures and irrationalities was aimed at the past or at the soon-to-disappear present. Each critique was also, in its hope for penal reform, a kind of hymn to the future. Nowadays, punishment appears to lack a future—or at least a vision of one which might be different and preferable to that which currently prevails.[5]

Part of the problem is what Stone calls 'the overwhelming evidence of . . . social dysfunction'—the by now well-known catalogue of punishment's inefficiencies (the failure of fines, probation, community corrections, and custodial measures alike substantially to reduce crime rates, the tendency of prison to create recidivists, the high social costs of penologically ineffective measures) and all the apparent irrationalities which seem to be the stock-in-trade of criminal justice. But these 'failures' can only partly explain why punishment seems increasingly problematic. In normal circumstances an established institution can finesse its failures. It can explain them away in terms which do not call into question the foundations of the organization—such as the need for more resources, minor reforms, better staff, more co-operation from other

[4] L. Stone, *The Past and the Present Revisited* (London, 1987), p. 10. On the 'failure' of punishments, see also S. Cohen, *Visions of Social Control* (Cambridge, 1985), p. 254, and D. Rothman, 'Prisons: The Failure Model', *Nation* (21 Dec. 1974), p. 647.
[5] On the crisis of penal ideology, see A. E. Bottoms and R. H. Preston (eds.), *The Coming Penal Crisis* (Edinburgh, 1980), and F. Allen, *The Decline of the Rehabilitative Ideal* (New Haven, 1981).

agencies, and so on. Most importantly, it can normally point to a future programme in which these problems will be better managed and the institution will reform itself. All social institutions have a margin of failure or ineffectiveness, but in normal circumstances this will be more or less tolerated without calling the institution itself into question. If the institution is meeting normal expectations and if its overall direction and basic legitimacy are unchallenged, then such failures are of no great consequence.

But in the case of modern punishments—whether custodial or non-custodial —a self-confidence in the established principles and an ability to redefine problems in institutional terms are currently lacking. Throughout the 1970s and 1980s the penal institutions of the United Kingdom, the United States of America, and many other Western nations have experienced a crisis of self-definition. In normal circumstances the administrators and employees of any penal system understand and justify their own actions within an established ideological framework—a working ideology. This official ideology is the set of categories, signs, and symbols through which punishment represents itself to itself and to others. Usually this ideology provides a highly developed rhetorical resource which can be used to give names, justifications, and a measure of coherence to the vast jumble of things that are done in the name of penal policy. Not the least of its uses is to supply the means to explain (or explain away) failures and to indicate the strategies which will, it is hoped, prevent their recurrence. For much of the present century, the term 'rehabilitation' was a key element of official ideology and institutional rhetoric. This all-inclusive sign provided a sense of purpose and justification for penal practice and made punishment appear meaningful for its various audiences. Today, however, this unifying and uplifting term is no longer the talismanic reference-point it once was. Following a sustained critique, the notion of rehabilitation has come to seem problematic at best, dangerous and unworkable at worst. In many jurisdictions the term—and the framework which it implies—has been struck from the official vocabulary. Elsewhere it is used cautiously and without confidence, in the absence of any effective substitute. Penal institutions have thus been deprived of the idiom, and indeed the mythology, around which modern punishment had anchored its self-definition.[6] For nearly two decades now those employed in prisons, probation, and penal administration have been engaged in an unsuccessful search to find a 'new philosophy' or a new 'rationale' for punishment. They have been forced to rethink what it is they do, and to reopen foundational questions about the justifications and purposes of penal sanctions, without so far having found a suitable set of terms upon which to rebuild an institutional identity.[7]

---

[6] It is worth adding that the normalizing apparatus of enquiry, individualization, and classification which was developed in the treatment era has not been dismantled along with the abandonment of the ideal. On this, see Cohen, *Visions of Social Control.*

[7] Numerous proposals for a new penal policy framework have emerged during the last two

If this were merely a matter of official rhetoric, or of the precise form which penal objectives should take, then we might expect a solution to be more readily available. Penal policy is, after all, a rich and flexible tradition which has always contained within itself a number of competing themes and elements, principles and counter-principles. Thus, over the last century and a half, its key terms have been developing and fluid rather than fixed, producing a series of descriptions—'moral reform', 'training', 'treatment', 'correction', 'rehabilitation', 'deterrence', 'incapacitation'—for what it is that penal sanctions do. But what seems to have come into question now, after the acknowledged failure of the most developed form of correctionalism, and in a period when Enlightenment social engineering has become deeply unfashionable, is a basic principle of modern punishment—namely the presumption that crime and deviance are social problems for which there can be a technical institutional solution. Indeed it is highly significant that the slogan which most marked this crisis of penal confidence was the phrase 'Nothing Works'—a statement which clearly conveys the instrumental means-to-an-end conception of punishment which marks the modern era.[8] Ever since the development of prisons in the early nineteenth century, and particularly since the emergence of a penological profession later in that century, there has been an implicit claim—and eventually a public expectation—that the task of punishing and controlling deviants could be handled in a positive way by a technical apparatus. It seems to me that this basic claim has now been put in question.

The question that arises today is not one of institutional adjustment and reform. It is a more basic question which asks whether the social processes and ramifications of punishment can be contained within specialist institutions of any kind. This is, in a sense, a crisis of penological modernism. It is a scepticism about a penal project that is as old as the Enlightenment with its vision of punishment as one more means of engineering the good society, of organizing institutions so as to perfect mankind. After more than two centuries

decades, the most important of them being the 'justice model' of sentencing, the 'humane containment' conception of imprisonment, and a conception of probation and community supervision as 'help' and 'support' rather than treatment. See N. Morris, *The Future of Imprisonment* (Chicago, 1974); A. von Hirsch, *Doing Justice* (New York, 1976); R. King and R. Morgan, *The Future of the Prison System* (Aldershot, 1980); and A. E. Bottoms and W. McWilliams, 'A Non-Treatment Paradigm for Probation Practice', *British Journal of Social Work*, 9 (1979), 159–202. Other proposals include 'selective incapacitation', a modified version of rehabilitation, and a 'minimalist' or even 'abolitionist' approach to criminal justice. See P. Greenwood, *Selective Incapacitation* (Santa Monica, 1982); F. T. Cullen and K. E. Gilbert, *Re-affirming Rehabilitation* (Cincinatti, 1982); N. Christie, *Limits to Pain* (Oxford, 1982), and H. Bianchi and R. van Swaaningen (eds.), *Abolitionism: Towards a Non-Repressive Approach to Crime* (Amsterdam, 1986).

[8] The slogan refers to the celebrated article by Martinson which surveyed the treatment research literature and reached a largely negative conclusion about the general efficacy of treatment programmes in penal settings. See R. Martinson, 'What Works?—Questions and Answers about Prison Reform', *The Public Interest*, 35 (1974). For a similarly negative evaluation of the British evidence, see S. R. Brody, 'The Effectiveness of Sentencing', *Home Office Research Unit Study*, 35 (London, 1976).

of rational optimism, even our 'experts' have begun to recognize the limits of social engineering and the dark side of social order. Our engineered world is facing its imperfections and is less optimistic, less confident. In the penal debates of the 1980s, we hear again, for the first time in almost two centuries, the re-emergence of basic moral and organizational questions. Lacking a new vocabulary, and dissatisfied with the modern institution's own terms, much of this discussion has looked back to the period immediately before the modern penal era. Contemporary proponents of 'the justice model' or of 'general deterrence' have revived the liberal discourse of eighteenth-century juris-prudence, raising basic questions about the right to punish, the limits on state power, the responsibility and dignity of the offender, the nature of criminality, the depiction of human nature, and so on. There have also been important attempts to reintroduce questions which had previously been silenced by institutional operations, such as the role of the victim, or the responsibilities of the community in causing and preventing criminality. Notably too, there has been a re-emergence of moral arguments that claim that punitive (as opposed to correctional) measures can be a proper and defensible form of reaction to crime, a form of thinking which has been markedly absent from most twentieth-century penal discourse.

These newly revived forms of thinking about punishment are significant, not because they represent solutions to the current malaise, but because they indicate the extent of it. In returning to the consideration of basic moral and political questions, these discussions indicate the fading of our penal institutions' ability to naturalize their practices and depict the world in their terms. Questions about the meaning of punishment do not, these days, get immediately translated into the established terms of an institutional ideology. They are instead perceived as troublesome and unsettled. And of course in these circumstances, such questions begin to emerge with more and more frequency.

It is not, then, only social scientists who are nowadays led to doubt the grounding and rationale of modern modes of punishment. The very staff of the criminal justice institutions are themselves increasingly perplexed as to what they are about. Consequently, it is not an idle or an 'academic' question that is being pursued when we seek to understand the foundations, forms, and effects of penal measures as they exist today. It is, on the contrary, a pressing practical issue.

Like all books, then, this one is a product of its times and circumstances. The past two decades have been years in which we seem to have come up against the limits of a certain way of thinking and acting in the field of punishment. Like many others, I have been led to reflect upon the roots of penal policy, and its social ramifications, instead of getting on with the job of improving and refining it. Indeed, at a time when penology was marked by sadly diminishing returns, this reflection upon fundamentals has been the abiding fascination of an otherwise narrow and unsettling field of study. The last 10 years or so have seen a sudden take-off in the number of studies in the history and sociology of punishment, no doubt because these forms of research are strongly drawn towards areas which appear currently to be problematic or undergoing transition. Indeed this new work on the foundations of punishment is in marked contrast to what went on before. In the mid-1950s, at the height of the correctional era in the USA, Donald Cressey asked why the sociology of punishment was such a neglected area of study—particularly, he might have added, given the landmark contributions of earlier writers such as Montesquieu, De Tocqueville and Durkheim.[9] Thirty years later and with the benefit of hindsight we can answer that in these years a technical penology, working within the institutions, was able to dominate the field and to limit the range of questions which appeared appropriate or worth while. It was a period of 'normal science', operating in circumstances where the axioms and problems had been authoritatively stated, and all that remained was to work out the details and fine-tune the institutional machinery. Now, however, when penologists have lost faith in the institutional project and have become critical and self-reflective, they are beginning once again to reassess the axioms upon which punishment is based. In this task, social theory and history prove more useful than penology, and increasingly these are the forms of enquiry which are being brought to bear.

Faced with the kinds of problems which I have described, one response would be to turn once again to the issue of justification and re-examine the normative arguments supplied by the philosophy of punishment. This, indeed, has been the course adopted by many writers in this field who feel that a careful reading of moral philosophy—usually of a liberal variety—can somehow supply the guidelines for a new and more acceptable programme of penal policy.[10] But in my view, there are reasons why such a project is both premature and misdirected. It seems to me that at present we lack a detailed appreciation of the nature of punishment, of its character as a social institution, and of its role in social life. The philosophies of punishment, at least in their traditional form, are based upon a rather idealized and one-dimensional image of punishment: an image which poses the problem of punishment as a variant of the classic liberal conundrum of how the state should relate to the individual.[11] But if, as I suspect, this image is an impoverished one, and fails to capture the full dimensions and complexities of punishment, then the solutions offered by philosophy are unlikely to match up to the problems of the institution. What is needed now is really a preliminary to philosophy—a descriptive prolegomenon which sets out the social foundations of punishment, its characteristic modern forms, and its social significance. Only on this basis

---

[9] D. R. Cressey, 'Hypotheses in the Sociology of Punishment', *Sociology and Social Research*, 39 (1955), 394–400.

[10] See e.g. von Hirsch, *Doing Justice* (New York, 1976) and P. Bean, *Punishment* (Oxford, 1981).

[11] On the connections between the philosophy of punishment and the political philosophy of liberalism, see N. Lacey, *State Punishment* (London, 1988). On the deficiencies of the current philosophical approaches to punishment, see D. Garland, 'Philosophical Argument and Ideological Effect', *Contemporary Crises*, 7 (1983), 79–85.

can philosophies be developed which adequately address the normative problems of this complex institution. Quite simply, we need to know what punishment is in order to think what it can and should be.

2. THE SOCIOLOGY OF PUNISHMENT

The present study is thus conceived as a work in the sociology of punishment or, more precisely, in the sociology of criminal law, criminal justice, and penal sanctioning.[12] Moving from the premiss that penal phenomena in modern society are problematic and badly understood, it seeks to explore the penal realm in all its different aspects, reopening basic questions about punishment's social foundations, seeking to chart its functions and its effects. Its ultimate aim is to uncover the structures of social action and the webs of cultural meaning within which modern punishment actually operates, thereby providing a proper descriptive basis for normative judgments about penal policy.

I take the sociology of punishment, broadly conceived, to be that body of thought which explores the relations between punishment and society, its purpose being to understand punishment as a social phenomenon and thus trace its role in social life. Being concerned with punishment and penal institutions, it shares its central subject-matter with 'penology', but is distinguishable from the latter by virtue of its wider parameters of study. Whereas penology situates itself within penal institutions and seeks to attain a knowledge of their internal 'penological' functioning (throughout the nineteenth century 'penology' was a synonym for 'penitentiary science'), the sociology of punishment views the institutions from the outside, as it were, and seeks to understand their role as one distinctive set of social processes situated within a wider social network.

Writings which take this latter, sociological, form have existed since at least the mid-eighteenth century—emerging then, as now, at a time when the established institutions of punishment were coming under critical attack. In *The Spirit of the Laws*, Montesquieu pointed to the connections of structure and of belief which tied forms of punishing to forms of governing in a distinctive and revealing way: 'It would be an easy matter', he wrote, 'to prove that in all, or almost all, of the governments of Europe, punishments have increased or diminished in proportion as these governments favoured or discouraged liberty.'[13] From there he went on to sketch in outline the political and

---

[12] Unfortunately we currently lack any widely used generic term which usefully describes the whole process of criminalizing and penalizing with which I intend to deal. In previous works I have adopted the term 'penality' to refer to the complex of laws, processes, discourses, and institutions which are involved in this sphere, and I will use it throughout the present study as a synonym for legal punishment in this broad sense. In some contemporary literature, the term 'social control' has come to be used in a similar way, see Cohen, *Visions of Social Control*, p. 3. I have, however, avoided this usage because 'social control' usually refers to a much wider range of practices, and also because, as we will see, I wish to argue that 'punishment' should not be thought of purely in terms of 'control'.

[13] Baron de Montesquieu, *The Spirit of the Laws* (Edinburgh, 1762), p. 88.

psychological dynamics which produce these connections, thus giving a sociological as well as a normative quality to his conclusion that 'the severity of punishment is fitter for despotic governments, whose principle is terror, than for a monarchy or republic, whose spring is honour and virtue'.[14] Almost a century later, Alexis de Tocqueville continued in this vein, though his study of the American penitentiary system suggested a more complex and ironic link between political liberalism and penal discipline. Pointing to an irony which would be rediscovered by subsequent writers such as Rothman and Foucault, he wrote in the 1830s that 'while society in the United States gives the example of the most extended liberty, the prisons of the same country offer the spectacle of the most complete despotism'.[15] In his subsequent study of *Democracy in America*, de Tocqueville would build upon this social insight afforded by punishment to show the subtle dialectic of freedom and restraint which operated within American society as a whole. These connecting insights, showing how punishment forms part of a wider culture, shaping and being shaped by it, have been the continuing hallmark of work of this kind. Indeed the issues posed by Montesquieu and de Tocqueville continue to be discussed and researched today.[16]

Despite these suggestive early works, however, the sociology of punishment has not become a well-developed area of social thought. With the partial exception of institutional studies of imprisonment, where a strong sociological research tradition has been founded,[17] the corpus of works is disparate and uneven in quality, and lacks any settled research agenda which can command widespread assent and promote a sense of collective endeavour. Instead what one finds is a series of disjointed and unconnected studies, emanating from a diverse range of projects and intellectual traditions, and adopting quite different angles of approach to the study of punishment. Within this series of studies there are works of the highest intellectual calibre—like those of Émile Durkheim, Michel Foucault, or George Herbert Mead—and also other important studies by authors such as Rusche and Kirchheimer, Michael Ignatieff and Douglas Hay, all of which have provoked follow-up studies, criticism, and a fairly large secondary literature. But despite the fact that these studies all take punishment as their object and offer sociological explanations and characterizations of penal phenomena, they do not by any means form a coherent body of research. On the contrary, the sociology of punishment is presently constituted by a diverse variety of 'perspectives', each of which tends

[14] Ibid.

[15] G. de Beaumont and A. de Tocqueville, *On the Penitentiary System in the United States* (Philadelphia, 1833), p. 47.

[16] See e.g. T. L. Dunn, *Democracy and Punishment: Disciplinary Origins of the United States* (Madison, 1987).

[17] See D. Clemmer, *The Prison Community* (New York, 1940); R. Cloward *et al.*, *Theoretical Studies in Social Organisation of the Prison* (New York, 1960); G. Sykes, *The Society of Captives* (Princeton, 1958); T. Morris and P. Morris, *Pentonville* (London, 1963); J. B. Jacobs, *Stateville: The Penitentiary in Mass Society* (Chicago, 1977); E. Goffman, *Asylums* (Garden City, NY, 1961).

to develop its researches in virtual disregard of other ways of proceeding. In effect, the sociology of punishment is reinvented with each subsequent study, so that on each occasion we are presented with a new conception of the phenomena to be studied and the proper questions to be posed.

To some extent this clash of perspectives and absence of a settled paradigm is an endemic characteristic of all sociology, and has to do with the incorrigibly 'interpreted' nature of its object. But there are also a number of reasons why this situation seems particularly aggravated in the sociology of punishment. In the first place, punishment—unlike other areas of social life such as religion, industry, or the family—has not been the site of intensive sociological enquiry, and has not been subjected to the rationalizing processes of discipline formation that modern scholarship normally entails. There are as yet no established textbooks or course descriptions which pattern the conduct of study in this field, or situate particular studies within an overarching discipline. Related to this is the fact that many of the leading studies in this area have been undertaken as aspects of a larger and different intellectual project, rather than as contributions to the sociology of punishment itself. For both Durkheim and Foucault, for example, punishment serves as a key with which to unlock a larger cultural text such as the nature of social solidarity or the disciplinary character of Western reason. Their concern has not been to help develop a comprehensive understanding of punishment—and although they do in fact contribute to such an understanding, this has been a by-product of their work rather than its central purpose. Few of the major authors in this field have conceived of themselves as partaking in a joint project or sharing a basic set of concerns and so there is little attempt to promote integration or synthesis. There has also been a tendency for different perspectives to be viewed—or to view themselves—as being in complete conflict with one another. This sense of incompatibility most often emerges where specific analyses of punishment are derived from global social theories—such as Marxism, or Durkheimian functionalism—which are, quite properly, viewed as being competing meta-conceptions of society and its dynamics. Moreover, in the clash between one perspective and another, analytical differences often take on an ideological inflection as well—making communication between perspectives that much less likely.

To some extent these different approaches do indeed represent serious and unbridgeable disagreements about the character of the social world and the place of punishment within it. No amount of scholarly co-operation will efface the fact that sociology's objects are essentially contested and open to competing interpretations. But as things stand in the sociology of punishment, it is not at all clear where the key disagreements lie, or indeed to what extent different perspectives are in fact complementary rather than being in competition, at least at some levels of analysis. Two points are worth making in this respect— one about the nature of theory, and the other about levels of analysis.

It is, at present, possible to point to at least four distinctive theoretical perspectives within the sociology of punishment, three of them already established, and a fourth which is in the process of emerging. The Durkheimian tradition stresses punishment's moral and social–psychological roots as well as its putative solidarity-producing effects. Marxist studies highlight punishment's role in what it takes to be class-based processes of social and economic regulation. Michel Foucault's work has argued that disciplinary punishments operate as power–knowledge mechanisms within wider strategies of domination and subjectification, while the work of Norbert Elias has prompted writers such as Spierenburg to situate punishment within an analysis of changing sensibilities and cultural mentalities. None of these interpretative perspectives is absurd or without merit. They each make serious claims for our attention because they each have something important to say about their object of study. Moreover, as even this brief characterization suggests, they are each concerned to bring into view different aspects of what turns out to be a rather complex set of penal phenomena. Each of them has a capacity to make visible particular aspects of a possibly complicated and many-sided reality and connect these aspects to wider social processes. Each mode of enquiry sets up a particular image of punishment, defining it in a particular way, highlighting some of the aspects, while inevitably obscuring or neglecting others.

If we treat these interpretations as representing a variety of perspectives—each one employing a different angle of approach and a shifting focus of attention—then there is no in-principle reason why they should not be brought together to help us understand a complex object in its various aspects and relations. However it is all too common for questions of interpretation—which are capable of multiple answers—to be understood as questions of ontology or of causal priority, in which case only a singular response will suffice. Once this occurs, and we assume that all theories are attempts to answer the questions 'what is the essential nature of punishment?' or 'what is *the* cause of punishment?' then we are always forced to choose between one or the other theoretical account. The result is an approach which tends to be needlessly reductionist and one-dimensional in its understanding.[18]

My point is simply that if we avoid this philosophical essentialism, then it is not clear that such choices are always necessary. Theories are conceptual means of interpreting and explicating information. They come into competition only when they offer alternative and incompatible explanations for the same data. Since one theory effectively supersedes another only when it explains the same range of data and problems more plausibly, it is by no means clear how the various theories of punishment stand in relation to each other. Indeed, in the sociology of punishment, theories have not been superseded so much as passed over in preference for other lines of questioning.

[18] As William Gass puts it, 'when we try to think philosophically about any human activity, we tend to single out one aspect as the explanatory center, crown it, and make every other element into a courtier, mistress, or servant'. W. Gass, 'Painting as an Art', *New York Review of Books*, 35: 15 (13 Oct. 1988), p. 48.

The point I wish to make about levels of analysis is rather similar. It is certainly the case that grand social theories such as those developed by Marx, Durkheim, or Elias give incompatible accounts of the central dynamics of social life. (Foucault's work is incompatible for the different reason that it denies the validity of theories pitched at this global level.) If it were the case that the analyses of punishment which derive from these various traditions were no more than miniaturizations of the larger global theories then all the incompatibilities would be reproduced at this more detailed level. But this in fact is not the case. Specific analyses which are launched from within a certain set of axioms will tend to ask distinctive questions, and focus upon particular aspects of the phenomenon under study, in accordance with the dictates of the general theory. But the findings produced in this way will not be mere reproductions of the global social theory—unless, of course, we are dealing with deductive dogmatics, in which case the theory is not being 'applied' but merely repeated.

Concrete spheres of social life, such as punishment are never exact microcosms of the social structures depicted by general theory. Outside Leibnizian philosophy—in which every monadic element is an essential expression of the whole—each particular sector of society can be assumed to display its own peculiar mechanisms and dynamics. And so, in any process of theoretical interpretation which is open to empirical information, the concrete character of the phenomenon should help determine the analytical results as much as the set of axioms which launched the enquiry. This being the case, the specific findings of any theory brought to bear upon punishment may or may not be compatible with others produced from within a different interpretative perspective. The question of their relationship is always an empirical one, and is not settled in advance. Thus, for example, Marxist analyses may discover ways in which penal practice reinforces class divisions and ruling-class dominance, and Durkheimian studies may point to other elements of the penal process which appear to express sentiments or reinforce solidarities which are not class based. Unless one assumes that penal practice is all of a piece, with a single, unitary meaning—that it is all a matter of class, or all a matter of cross-class solidarity—there is no reason to reject either analysis out of hand. Instead what is required is a more subtle, in-depth analysis which examines how these two aspects seem to coexist within the complex set of practices which make up the penal realm. In the pages which follow, I will attempt to explore such issues and see to what extent a more comprehensive sociology can be constructed out of the specific interpretations which currently exist.

If, then, we are committed to a comprehensive examination of the structures and meanings of punishment in modern society, there appears to be no ready-to-hand general framework within the sociology of punishment which will allow us to pursue this enquiry. Instead we find a range of interpretative traditions, each one projecting a slightly different image of punishment and its connection with the rest of the social world, and each one bearing an as-yet-indeterminate relationship to the others. Given this situation, the best strategy appears to be one which is inclusive and open to synthesis, at least in the first instance. My intention is therefore to work through each of the existing theoretical traditions in turn, treating each tradition not as a rigid model or comprehensive account, but as a source of specific perspectives and partial interpretations. My method will be to identify and pursue the distinctive questions that each one poses and to examine what they have to say about the foundations, functions, and effects of punishment, and how this helps us understand punishment today. This will go beyond mere exposition, not least because much of the theory of punishment lies buried within detailed historical narratives, or else exists in a rudimentary form which needs to be worked up and refined. Moreover, I will frequently press arguments and lines of analysis beyond their original scope and sketch out new modes of interpretation wherever the established theories appear inadequate. The aim of this approach is to bring to light as many facets of punishment as possible, and also to bring the different interpretations into conversation with one another, so that their differences can be precisely specified and their complementary aspects can be shown as such. The outcome, it is hoped, will be a balanced synopsis of what the sociology of punishment has to offer, and a suggestion of how these ideas help us to understand the nature of punishment today.

The sociological accounts of punishment that we currently possess have each isolated and abstracted a particular aspect or facet of punishment and have provided powerful analyses based upon this. But although such interpretations can often be brilliantly illuminating and insightful, they are also prone to be partial and somewhat one-sided. One symptom of this is the tendency of historians of punishment, seeking to convey a rounded sense of the institution as it is operated at a particular time and place, to write *against* such theories, showing their monolithic interpretations to be incomplete at best, and completely untenable at worst. But the real point of their complaint is not that historians do not need theory. It is that theories which are too narrow in compass simply act as an obstacle to understanding and need to be replaced by better theories which will be more adequate to their task. A measure of abstraction is a necessary first step in the analysis of any complex phenomenon, and it is not unusual for a field of knowledge in its early stages of development to be characterized by competing abstractions and monocausal forms of explanation. But the ultimate objective of research must be to return to the concrete, to integrate and synthesize different abstractions in a way that simulates the overdetermination of real-world objects and approximates their complex wholeness. It seems to me that the sociology of punishment is now reaching that stage of maturity where it should be striving for integrated, pluralistic interpretations—interpretations which can come closer to accounting for the complexity and variegated detail which both historians and contemporary penologists repeatedly encounter.[19]

[19] Such an endeavour will not settle, once and for all, interpretative disputes, but it ought to

The present project then, is an attempt to extend and synthesize the range of interpretative material that currently forms the sociology of punishment, and to build up a more complete picture of how punishment might be understood in modern society. The writings of Foucault, Marx, Durkheim, or Elias excel in the tenacious, dogged pursuit of an explanatory theme—making a wilful attempt to drive a mode of thinking as far as it will go. As a means of discovery, or a way of producing new interpretative insight, this method can hardly be bettered, though, as we have seen, a kind of peripheral, contextual blindness is sometimes the price of this intensely focused vision. In the present study, however, different methods and values come to the fore. Its concern is to be balanced and perspicacious, synthesizing and comprehensive, and in so doing it will necessarily qualify the claims of these theorists, and suggest the limitations of their accounts. But it should perhaps be stressed that this book is not about the limitations of other theorists. It is about the constructive enterprise that their single-minded theorizing has made possible.

3. Punishment as an object of study

Having discussed the various interpretative stances adopted towards punishment, it is perhaps time to say something about punishment itself. The first point to note here is that 'punishment', despite this singular generic noun, is not a singular kind of entity. Indeed it seems likely that some of the variation of interpretative results which one finds in the sociology of punishment has to do with the nature of the thing analysed, rather than with the analytical process brought to bear upon it. We need to remind ourselves, again and again, that the phenomenon which we refer to, too simply, as 'punishment', is in fact a complex set of interlinked processes and institutions, rather than a uniform object or event. On close inspection, it becomes apparent that the different interpretative perspectives have tended to focus in upon quite different aspects or stages of this multifaceted process. Thus when Pashukanis discusses the ideological forms of the criminal law, Durkheim focuses upon condemnatory rituals, Foucault shifts attention to institutional routines, and Spierenburg points to the sensibilities involved, each of them is, in effect, moving back and forth between different phases of the penal process, rather than producing different interpretations of the same thing. Unfortunately though, such differences of focus have often been disguised by a lack of analytical specificity and by the failure of individual theorists to place their own work in the context of other interpretations. Given the synthesizing concerns of this study, it is important that it begins by discussing this question in some detail, and that in subsequent

focus them more precisely and make them more productive. As Clifford Geertz says of cultural anthropology, it 'is a science whose progress is marked less by a perfection of consensus than by a refinement of debate. What gets better is the precision with which we vex each other.' C. Geertz, 'Thick Description: Toward an Interpretive Theory of Culture', in id. *The Interpretation of Cultures* (New York, 1973), p. 29.

analyses it avoids this tendency to discuss 'punishment' as if it were all of a piece.

An observation made by Friedrich Nietzsche can serve to orient our discussion.

I would say that in a very late culture such as our present-day European culture the notion 'punishment' has not one but a great many meanings. The whole history of punishment and of its adaptation to the most various uses has finally crystallized into a kind of complex which it is difficult to break down and quite impossible to define. . . . All terms which semiotically condense a whole process elude definition; only that which has no history can be defined.[20]

Punishment, then, is not reducible to a single meaning or a single purpose. It is not susceptible to a logical or formulaic definition (as some philosophers of punishment would have it) because it is a social institution embodying and 'condensing' a range of purposes and a stored-up depth of historical meaning. To understand 'punishment' at a particular time, as Nietzsche says, one has to explore its many dynamics and forces and build up a complex picture of the circuits of meaning and action within which it currently functions. This is precisely what the present study aims to do. But if such an investigation is to be undertaken, then clearly some parameters or co-ordinates of study have to be outlined—not as a substitute for empirical enquiry but as a guide to it. It is in this sense, and with this purpose, that I offer the following identification of my object of study.

Punishment is taken here to be the legal process whereby violators of the criminal law are condemned and sanctioned in accordance with specified legal categories and procedures. This process is itself complex and differentiated, being composed of the interlinked processes of law-making, conviction, sentencing, and the administration of penalties. It involves discursive frameworks of authority and condemnation, ritual procedures of imposing punishment, a repertoire of penal sanctions, institutions and agencies for the enforcement of sanctions and a rhetoric of symbols, figures, and images by means of which the penal process is represented to its various audiences. Two things should follow from this fact of internal differentiation. The first is that discussions of 'punishment' can have a whole range of possible referents which are all properly part of this institutional complex. The second is that the penal process is likely to exhibit internal conflicts and ambiguities, stemming from its fragmented character. As noted above, I have tried to capture this sense of internal complexity by proposing the generic term 'penality' to refer to the network of laws, processes, discourses, representations and institutions which make up the penal realm, and I will use this term as a more precise synonym for 'punishment' in its wider sense.

This focus upon the legal punishment of criminal law offenders means that although punishment also takes place outside the legal system—in schools,

---

[20] F. Nietzsche, *The Genealogy of Morals* (New York, 1956), p. 212.

families, workplaces, military establishments, and so on—these forms of punitive practice will largely be left out of the present study. Punishment in some form or other is probably an intrinsic property of all settled forms of association and there is much to be learned from viewing punishment in these various social settings. Despite being derivative in a certain sense—in that all penal domains in modern society depend upon the delegation of authority from the sovereign legal order—these forms have their own specificity and are not mere imitations of state punishments. They will, however, be considered here only where their discussion can further our understanding of the legal order of punishment and not as a topic in themselves.[21] Nor will this study concentrate upon the non-legal but often routine forms of punishment which occur in modern criminal justice—for example, the informal rituals of humiliation involved in some police work or the implicit penalties involved in the prosecution process—since my primary concern will be those punishments which are authorized by law.[22] This may appear to be a serious exclusion, since the informal actions of police, prosecutors, and state officials clearly play a large role in crime-control and constitute an important aspect of state power. However, my concern here is to understand legal punishment and its social foundations, not to chart the repertoire of deterrents that are in use, nor to trace all of the forms in which state power is exercised through the criminal justice apparatus.

The location of state punishment within a specifically legal order gives punishment certain distinctive characteristics which are not a feature of punishments in other social settings. For example, the sovereign claims of the law give legal punishments an obligatory, imperative, and ultimate nature which are unmet with elsewhere. Similarly, the forms of law, its categories, and principles are important in shaping penal discourses and procedures—as we will see when we discuss the work of Pashukanis in Chapter 5—though it should be stressed that penal institutions such as the prison are sometimes legally authorized to adopt procedures which fall far short of the normal juridical standards, for example, on due process in disciplinary hearings. Location within a legal order, then, is one determinant of punishment's forms and functions, but is by no means the only determinant involved.

Although legal punishment is understood to have a variety of aims, its primary purpose is usually represented as being the instrumental one of reducing or containing rates of criminal behaviour. It is thus possible to conceive of punishment as being simply a means to a given end—to think of it as a legally approved method designed to facilitate the task of crime control. Nor is this an uncommon or particularly inadequate perception of punishment.

---

[21] For an attempt to study punishment in a wider compass, looking at its use in areas other than the criminal law, see C. Harding and R. W. Ireland, *Punishment: Rhetoric, Rule and Practice* (London, 1989). Also A. Freiberg, 'Reconceptualizing Sanctions', *Criminology*, 25 (1987), 223–55.

[22] See on this M. Feeley, *The Process is the Punishment* (Beverly Hills, 1979), and J. Skolnick, *Justice Without Trial* (New York, 1966).

Crime control is indeed a determinant of penal practice and this ends–means conception is widely adopted both by penologists and by philosophers of punishment. This instrumental, punishment-as-crime-control conception has, however, been unattractive to sociologists of punishment. These sociologists have usually perceived a sense in which punishment's significance or social function runs beyond the narrow realm of crime control, and they consider such an instrumentalist conception to be an unjustified narrowing of the field of study. Indeed, in some instances, certain theorists have gone so far as to deny punishment's crime-control function altogether, arguing that penality is not well adapted to this particular end, and that therefore some other end must be posited to explain its character. The most celebrated instance of this is Émile Durkheim's declaration that 'if crime is not pathological then the purpose of punishment cannot be to cure it', but similar positions are adopted by writers such as Mead, Rusche and Kirchheimer, and, more recently, Michel Foucault. Each of these writers points to the 'failure' of punishment as a method of crime control and argues that it is badly adapted to this end, before going on to discuss alternative ways of understanding the phenomenon.

In a sense, this kind of approach is liberating for anyone who wishes to think about punishment, since it frees us from the need to think of punishment in 'penological' terms and opens up the question of penality's other social functions. There are, however, serious problems with such a position, despite its obvious attractions. For one thing, it continues to think of punishment as a means to an end: if not now the end of 'crime control' then some alternative telos, such as social solidarity (Durkheim) or political domination (Foucault). But this 'purposive' or teleological conception of a social institution makes for bad sociology. Not only is it quite possible, as Nietzsche points out, for a single, historically developed institution to condense a whole series of separate ends and purposes within its sphere of operation. It is also the case that institutions are never fully explicable purely in terms of their 'purposes'. Institutions like the prison, or the fine, or the guillotine, are social artefacts, embodying and regenerating wider cultural categories as well as being means to serve particular penological ends. Punishment is not wholly explicable in terms of its purposes because no social artefact can be explained in this way. Like architecture or diet or clothing or table manners, punishment has an instrumental purpose, but also a cultural style and an historical tradition, and a dependence upon 'institutional, technical and discursive conditions'.[23] If we are to understand such artefacts we have to think of them as social and cultural entities whose meanings can only be unravelled by careful analysis and detailed examination. As in all spheres of life, a specific need may call forth a technical response, but a

---

[23] The quotation is from P. Q. Hirst, *Law, Socialism and Democracy* (London, 1986), p. 152, where Hirst argues that '. . . means of punishment are *artefacts of social organization*, the products of definite institutional, technical and discursive conditions in the same way as other artefacts like technologies or built environments. Artefacts can be explained not by their individual "purpose" alone but by the ensemble of conditions under which such constructions or forms become possible.'

whole process of historical and cultural production goes into the shaping of that 'technique'.

The need to control crime in its various forms, and to respond to the depredations of law-breakers is thus only one of the factors which helps shape the institutions of penality. It is, no doubt, an important one, and it would make little sense, for example, to analyse US penal policy without bearing in mind the levels of crime experienced in the USA, and the social and political consequences which follow from this. But even if one could disentangle 'real' crime rates from the processes of policing, criminalizing, and punishing (through which we generate most of our knowledge of crime—and at least some of its actuality), it is clear enough that criminal conduct does not determine the kind of penal action that a society adopts. For one thing, it is not 'crime' or even criminological knowledge about crime which most affects policy decisions, but rather the ways in which 'the crime problem' is officially perceived and the political positions to which these perceptions give rise. For another, the specific forms of policing, trial, and punishment, the severity of sanctions and the frequency of their use, institutional regimes, and frameworks of condemnation are all fixed by social convention and tradition rather than by the contours of criminality. Thus to the extent that penal systems adapt their practices to the problems of crime control, they do so in ways which are heavily mediated by independent considerations such as cultural conventions, economic resources, institutional dynamics, and political arguments.[24]

Thinking of punishment as a social artefact serving a variety of purposes and premised upon an ensemble of social forces thus allows us to consider punishment in sociological terms without dismissing its penological purposes and effects. It avoids the absurdity of thinking about punishment as if it had nothing to do with crime, without falling into the trap of thinking of it solely in crime-control terms. We can thus accept that punishment is indeed oriented towards the control of crime—and so partly determined by that orientation—but insist that it has other determinants and other dynamics which have to be considered if punishment is to be fully understood.

Punishment, then, is a delimited legal process, but its existence and operation are dependent upon a wide array of other social forces and conditions. These conditioning circumstances take a variety of forms—some of which have been explicated by historical and sociological work in this field. Thus, for example, modern prisons presuppose definite architectural forms, security devices, disciplinary technologies, and developed regimes which organize time and space—as well as the social means to finance, construct, and administer such

---

[24] For a discussion of research attempts to isolate the impact of crime rates upon penal policies, see W. Young, 'Influences Upon the Use of Imprisonment: A Review of the Literature', *The Howard Journal*, 25 (1986), 125–36. D. Downes, in his comparative study of penal policies in The Netherlands and England and Wales, shows that in a period when both countries experienced rising crime rates, England and Wales resorted to a policy of increased imprisonment while The Netherlands effected a substantial decarceration. D. Downes, *Contrasts in Tolerance* (Oxford, 1988).

complex organizations.[25] And as recent work has shown, specific forms of punishment are also dependent for their support upon less obvious social and historical circumstances including political discourses and specific forms of knowledge,[26] legal, moral, and cultural categories,[27] and specific patterns of psychic organization or sensibility.[28] Punishment may be a legal institution, administered by state functionaries, but it is necessarily grounded in wider patterns of knowing, feeling, and acting, and it depends upon these social roots and supports for its continuing legitimacy and operation. It is also grounded in history, for, like all social institutions, modern punishment is a historical outcome which is only imperfectly adapted to its current situation. It is a product of tradition as much as present policy: hence the need for a developmental as well as a functional perspective in the understanding of penal institutions. It is only by viewing punishment against the background of these wider forms of life and their history that we can begin to understand the informal logic which underpins penal practice. In consequence, we should be prepared to find that this 'logic' is the social logic of a complex institution built upon an ensemble of conflicting and co-ordinating forces, rather than the purely instrumental logic of a technical means adapted to a given end.

The outline definition I have just provided, or something very like it, is the unstated point of departure for most sociological analyses of punishment. Different interpretative traditions take up different aspects of the phenomenon, and devote themselves to filling in the substantive content of one or other of the connections and relationships that I have sketched out in formal terms. My own discussion begins with the presumption that these various interpretations are not necessarily incompatible in every respect. Indeed, given the complexity of the social institution of penality, it is likely that what currently appear to be conflicts of interpretation may turn out to be more or less accurate characterizations of an institution which is itself 'conflicted'. By working through these various perspectives, measuring the worth of their arguments, and applying their interpretations to the contemporary scene, I intend to build up a more comprehensive and recognizable picture of the field of penality and its social supports. Wherever the existing interpretative perspectives fail to address aspects of punishment which I take to be important, I will endeavour to generate my own interpretations, drawing upon the work of other social theorists where necessary. Similarly, I will not feel constrained to discuss at length interpretative positions which appear in the literature but which I judge to be inadequate or inaccurate. My primary aim is to understand the

---

[25] See M. Foucault, *Discipline and Punish* (London, 1977); R. Evans, *The Fabrication of Virtue* (Cambridge, 1982); and G. Rusche and O. Kirchheimer, *Punishment and Social Structure* (New York, 1939, 1968).

[26] Foucault, *Discipline and Punish*; D. Garland, *Punishment and Welfare* (Aldershot, 1985).

[27] J. Langbein, *Torture and the Law of Proof* (Chicago, 1976); J. Bender, *Imagining the Penitentiary* (Chicago, 1987).

[28] P. Spierenburg, *The Spectacle of Suffering* (Cambridge, 1984); D. Garland, 'The Punitive Mentality: Its Socio-Historical Development and Decline', *Contemporary Crises*, 10 (1986), 305–20.

reality of punishment, not to offer a full account of the literature which has grown up around it.

One final point should be made before embarking upon this enterprise. Much of the sociology of punishment proceeds as if the key questions always concerned the social and historical determinants of punishment, asking 'how are penal measures shaped by their social and historical context?' This, it seems to me, is only half the story. In the present book I will be concerned to emphasize the ways in which penality shapes its social environment as much as the reverse. Penal sanctions or institutions are not simply dependent variables at the end of some finite line of social causation. Like all social institutions, punishment interacts with its environment, forming part of the mutually constructing configuration of elements which make up the social world. All the classic sociological writings—from Durkheim to Foucault—are clear about this, and this dialectic will be emphasized throughout the present work. This, indeed, is one of the reasons why the sociological study of punishment is so potentially valuable. It tells us how we react to disorderly persons and threats to the social order—but also, and more importantly, it can reveal some of the ways in which personal and social order come to be constructed in the first place.

2

Punishment and Social Solidarity
The Work of Émile Durkheim

Émile Durkheim's legacy to the sociology of punishment is an ambiguous one. On the one hand, Durkheim did more than anyone else to develop a sociological account of punishment and to emphasize the social importance of penal institutions. On the other hand, many of his interpretations appear flawed in important respects and, recently at least, have been pushed aside by more critical accounts of the phenomena. My intention in this chapter and the next is to rework the Durkheimian legacy, showing that despite its faults it has important insights to offer. I will be arguing that despite the limitations of Durkheim's theory and the conceptual vocabulary in which it is phrased, his work nevertheless opens up perspectives and indicates connections which can help us come to terms with the foundations of punishment and some of its social functions and meanings. My discussion of Durkheim's work is thus undertaken not as an end in itself but as a first step towards the construction of a more adequate framework for the analysis of penality.

1. AN INTRODUCTION TO DURKHEIM'S SOCIOLOGY

More than any other social theorist, Durkheim took punishment to be a central object of sociological analysis and he accorded it a privileged place in his theoretical framework, returning to it again and again as his life's work progressed. This analytical concern with punishment came about because, for Durkheim, punishment was an institution which was connected to the very heart of society. Penal sanctioning represented for him a tangible example of the 'collective conscience' at work, in a process that both expressed and regenerated society's values. By analysing the forms and functions of punishment, the sociologist could gain systematic insights into the otherwise ineffable core of the moral life around which community and social solidarity were formed. Thus, in the processes and rituals of penality, Durkheim claimed to have found a key to the analysis of society itself.

Durkheim, of course, had a very specific conception of society and pursued a particular line of sociological enquiry. He was concerned, above all, to uncover the sources of social solidarity which were, for him, the fundamental conditions of collective life and social cohesion. For Durkheim, society and its patterned forms of mutual interaction can only function if there first exists a shared framework of meanings and moralities. Without such a framework, social life is inconceivable, as even the most elementary exchanges between individuals require an agreed set of norms within which they can take place. These social norms and 'collective representations' are not fortuitous or self-determining, but are instead an aspect of the forms of social organization and interaction which exist at any particular time. As Durkheim puts it at one point, 'the morality of each people is directly related to the social structure of the people practising it'.[1]

The culture and ethics of any society are thus grounded in a particular social organization, thereby forming a functioning social whole. Emergent patterns of social interaction give rise at the same time to shared classification on the part of those involved, so that the categories of conscience and consciousness are constructed in ways which accord with the realities of group life. These emergent categories in turn form the collective framework through which social life can routinely exist and through which individuals are bonded to each other and to society in a cohesive way. In Durkheim's conception, societies thus consist of material forms of life which are understood, sanctioned, and sanctified through the cultural categories to which they give rise. The moral (or mental) aspects and the social (or material) aspects of group life are seen as mutually conditioning and constitutive, and, in normal circumstances, they function together as different dimensions of a cohesive social whole.

It is this distinctive conception that makes Durkheim's work at once a social science and also a 'science of ethics'. His sociology is, above all, concerned with those distinctive moral bonds which for him constitute the truly social aspects of human life. His fundamental object of analysis is the relationship between social moralities and their conditions of existence. This also forms the basis of his 'holistic' approach to society, and his concern to understand aspects of social life in terms of their functional significance for the social whole. Finally, this conception of the moral and the social as two sides of the same coin allows Durkheim to take a particular social practice—such as punishment—and view it as a moral phenomenon operating within the circuits of the moral life, as well as carrying out more mundane social and penal functions.

Within this general understanding of society, Durkheim's more specific concern was to come to terms with the changing forms of solidarity which emerged as societies evolved and their basic structure and organization began to change. In particular, he sought to understand the sources of solidarity in modern societies where the rise of individualism, the specialization of social functions, and the decline of universal religious faith gave the impression of a world without shared categories. His interpretation of this modern situation differed profoundly from that of social conservatives who feared that society was destined to tear itself apart in the clash of individual interests, and who advocated a return to traditional forms of morality and religious faith. On the other hand, he also opposed the views of social utilitarians such as Herbert Spencer who argued that modern society could survive without need of any collective morality, since the untrammelled pursuit of private individual interest would itself produce collective welfare and stability. Against these views, Durkheim asserted that society did indeed require a moral framework,

---

[1] É. Durkheim, *Moral Education* (New York, 1973), p. 87.

but that its form and content had to reflect the current conditions of social organization. In large part, he claimed, the division of labour itself had already given rise to a suitable modern morality, centred around the cult of the individual and a cluster of associated values such as freedom, rationality, and tolerance. These moral conceptions had emerged hand in hand with the restructuring of society brought about by industrialization, specialization, and secularization and were already embodied in the thinking and action of individuals. In effect, modern society had begun to produce the morality it required, but it had not done so self-consciously, and further moral developments would be required before the new conditions of social life were fully reflected and made meaningful in the realm of social ethics.[2] The role of sociology was, in Durkheim's view, to produce this modern self-consciousness—to identify the forms of morality to which modern society gave rise, and to facilitate their full development. Its task was thus to identify the sources of social health and to show what action would be needed to promote the optimum functioning of the social organism.

Durkheim's view of society, including modern society, thus centres upon his conception of the moral order and its vital role in social life. He is concerned to show how this moral order functions to constitute individuals and their relationships, how it forms a symbolic centre around which solidarities are formed, and how it is itself transformed over time in keeping with the development of the social division of labour and the material conditions of group life. But the notion of a moral order is, of course, an abstraction—a generic term for a multitude of specific intuitions and categories shared by the members of a community. It is a 'social fact', but not one which can be directly observed or studied in a scientific mode. Consequently, Durkheim was forced to analyse this crucial moral entity indirectly, by reference to other, more tangible, social facts which bore its imprint and were most closely associated with it. In his later works, and in respect of simple societies, Durkheim would turn to religious rites and primitive classifications as a means of studying solidarity through the forms of its expression. But the 'visible index' which he adopted first of all, and which he found most valuable in the analysis of modern society was that of law, and in particular the kinds of *sanctions* which each law entailed.[3]

In his classic work, *The Division of Labour*, and again in several subsequent essays and lectures, Durkheim conceives of punishment as a straightforward embodiment of society's moral order, and an instance of how that order represents and sustains itself. We are thus presented with a detailed account of punishment's functioning and moral significance (in *The Division of Labour* and

---

[2] See É. Durkheim, *The Division of Labor in Society* (New York, 1933), p. 228.

[3] See Durkheim, *The Division of Labor*, p. 64. Durkheim argues that the penal sanctions characteristic of 'repressive law' are a manifestation of a strong *conscience collective* and mechanical solidarity. The non-penal sanctions of 'restitutive' law are, on the other hand, indicative of the organic solidarity associated with a developed division of labour.

again in *Moral Education*) as well as a lengthy discussion of the historical evolution of punishment and its connections with the evolution of social types (in 'The Two Laws of Penal Evolution'), all the time connecting the facts of penal practice to the essential constituents and processes of social life. Durkheim thus provides a full-scale sociological account of punishment as a kind of by-product of his concern to substantiate and elaborate his general social theory. Moreover, it is an account which is remarkable in a number of respects, not least in attributing to punishment a moral seriousness and a functional importance for society which far outweigh its contribution as a means of controlling crime.

This Durkheimian conception of punishment, at least in its simplest form, is well known in the sociological and penological literature. Nevertheless, it is rarely taken very seriously as a means of interpreting the forms of punishment in modern society. This is so for several reasons. First of all, Durkheim's account of punishment is clearly generated by his general social theory, and, in a number of important respects, is dependent upon it. This general theory is now widely acknowledged as being deeply problematic at key points, and dissatisfaction with this framework has led many to reject the Durkheimian approach to the study of punishment.[4] Secondly, Durkheim's discussion of punishment implies, and at one point explicitly presents, an evolutionary account of the history of penal law. Subsequent historical studies have shown Durkheim's penal history to be based upon inadequate and misleading data and to present a developmental pattern which is, at least in some respects, quite untenable. Finally, Durkheim's account of punishment seems, at least at first sight, to be more in keeping with 'primitive' than with modern societies. Much of the penological material which he uses is drawn from ancient or small-scale societies—he talks of aborigines, of the laws of Manou, of the ancient Hebrews—and his characterization of penal processes seems to be grounded within this pre-modern world. Thus, in his account, punishment is depicted as a group phenomenon of great intensity. It is supposedly propelled by irrational, emotive forces which sweep up society's members in a passion of moral outrage. Its procedures are depicted as ceremonial rituals with un-mistakeably religious overtones, undertaken to reaffirm group solidarities and restore the sacred moral order violated by the criminal. Diverting as these scenes may be to the modern reader, they seem to speak more to another world—perhaps a primitive 'anthropological' world—than to the realities of penal practice today. Faced with the mundane appearance of our very utilitarian, very bureaucratic, very professionalized, and very profane institutions of punishment, Durkheim's vision can seem altogether inappropriate.

All these considerations have tended to make Durkheim's interpretation of punishment well known but little used. And like all theories which survive in

---

[4] See e.g. my 'Durkheim's Theory of Punishment: A Critique' in D. Garland and P. Young (eds.), *The Power to Punish* (London, 1983), which is at pains to reject the Durkheimian framework, even though it stresses some positive aspects of Durkheim's work.

classroom textbooks rather than in research and serious discussion, this important interpretation has come to be more and more bowdlerized as time has gone on. The extensive discussion of Durkheim's work which I will present here is an attempt to recapture the subtleties and insights of his theory of punishment and to present them in ways which are relevant to an understanding of the present. As suggested in the previous chapter, my exploration of Durkheim's theory of punishment will assume that it is not entirely determined by his general social theory, so that aspects of the former will be able to survive the criticism aimed at the latter. My contention will be that Durkheim's questions about the moral basis of penal law, about the involvement of onlookers in the penal process, about the symbolic meanings of penal rituals, and about the relationship of penal institutions to public sentiment, are all questions which are worthy of our close attention, even when the answers which Durkheim suggests are not themselves convincing. I will also assume that Durkheim's theory is primarily an account of the motives, functions, and significance which attach to legal punishment rather than an account of its historical development. It is thus perfectly possible to reject his historical account while retaining important aspects of his theory. Finally, I will approach and evaluate Durkheim's interpretation of punishment not as a once-upon-a-time account but as a means of understanding punishment *today*, in modern society.

Certainly there are compelling reasons to doubt the immediate relevance of Durkheim's interpretation. We now live within a developed division of labour, and in a contested moral order where collective public ritual no longer has a very prominent place. 'Society' no longer punishes—if it ever did—but instead delegates this function to a state apparatus and to specialist institutions on society's margins. Emotive acts of vengeance have long since become taboo—at least in official conduct—and have been displaced by what appear to be rational processes of crime control; and so on. But these discrepancies form an interpretative challenge rather than a refutation; they show the work which has to be done if we are to think through Durkheim's theory to an understanding of its field of application. Durkheim was well aware of the differences between simple and advanced societies—his whole life's work was devoted to understanding such changes. And, in full awareness of these differences, he insisted that his interpretation of punishment was appropriate to modern societies as well as to primitive ones. His argument is that despite the appearance of modern punishment, and whatever the contrary intentions of its administrators, the elementary characteristics he identified in primitive societies still underpin our practice and give it its true meaning. Durkheim claims to be speaking to us and to our society, though like his contemporary Sigmund Freud, he is well aware that we will resist his propositions and find them strange.

In the pages which follow I will first give an exposition of the theory of punishment which is developed in Durkheim's work, and then later pursue in more detail the individual themes and elements which compose this overall account. The first, expository section which forms the rest of this chapter will endeavour to give an accurate paraphrasing of Durkheim's work, taking care to stick to the texts and trying to reconstitute their meaning. The chapter which follows on from this, though, will be much more exploratory, and will be concerned to think through Durkheim's questions and analyses, using the work of other theorists as well as contemporary material on punishment to explore their validity and relevance today.

Punishment is discussed at many points in Durkheim's work but there are three major texts which set out his theory at length: *The Division of Labour* (1895), 'Two Laws of Penal Evolution' (1902), and the university lectures which came to form *Moral Education* (1902–3). Although each of these texts comes at the problem from a slightly different angle, and each one develops and refines the theory in certain ways, the underlying essentials of the theory of punishment are consistently presented and unchanging throughout. Moreover, many of Durkheim's other texts—particularly *The Elementary Forms of the Religious Life* and *Primitive Classifications*—contain discussions (for example, of the nature of the sacred, of ritual practices, of collective representations) which illuminate while remaining consistent with the basic elements of his account of punishment. Wherever it seems helpful, I will use these later texts to explicate or enlarge upon Durkheim's earlier conceptions.

2. THE THEORY OF PUNISHMENT IN *THE DIVISION OF LABOUR*

The Division of Labour is Durkheim's masterpiece, in the original sense of that term. It is the early text which sets out the fundamental problems which will form his life's work and which provides the necessary intellectual tools for their analysis. In it, Durkheim's central concern is with the changing nature of social morality and social solidarity, and his extensive discussion of punishment is undertaken as a means of illuminating that larger problem.

Durkheim sees punishment as a social institution which is first and last a matter of morality and social solidarity. The existence of strong bonds of moral solidarity are the conditions which cause punishments to come about, and, in their turn, punishments result in the reaffirmation and strengthening of these same social bonds. Durkheim is, of course, aware that these moral aspects are not uppermost in our social experience of penal practice. Like most institutions, punishment is generally understood in terms of its mundane, instrumental tasks—the control of crime, the enforcement of law, the restraint of offenders, and so on. But then much of social morality is, for Durkheim, unspoken, latent, taken for granted. Indeed it is a characteristic of modern society that the moral bonds which tie individuals together are embodied within acts such as contracts, exchanges, or interdependencies which appear, on their surface, to be purely matters of rational self-interest. Durkheim's analysis of punishment —like his analysis of the division of labour itself—is thus a deliberate and counter-intuitive attempt to bring into view these submerged moralities and thereby to elucidate punishment's moral significance and moralizing social functions. As we have seen, Durkheim's concern in pointing to the moral content of instrumental action was to make this morality more self-conscious and thereby allow it to be better preserved and developed. It seemed to him that such a task was particularly urgent in the penal realm because, as Durkheim frequently mentions, many turn-of-the-century penologists were intent upon removing all traces of moral censure from penal law, and giving it a purely technical character as a form of treatment and rehabilitation.

How, then, are we to understand punishment as a moral form of social action? In what precise sense is punishment a cause and yet also an effect of social solidarity? Durkheim begins his discussion of punishment with an analysis of the crimes against which punishments are used. Crimes, as he points out, are not 'given' or 'natural' categories to which societies simply respond. The content of such categories changes from place to place and from time to time and is a product of social norms and conventions. Moreover, crimes are not always or everywhere equivalent to acts which are harmful to society, or contrary to the public interest. They are not, then, merely prohibitions made for the purpose of rational social defence. Instead, Durkheim argues that crimes are those acts which seriously violate a society's *conscience collective*.[5] They are essentially violations of the fundamental moral code which society holds sacred, and they provoke punishment for this reason. It is because criminal acts violate the sacred norms of the *conscience collective* that they produce a *punitive* reaction. Where social rules of a less fundamental nature are violated, the violators can be sanctioned by other means—for example by means of restitutive laws and regulatory sanctions. But crimes are, in effect, moral outrages which 'shock' all 'healthy consciences' and give rise to a demand for punishment rather than any lesser form of social reaction.[6]

So far, Durkheim has argued that it is the connection with sacred things and fundamental values which gives crime a grave moral significance and which necessitates a punitive response. At this stage, he pauses to qualify the argument in one important respect. He points out that while most criminal offences are recognizably violations of cherished moral values, there is also a class of criminal acts which do not strike all 'healthy consciences' as outrageous and yet are deemed criminal none the less. The crimes in question are offences against the state, which, he says 'are more severely repressed than they are

[5] Durkheim defines 'the *conscience collective* or *commune*' as 'the totality of beliefs and sentiments common to the average citizens of the same society [which] forms a determinate system which has its own life'. Durkheim, *The Division of Labor*, p. 79. For a discussion see S. Lukes, *Émile Durkheim: His Life and Work* (London, 1973), pp. 4–6, and also S. Lukes and A. Scull (eds.), *Durkheim and the Law* (Oxford, 1983), introd.

[6] Durkheim, *The Division of Labor*, p. 73. Durkheim here simply assumes the existence of criminal acts as a feature of society. In his book *The Rules of Sociological Method* (New York, 1938) he argues that acts which breach social norms will necessarily be a feature of any society. This is the famous 'crime is normal' argument, which links up with the one developed here.

strongly reproved by general opinion'.[7] The existence of such crimes seems to raise problems for Durkheim's theory, because it suggests that not all crimes are violations of the *conscience collective*. As he points out, the definition of such conduct as criminal and punishable might be thought of as being an act of the governmental power, operating independently of collective sentiments, thus denying the absolute bond which Durkheim posits between legal punishment and collective morality. However he resolves this difficulty by arguing that the state is, in effect, the guardian of the collective sentiments, whose 'primary and principal function is to create respect for the beliefs, traditions and collective practices: that is, to defend the common conscience against all enemies within and without'.[8] The state is thus conceived as a kind of secular priesthood, charged with protecting sacred values and keeping the faith. It becomes the 'symbol and living expression' of society's collective beliefs—'the collective type incarnate' so that offences against its powers are viewed as offences against the *conscience collective* itself.[9] The linkage between punishment and collective sentiments thus survives intact after all.

One must ask, however, why it is that violations of collective sentiments must always result in a punitive response. What causes crimes to be *punished* rather than dealt with in some other way? In making this step in the argument Durkheim provides a complex and intriguing discussion which touches upon the nature of sacred things, the psychology of moral outrage, and the social-psychological mechanisms which give force and authority to social conventions. We should therefore take some care to grasp precisely what he is saying. The starting-point for his discussion is the insistence that at least some criminal laws have the status not merely of conventions or regulations but of sacred prohibitions which command widespread assent: 'what gives penal law its peculiar character is the . . . extraordinary authority of the rules which it sanctions.'[10] According to Durkheim, the violation of sacred values always produces an outraged response. The criminal act violates sentiments and emotions which are deeply ingrained in most members of society—it shocks their healthy consciences—and this violation calls forth strong psychological reactions, even among those not directly involved. It provokes a sense of outrage, anger, indignation, and a passionate desire for vengeance.

So penal law rests, at least in part, upon a shared emotional reaction caused by the criminal's desecration of sacred things. But despite the importance of this point for Durkheim's theory, his psychological account of such reactions is actually fairly cursory. He stresses that our commitment to these collective values has the character of a deeply held religious attachment. They are 'strongly engraven' on our consciences, 'cherished', 'deeply felt'. They occupy a position of depth in our psychic organization, and are thus fundamental to who we are. Unlike abstract ideas, to which we attach ourselves on only a superficial level, and in which we can tolerate contradiction, these deeper

---

[7] Durkheim, *The Division of Labor*, p. 82.
[8] Ibid. 84.   [9] Ibid.   [10] Ibid. 141.

moral feelings have a force and importance which brooks no disagreement: '. . . when it is a question of a belief which is dear to us, we do not, and cannot, permit a contrary belief to rear its head with impunity. Every offence directed against it calls forth an emotional reaction, more or less violent, which turns against the offender.'[11]

Crimes are offences against society's sacred moral order which in turn corresponds to deeply held sentiments within society's individual members. Crimes are thus a violation of society's morality *and* a personally felt outrage against every 'healthy' individual. The result is a passionate, hostile reaction on the part of the public which demands the offender be punished. For Durkheim, then, 'passion . . . is the soul of punishment', and vengeance is the primary motivation which underpins punitive actions.[12]

In order to substantiate this contention, Durkheim turns to the actual penal practices of various societies, and shows how such vengeful passions manifest themselves. Less cultivated societies exhibit this trait clearly enough, he says, since they tend to 'punish for the sake of punishing' and 'without seeking any advantage for themselves from the suffering which they impose'.[13] In such societies, punishments continue, unlimited by other considerations, until all passion is spent, often pursuing the criminal beyond death itself or else spilling over on to the punishment of innocents such as the offender's family or neighbours. In modern societies, one has to look harder to see the operation of these vengeful passions in punitive action, since such emotions have been officially denied and displaced by more reflective, utilitarian concerns. Nowadays we claim that it 'is no longer wrath which governs repression, but a well premeditated foresight'.[14] But Durkheim insists that it is merely our understanding of punishment which has changed, not its reality: 'the nature of a practice does not change because the conscious intentions of those who apply it are modified. It might, in truth, still play the same role as before, but without being perceived.'[15] As proof of the continuing role of vengeance in modern punishment he points to our continuing retributive concern to make the punishment fit the crime, as well as to 'the language of the courts' which continues to express a strong concern with public denunciation.[16] Modern penal systems may try to achieve utilitarian objectives, and to conduct themselves rationally and unemotively, but at an underlying level there is still a vengeful, motivating passion which guides punishment and supplies its force. According to Durkheim, 'the nature of punishment has not been changed in essentials'. All that can be said is that

[11] Ibid. 97–8.
[12] Ibid. 86.
[13] Ibid. 85–6.
[14] For this passage I have used the new trans. by W. D. Hall, of *The Division of Labour* (London, 1984) quoted in Lukes and Scull (eds.), *Durkheim and the Law*, p. 60, in preference to the Simpson trans. to be found at p. 86 of *The Division of Labor* (New York, 1933). Elsewhere I rely upon the Simpson version.
[15] Durkheim, *The Division of Labor*, p. 87.   [16] Ibid. 88.

the need for vengeance is better directed today than heretofore. The spirit of foresight which has been aroused no longer leaves the field free for the blind action of passion. It contains it within certain limits; it is opposed to absurd violence, to unreasonable ravaging. More clarified, it expends less on chance. One no longer sees it turn against the innocent to satisfy itself. But it nevertheless remains the soul of penality.[17]

Thus for both modern and primitive societies, Durkheim presents a very forceful and distinctive interpretation of punishment. To think of punishment as a calculated instrument for the rational control of conduct is to miss its essential character, to mistake superficial form for true content. The essence of punishment is not rationality or instrumental control—though these ends are superimposed upon it—the essence of punishment is irrational, unthinking emotion fixed by a sense of the sacred and its violation. Passion lies at the heart of punishment. It is an emotional reaction which flares up at the violation of deeply cherished social sentiments. And although institutional routines will modify these accesses of rage, and strain to use them in a productive way, the dynamic and motivating force of punishment is emotional and unreflecting: it is an authentic act of outrage. The force and energy of punishment, and its general direction, thus spring from sentimental roots—from the psychic reactions commonly felt by individuals when sacred collective values are violated. So although the modern state has a near monopoly of penal violence and controls the administration of penalties, a much wider population feels itself to be involved in the process of punishment, and supplies the context of social support and valorization within which state punishment takes place.[18] Thus while some accounts of punishment see only two parties involved in punishment—the controllers and the controlled, Durkheim insists upon a crucial third element—the onlookers, whose outraged sentiments provide a motivating dynamic for the punitive response.

So far, Durkheim's account of punishment has been primarily motivational and psychological—though he does ground these psychic elements within a theory of sacred social values. It depicts punishment as an expressive institution —a realm for the expression of social values and the release of psychic energy. Strictly speaking, it has no 'objective' or 'intended goal'. It is not a means to an end. Punishment simply occurs in the nature of things. It is a collective reaction sparked off by the violation of powerful sentiments—like the sparks that fly when someone disturbs an electric current. But this much forms only half of Durkheim's account, for it is at this point that he moves to a fully sociological explanation and describes how these individual passions produce, in the aggregate, a more powerful and more useful social outcome.

[17] Durkheim, *The Division of Labor*, p. 90.
[18] Ibid. 102. 'As for the social character of this reaction, it comes from the social nature of the offended sentiments. Because they are found in all consciences, the infraction committed arouses in those who have evidence of it or who learn of its existence the same indignation. Everybody is attacked; consequently everybody opposes the attack.'

The passions provoked by crime are, in their immediate origin, the spontaneous reactions of individuals. But in being voiced collectively and at the same time, these reactions reinforce each other and give rise to an important social consequence. In effect, 'crime brings together upright consciences and concentrates them'.[19] It serves as an occasion for the collective expression of shared moral passions, and this collective expression serves to strengthen these same passions through mutual reinforcement and reassurance.[20] In effect, the social reality of the moral order is demonstrated by this collective, punitive response and is thereby further strengthened. The important point that Durkheim is making here is that the moral order of society—and hence its solidarity—rests entirely upon its sanctioning in social convention. When crimes occur which violate the norms of social life, these norms are weakened and shown to be less than universal in their binding force. The effect, however, of the upswelling of a collective passionate reaction to such crimes is to give a powerful demonstration of the real force which supports the norms, and thereby reaffirm them in the consciousness of individual members. This functional outcome effectively completes a virtuous circle set off by crime. The existence of a sacred moral order gives rise to individual sentiments and passionate reactions, which in turn demonstrate the existence and reinforce the strength of the sacred moral order. Crime and punishment, for Durkheim, are important in so far as they set this moral circuitry in motion.

So, having begun by emphasizing the emotional, expressive, non-utilitarian roots of punishment, Durkheim then introduces what one might call his paradox of higher utility. For he proceeds to argue that punishment does, after all, achieve a definite end or objective. But it is not the petty calculation of social controllers which makes punishment useful—these attempts rarely succeed in their control and reform ambitions. Instead it is the common expression of outrage that turns out to have a spontaneously functional effect. These outbursts of common sentiment—concentrated and organized in the rituals of punishment—produce an automatic solidarity, a spontaneous reaffirmation of mutual beliefs and relationships which serve to strengthen the social bond:

Although [punishment] proceeds from a quite mechanical reaction, from movements which are passionate and in great part non-reflective, it does play a useful rôle. Only this rôle is not where we ordinarily look for it. It does not serve, or else only serves quite secondarily, in correcting the culpable or in intimidating possible followers. From this point of view its efficacy is justly doubtful and, in any case, mediocre. Its true function is

---

[19] Ibid. 102.
[20] 'We have only to notice what happens, particularly in a small town, when some moral scandal has just been committed. They stop each other on the street, they visit each other, they seek to come together to talk of the event and to wax indignant in common. From all the similar impressions that are exchanged, from all the temper that gets itself expressed, there emerges a unique temper, more or less determinate according to the circumstances, which is everybody's without being anybody's in particular. This is the public temper.' Ibid. 102.

to maintain social cohesion intact, while maintaining all its vitality in the common conscience.[21]

Punishment then, like all moral phenomena (including human beings themselves), has a dualistic character.[22] It is at once a matter of individual psychic emotion and, at the same time, one of collective social morality. These two aspects coexist within a functional spiral which helps create and re-create social cohesion. This, for Durkheim, is the character of punishment in all societies—modern or primitive.

For the sake of balance, one ought to stress that punishment is by no means the sole process which contributes towards social cohesion—religious rituals, family life, education, economic exchange all have similar consequences. And it is also worth noting that solidarity-through-punishment is clearly more important in some societies than in others, as Durkheim himself points out.[23] It is the thesis of *The Division of Labour* that penal law, and the common conscience which it enforces, play a central role in the cohesion of simple societies—it is in fact the very basis of mechanical solidarity. In modern, organic society, on the other hand, the division of labour becomes the predominant source of solidarity—'the principal bond'—so that penal law and common values come to play a much reduced but none the less essential rôle.[24] In effect, the *conscience collective* of modern societies ceases to be a pervasive, intensive force which demands a religious conformity in every sphere of life. Instead it occupies a much shallower, but none the less important sphere operating as the guardian of those fundamental values (such as 'freedom' and 'individualism') around which modern moral and social diversity flourish. As Durkheim puts it, '. . . the common conscience is [not] threatened with total disappearance. Only, it more and more comes to consist of very general and very indeterminate ways of thinking and feeling, which leave an open place for a growing multitude of individual difference'.[25] In this sense then, '. . . mechanical solidarity persists even in the most elevated societies', and along with this solidarity there persists the fact of penal law and of punitive responses to crime.[26]

The final point concerning punishment in *The Division of Labour* draws attention to the *organized* nature of this collective punitive response. Durkheim describes how the spontaneous social action of the outraged community comes to be institutionalized in the form of a tribunal and a penal apparatus, charged with the expression of public feeling and the carrying out of the punishment itself. Once established, this governmental agency continues to draw its force and authority from the common conscience: its powers are thus derivative and

[21] Durkheim, *The Division of Labor*, p. 108.

[22] On Durkheim's conception of human nature see 'The Dualism of Human Nature and its Social Conditions' in K. H. Wolff (ed.), *Essays on Sociology and Philosophy* (New York, 1964).

[23] 'The part that [punishment] plays in the general integration of society evidently depends upon the greater or lesser extent of the social life which the common conscience embraces and regulates.' Durkheim, *The Division of Labor*, p. 109.

[24] Ibid. 173.   [25] Ibid. 172.   [26] Ibid. 186.

based in public feeling. At the same time though, the fact of institutionalization has important consequences. It gives added strength to the moral order by 'realizing' it in practical and continuing ways. It also ensures the existence of routine procedures and formal occasions which will help evoke the proper moral response to criminality, while simultaneously moderating the expression of moral passions and putting them to proper use. But where other theorists would interpret these developments as the supplanting of emotion by calculation, rationality, and administrative forms, Durkheim holds on to his conception of punishment by viewing these institutions in a different light. For him, the institutions of penality function less as a form of instrumental rationality and more as a kind of routinized expression of emotion, like the rituals and ceremonies of a religious faith.

3. THE TWO LAWS OF PENAL EVOLUTION

The discussion of punishment presented in *The Division of Labour* gives an extended account of the sources, the functioning, and the social significance of 'penal law'. It says nothing at all, however, about the actual *forms* of punishment —about the apparatuses, institutions, and substantive measures through which 'punitive reactions' are concretely realized. Nor does it provide punishment with a history. Apart from noting that modern societies are more circumspect about the act of punishing, and no longer do so in 'so material and gross a manner' as formerly, there is no discussion whatsoever of historical change.[27] In fact, Durkheim's only concern with such matters in this section of *The Division of Labour* is a negative one. He strenuously denies the relevance of history in respect of penality's functioning and its essential underlying character, claiming that, despite all appearances: 'punishment . . . remains for us what it was for our fathers.'[28]

A theory of punishment which gives no place to historical change and says nothing about penal forms leaves too many questions unanswered, so it is no surprise to find Durkheim returning to these issues some years later in an essay 'The Two Laws of Penal Evolution', first published in 1902. Without announcing itself as such, this paper is essentially an attempt to round out the original theory of punishment, showing how the facts of penal history can be brought within its terms and interpreted in accordance with them. It thus represents an extension and a substantiation of the earlier work; a kind of empirical demonstration of the theory's explanatory power. With the exception of one important qualification—to do with the effects upon punishment of absolutist governments—the basic theoretical framework of the original is preserved intact, while its implications and insights are considerably extended.

In essence, Durkheim's essay addresses a paradox. It is faced with the evident historicity of punishment—the abundant evidence which shows that

---

[27] Ibid. 89.   [28] Ibid.

penal methods have changed substantially over the course of time—but it also wishes to defend a thesis which asserts the ahistorical, unchanging character of punishment as a social process. The resolution of the problem lies in the argument that since the nature of social organization and the *conscience collective* change over time, such changes considerably alter the kinds of sentiments and passions provoked by criminal violations. Different passions, as well as different forms of social organization, give rise to different penal forms, so that although punishment is still an expression of collective sentiments, and a means of reinforcing them, the *forms* which it takes will have altogether changed. Durkheim's thesis is thus considerably refined by distinguishing between the forms and the functions of punishment. It now states, in effect, that it is the underlying mechanisms and functions of punishment which stay constant, while its institutional forms undergo historical change. However, in order to reach this position, Durkheim has to demonstrate precisely how different forms of collective morality give rise to different forms of punishment. This demonstration forms the substance of his essay.

The major changes which penal history displays are of two kinds, according to Durkheim. The intensity of punishment has tended to become less, as societies have become more advanced and, at the same time, deprivation of liberty by imprisonment has emerged as the preferred form of punishment, replacing the various capital and corporal methods which pre-existed it. The general pattern of evolution which he describes is thus one of decreasing penal severity and increasing reliance upon the prison, the two movements going hand in hand with each other and with the wider evolution of societies from 'simple' to 'advanced' social types. The general pattern is not, however, definite or uninterrupted. He is careful to point out that 'the succession of societies does not take a unilinear form', since societies develop at different rates and from different starting-points.[29] More importantly, he also argues that another, separate factor—the nature of political power—can independently influence punishment and bring about counter-evolutionary changes in its form. I will discuss this 'extraneous' influence in a moment, but first it is necessary to show how the general pattern is explained.

Durkheim accepts the conventional historical opinion of his contemporaries that 'intense' or 'severe' punishments are generally characteristic of simple societies, and that modern-day societies have become considerably more lenient in their penal methods. As confirmation of this he presents a catalogue of the atrocities and forms of suffering inflicted by the penal codes of various ancient societies, though this is more by way of an illustration than an empirical proof. A typical example is the following: 'among the various tribes of Syria', Durkheim tells us, 'criminals were stoned to death, they were shot full of arrows, they were hanged, they were crucified, their ribs and entrails

---

[29] É. Durkheim, 'Two Laws of Penal Evolution', *Année sociologique*, 4 (1901), 65–95. Repr. as ch. 4, 'The Evolution of Punishment', in Lukes and Scull (eds.), *Durkheim and the Law*. The quotation in the text is from p. 103 of Lukes and Scull.

were burned with torches, they were drawn and quartered, they were hurled from cliffs . . . or they were crushed beneath the feet of animals, etc.'[30] By itself, this is insufficiently precise to give an adequate understanding of Syrian penal practices (one wishes to ask were all criminals treated in this way? Were other, lesser methods also used? Which sanctions were most common? And so on) but in showing the use of methods which would be considered excessive or barbaric in late-nineteenth century France, it seems to give some support to the conventional view.

According to Durkheim, simple societies have resorted to draconian penal measures because of the intensity of the *conscience collective* which prevails in such societies. Their characteristic social morality is itself severe, rigid, and demanding, being wholly religious in form and representing all of its rules as transcendental laws, authorized by the gods. Within such societies, individuals are deeply imbued with a sense of the sacred character of social rules, and conformity to the rules is regarded as a sacred duty which is rigorously policed. Indeed, since social solidarity here rests mainly upon the sharing of collective beliefs—there being no extended division of labour to produce organic solidarities—Durkheim implies that the very existence of society itself depends upon their strict enforcement. In these circumstances any violation of the common conscience becomes a grave threat to society and an affront to deeply held religious beliefs. It consequently provokes an intensely violent reaction which manifests itself in suitably violent penal forms. The vehemence and torments of early penal systems are thus the product of a religious morality which can brook no opposition for fear of avenging gods and social collapse.

In contrast, the collective sentiments which exist in more advanced societies are less demanding and occupy a less prominent place in social life. As we saw earlier, modern organic societies are characterized by moral diversity and the interdependence of co-operating individuals, each of whom is to some extent differentiated and unique. The collective beliefs which these individuals share do not have the character of intensive religious prohibitions which regulate all spheres of life by strict decree. Instead, the common beliefs emphasize, above all, the value of the individual and correlative virtues such as freedom, human dignity, reason, tolerance, and diversity. Such values, being collective and inscribed in the foundations of social life, are still accorded a kind of transcendental status, and are deeply cherished in the consciences of individuals. But the tone and quality of these sentiments are markedly different from the stern, religiously sanctioned beliefs of earlier times. By its very nature, this new moral faith invites reflection and rational consideration in ethical matters: it no longer represents itself as the imperious will of gods who must be unquestioningly obeyed. As a consequence, social morality has a different psychological resonance—a different place in the psychic structure—and so gives rise to a more moderate reaction whenever its tenets are violated.

---

[30] Ibid. 108.

Durkheim indicates this crucial difference by means of a distinction between 'religious criminality' and 'human criminality'. Virtually all offences against the *conscience collective* of a simple society have the status of 'religious criminality'. As such, these offences provoke a veritable horror amongst the reverential onlookers, whose revulsion at this abomination, and whose fear of its consequences, drive them to take violent measures against the criminal. Religious passions are thus the source of atrocious punishments, and indeed it is precisely because a deity has been attacked that such punishments seem to show little concern for the offender's suffering, 'for what is an individual's suffering when it is a question of appeasing a God?'[31] By contrast the criminality typical of secular, modern societies is 'human criminality', i.e. offences against persons and their property. Such crimes still provoke strong reactions, and still give rise to a public demand for punishment, but, as we have seen, the sentiments involved in this reaction are qualitatively different, since '. . . the offence of man against man cannot arouse the same indignation as an offence of man against God'.[32] Moreover, with the rise of humanism and individualism, a new dialectic finds its way into punishment. For, as Durkheim points out, the same moral sentiments which are outraged when an individual is offended against are moved to sympathy at the sight of the offender's own suffering when he or she is punished. The consequence is that '. . . the same cause which sets in motion the repressive apparatus tends also to halt it. The same mental state drives us to punish and to moderate the punishment. Hence an extenuating influence cannot fail to make itself felt.'[33] The combined result of these interlinked changes is to make the average intensity of punishments in modern societies much less than was formerly the case.

The intensity of punishment, then, is seen to be a direct consequence of the nature of the *conscience collective*, and the development of a modern, secular morality tends automatically to bring about a general diminution in the severity of penal measures. Durkheim stresses that this evolution represents a change in the quality of the collective sentiments rather than a simple weakening of their strength. 'It is no longer that lively emotion, that sudden explosion, that indignant bewilderment aroused by an outrage directed against a being whose value immeasurably surpasses that of the aggressor; it is more that calmer and more reflective emotion provoked by offences which take place between equals.'[34] The collective sentiments of modern societies are not a watered-down version of an older morality: they form a wholly different mentality, with different practical consequences.

It is in terms of the quality of collective sentiments and their consequences for penal measures that we can understand, also, the major qualification Durkheim introduces into his evolutionary account. He points out that the correlation between social types and the intensity of punishment is complicated by another, independent factor, namely, the emergence of absolutist political

---

[31] Durkheim, *The Division of Labor*, p. 124.
[32] Ibid. 125.   [33] Ibid. 126.   [34] Ibid. 130.

regimes. Absolutist governments are characterized by an absence of limiting restraints on their powers, a capacity to assume an ascendancy over the rest of society, and a tendency to treat individual subjects as if they were the property of the state rather than its citizens. Such governmental forms can occur in any social type, so they are independent of the general pattern of change which leads societies to become more organic and punishments to become more lenient. The relevance of absolutism to this discussion is that absolutist governments are notoriously prone to the use of draconian modes of punishment. As Durkheim notes, 'the apogee of the absolute monarchy coincides with the period of the greatest repression'.[35]

Absolutism thus has the same consequences for punishment as do the collective sentiments of simple societies, even though they appear to exist independently of one another, so Durkheim is forced to confront this problem of a separate cause for the same effect. In the event, his solution is disarmingly simple. He argues that the power and charisma of an absolute ruler gives rise to a kind of religious aura which surrounds this apparently superhuman power. The revival of the religious idiom imparts a divine quality to laws and, thus, a sacrilegious quality to their violation which in turn increases the violence with which crimes are punished:

wherever the government takes this form, the one who controls it appears to people as a divinity. When they do not make an actual God of him, they at the very least see in the power which is invested in him an emanation of divine power. From that moment, this religiosity cannot fail to have its usual effects on punishment.[36]

In effect then, punishment is always to be understood in terms of the quality of collective sentiments, though the latter may be shaped by governmental forms as well as by the structures of social organization and morality. Absolutist governments in advanced societies are an obvious example of this double conditioning, but Durkheim also illustrates the obverse case in his discussion of the ancient Hebrews. Here he notes that the Hebrew penal code was more lenient than one would expect in such an undeveloped social type, and accounts for this by pointing to the non-absolutist political organization of that society, and the fact that 'the temper of the people remained profoundly democratic'.[37] By linking democracy to leniency of punishments, and tyranny to severity, Durkheim effectively restates Montesquieu's doctrine of the politics of punishment, though he does so within a much more developed theory of how these linkages are made.

So far, Durkheim's discussion of the changing form of penal measures has been exclusively concerned with the 'intensity' or the 'quantity' of punishment involved. A very large and disparate catalogue of ancient punishments involving all sorts of different techniques, arrangements, and symbolic meanings are treated simply as examples of 'severe' punishment, while the various forms of modern punishment, particularly imprisonment, are reduced to so many

[35] Ibid. 112.   [36] Ibid. 129.   [37] Ibid. 109.

examples of 'leniency'. One should not be surprised at this. Durkheim's theory views vengeful emotion as the immediate source of punishment, so he is easily led to see penal forms in terms of the amount of violent passion they seem to manifest. We should, however, be aware that there are always other dimensions involved in the forms which penal measures take. Penal sanctions always have a specific organization and a specific institutional form. They inflict suffering in a particular way, using particular techniques, distinctive procedures, and particular symbolic forms of self-representation. Concrete sanctions are never just a matter of more or less intensity.

Durkheim's second 'law of penal evolution' begins to address this further problem of the 'quality' rather than the 'quantity' of punishment. It states that: 'deprivations of liberty, and of liberty alone, varying in time according to the seriousness of the crime, tend to become more and more the normal means of social control.'[38] However, for the most part, he tends to treat the prison as an example of modern leniency in punishing, rather than a specific penal measure with definite attributes. He begins by pointing out that a consequence of punishment's tendency to become more lenient as societies developed was the eventual necessity of abandoning practices such as executions, mutilations, tortures, etc. and replacing them with less severe measures. The new institution which tends to replace the old atrocities—the prison—is, according to Durkheim, itself the product of the same processes which tend to decrease the severity of punishment. The break-up of undifferentiated societies and the development of individualism ended the ethic of collective responsibility and also increased social mobility, necessitating the use of places of detention for offenders awaiting trial. At the same time another social process—the differentiation of the organs of government—began to manifest itself in the construction of functional buildings (the manorial castle, the royal palace, fortresses, city walls, and gates) and the development of military and administrative capacities which would eventually provide the architectural and managerial conditions necessary for incarceration. Thus the social need for a place of detention became marked at the same time (and from the same causes) as the material conditions for such an institution. Once established, the prison lost its purely preventive or custodial character and took on more and more the character of a punishment in itself. Gradually, says Durkheim, it became the 'necessary and natural substitute for the other punishments which were fading away'.[39]

In many respects this is a limited and disappointing account of the rise and social basis of a major modern institution. The connections which Durkheim makes between the prison and the modern forms of organization and morality are superficial and rather obvious, when one might have expected a more penetrating discussion. The targeting of 'liberty' as the object of punishment, the intensive focusing upon the individual in prison cells, the efforts at moral reform characteristic of penitentiary regimes, or indeed the de Tocquevillian

---

[38] Durkheim, *The Division of Labor*, p. 114.   [39] Ibid. 120.

irony which leads liberal democratic societies to institute the despotic tyranny of prison regimes—all these issues seem to present themselves as obvious and urgent questions, which at least in principle are fully explicable within Durkheim's theoretical framework. Yet they are not even touched upon here or elsewhere in Durkheim's work.

Durkheim ends this historical essay with a paragraph which refers not to the past but to the present. Recalling his general argument that penal forms are caught up in and changed by the evolution of social moralities, he suggests that this process of change 'explains the state of crisis in which the penal law of all the civilized peoples is found'.[40] Moreover, he goes on to indicate, albeit a little obliquely, that imprisonment—which throughout the whole essay had stood as the exemplary form of modern punishment—is increasingly an anachronism which is out of keeping with the framework of contemporary life: 'we have arrived at the time when penal institutions of the past have either disappeared or are surviving by not more than force of habit, but without others being born which correspond better to the new aspirations of the moral conscience.'[41] Quite what Durkheim means by this statement is not apparent from the essay which proceeds it. We are not told in what ways the current forms of punishment—presumably meaning the deprivation of liberty—are out of correspondence with the new moral conscience. Nor are we pointed to new penal measures which might better express these collective sentiments. Indeed by raising this important question Durkheim simply draws attention to his own failure to specify in detail the kind of links which pertain, or should pertain, between penal forms and social sentiments.

Durkheim in fact returned to this question very soon afterwards, though in a different context and in a different fashion. In his Sorbonne lectures on moral education of 1902–3 in which he discussed the role of the school in socializing individuals, he was led to consider the proper forms of punishment which would be appropriate to such a task. In the course of that discussion Durkheim further elaborated his theory of punishment and also proposed a number of more precise specifications as to the forms which penal measures should take. It is to that discussion that I now finally turn.

4. Punishment as moral education

Durkheim's most detailed and concrete discussion of punishment is also, paradoxically, the one which is least well known to sociologists and penologists. In all the literature on Durkheim and punishment there is barely a single reference to what might be considered his final theoretical statement on the matter. This statement occupies fully three chapters of his work on *Moral Education* and provides us with his most fully developed, and also his most subtle account of the moral importance and effects of punitive measures. The

---

[40] Ibid. 131.   [41] Ibid.

setting for this discussion is much more specific than in previous works, since Durkheim is here concerned to describe the principles and pragmatics of schoolroom education, but in fact this turns out to be a perfect setting for Durkheim to indicate the specific implications of his theoretical work. As he conceives it, the task of modern education is to develop a secular, rational morality and to find the best means of socializing the child into this new *conscience collective*. The role of punishment in this setting is thus precisely the same as its role in the wider society—it is an expression and an enforcement of social morality—so his discussion of punishment in the classroom is undertaken as an extension of the theory which he had developed in his earlier work.

An important aspect of Durkheim's argument is that modern secular moralities—which are open to rational discussion and do not depend upon the mysticism and blind faith characteristic of religions—are none the less perceived to be in some way 'sacred' and 'transcendental'. Even in modern society, 'the domain of morality is as if surrounded by a mysterious barrier which keeps violators at arm's length, just as the religious domain is protected from the reach of the profane. It is a sacred domain.'[42] This sense of the 'transcendent' is, in Durkheim's view, the authority of society and social conventions as experienced by the individual, but it is none the less powerful for being recognizably 'man-made' rather than divine. Precisely because such beliefs and sentiments are perceived as transcending the individual, any violation or infringement of their rules prompts the same violent reprobation 'that the blasphemer arouses in the soul of the believer'.[43] As Durkheim has shown us before, offences against society's sacred domain provoke a passionate and a punitive response. But, as he points out more clearly in this context, punishment cannot by itself *create* moral authority: on the contrary, punishment implies that authority is already in place and has been breached.[44] The creation of that authority and sense of the sacred is, in fact, a work of moral training and inspiration which goes on in the family, in the school, and elsewhere throughout society. Punishment can only protect and regenerate what is already well constituted by other means—it is ancillary to moral education, not its central part.

But if punishment is not the centre of social morality it is none the less an essential and necessary component of any moral order. For, as Durkheim takes pains to point out, it has a crucial role in preventing the collapse of moral authority. It ensures that, once established, the moral order will not be destroyed by individual violations which rob others of their confidence in authority. Punishment is thus a way of limiting the 'demoralizing' effects of deviance and disobedience. As he puts it at one point: 'punishment does not

---

[42] Durkheim, *Moral Education*, p. 10.   [43] Ibid. 9.

[44] As M. Kennedy points out, without already-established rules and forms of authority, 'punishment' does not exist. It becomes merely retaliatory injury. See M. Kennedy, 'Beyond Incrimination: Some Neglected Aspects of the Theory of Punishment', in W. J. Chambliss and M. Mankoff (eds.), *Whose Law? What Order?* (New York, 1976).

give [moral] discipline its authority, but it prevents discipline from losing its authority, which infractions if they went unpunished, would progressively erode.'[45] Punishment's role is to demonstrate the reality and actual force of moral commands. Conventional rules can only command the prestige and the authority of sacred things if it is shown that violators will indeed be punished, and that the moral order has the strength to withstand direct attacks. Social relations are thus like credit relations in this respect—they depend upon trust and upon being underwritten and guaranteed by a powerful agency. Breach of trust, or doubts about the strength of the guarantor, can quickly lead to a collapse of the credit system. Consequently, individual offences must be punished, not just because of the individual harm that they do, but because of the ramifications such violations might have at the level of the moral order itself. There is thus a kind of 'system requirement' for punishment which is most obvious in the classroom, where moral order is fragile and dependent upon the teacher's actions. In the case of society at large the same system requirement exists, though it may be less easy to observe or to evidence. As Durkheim puts it,

a moral violation *demoralizes*. . . . the law that has been violated must somehow bear witness that despite appearances it remains always itself, that it has lost none of its force or authority despite the act that repudiated it. In other words, it must assert itself in the face of the violation and react in such a way as to demonstrate a strength proportionate to that of the attack against it. Punishment is nothing but this meaningful demonstration.[46]

Durkheim insists that this reassertion of the moral order is the primary function of punishment, both in the classroom and in the courts. He is aware, however, that this functional effect at the level of the system, is, in a sense, automatic, and is not always well understood by the administrators of punishment—whether they are teachers or criminal court judges. Consequently, he wants to argue that this 'meaningful demonstration' of moral strength should be the primary *objective* of punishing, as well as its primary function. This is to say, he wants punishers to become conscious of punishment's real moral function, and to make this the focus of their endeavours. He therefore provides an argument which moves from the abstractions of punishment's social functioning (which was his topic in previous works) to the concrete particulars of how we ought to punish in specific cases.

He begins this argument by denying the conventional idea of punishment as a deterrent instrument which can coercively control individual conduct. There is, he says, evidence to show that 'the prophylactic influence of punishment has been exaggerated beyond all reality', and it is easy to see why.[47] By themselves, threats of unpleasant consequences have no moral content. They merely present practical obstacles which stand in the way of the criminal's desires. As such these are no more than '. . . the professional risk of the

---

[45] Durkheim, *Moral Education*, p. 167.
[46] Ibid. 166.   [47] Ibid. 162.

delinquent career'.[48] Of course, the penal consequences of crime can be onerous, but there are also real hardships involved in resisting temptation and doing one's duty, so that temptation will often win out if an amoral calculation of interest is all that is involved. Utilitarian regulation of this sort can at best provide a limited form of control—'a police procedure . . . guaranteeing only overt and superficial propriety'.[49] Such threats act 'from the outside and on externals'—they 'cannot touch the moral life at its source'.[50] Moreover, amoral punishments of this sort can actually be counter-productive. They risk 'eliciting bad feelings' and do nothing to improve the moral qualities of the person involved.[51]

In the light of these considerations, Durkheim argues, we ought to give up thinking of punishment as a utilitarian instrument and instead consider it in its true role, as an expressive form of moral action.[52] The proper task of punishment is to uphold moral sensibilities by censuring all offences against them. In essence punishment is a means of conveying a moral message, and of indicating the strength of feeling which lies behind it. Its point is 'not to make the guilty expiate his crime through suffering or to intimidate possible imitators through threats, but to buttress those consciences which violations of a rule can and must necessarily disturb in their faith'.[53] Once we understand that this is what punishment is actually about, it has important consequences for the way we think about concrete sanctions. Thus it becomes apparent, for example, that 'pain . . . is only an incidental repercussion of punishment; it is not its essential element'.[54] We inflict various degrees of suffering and hardship upon the offender, not for what they can achieve in themselves, but in order to signalize the force of the moral message being conveyed. Physical harms, prison cells, monetary penalties, and stigmatization are thus for Durkheim so many concrete signs by which we express disapproval, reproach, and the power of the moral order. In an important sense, then '. . . punishment is only the palpable symbol through which an inner state is represented; it is a notation, a language through which either the general social conscience or that of the teacher expresses the feeling inspired by the disapproved behaviour'.[55]

Given the reproachful message that it must convey, this practical language of punishment—the specific devices through which a sanction is realized— cannot do other than take painful and unpleasant forms. But Durkheim emphasizes that these punitive devices are only the incidentals of punishment. They are a means of expressing a moral condemnation and should be designed, above all, to serve that purpose. Penal forms which are not properly

[48] Durkheim, *Moral Education*, p. 162.
[49] Ibid. 161. For recent discussions of deterrence and its limited efficacy, see G. Hawkins and F. Zimring, *Deterrence: The Legal Threat in Crime Control* (Chicago, 1973), and D. Beyleveld, *A Bibliography on General Deterrence Research* (Westmead, 1980).
[50] Durkheim, *Moral Education*, p. 161.   [51] Ibid. 163.
[52] For a discussion of the expressive functions of punishment, see J. Feinberg, *Doing and Deserving* (Princeton, 1970), ch. 5.
[53] Durkheim, *Moral Education*, p. 167.   [54] Ibid.   [55] Ibid. 176.

expressive in this way, but are instead designed to be effective as deterrents or else to cause maximum suffering, are thus inappropriate. They distort punishment's true purpose and ought not to be used. Put simply, Durkheim's point is that the method must not undercut the message. Penal sanctions cannot help but be unpleasant, but this aspect of suffering should be reduced to a minimum.

At this point, Durkheim is prompted to introduce a new consideration into his theory of punishment. Previously the force of the punitive reaction was determined by the passions which were provoked by the offence. But in phrasing his idea of punishment in this new metaphor of a *communication*, Durkheim is led to consider another element in the operation: the receptivity of the audience.[56] If a forceful moral reproach is to be communicated, its audience must understand its meaning and feel its force. The language of penality must suit the participants, and must be comprehensible to them. Consequently, the practical language of punishment—or rather the concrete sanctions through which moral reproach is realized—will depend upon the *sensibilities* of the society in question. In some societies, he suggests, 'individual sensibilities are hard to affect' and so 'it may be necessary for blame . . . to be translated into some violent form'.[57] However, in more advanced societies, where sensibilities are more refined, 'ideas and feelings need not be expressed through such grossly physical procedures'.[58] As a case in point, Durkheim argues that corporal punishment is unconscionable in a highly civilized society, except in the training of infants who are still too young to possess a moral sense. Corporal punishment is unnecessary as a means of 'getting through' to individuals, since our modern sensibility has provided us with 'more delicate nervous systems which respond even to weak irritants'.[59] Moreover it cannot convey a clear moral message because its very method of doing so violates one of our central moral values—the respect for persons. Thus this kind of sanction 'weakens on the one hand sentiments which one wishes to strengthen on the other'.[60]

The account of punishment which we find here in *Moral Education* is both important and revealing. It refines Durkheim's account of punishment's functioning, and shows how his theory relates to the practical use and design of penal sanctions. It also introduces a concern with changing sensibilities which are shown to be important in the determination of punishments, though no attempt is made to link the history of sensibilities to the history of the *conscience collective*. It is revealing because it shows much more clearly than before why

---

[56] On punishment as moral communication, see A. Duff, *Trials and Punishments* (Cambridge, 1986). Duff bases his arguments not upon Durkheim's sociology but instead upon Kant's philosophy. See also J. R. Lucas, *On Justice* (Oxford, 1980), pp. 131–4.

[57] Durkheim, *Moral Education*, p. 182.

[58] Ibid. This point about changing sensibilities is not further pursued in Durkheim's work. It will, however, be discussed at some length when I deal with the work of Norbert Elias and its implications for the study of punishment.

[59] Durkheim, *Moral Education*, p. 182.   [60] Ibid. 183.

Durkheim has so little to say about the actual apparatus and instrumentalities of punishment. It shows why he discusses only the external forms of punishment (which are directed at the public—and are moralizing signs)—not the *internal* forms (which touch only the inmates or offenders and are largely control orientated rather than moral). Durkheim's concern is not to understand punishment in all its aspects but merely to point out its moral content and its moralizing social effects. Penality's coercive apparatus of threats, physical restrictions, monetary penalties, and so on are interesting to him only as so many means of conveying moral passions and moral messages. Prisons, being relatively lenient devices, convey a particular kind of moral sentiment—a rather humanistic, modern one as it turns out—while stonings, mutilations, and tortures express a different quality of emotion and, behind that, a more primitive, religious mentality. In so far as these penal measures are also specific devices for asserting disciplinary regimes or direct forms of behavioural control, they are no longer truly moral phenomena and they fall below the horizon of analysis. Durkheim's ideal punishment is one of pure expression, a moral statement which expresses condemnation without pursuing any lesser goals. As he says at one point, '. . . the best punishment is that which puts the blame . . . in the most expressive but least costly form possible'.[61]

More importantly, we can now see that his whole analysis of punishment in society is organized around this ideal figure. His theory considers punishment only in so far as it is a moral phenomenon. It is orientated towards the explication of punishment's moral content and its moral consequences and asks how does punishment function in the circuits of moral life? To the extent that punishment has *other* meanings, other sources, and other effects, Durkheim's work has little or nothing to say of these. Ironically then, although Durkheim opens up new and important questions concerning the semiotics of punishment —its communicative propensities, its symbolic resonance, its metaphoric capacity to speak of other things—and concerning the cultural foundations upon which punishment is based, his own reading of these phenomena is severely restricted by the theoretical framework within which these questions arise.

Such a conclusion should not surprise us. As I pointed out at the start of this chapter, Durkheim explores punishment as a means of understanding the moral life of society and its mode of operation. He makes no claim to have provided a comprehensive theory of punishment and that was never his concern. Nevertheless, what Durkheim *does* say about punishment is important and often compelling. We need to consider to what extent his interpretation— partial though it is—can help us make sense of penality today.

<hr>

[61] Quoted in the editor's introduction to Durkheim, *Moral Education*, at p. xvi, this is a trans. from the original French text. *L'Éducation morale* (Paris, 1925), p. 232.

3

Punishment and the Construction of Authority
A Reworking of Durkheimian Themes

It will be apparent by now that Durkheimian theory presents a distinctive and sometimes counter-intuitive reading of punishment's social meaning. Instead of taking penality at its face value as an instrument of crime control, Durkheim looks for the submerged moral content embodied in punishment, and having uncovered and elaborated this moral dimension, he presents it as being the fundamental basis of society's penal practice. Punishment, for Durkheim, is above all a moral process. It is propelled by moral sentiments, its forms symbolize and express moral judgments, and its effects are primarily to reaffirm the moral order. In effect, punishment sets up a kind of moral circuitry, channelling the energy of collective sentiments into a self-sustaining and socially binding circle of affirmation. It is one mechanism among others in the complex circuits of social solidarity.

This theory of punishment-as-moral-process is composed of a number of distinctive elements which I propose to discuss one by one, though it should be clear that these elements, in Durkheim's view, are interdependent and mutually sustaining. These are: the idea of the sacred, as it applies to collective sentiments; punishment's necessary role in the maintenance of these sacred sentiments; the passions which drive punishment and provide its social support; the rituals which express these passions and enact penal measures; the collective involvement of the community in punishment; and, finally, the social effects which punishments are said to produce. These components, taken together, amount to a specific theory of punishment's functional role in social organization, and this theoretical claim will also be given critical attention in the pages which follow.

Each of these components of Durkheim's theory presents difficult problems of understanding and application. In many instances Durkheim's own formulations will be found to be unacceptable or in need of modification, and the relevance of his concepts for an interpretation of the present is not always at first sight apparent. But for all its problems, Durkheim's reading of punishment opens up important aspects of the penal complex and reveals dynamics and dimensions which are not otherwise visible. We need to hold on to these insights, and pursue them into the present, developing them in whatever ways this task requires. Accordingly, the discussion which follows will be positive and constructive rather than dismissive. It will seek to qualify or reconstruct Durkheim's arguments where necessary, to think through the relevance of his concepts for the present, and to indicate where his formulations need to be taken together with other considerations to produce a more comprehensive account of penality.

1. The importance of history

Before going on to discuss these central elements of Durkheim's theory, it will be useful to make a few preliminary observations that can serve to orientate that discussion. One of the most resounding and recurrent criticisms of Durkheim's theory of punishment concerns itself with a number of serious errors which appear in his historical account of penal evolution. A whole series of studies have pointed out that Durkheim greatly overstates the importance of 'repressive' law in early societies and understates its role in advanced ones.[1] Related to this is his misunderstanding of the normative frameworks to be found in primitive societies, many of which are based upon flexible reciprocities and co-operation rather than harsh religious conformity.[2] His periodization of the historical record is also much criticized, since he lacks any conception of intermediate stages between 'the primitive' and 'the advanced' and is consequently led to classify together societies which are in most respects utterly disparate. Most tellingly, it has been shown that quite different frameworks of social relations and penal measures sometimes operate simultaneously and in competition with one another within the same social formation. Thus, for example, throughout the early modern period of European history, traditions of 'community law' (and their restitutory, reconciliatory, compensation-based forms of sanctioning) were in ongoing competition with an emerging tradition of 'state law' (which emphasized repressive sanctions and punitive justice). The conflict between these traditions was not simply a matter of the old being replaced by the new, as Durkheim's evolutionism would imply, but was instead a fundamental and far-reaching struggle over ways of organizing social and legal life.[3]

The historical development of punitive forms, then, did not take the trajectory suggested by Durkheim, nor were its dynamics precisely those which he described. Instead of being an emergent property of an evolving social solidarity, penal forms were the contested outcome of an ongoing struggle between different social forces and different visions of society—a

---

[1] See S. Spitzer, 'Punishment and Social Organization: A Study of Durkheim's Theory of Evolution', *Law and Society Review*, 9 (1975), 613–37; R. D. Schwartz and J. C. Miller, 'Legal Evolution and Societal Complexity', *American Journal of Sociology*, 70 (1964), 159–69; L. S. Sheleff, 'From Restitutive Law to Repressive Law: Durkheim's *The Division of Labor in Society* Revisited', *Archives européenes de sociologie* (*European Journal of Sociology*), 16 (1975), 16–45; Lukes and Scull (eds.), *Durkheim and the Law*, introd.; P. A. Sorokin, *Sociocultural Dynamics*, ii (New York, 1937); P. N. Grabowsky, 'Theory and Research on Variations in Penal Severity', *British Journal of Law and Society*, 5 (1978), 103–14.

[2] See e.g. B. Malinowski, *Crime and Custom in Savage Society* (Totowa, NJ, 1966), and id., *Argonauts of the Western Pacific* (London, 1922).

[3] '. . . the gradual displacement of the [community law] by the [state law], a process which began in the tenth century and lasted until the nineteenth century, was one of the central (yet most neglected) developments of European history, constituting a revolutionary change in legal methods and techniques of social control.' B. Lenman and G. Parker, 'The State, the Community and the Criminal Law in Early Modern Europe', in V. A. C. Gatrell, B. Lenman, and G. Parker, *Crime and the Law: The Social History of Crime in Western Europe Since 1500* (London, 1980), p. 23.

point confirmed by histories of penal change in the modern period.[4] In some respects, Durkheim's discussion of 'absolute power' and its 'independent' role in the evolution of punishments might be taken as a hint in the direction of a history where political forces struggle to remake social relations and beliefs. But in fact Durkheim overlooks the possibility of a clash between the ideological claims of absolutism and the *conscience collective* of the society concerned, presuming that the two will somehow merge to form a unified and coherent system of authority and belief. However one looks at it, Durkheim's historical account is too much a story of smooth evolution and functional adaptation to fit with the facts.

By and large then, the historical critique of Durkheim's work is sustained and unanswerable. But, for reasons that are important to understand, this historical critique makes only a limited impact upon Durkheim's theory of punishment. It shows that Durkheim has failed to substantiate his functional theory by his use of historical illustrations, not that such a substantiation could not, in principle, be achieved. It seems clear that Durkheim's primary concern is to present an account of punishment's moral functioning within an established social order, not to detail the concrete processes which are involved in penal change. In emphasis at least, his analysis is 'functional' rather than 'historical'; synchronic rather than diachronic. His 'history' of penal evolution is not, in fact, a history at all, at least not in the normal sense of an investigation which highlights process, change, and transition. It is rather a discussion of two historically successive social types—the mechanical and the organic—each being discussed as a unified functioning entity, entire unto itself, with its own specific forms of solidarity and of punishment. His concern is not to show how the historical transition was made between these two social forms—hence his neglect of all intermediate stages—but rather to make the sociological point that different forms of solidarity give rise to different forms of punishment. The fact that Durkheim 'gets it wrong' concerning the precise nature of these different societies, concerning the specific penal and social forms characteristic of each, or in respect of the trajectory of historical change does not, in itself, disturb his primary claim, which is to have provided a functional account which links forms of punishment to forms of solidarity.

The very fact that this historical critique fails to strike at the heart of Durkheim's work is in itself most revealing, for it shows very clearly the extent to which Durkheimian theory lacks a genuine historical consciousness and a genuine sense of social conflict. As we will see in the following discussion, his analyses—particularly of key concepts such as the *conscience collective*—too often proceed as if these were given, uncontested facts of social life. This brief consideration of these historical points brings into view the extent to which the 'moral order' or 'legal system' of any society are in fact the outcome of historical struggles and a continuing process of negotiation and contestation.

[4] See M. Ignatieff, *A Just Measure of Pain: The Penitentiary in the Industrial Revolution* (London, 1978), and Garland, *Punishment and Welfare*.

Durkheim's positivist attitude to social facts and his evolutionary functionalism should not be allowed to hide the fact that specific forms of society do not simply 'emerge': they are a fragile and contested outcome of struggles between competing social groups and forms of life, often with their own inherent conflicts and contradictions.

2. Rethinking ~~the conscience~~ collective

Forming the foundation-stone of Durkheim's theory of punishment is his conception of a common moral order which he terms the *conscience collective*. This 'common conscience' defines what is and is not criminal; it is the ultimate source of the passionate reaction which motivates punishment; and it is also the beneficiary of the punitive process, being strengthened and reaffirmed by the social response to crime. Despite its crucial place in his argument, the concept of the *conscience collective* is never fully elaborated in Durkheim's work. It has the status of a given social fact, a foundational entity, upon which other social phenomena rest. It is described as 'the totality of beliefs and sentiments common to average citizens of the same society' and we are told that it forms 'a determinate system which has its own life'.[5] Unfortunately, and in keeping with Durkheim's general style of argument, we are not told how this common conscience comes into existence: we learn nothing about the history or conditions of emergence of this crucial entity. Instead of investigating the historical production of a common mentality, Durkheim simply takes this as being a necessary component of any established, functioning society. It is a point of departure for his enquiry and is thus excluded from the enquiry itself. This positing of a *conscience collective* is one of the most contentious and problematic aspects of Durkheim's social thought, and it clearly has ramifications for his theory of punishment. For our purposes, we need to ask in what sense, if any, is it valid to talk of a *conscience collective* in modern societies, and can modern punishment be understood in such terms?

The first point that needs to be made is that the existence of a level of orderliness and law-abiding conduct in society does not necessarily imply that underlying such conduct is a mass commitment to shared moral norms. As many critics have pointed out, much law-abiding behaviour is amoral or 'utilitarian' in nature—based more upon the avoidance of sanctions than a commitment to the morality which these sanctions enforce.[6] This is particularly true in situations of social conflict, where the law embodies the interests and aspirations of some groups but not others. For Durkheim, utilitarian obedience and interest-based laws are signs of demoralization and transition. A state which does not represent the collective sentiments of the whole society is, in his view, 'pathological' and cannot last for long. But the evidence of the con- temporary world suggests just the opposite: long-term group conflict—based

---

[5] Durkheim, *The Division of Labor*, p. 79.
[6] See A. Giddens, *Durkheim* (Hassocks, Sussex, 1978), ch. 6.

upon class, race, sex, regional identity, and ideology—is an inherent quality of most, if not all, modern societies, yet these same societies are able to function, persist through time, and reproduce themselves. It is therefore perfectly possible for a level of order to be maintained without there being any universal commitment to the morality of that order.

Of course Durkheim does not suggest that societies exhibit a total consensus or absence of social conflict: one of the defining features of modern society is, for him, the fact of social differentiation and the continuing need for the adjustment of interests and the resolution of conflicts. His contention is rather that underneath the surface of clashing interests and social difference there is in operation a moral framework which holds competing interests together and provides a basis for their resolution. It is at this deeper level of agreement that the *conscience collective* exists, and the continuing importance of criminal law is that it embodies those underlying values and symbolizes their force. Durkheim is no doubt right to presume that the very idea of a society presupposes a minimum of mutual agreement. As Mary Douglas puts it: 'not just any busload or haphazard crowd of people deserves the name of society: there has to be some thinking and feeling alike among members.'[7] But even in respect of this deeper level of moral belief, there are compelling reasons to doubt Durkheim's arguments and to qualify the conclusions which he derives from them.

Durkheim posits this deep framework of shared sentiments as an emergent property of social organization. A particular form of social life—whether a rudimentary organization or a specialized division of labour—brings with it a moral framework which binds individuals to each other and to its conventions and institutions. The problem of social order, for Durkheim, is primarily one of socializing each new generation of individuals into this way of life and the moral structures which support it. (A secondary problem is to ensure that the moral order is well adapted to the extant forms of social organization.) Socializing individuals into 'society' is thus the key problem area for Durkheim, and his sociology concentrates upon the problems which arise from a failure of individual socialization—problems such as crime, suicide, anomie, demoralization, and the collapse of social authority. But in focusing upon this interface between society and the individual, Durkheim neglects another major axis of social life and social conflict—namely the relationship between competing groups. In all but the most simple social formations, different social groups have existed and have struggled with one another to realize their own vision of social life and its proper organization. The forms of social relations and moral beliefs that come to dominate in any society are thus the outcome of an ongoing process of struggle and negotiation. They are not a given characteristic of a particular social type, nor are they the inevitable product of functional evolution. If a particular form of society and collective sentiment becomes

[7] Douglas, *How Institutions Think*, p. 9.

established at a point in history, this must be seen as the (perhaps temporary) outcome of a struggle between competing powers and forces, rather than the 'appropriate' or 'functional' condition for such a social type. Moreover, unless the dominant social groupings can destroy all opposition, new groups and forces will continually rise up to challenge the established order in one respect or another. It is therefore a characteristic of social order that it is continually being negotiated and contested. Establishing society is not just a problem of socializing deviant individuals, it is also, and crucially, a matter of subduing competing social movements and social groups.

This basic point has important consequences for Durkheim's account. It means, firstly, that in most societies the *conscience collective* may be a much more problematic category than Durkheim allows, and that even where an established moral order does exist, it does so by virtue of a successful struggle against competing forms of order. An individual is thus socialized not into 'society' as such, but into a specific form of social relations which has come to dominate over alternative forms. We should perhaps talk of a 'ruling morality', or a 'dominant moral order', rather than the *conscience collective*. Secondly, if the *conscience collective* is not a given or automatic feature of society, then we need to know how it came to exist in its particular form. History thus becomes essential for its understanding, and not just a supplementary illustration of its changing forms. We need to understand the forces which brought this moral order into being, in this particular form, and in competition with alternative possibilities which may have existed.

To reintroduce historicity in this way serves to point out that any 'given' moral order is in fact actively constructed by social forces, in a context of competing alternatives. It thus draws attention to the ideological work that has to be done to maintain a particular moral order in dominance—the need for ruling ideas to be persuasive and to establish their hegemony over oppositional value systems. Durkheim clearly recognizes the need for moralizing work—the *conscience collective* has to react against violators, reaffirm its claims, uphold its authority, and so on. But for him the point of this work is to avoid 'demoralization' or the collapse of moral authority. He fails to acknowledge that an equally persistent concern on the part of the authorities is to avert the challenge of competing moralities and competing social groups. We see this most clearly when Durkheim discusses the role of the state in respect of collective sentiments. As I noted earlier, Durkheim views the state as a preserver of the people's customs—a conservative force which guards and maintains the collective sentiments which already exist in the people. It is possible that this description may fit a primitive society, tentatively establishing an institutional structure, though even here it seems doubtful. But it is hard to see how Durkheim's description could apply to the revolutionary governments which established themselves in France after 1789, in Russia in 1917, or even to the governments of Thatcher, Reagan, and Gorbachev in the 1980s. Leading groups in society, acting through the state and through civil institutions, are continually engaged in the remaking of social relations and collective sentiments in accordance with their particular programmes of political action. Typically these active forces claim to be expressing the sentiments of the people, or the true customs and traditions of the land, but such claims are the rhetorical stock-in-trade of political persuasion. It is hardly credible to accept such claims in the implicit way that Durkheim does.

So, instead of depicting the *conscience collective* as an emergent property of 'society-as-a-whole', we ought to conceive of a dominant moral order which is historically established by particular social forces. This is precisely the sense of the terms 'dominant ideology' and 'hegemony' which have been developed, primarily in the Marxist tradition, in order to deal with this issue, and it may be that these concepts provide a better guide to the political determinants and effects of social morality. But before switching in this way from one approach to another we should ensure that nothing of importance is lost in translation. Because, for all its faults, the Durkheimian concept does point to certain facts which are of vital importance, and which tend to drop out of sight when Marxist alternatives are used.

The first point is that even though social moralities are actively enforced by particular social groupings, Durkheim is surely right to argue that these normative regimes are not entirely a matter of alien imposition; that they do, in part, correspond with the deeply felt beliefs of common people. At least in the case of stable societies, which are not undergoing revolution or in a state of civil war, the laws and established moral codes will always be built around values and categories which are shared to a greater or lesser extent by the individual members of the society. In the case of modern democratic polities, the dominant morality is neither an alien imposition from above nor an authentic expression of values from below, but instead a compromise formation which takes up a position somewhere between these extremes. When ascendant social élites legislate their preferred categories into laws and institutional practices, they do not, except in exceptional circumstances, ignore the moral culture of the mass of the people. To do so is to invite deep resistance and hostility, and undermine the degree of voluntary co-operation that all stable authority requires, so that even autocratic rulers are in part bound, as Durkheim claims, by collective sentiments. To the extent that government is representative and subject to an effective mass franchise, the space for violating customary beliefs is still less. But if legislative élites cannot afford to ignore or overturn those values which have a place in the hearts of the citizens, they are usually in a position to transform them in certain ways or to give them particular inflections. In effect, politics becomes a matter of working upon existing social relations and moralities so as to lead them in new directions and reshape them in accordance with a particular politics.[8] This process of change is assisted by the fact that the *conscience collective* of any society consists of a

[8] See G. Stedman Jones, *Languages of Class* (Cambridge, 1982).

vaguely specified set of core values rather than a system of fully articulated moral rules. These core values may be interpreted in various ways and will be differently understood by different sectors of the population, so that the art of political change becomes one of articulating a new morality while claiming to ground it in the values which everyone holds. The extent to which laws and official practices appear to coincide with the existing sentiments of society's members, or depart from them, will thus vary not just with the state's reforming ambitions and its need for mass support, but also with its ability to represent its actions in traditional terms.

Durkheim is surely right to argue that the sentiments of 'the average conscience' normally find some expression in society's laws and moral codes, and that these sentiments supply a popular force which supports and legitimates authority. Collective sentiments are thus real entities rooted in the emotional and moral make-up of individuals and operating as important social forces in their own right: they should not be excluded from analysis or presumed to be ineffective in shaping social policies and social action. But what Durkheim fails to see is the extent to which these deeply held sentiments are the object and outcome of a historical process of political struggle. Laws and state actions do not simply 'express' such sentiments—they also seek to transform and reshape them in accordance with a particular vision of society. Such changes, when they occur, are often slow and require extensive ideological work, but the moral sentiments which are internalized by individuals do change over time, as new normative codes are legislated and new generations are socialized in accordance with them.

In the light of all this, we must seriously question Durkheim's claim that laws and legal sanctions are the 'visible symbol' and faithful expression of something called the *conscience collective*. Popular sentiments—which may be diffuse and ambivalent—act as a political conditioning factor upon legislation and legal decisions rather than as a direct determinant of them. Consequently, the 'fit' between laws and collective sentiments will always be loose and imperfect—some laws may indeed be an 'index' of social sentiment, while others may fly in the face of it. More importantly, perhaps, legal enactments cannot be seen as a simple expression or representation in law of collective values, since laws are themselves an important force in the construction and organization of the latter. In general, social sentiments and laws are, in effect, mutually interacting and conditioning rather than related as cause and effect.

3. THE IDEA OF THE SACRED

The other aspect of Durkheim's argument which tends to get lost if one thinks instead in terms of 'ideology' and 'hegemony', is the important idea of 'the sacred' which Durkheim ties into his description of the *conscience collective* and the laws which symbolize it. His argument here applies to primitive, 'mechanical' societies where laws and collective sentiments are clearly framed within a religious idiom and are deemed to be shaped by divine decree, but it also extends to advanced, secular societies where the idea of the sacred continues to be an essential aspect of the moral order and its expressions. Durkheim insists that a transcendental quality is still ascribed to the fundamental values of modern society, the power of which is still experienced by society's members long after religious belief has been exchanged for secular rationalism. Despite the fact that morals are now understood—on an intellectual plane—as being a product of social convention and convenience, they continue to impress individuals—at least emotionally—as being somehow elevated, supernatural, having a power and a quality which places them on a higher plane of existence. The attitude that is adopted towards such 'sacred' entities is not one of everyday utilitarian calculation. They are not simply rules like any others to be rationally understood and instrumentally obeyed. Instead, they strike the individual as superior to him or her, and inspire feelings of deep respect, awe, love, and even dread. The attitude adopted towards these objects is precisely that of the religious believer towards his or her god, so that even in a secular, differentiated, modern society, one still finds the psychological patterns and emotional commitments of absolute, unthinking faith.

There is good reason to believe that this quality of sacredness—or something very like it—does indeed exist in modern societies and forms an important element in the operation of social and legal authority. Certainly other sociologists have frequently agreed with such a finding. Working from a very different sociological perspective, Max Weber, for example, argued that there is no legitimate authority without an element of 'charisma'—charisma being Weber's term for the quality of extraordinary power and grace which is widely ascribed to certain individuals or institutions, and which is the equivalent here of Durkheim's 'sacredness'. However, one should perhaps question Durkheim's understanding of the source of this transcendental power, and its social implications. Durkheim attributes this sacred quality to a (largely unconscious) recognition, by the individual, of the claims of 'society' as a superior force. In his view, 'sacredness' emerges from the awe-inspiring gap between the individual and the social and it attaches to those categories which appear fundamental to the existence of the latter. While agreeing with much of this, other sociologists such as Edward Shils and Clifford Geertz find the source of 'sacredness' or 'charisma' not in 'society itself' but instead in the practices and self-representations of those ruling élites and power-holders who claim to act in the name of society—which is not at all the same thing.

Shils, for example, argues that charisma attaches to those acts which are involved with the symbolic centre of society.[9] This 'center' is Shils's term for the arena where society's ruling forces and leading institutions come together— the place where the action is, and where those events occur which most

[9] E. Shils, *The Constitution of Society* (Chicago, 1982), part 2, 'The Sacred in Society'.

powerfully affect individuals' lives. In effect, charisma attaches to power rather than to 'society'. Clifford Geertz's work on 'the inherent sacredness of sovereign power' also leads in this direction.[10] His ethnographies of the forms of symbolic display and self-representation adopted by different rulers show very clearly that 'sacredness' is a quality produced—and recognized—in the ritual manifestations of power, and that sacred categories owe more to the chosen idiom and symbolics of power than to the objective needs of society:

> at the political center of any complexly organized society . . . there is both a governing elite and a set of symbolic forms expressing the fact that it is in truth governing. No matter how democratically the members of the elite are chosen . . . they justify their existence and order their actions in terms of a collection of stories, ceremonies, insignia, formalities, and opportunities that they have either inherited or, in more revolutionary situations, invented. It is these—crowns and coronations, limousines and conferences—that mark the center as center and give what goes on there its aura of being not merely important but in some odd fashion connected with the way the world is built.[11]

Durkheim, then, is right to see an 'aura'—or as he puts it 'a mysterious barrier'—around aspects of social morality, and to emphasize the psychological and social reality of its effects.[12] But this 'sacredness' will attach not to the moral foundations of 'society' as such, but instead to those norms and rituals of power which are crucial to a particular version of social order.

When Durkheim discusses the *conscience collective* in modern society—and hence too, the realm of the sacred—he is referring to a realm which is much narrower than in former times. As he clearly recognizes, many of our modern rules of conduct and legal prescriptions are merely conventional norms designed to ensure the harmonious working of the division of labour and the myriad interactions and exchanges which it entails. These 'restitutive' norms and rules of law do not strike us with the force of sacred entities—they have no grounding in our emotional or ethical intuitions and so 'do not correspond to any sentiment in us'.[13] Rules and laws such as these—which Durkheim regards as a corollary of the division of labour—do indeed produce a form of solidarity based upon interdependence and mutual reliance. But this organic solidarity is always dependent upon and underpinned by the deep moral sentiments which people continue to hold in common—by the samenesses which in a crucial sense hold people together and permit their diversities. Thus the common conscience does not disappear with the emergence of modern differentiated society. Instead it changes its form, and becomes the moral guarantor of organic solidarity. As we saw in the last chapter, the values which feature in this new moral framework are not fine grained and highly specific as in the religious codes of older societies—instead they consist of generic, foundational values, such as respect for the individual, freedom, reason,

---

[10] C. Geertz, 'Centers, Kings and Charisma: Reflections on the Symbolics of Power', in id., *Local Knowledge: Further Essays in Interpretive Anthropology* (New York, 1983).
[11] Ibid. 124.
[12] Durkheim, *Moral Education*, p. 10.   [13] Durkheim, *The Division of Labor*, p. 112.

tolerance, and so on. But, despite all the diversity which these sentiments permit, they themselves may not be violated with impunity. As before, the *conscience collective* is protected by a strict code of penal law, which—unlike most law in modern society—*does* evoke deep-seated emotions and a sense of the sacred. Thus in a world of secular diversity, punishment continues to protect a residual sphere of sacred values, and draws its force and significance from this fact.

We have seen that Durkheim's concept of the *conscience collective* is problematic, and that legal enactments cannot be understood as a faithful index of a shared moral order. But what are we to make of this more restricted case? Do violations of the criminal law strike at genuinely shared and deeply felt sentiments? Is the penal code an authentic representation of the popular sense of the sacred? The answer to this is that, once again, the legal code in question is a compromise formation which at any one time will partly reflect the felt needs and sentiments of the population and partly express the strategic concerns and conflicts of the legislative élite. Of course the representativeness of different penal codes will vary, but in general they will tend to take up the moral concerns of the citizenry and give them a particular inflection, or else ally them with prohibitions which are less genuinely shared. Criminal codes protect the basic requirements of social order—security, personal safety, the liberty of the individual, the protection of property, and so on—and these are values which are indeed deeply held and widely shared. In that sense, a basic correspondence will generally exist between criminal law and popular sentiments. But the specific provisions of the criminal law interpret these basic values in particular ways, and also fan out beyond them to proscribe forms of conduct which do not 'shock all healthy consciences'. There may be basic agreement that rape, or murder or robbery or burglary is morally repugnant and should be proscribed, but there may also be widespread disagreement as to the proper way to punish these offences, and little or no agreement regarding other kinds of offences (such as drink-driving, white-collar crime, domestic violence, tax evasion) or even in the precise interpretation of those basic ones (should homicide include vehicular killings? infanticide? abortion?). And agreement 'in essentials' is very different from agreement in specifics, particularly given that criminal law revolves around specific decisions as to the criminality of the action, the seriousness of the offence, and the appropriateness of any particular punishment.

It is also the case in this as in any other field of law, that the relationship between social sentiments and legal enactments is interactive rather than unidirectional. Over time, the legal prohibition and punishment of specific acts can induce changes in popular sentiment, so that what was once felt by the public to be tolerable may come to be morally and then emotionally condemned. Criminal law can thus lead as well as follow 'public opinion'. More importantly —because more frequently—penal codes do not radically change public sentiments so much as impose a particular ordering and organization upon them. As we shall see in our discussion of penal rituals, the routines of punishment provide a practical education in moral feeling for the public at large. Specific penal decisions—to punish an offence with life imprisonment, to penalize another with a fine—afford a vivid public display of the expected moral response to particular crimes. Handed down by our leading institutions with an aura of *gravitas* and moral seriousness, these decisions set the tone for the public's response at the very moment that they claim to express it. And while sentencers and legislators will occasionally misjudge their actions, and provoke a backlash of popular disagreement, their actions more usually prefigure popular sentiment and give it a degree of definition which it would otherwise lack. As James Fitzjames Stephen once put the point: '. . . the sentence of law is to the moral sentiment of the public in relation to any offence what a seal is to hot wax.'[14]

The legal acts of punishment which command overwhelming public assent and suggest a close fit between law and common sentiment are those which deal with heinous criminal acts of the most self-evident kind. Child murderers, multiple rapists, terrorist bombers, and the perpetrators of suchlike atrocities provoke a widespread and genuine outrage which needs little coaching from the authorities. But the groundswell of collective outrage and sentiment which occurs in these relatively rare (but widely reported) cases should not be mistaken for agreement in every other particular. The relationship of penal law to common sentiments may vary within the broad parameters that I have mentioned, and thus is always a matter for empirical enquiry. Durkheim is simply wrong to assume that the two are normally identical, though any suggestion of their complete independence would be equally misleading.

4. THE SOCIAL NECESSITY OF PUNISHMENT

One major implication which Durkheim draws from his theory that punishment is bound up with society's sacred moral order is the argument that punishment is a social necessity. His argument here is that punishment is never merely a reaction to particular crimes and the direct harms that they cause, because in addition to this immediate crime-control function punishment also has a system-maintaining function which, in sociological terms, is more essential. In reacting to particular crimes, punishment has the task of upholding the overarching moral order and of preventing its erosion and collapse, so even where the costs of punishing an offence appear greater than the direct harms caused by it, there is always another consideration weighing in the balance which indicates that punishment is required.

A useful way of thinking about Durkheim's point is to say that the social process of punishment is a matter of *governance* and not just of *management*. 'Management', as Philip Selznick argues, 'suggests rational, efficiency-minded,

[14] J. F. Stephen, quoted in J. Feinberg and H. Gross, *Philosophy of Law* (Encino, Calif., 1975), p. 543.

goal-driven organization. This is the realm of administrative rather than political decisions. Ends are characteristically taken as given, and every act is justified by the contribution it makes to these ends. Everything else is a distraction.'[15] 'Governance', on the other hand, cannot limit itself to the single-minded pursuit of expediency and narrowly defined goals. It implies a broader responsibility for the overall maintenance of a social system, the requirements of which are more complex and more political: 'governance takes account of all the interests that affect the viability, competence and moral character of an enterprise, the strategies of governance are basically political. They have to do with forming public opinion, accommodating interests, and determining what ends should be chosen and by what means pursued.'[16]

It may be, as Shearing and Stenning argue, that private policing and security firms, which serve their employer's corporate interests rather than the interests of the state or the public, can pursue an amoral, managerial use of punishment, invoking it only when it appears expedient and cost-effective to do so.[17] And it may also be true that particular state agencies—such as the police—are sometimes drawn towards a managerial 'crime-control' approach in their decision-making, because of the scarcity of resources and the pressure for immediate and visible 'results'.[18] But Durkheim seems correct in supposing that, in general, the social process of punishing offenders is undertaken as a question of governance, and takes the maintenance of moral order and legal authority as the broad context within which particular decisions must be set.

In Durkheim's view a failure to punish violations of the *conscience collective* undermines the collective force of social morality and runs the risk of demoralizing citizens. In the light of the previous discussion, I would qualify this by saying that a significant failure to punish can undermine the sovereignty and authoritativeness of a particular legal and moral order and the ruling powers which support it.[19] Nevertheless, the point remains that punishment, routinely applied, is more than an instrument of crime control. It is also a sign that the authorities are in control, that crime is an aberration and that the conventions which govern social life retain their force and vitality. A failure to punish violators, or—what amounts to the same thing—a failure to impose an effective lawful order, can quickly result in the erosion of political authority, as can be seen in certain areas of Northern Ireland, the Lebanon, and even some

---

[15] P. Selznick, *The Moral Commonwealth*, unpub. MS (Feb. 1988), p. 663.

[16] Ibid. 664.

[17] C. Shearing and P. Stenning, 'From the Panopticon to Disney World: The Development of Discipline', in A. Doob and E. Greenspan (eds.), *Perspectives in Criminal Law* (Aurora, 1984).

[18] See e.g. Skolnick, *Justice Without Trial*, and A. Blumberg, *Criminal Justice* (Chicago, 1967).

[19] In fact most violators of the law are not punished because they are not caught, and the stability of modern states seems not unduly troubled by this. The significant cases are those which, because of their character or frequency, gain public attention and are seen to have implications for the state's ability to deliver 'security' and 'order'.

sections of the larger cities in the USA.[20] In punishing offenders a legal order is reaffirming the generality of its power as well as curbing the conduct of criminals.

We should be careful, though, to avoid supposing that the sign-of-authority function and the crime-control function are somehow distinct and unrelated. If punishments (and the threat of punishments) were routinely imposed but were entirely ineffective in containing crime, then this too could undermine the claims of the moral order and the political powers which pose as its guarantor. Ralf Dahrendorf has recently set out an argument which echoes the Durkheimian thesis and reminds us that sanctions have to have a certain force and effectivity if they are to have this system-maintaining effect. Dahrendorf argues that, since the Second World War, the sanctions used against offenders in Europe and North America—particularly against adolescents and first offenders— have become so 'emasculated' and lenient that they have contributed to the collapse of the authoritative social order. This weakening of sanctions, he claims, has continued to the point of 'impunity'—weak sanctions being an equivalent to waived sanctions—with all the anomic consequences predicted by Durkheim. As Dahrendorf puts it, 'impunity, or the systematic waiver of sanctions, links crime and the exercise of authority. It tells us something about the legitimacy of an order. It is an indication of decomposition . . .'[21]

The implication of Dahrendorf's argument is, at least in part, that the 'toughening up' of punishments is a necessary step if social and moral authority is to be restored in modern society, and Dahrendorf relies heavily on Durkheim's thesis as support for his view. In fact, though, Dahrendorf goes considerably further than Durkheim in this respect, and gives punishment and penal severity a more prominent role in the production of authority than Durkheim's theory ever does. Punishment, for Durkheim, is necessary as a last resort, and must be used when obedience cannot be induced by other methods. But his theory says nothing specific about the amount or intensity of punishment required, since this will always depend upon the circumstances. Clearly the force and form of the sanction will have sufficiently to convey the message that the 'authorities' are in control, but Durkheim insists that punishment cannot by itself *produce* authority, however harshly it strikes: it can only reinforce a moral order which is already, authoritatively, *there*. The inter-action between authority and punishment is thus a complex one. Punishment is used most frequently where authority is weakest—but in such cases it has least effect. Alternatively, a strong and legitimately established moral order requires only token sanctions to restore itself and deal with violators. Durkheim would not go so far as Nietzsche—who claimed that a self-confident society 'flushed with . . . a sense of power' could afford to let its offenders go

[20] J. Q. Wilson and G. Kelling's essay, 'Broken Windows', examines the processes involved in respect of neighbourhoods which suffer from high levels of crime and low levels of effective policing. *Atlantic Monthly*, March 1982, pp. 29–38.
[21] R. Dahrendorf, *Law and Order* (London, 1985), p. 20.

unpunished.[22] But he certainly implies that punishment is largely ineffective except where authority is already strong. Thus the more authoritative, stable, and legitimate the political–moral order, the less need there is for terroristic or force-displaying uses of punishment.

Durkheim's claim about the 'social necessity' of punishment is thus a limited one and should be understood as such. It should not make us complacent about the use of punishment in society, nor lead us to view it as 'good for society' except in this minimal, last-resort capacity. As Durkheim realized, the precise determination and use of penal sanctions must always be a matter of politics, depending upon levels of authority, legitimacy, and tolerance, as well as sensibilities and reforming energies. As he put it in *The Division of Labour*: 'in saying that punishment such as it is, has a *raison d'être*, we do not intend to suggest that it is perfect and incapable of betterment . . . the matter is only a question of justification in the large.'[23]

5. PUNITIVE PASSIONS

Durkheim says of punishment that it is functionally required and useful at the level of the social order, but is in fact mechanically, non-purposively, produced. Punishment is driven, in the first instance, by collective moral outrage rather than strategic planning. Its motivation comes 'from below' rather than from above.[24] In fact, Durkheim came to modify this 'bottom-up' account of punishment's dynamics when he allowed that the state and its penal institutions nowadays 'graduate' this spontaneous passion, and direct its energies in a more self-conscious pursuit of efficiency. Nevertheless, he is adamant that the passions of outrage and indignation felt by 'healthy consciences' continue to provide the primary motivational energy which prompts and supports legal punishments. The state merely takes control of a penal process which remains rooted elsewhere.

Durkheim's emphasis upon the popular, emotional dynamics of punishment has not been much repeated in other sociological accounts of the phenomenon. In the work of Foucault or Rusche and Kirchheimer, or in the large 'sociology of control' literature of the 1970s and 1980s, there is virtually no discussion of such issues. Punishment is seen instead as a strategic measure undertaken by the state, and the focus is upon the political calculations which underlie penal practice, rather than the popular emotions which it conveys. Part of the reason for this is that these critical accounts want to imply that the state, or the ruling class, or the disciplinary machine, is the punishing subject and that penal sanctions are deployed without the real consent or support of the population at large. To the extent that 'the people' go along with this, it is seen as being a

---

[22] Nietzsche, *The Genealogy of Morals*, p. 205.

[23] Durkheim, *The Division of Labor*, p. 109.

[24] This happy coincidence between private interest and public good is also noted by Adam Smith in his *The Theory of the Moral Sentiments* (Oxford, 1976; orig. publ. 1759).

matter of false consciousness and misdirected anger—the real source of punishment is the ruling élite. But such an implication is surely implausible, at least in its simple form. Deeply held sentiments regarding crime and punishment undoubtedly exist throughout the population and are forcefully and frequently expressed. Whether these be judged 'authentic' and self-generated or 'false' and ideologically constructed, makes no difference whatsoever to their reality and social force. Nor is it useful for critics of penality to ignore such facts, for if such sentiments do exist, and give support to current penal practices, then penal reformers will have to address themselves directly to popular feelings if they intend to produce real change.

As we saw in the last chapter, Durkheim describes the sentiments which motivate punishment as consisting in the more or less lively emotions of horror, moral outrage, and righteous indignation. These are the shocked reactions of a community of believers when confronted with powerful acts of blasphemy and sacrilege, and they carry a force of rage and energy which springs from the believer's depth of commitment. The emotions in question are thus forceful and aggressive, but they have about them a moral tone and a quality of righteousness—they are socially derived and in a sense 'altruistic' sentiments rather than the base instincts of individuals. In his discussion of moral sentiments and the nature of human 'sympathies', Adam Smith gives an account of the punitive passions which is very closely related to Durkheim's, and which, in some respects, extends the latter's description in important ways. Like Durkheim, Smith refers to the 'anger', 'abhorrence', 'aversion', and vengefulness which criminal acts evoke in the hearts of other members of the community, but he sharpens this description by identifying a single quality of sentiment as the key dynamic of punitive action. '[T]he sentiment which most immediately and directly prompts us . . . to punish, is', he says, '*resentment*'.[25]

Resentment, according to Smith, is the sentiment of sympathy felt by the 'impartial spectator' whenever he or she learns of the suffering of someone who has been the victim of a wrongdoing. Being prompted by proper moral sentiments, resentment is distinguishable from mere hatred or dislike and is, in fact, a more active emotion than either of the latter. Resentment moves the 'indifferent bystander' to feel strongly that action must be taken to put right the injustice, that, in short, 'something must be done'. Smith, of course, gives an individualistic turn to his account of this social process—it is sympathy for another individual which prompts social justice, rather than a Durkheimian respect for society's laws—but like Durkheim he is careful to give resentment a moral quality, and to distinguish it from simple vengefulness or individual aggression. Smith denies the conventional view that resentment is 'the most odious, perhaps, of all the passions' and he argues that proper resentment is always measured and proportionate to the victim's suffering. Any punitive

---

[25] A. Smith, *The Theory of Moral Sentiments*, p. 68.

reaction which goes beyond this moderate desire for justice will itself be resented by reasonable members of the community.[26] In point of fact, Smith believed that 'the greater part of mankind are incapable of this moderation' and are all too prone to 'rude' and 'undisciplined' violence. But in civilized society, those individuals who are responsible for administering justice and imposing punishments do so, and do so justly, under the motivation of a distinctively moral sentiment called resentment.

To the modern, post-Freudian imagination, these accounts of punitive emotion seem altogether too sanitized and free from base desire. There must be more than a suspicion that their concern to show punishment's part in social health led these writers too easily to assume that punitive sentiments are therefore 'healthy' and 'moral'. By way of an antidote to this, we should consider the work of Friedrich Nietzsche, whose *Genealogy of Morals* presents a very much darker interpretation of the sentiments which motivate punitive justice. For Nietzsche, there is more than dutiful moral sentiment in the fact of punishment—there is positive pleasure. To punish another is to gratify the impulses of sadism and cruelty which a will to power over others produces in the human psyche. 'To behold suffering gives pleasure', he says 'but to cause another to suffer affords even greater pleasure. This severe statement expresses an old, powerful, human, all too human sentiment.'[27] As usual in Nietzsche's vision, the least noble sentiments are to be found among the common people, the lower classes, 'the herd'. But in the case of punishment, there is a specific explanation for this social distribution of cruel delight—for the act of punishing implies a measure of power which is the more enjoyed the less often it is experienced. 'In "punishing" the debtor, the creditor shares a seignorial right. For once he is given a chance to bask in the glorious feeling of treating another human being as lower than himself—or, in case the actual punitive power has passed on to a legal "authority", of seeing him despised and mistreated.'[28]

As the last sentence of this passage indicates, the pleasures of punishment are nowadays vicarious rather than direct, since in modern society it is the state which punishes, using the punitive machinery for its own purposes and utilities. But, Nietzsche argues, even as an instrument of state power, punishment continues to be a muted festival of cruelty in which the population may indulge its base emotions and its indirect enjoyment of power. Of course the penal institutions of modern society deny their association with cruelty, and popular sadism is frowned upon by the high-minded moralists of the community, but Nietzsche insists that beneath this hypocrisy—or perhaps in what Freud would call the unconscious—these passions continue to exist: '. . . pleasure in cruelty is not really extinct today; only, given our greater delicacy, that pleasure has had to undergo a certain sublimation.' It has to be 'translated into imaginative and psychological terms in order to pass muster before even the tenderest hypocritical conscience'.[29]

---

[26] Ibid. 76. [27] Nietzsche, *The Genealogy of Morals*, p. 198.
[28] Ibid. 196–7. [29] Ibid. 200.

Disturbing as these passages are, it would be hard to deny that these sentiments or something very like them still have a place within the emotive range surrounding modern punishment.[30] Nevertheless, it seems clear that Nietzsche's account is as partial and one sided as that of Durkheim or Smith. If we examine the sentiments typically expressed by reformers, by penal agents, and by the different sectors of the public, it quickly becomes clear that the punishment of offenders is capable of evoking a whole range of feelings from sympathy and compassion to anger and indignation. When confronted with this complex range of emotions it makes little sense to begin by reducing this diversity to a single sentiment or feeling-tone. Nor does it seem useful to argue whether the predominant sentiment is high or low in some moral hierarchy, since a key aspect of emotional life—in this sphere as in many others—is the fact of ambivalence: i.e. the coexistence of contradictory impulses and emotions towards the same object. Psychological attitudes are often a fusion of high moral sentiment and the immorality of ulterior motive, so the last thing we should expect is that punitive emotions will prove to be simple or single-minded.

In his analysis of 'The Psychology of Punitive Justice', George Herbert Mead begins to explore the complex psychological dimensions of the public response to criminal offenders. He argues that the righteous indignation which society's members feel towards the criminal aggressor is, in effect, a cultural sublimation of the self-assertive instincts and destructive hostilities which lie behind social co-operation and competition. As he puts it, 'the cry of thief or murder is attuned to profound complexes, lying below the surface of individual effort'.[31] Normally, such hostilities are restrained by the internalized social inhibitions upon which social life depends, but the rituals of criminal procedure provide an authorized occasion for their release. Taking part in the emotional defence of 'society's interests' against criminal depredations, the individual's aggressions against the 'outsider' are aroused and reinforced, as is his or her identification with the in-group and the interests which are at stake. According to Mead, it is this process of group-reinforced identification, and its release of aggressions, which gives to punitive emotions their characteristic zeal and energy. The temporary disappearance of inhibition—allowing an unrestrained love of the group and hatred of its enemies—'means a removal of resistance and friction and adds exhilaration and enthusiasm to the expression of one of the most powerful human impulses'.[32] This Meadian analysis is, of course, very close to the Durkheimian one in its positive psychological aspect—hostility towards the criminal helps promote solidarity and love between the citizens. But the two accounts diverge because Mead stresses that it is the underlying

---

[30] See the discussion of this in ch. 10.
[31] G. H. Mead, 'The Psychology of Punitive Justice', *American Journal of Sociology*, 23 (1918), p. 591.
[32] Ibid. 598.

psychic forces of mutual hostility and self-assertion which supply the emotional energy for punishment and colour the form which it will take.

The ambivalence which Mead hints at when he describes the punitive emotion as socially displaced and uninhibited aggression—rather than dutiful moral outrage—is also the distinctive centre of most Freudian accounts of punishment's psychology. For the psychoanalyst, the mechanisms of instinct, inhibition, repression, and release are very much as Mead describes them, and punishment presents 'a socially acceptable outlet for our own aggressions'. According to this view, 'the institution of punishments represents a compensation, as it were, for the restrictions one puts on one's own sadism, and the identification of the righteous member of the community with the latter's punishing functions, helps him to live out his own aggressions in an acceptable fashion'.[33] We are back, in other words, to the position set out by Nietzsche. However, at least for some Freudians, there are other layers of psychic involvement which interest the righteous citizen in the criminal and his or her punishment. It is sometimes suggested, for example, that the fascination which criminal exploits have for many of the public—as shown in popular reading and viewing habits, and the unquenchable thirst for crime news—is a gratification of repressed aggressions and sexual desires which continue to inhabit the socialized citizen. The range of feelings evoked by a criminal who seems to live out such desires can thus include identification and vicarious gratification as well as horror and repugnance. Indeed, the punitive energy shown by some individuals towards criminals can be interpreted as a guilty and masochistic response to their own tendency to fantasize an identification with the criminal's exploits.[34]

Interpretations such as these are inherently controversial and carry little weight outside of individual case histories based upon reliable clinical evidence. Nor do I seek to generalize from them here. But the conflicting emotions and ambivalences, which depth psychology suggests, do serve to show the range and complexity of the emotions involved in this area. Fascination, intense curiosity, guilty pleasure, and indignant aggression may form part of the normal response to crime, even if these are not the sentiments which are publicly expressed.

Nor should reference to Freud and to sublimated desires make us forget the 'civilized sentiments' which bring about this sublimation and form a counterpoint to hostile attitudes.[35] The Western Judaeo-Christian culture which has helped form modern penal institutions and which continues to shape penal policy, also draws upon the most elevated sentiments and moral attitudes. One has only to look at the charitable and philanthropic practices which have

---

[33] F. Alexander and J. Staub, *The Criminal, the Judge and the Public* (London, 1931), p. 221.

[34] For a subtle discussion of this phenomenon, in a historical case-study, see L. Faller, *Turned to Account: The Forms and Functions of Criminal Biography in Late Seventeenth and Early Eighteenth Century England* (Cambridge, 1987), ch. 1.

[35] See ch. 10.

grown up around penal institutions, or at the penological teachings of religious and humanistic movements to see that, whatever else they involve, they do articulate sentiments such as sympathy, love, and pity and promote attitudes of benevolence, forgiveness, and mercy. If, then, we follow Durkheim's lead and explore the emotional context within which penal practice occurs, we should be clear that we are faced with a complex and ambivalent field of forces, rather than the uniform collective passion which he implies.

However we understand the character and sources of these emotions—and I shall return to this problem in later chapters—it seems clear that in contemporary societies criminal conduct continues to produce emotive responses, and that, at least in psychological terms, there is still a considerable collective involvement and public interest in the business of crime and punishment. Crime-reporting and the relaying of sentencing decisions take up a high proportion of space in the popular press and media. 'Law and order' issues evoke strong feelings among the electorate. Crowds of angry—or merely curious—people gather around police stations or court-rooms where notorious offenders are held, and it is not unknown for jubilant, voyeuristic crowds to assemble outside prisons where judicial executions are being carried out. And whenever such 'popular emotions' are displayed there will be journalists on hand to relate the event to a more passive (but still interested) readership elsewhere. So punishment continues to be 'an emotive issue', as the politicians say, but in fact our culture imposes heavy restraints upon such emotions, and ensures that the forms and possibilities of their expression are carefully structured and controlled. 'Vengeance', for example, is no longer an acceptable sentiment to be voiced in this context. As Susan Jacoby and others have shown, the vengeful demand for retaliation came to be regarded as uncivilized and unworthy during the nineteenth century, so that anger directed towards the criminal must now adopt a more polite form of expression if it is to be heeded.[36] In fact 'punitiveness', as such, has come to be a rather shameful sentiment during the twentieth century, at least among the educated élite, so that arguments about prison conditions, severity of sentences, or the justice of the death penalty tend to be couched in utilitarian terms—even when it seems apparent that hard treatment is what is wanted, not 'useful effects'.

As for their possibilities of expression, popular sentiments regarding punishment do not have a direct role in the modern process of punishment—except where lynch mobs defy the state's monopoly over penal sanctions. With the limited exception of juries and lay justices—whose roles are strictly defined— 'public opinion' and 'community feelings' enter into the process of justice only in an oblique fashion. They provide a general context of support for the laws and institutions which exist—or for new measures which rely upon electoral endorsement—and they are referred to as a proper 'consideration' in the formation of policy and in individual sentencing decisions. In that sense, the

---

[36] S. Jacoby, *Wild Justice: The Evolution of Revenge* (London, 1985).

public acts as a kind of stage army in the criminal justice process—being referred to and invoked more often than it gets involved in the action. Social sentiments form the specific 'climate of opinion'' or *mentalité* in which penal institutions operate—they are a general structuring context, rather than the particular causes of specific penal acts. But even this broad structuring role has to be qualified, because as we saw earlier, the relationship between public sentiment and state practice is an interactive one. Sentiments are elicited and evoked, trained and organized, by the very institutional practices which they come to support.

6. The rituals of punishment

In seeking to understand this process whereby disparate social sentiments are brought to life and given a specific focus, we must turn to the study of penal rituals and their social organization. As Durkheim tells us—in his studies of religion as well as those on punishment—it is through periodical ritual practices that social sentiments maintain their force and vitality. These rituals punctuate normal social life and provide a specific framework for the expression and release of popular emotion. For Durkheim, the rituals of criminal justice—the court-room trial, the passing of sentence, the execution of punishment—are, in effect, the formalized embodiment and enactment of the *conscience collective*. In doing justice, and in processing criminals, these procedures are also giving formal expression to the feelings of the community— and by being expressed in this way those feelings are both strengthened and gratified. Penal rituals are thus, for Durkheim, a means of representing and reinforcing a morality that already exists. Other anthropologists, however, go further than this and give rather more emphasis to the *creative* effect of ritual with respect to sentiment.[37] Rituals do not just 'express' emotions—they arouse them and organize their content; they provide a kind of didactic theatre through which the onlooker is taught what to feel, how to react, which sentiments are called for in that situation. Rituals—including the rituals of criminal justice—are ceremonies which, through the manipulation of emotion, prompt particular value commitments on the part of the participants and the audience and thus act as a kind of sentimental education, generating and regenerating a particular mentality and a particular sensibility. Not every criminal case does this, of course, though ritualistic elements are involved in even the most mundane, 'conveyor-belt' procedures. But there are what one might describe as 'show-case' trials and punishments—solemn, emotionally charged affairs of high drama and real import—which tend to be the ones which are relayed by the media to the public to represent the meaning of justice.

[37] See e.g. V. Turner, *The Ritual Process* (Ithaca, NY, 1977); C. Geertz, *Negara: The Theatre State in Nineteenth Century Bali* (Princeton, NJ, 1980); K. Thomas, *Religion and the Decline of Magic* (London, 1971).

The public is not immediately involved today in the direction or administration of punishment. Rather it forms the audience of onlookers to which penal rituals appeal and which, in turn, responds with emotional commitment and support (or, less often, with criticism and protest). These ritual occasions thus form the focus for the diffuse concerns, worries, and emotions that constitute the public temper in regard to crime. People look to such procedures not just as instrumental mechanisms which will process the single offender in question, but as symbolic reassertions of order and authority which help deal with the feelings of helplessness, disorder, and insecurity which crime introduces into their lives. In witnessing the penal ritual—whether directly or through second-hand reports—citizens are led to experience for themselves the emotional drama of crime and its resolution in punishment. It is a social occasion which simultaneously structures individual sentiment and gives it cathartic release.

The penal process, in other words, must be seen as a means of evoking, expressing, and modifying passions, as well as an instrumental procedure for administering offenders. As well as 'getting things done' with respect to crime control, penal rituals are concerned to manipulate symbolic forms as a means of educating and reassuring their public audiences. The symbols which are invoked in these ceremonies—like all public symbols—'function in concrete situations to organize perceptions (meanings, emotions, concepts, attitudes)' and thus to shape cultural ethos and private sensibility.[38] In this way, punishments help structure our customary discourses and practices of 'blaming', 'holding responsible', and thinking about deviance. They provide moral guidance, patterns of discernment, and languages of condemnation which have wider social effects in organizing conduct in all walks of life, as well as their role in feeding back more directly their support for the established institutions of punishment.[39]

The literature of social psychology provides several analyses of penal rituals which suggest how the formal organization and procedures of these rites help produce their symbolic and emotive effects. Harold Garfinkel's classic account of court-room ritual interprets it as a 'degradation ceremony' in which 'moral indignation serves to effect the ritual destruction of the person denounced' by defining the accused as, in effect, an enemy of the people and their ultimate values.[40] This analysis has subsequently been extended by Pat Carlen, whose study of the court-room showed how its spatial organization, its temporal routines, and its linguistic codes all help structure the status of the parties

[38] C. Geertz, 'Deep Play: Notes on the Balinese Cockfight', in id., *The Interpretation of Cultures* (New York, 1973), p. 449.

[39] The importance of penal ritual in shaping public perceptions is stressed by Edwin Sutherland in his account of why 'white-collar' and 'corporate' crime is so leniently dealt with in modern societies. Sutherland argued that public resentment against such offences remained largely unorganized and unfocused because they were dealt with by civil law procedures and not by the penal rituals of the criminal law. See E. H. Sutherland, *White-Collar Crime* (New York, 1949).

[40] H. Garfinkel, 'Conditions of Successful Degradation Ceremonies', *The American Journal of Sociology*, 61 (1956), 420–4.

involved, and the symbolic meaning of the event.[41] In George Herbert Mead's account, the court-room procedure is designed to evoke in its audience the twin emotions of 'respect for the law' and 'hatred for the criminal aggressor'.

[T]he court procedure emphasizes this emotional attitude. The state's attorney seeks a conviction. The accused must defend himself against this attack. The aggrieved person and the community find in this officer of the government their champion. A legal battle takes the place of the former physical struggle which led up to the arrest. The emotions called out are the emotions of battle.[42]

And finally, Alexander and Staub add that '. . . court trials, especially those of capital crimes, frequently have the character of a public performance and serve as an outlet for our aggressions, even as gladiator battles of ancient Rome, or bullfights of some of the modern Latin races serve the same purposes'.[43]

These kinds of arguments are presented to show the ritual qualities and effects generally possessed by criminal justice procedures. But, of course, rituals are always highly specific social events: they always operate within a particular community of belief, grounding their practices within the social relations, authorities, and traditions of that community. Similarly, the symbolic forms which they use always derive their meaning and importance in the concrete circumstances of their use—rather than being universal or always recognizable. Historical studies of punishments show this clearly enough. The eighteenth-century English court scenes which Douglas Hay describes do not merely evoke the timeless majesty of the law and the heinousness of crime. Included in these elaborate rituals are symbolic celebrations of the power of religion, the importance of hierarchy, the local relations of status, deference, and paternalism, and of course the power of the state and its officials to lead, direct, and punish the multitude. The broad gestures and procedures here are recognizable as the instrumental actions of a modern court of law, but the symbolic languages in use, and the connotations of every sign and gesture, are distinctively English, local, and historically specific. Similar points can be made about the rites of execution described by Spierenburg in Amsterdam, Foucault in France, or Masur in the USA, or again about the politico-religious rituals of justice which Zeman describes in Puritan Massachusetts. All these conveyed specific meanings to their audience which the historian can only try with difficulty to reconstruct.[44]

It seems clear from these examples that the symbolic languages of penal

[41] P. Carlen, *Magistrates' Justice* (Oxford, 1976).

[42] Mead, 'The Psychology of Punitive Justice', p. 586.

[43] Alexander and Staub, *The Criminal, the Judge and the Public*, p. 222.

[44] D. Hay, 'Property, Authority and the Criminal Law', id. *et al.*, *Albion's Fatal Tree* (Harmondsworth, 1975); Spierenburg, *The Spectacle of Suffering*; Foucault, *Discipline and Punish*; L. Masur, *Rites of Execution: Capital Punishment and the Transformation of American Culture, 1776–1865* (New York, 1989); T. Zeman, 'Order, Crime and Punishment: The American Criminological Tradition', Ph.D. diss., University of California (Santa Cruz, June 1981).

rituals speak to specific communities at specific times and places rather than to the universal requirements of criminal justice or law enforcement. Moreover, the meanings and affirmations which emerge from these rituals refer outwards, beyond the court, to the social order itself and the particular relations, hierarchies, and ideologies which constitute it. In that sense a penal ritual is, as Durkheim believed, also and always a social ritual on a larger scale. As such, the success of the penal process, in evoking the proper emotions and public responses, will depend not just upon the justice of the particular case in hand, but also, and crucially, upon the coherence (or divisiveness) of the social order which surrounds it. Wherever a community is not completely homogeneous—which is to say virtually everywhere—there will tend to be different audiences for such public ceremonies and different responses to it. Some participants or onlookers will experience recognition, identity, and reinforcement of faith, while for others the ceremony may seem to reveal coercion rather than authority, an alien power rather than a shared belief. And of course it is always possible that a public ritual will misfire and produce unintended effects, either because its rites are improperly observed or because of wider conflicts in the social order. An executioner may botch his work, a judge may act unjustly, the law may be unpopular or the defendant may move the crowd to sympathy—evoking pathos, protest, and indignation against the authorities, rather than solidarity with them.

7. Public involvement and penal ritual today

What can be said about penal rituals as they operate in contemporary society? What are the ritual occasions? Who participates in them, and how? What idiom do they employ and which sentiments are evoked? What, in general, are the effects which they have? In the view of some commentators, such as Michel Foucault, ritualized procedures are more and more replaced today by regulative measures and instrumental disciplines. Modern society is based upon surveillance, rather than spectacle; and accordingly punishment becomes a matter of privatized regimes rather than public ceremonials.[45] It is also suggested that the diversity of modern culture, and particularly the absence of broad-based communities of belief, renders impossible the operation of meaningful public rituals, and destroys the basis for real communication on this level..It seems to me that such views are overstated, though they do point to an important truth about modern society. Public rituals, ceremonies, and spectacles continue to operate and to have important social effects, as anyone who has seen a royal coronation in the UK or a political party convention in the USA will already realize. But the form of such occasions has certainly changed, as has their relative place in the support and maintenance of the social order. Foucault and others are right to point to the elaborate machinery of control and regulation

---

[45] Foucault, *Discipline and Punish.*

which extends today to most spheres of life, disciplining and normalizing social conduct and relations. And no doubt this massive administrative capacity ensures a level of stability and orderliness which early modern states would envy. But, as was argued earlier, the organization of sentiment, emotion, and commitment remains an important aspect of any regime's legitimacy, and so public rituals continue to have a place in the modern world—even if their audience is divided and their idiom necessarily secular. (Nor should it be thought that the administrative machinery of social regulation is altogether devoid of ritual and symbolic significance. As I will argue in Chapter 11, bureaucratic actions and technical languages have their own gestural, rhetorical aspects.)

No attempt will be made here to analyse the details of contemporary penal rituals—such interpretations require close analysis and detail, and are best dealt with through individual case-studies. Instead I want just to indicate the positioning of ritual process in modern criminal justice, and the general patterns of its operation and effects. The first point to note in this regard is that the ritual aspects of the penal process tend nowadays to be confined to the court-room and the process of conviction and sentencing. The focus of public attention, and the locus of ritual display, is thus the *declaration* of punishment, rather than the process of punishment itself, which tends to be conducted in 'privatized' circumstances, away from public view.[46] This situation contrasts sharply with previous penal systems, where the execution of sentence was the highpoint of an extended public drama, taking place in full view of an assembled crowd—and the difference has some important social consequences.[47] The penal process of modern societies has become a fragmented, differentiated sequence of events, in which certain aspects are subjected to close public scrutiny and involvement, and others are left to the management of professionals who, for the most part, maintain a low visibility and control their own information output.[48] The courts have tended to become the forum where 'justice is done' and to which public attention is directed, while the other penal

[46] This modern distribution of attention is reflected in the patterns of news-reporting which surround criminal justice: '. . . prisons are relatively closed institutions for the purposes of news. It is rare to find a regular "prison beat" reporter. . . . Prisons are run in terms more of administrative discretion than of external review and accountability, and this veil of administrative decency has effectively kept out the news media. This observation is borne out by content studies that indicate that stories emanating from prisons, or about prisons, are rare statistically compared to court coverage and especially police coverage.' R. V. Ericson, P. M. Baranek, J. B. L. Chan, *Negotiating Control: A Study of News Sources* (Toronto, 1989), p. 11.

[47] See E. Canetti, *Crowds and Power* (Harmondsworth, 1973), p. 59, where Canetti argues that the modern 'crowd' is composed of the newspaper-reading public: 'Today everyone takes part in public executions through the newspapers. Like everything else, however, it is more comfortable than it was. We sit peacefully at home and, out of a hundred details, can choose those to linger over which offer a special thrill. . . . [W]e know more about the business than our predecessors, who may have walked miles to see it, hung around for hours, and in the end, seen very little.'

[48] This concern for a low profile is not always successful. In particular it is countered by the attempts of critics and journalists to bring the realities of punishment out from 'behind the scenes' and to expose any cruelties or procedural improprieties which occur in penal institutions.

institutions have come to be seen as technical apparatuses, more concerned with 'management' than with 'governance'.

If we look at the style and procedures of the two aspects of the system we can see the effect this differentiation has had. The court-room is open to the press and the public. It retains the elaborate formalities and ceremonial procedures appropriate to public ritual and symbolic display. Even in the lower courts, where crimes are mundane and the sentences routine, there is a ritual evocation of the symbols of justice and an implied address to the watching public. And the higher courts—which deal with more serious crimes and which are more frequently reported—continue to speak in the traditional language of moral rhetoric, concerning themselves with the culpability, guilt, and punishment of the offender, phrasing the issues in emotive moral terms and resorting to denunciatory diatribes and open condemnation. In the exchanges between the parties and in the deliberations of the judge, the 'community interest' and 'community feelings' are continually invoked, so that the onlookers become a symbolic part of the proceedings, rather than simply spectators at the event, and, in the case of jury trials, selected members of the public play a real part in the process of conviction. Similarly when the sentence is announced the implication is that it represents the community's judgment, rather than that of the sentencer. The court-room is thus a ritual in which society as a whole is deemed to participate. It is because of this ritual structure and moral rhetoric that the courts continued to appear 'punitive' even at the high point of the treatment era in the 1950s and 1960s: instead of becoming technical instruments of assessment and correction they continued to give a place to the expression of sentiment and public condemnation.

In contrast, the rest of the criminal justice system operates in a less decorous fashion, and is oriented more towards low-key management than to public ritual. Those penal institutions which actually carry out the sentences—prisons, probation and parole agencies, social work departments, fine-enforcers, etc.— tend to be closed to the public and the press, or at least to control the degree to which they are open. They tend to represent their operations in neutral, technical terms and adopt a managerial posture rather than a moral one. Once inside these institutions, offenders are dealt with as so many objects of administration, being evaluated in managerial terms as good or bad prisoners, and low or high risks, rather than as 'criminals' who have perpetrated evil acts. The sentiments of the public and strong community feelings are deliberately neutralized within this institutional process. Institutional staff see themselves not as moral condemners but as impartial managers, committed to unemotive conduct and bureaucratic regimes.[49] And while penal institutions exist within a punitive, emotive context, and have occasionally to bend to punitive demands, they experience this as an environmental constraint and contradiction—as being a disruption of their task rather than constitutive of it.

---

[49] See Jacobs, *Stateville*, and J. J. DiIulio, *Governing Prisons: A Comparative Study of Correctional Management* (New York, 1987).

There are, of course, institutional rituals associated with imprisonment and even with non-custodial sanctions—for example the induction process where new inmates are stripped of their own clothes and possessions, bathed, processed, and allocated an institutional identity—but rites of passage such as these are performed for an internal audience and for internal purposes: their primary aim is to assert institutional control, not to make a show for a watching public. Similarly, the language of penal administrators is predominantly technical, managerial, quasi-scientific. It is oriented to the performance of a specialist, professional task and tends to exclude the public and the punitive rather than invoke them.[50] Inevitably this, too, functions as a rhetoric of sorts, and conveys to the public—or that part of it which wishes to be informed—a definite imagery and symbolism. But unlike court-room symbolism, this penal rhetoric gives a primary place to utilitarian concerns such as effective control, cost efficiency, and bureaucratic rationality—moral condemnation is a sub-merged image rather than the predominant one.

This removal of punishment's institutions from the public and moral arenas is very much the subject of Michel Foucault's historical work, and I will discuss this in more detail later, but for now the point that needs to be made is that popular involvement in the execution of punishment (as opposed to its declaration) is today of a rather limited and abstract nature. By and large the institutions of punishment escape close scrutiny by the public. When new institutions are developed, or major reforms undertaken, it is politically requisite that these be represented in such a way as to gain the tacit support of the public—or at least they must avoid incurring the opposition of those parts of the public which are politically active. However, once the institutional structure is established its repertoire of sanctions becomes the conventional one and it quickly becomes a routinized, technical matter. So long as the existing sanctions appear to convey a punitive effect in a manner which is broadly in keeping with current sensibilities, there tends to be limited moral interest in the details of how punishments are actually carried out. The whole focus of public interest and emotional intensity falls upon the court ritual and the declaration of sentence. Thereafter, the offender—and the remaining penal process—is removed from public view. In consequence, the institutions of punishment have tended to become instrumental in their orientation rather than morally expressive: they have come to focus upon a narrow range of technical objectives—security, control, cost efficiency, etc.—rather than upon the wider social and moral values. Considerations of social value, morality, and justice tend to form the external environment for these institutions rather than to penetrate their walls and guide their detailed practices. It is only when scandals occur, or when reformers make current practices appear scandalous, that these

[50] In many jurisdictions, especially since the 1970s, efforts are made to involve 'the community' in the business of dealing with and resettling offenders, and many voluntary agencies and individuals play a part in this. Nevertheless, punishment remains a largely professional task, operating out of sight of the vast majority of the public.

details are opened up for public scrutiny—and, even then, considerations of cost efficiency and procedural propriety can often displace all other forms of evaluation.

Given this situation, the Durkheimian argument that punishments express collective sentiments and are shaped by them can be accepted in only a very limited form. Public sentiments lend support to penal measures only in a very broad and contextual way. Certainly a penal system must broadly accord with the sensibilities of the public and its sanctions must appear to convey condemnation in a sufficient and appropriate way. But the day-to-day conduct of penal practices is not readily visible to the public, nor is it the focus of much 'passionate' interest. The nature of those penal practices is determined not by public sentiment, or even by those representations of 'public opinion' which are manufactured by the media, but by a legislative machinery and an administrative staff which usually operate at a considerable remove from public scrutiny—except at times of reform or public scandal. The normal focus of community feeling is not concerned with determining the range of penal practices, so much as with whether or not individual offenders are appropriately sentenced within the conventional range. The public's concern with punishment, and the rise and fall of 'passionate reactions', tend to centre around the deployment of the available sanctions—who gets what sentence?— rather than with the details of what goes on in penal institutions.

8. THE EFFECTS OF PUNISHMENT

Durkheim's analysis of the functions of punishment leads us to reverse our usual understanding of the target population of penal measures and the effects which these measures have. Punishment is conventionally viewed as a necessary and more or less effective means of controlling society's deviant minority. But Durkheim rejects this view. He argues that the effect of penal sanctions upon offenders and those prone to offending 'has been exaggerated beyond all reality' and is, in fact, 'very limited'.[51] As we have seen, the limited efficacy of punishment in such cases arises because it fails to achieve truly moral consequences. Most offenders lack a 'healthy' moral conscience, so that, for them, punishment is merely a form of intimidation. At best, it can act as a kind of policing mechanism, enforcing 'overt and superficial propriety' but doing nothing to change the individual's disposition to anti-social conduct. Indeed, Durkheim argues that the more frequently punishment is used, the less effective it becomes, since it tends to destroy whatever shamefulness and moral feelings the individual had left.

This last point is well taken, and helps to explain the very high recidivism rates which are a feature of modern penal systems. Precisely because punishment involves moral condemnation, but cannot by itself produce moral attachment,

[51] Durkheim, *Moral Education*, p. 162.

it serves to alienate further offenders rather than to improve their conduct. Moral reproach produces guilt, remorse, and reform only where the offender is already a member of the moral community represented by the law, and, in such cases, self-reproach makes formal punishment more or less redundant. But in other cases, where attachment is weak and self-reproach is minimal, punishment is prone to have the opposite effect. As Friedrich Nietzsche puts it, 'by and large, punishment hardens and freezes; it concentrates, it sharpens the sense of alienation; it strengthens resistance'.[52] In such situations, '. . . what punishment is able to achieve, both for man and for beast, is increase of fear, circumspection, control over the instincts. Thus man is *tamed* by punishment, but by no means *improved*; rather the opposite.'[53]

For Durkheim, this kind of social constraint through intimidation is characteristic of a demoralized society. For him, the real bonds holding people together and regulating their conduct are always moral bonds, ties of shared sentiment and morality—hence his tendency to dismiss the importance of 'mere' control. But there is good reason to suppose that in modern societies—where moral community is often absent or fragmented, where large sectors of the population are only passive or ambivalent adherents to the dominant moral order, and where certain groups show a considerable disaffection from it—the role of 'mere' control and policing is much greater than Durkheim ever envisaged. Here it is not the occasional demoralized individual who exists outside of the *conscience collective*—it is rather whole groups and classes which are to some extent alienated, and whose co-operation with authority is based more upon a fear of consequences than upon dutiful moral commitment. In such circumstances, effective policing, extensive control, and an increased enforcement capacity come to be more important aspects of maintaining the social order than Durkheim's analysis would suggest.

This point is important because it indicates a deep connection between the development of an administrative form of penal sanctioning—premissed upon behaviour control rather than moral appeal—and the decline of moral community in modern society. It is precisely because much of the population—and especially the low-status sectors from which offenders are predominantly drawn—lives outside of, or in an ambivalent relation to, the dominant moral order, that punishments have become less public and less openly moral in tone.[54] Modern penal policy endeavours to transform conduct by threats, penalties, behavioural training, psychological adjustment, and the manipulation of environment—it seeks to improve and correct by technical means rather than by moral persuasion. These measures, as we have seen, are undertaken on the margins of society, out of sight of the public and without involving them in the operation. Unlike Puritan punishments, for example, where penal

---

[52] Nietzsche, *The Genealogy of Morals*, p. 214.   [53] Ibid. 216.

[54] For a discussion of the dimensions of moral disaffection and ambivalence as they relate to the criminal law, see Dahrendorf, *Law and Order*. On the wider question of the limits of any moral vocabulary in the modern world, see A. MacIntyre, *After Virtue* (Notre Dame, Ind., 1981).

measures were conceived as an aspect of community life and which aimed for the moral reintegration of the offender, modern penality is seen as a management problem, aimed at the containment of deviant groups who are, in all likelihood, beyond real integration.[55] One might say that, for the upright sections of the community—*les honnêtes gens*—punishment still adopts a moral form and a ritualistic expression in the sphere of the court and its judicial process. But for the underclass—for that large population which threatens to live outside the law because it lacks, and is perceived to lack, the incentives to be law-abiding which property, career, and status can provide—the practices of penality and policy adopt a more business-like, instrumental approach, concerned with the furtherance of effective control rather than the niceties of moral display. As we will see in later chapters, the work of Michel Foucault explores these instrumentalities of modern punishment in great detail, thus providing an important corrective and complement to Durkheim's one-sided approach.

But what of this moral dimension of punishment upon which Durkheim places so much stress? Do penal rituals actually produce the effects which Durkheim claims for them even if they are not the whole of punishment's social meaning? It will be recalled that Durkheim posits a 'higher utility' for punishment. He argues that its major effect—indeed its main social function— is to enhance social solidarity by reaffirming the force of collective sentiments. The ritualized procedure of criminal justice is, in effect, a form of 'secular communion', as Garfinkel puts it, which 'brings together upright consciences and concentrates them'.[56]

Other writers clearly support Durkheim in this respect, and this particular thesis has achieved the status of canonical knowledge in the sociological world. We know from the anthropological study of ritual process that solidarity among the participants is a characteristic effect of these social occasions—an effect described by some anthropologists as a latent function (signifying the cunning of social institutions) and by others as a conscious objective (signifying the cunning of the authorities who stage and perform the rituals).[57] Furthermore, the psychological pattern which Durkheim describes is a familiar and plausible one—we have all experienced the unifying effect of a common enemy, the pleasures of positive identifications and the uplifting sense of solidarity that comes from collective affirmation. So when the textbooks set out Durkheim's thesis, and note that studies by Mead, Garfinkel, and Kai Erikson confirm its validity, it is easy to assume that penal rituals do produce solidarity and to leave the matter at that.[58]

[55] For an account of criminal justice organized along Puritan lines, see Zeman, 'Order, Crime and Punishment'.

[56] Garfinkel, 'Conditions of Successful Degradation Ceremonies', p. 421 and Durkheim, *The Division of Labor*, p. 102. The published text of Garfinkel's essay, together with various reprints, talks of 'secular communism' (*sic*) which I take to be a slip.

[57] See Douglas, *How Institutions Think*, ch. 3.

[58] See J. M. Beattie, *Crime and the Courts in England, 1660–1800* (Princeton, 1986) for a good example of this Durkheimian interpretation being brought to bear upon the analysis of 17th-cent. punishments.

But, in point of fact, there is reason to be cautious about this assumption and to treat it as a matter of empirical contingency, rather than an axiomatic fact about the world. Indeed if one looks closely at the studies which are usually cited as support for Durkheim's thesis, it becomes apparent that they actually qualify it in important ways and lead one to doubt its generality. Take G. H. Mead's famous study of 'The Psychology of Punitive Justice', for example. This essay certainly affirms that punitive rituals evoke emotional responses in the onlookers which give rise to an effective form of solidarity. As Mead puts it, 'the revulsions against criminality reveal themselves in a sense of solidarity with the group, a sense of being a citizen'.[59] Through punitive justice we the public can experience 'the common will' and 'the feeling that we all stand together' to a degree that allows social solidarities to take precedence over the many conflicts and tensions which otherwise divide us.[60] As Mead declares, 'seemingly without the criminal, the cohesiveness of society would disappear'.[61] But the crucial term here is 'seemingly' because Mead's essay is, in fact, a powerful *critique* of punitive justice and a *refutation* of its social utility. Published in 1918, amidst the human carnage of the First World War, it is above all a Progressive's attack upon hostile social rituals and a plea for a constructive, recuperative approach to social problems.

It is not simply 'solidarity' which punitive justice promotes—it is a distinctive form of solidarity: 'the emotional solidarity of aggression'.[62] This is a cohesion based upon the release of individual aggressions in the form of a 'functional' group hostility, dedicated to the vanquishing of an enemy. And while this— like warfare itself—can undoubtedly bind a social group, it does so in a particular form and with definite social costs. As Mead insists, 'while . . . the attitude of hostility, either against the transgressor of laws or against the external enemy, gives to the group a sense of solidarity which most readily arouses like a burning flame and which consumes the differences of individual interests, *the price paid for this solidarity of feeling is great and at times disastrous*.[63] The dysfunctional consequences of punitive justice—or rather the social costs which it entails—are then described in some detail by Mead. He points out that the hostility aroused by criminal proceedings prevents us from dispassionately dealing with the causes of crime; that it promotes an unquestioning attitude towards the law and the social interests it maintains; and, more widely, that it directs our energies against scapegoat enemies instead of towards 'the reconstruction of social conditions'.[64] In effect, Mead shows us the other side of those emotions which Durkheim treats as straightforwardly functional, demonstrating their potential for destructive intolerance and escalating social violence, as well as for social cohesion. Indeed, Mead's critique reminds us that the passionate, punitive reactions which Durkheim describes are, quite literally, those of the religious zealot. And while deep religious commitment can form

---

[59] Mead, 'The Psychology of Punitive Justice', p. 586.
[60] Ibid. 587, and 569.   [61] Ibid. 591.   [62] Ibid.
[63] Ibid. 592 (emphasis added).   [64] Ibid. 602.

the basis for a stable social order, it can also give rise to intolerance, repression, schismatic division, and bitter social conflict.

A similar qualification is implied by Harold Garfinkel in his essay on 'Conditions of Successful Degradation Ceremonies'. Garfinkel takes it as axiomatic that 'moral indignation may reinforce group solidarity'—though note that he says 'may'—and that 'only in societies that are completely demoralized will an observer be unable to find . . . ceremonies' which are devoted to this purpose.[65] He then proceeds to analyse how such ceremonies are organized, and how they 'work' by the manipulation of symbol, meaning, and emotion. On the surface, this appears as a restatement of the Durkheimian thesis about functional effectivity of penal rituals, but in fact the essay shows the *difficulties* of effective denunciation as well as the methods by which it can be achieved. The structural preconditions and contextual requirements which Garfinkel describes as being necessary to a 'successful' denunciation are by no means easy to satisfy. By way of general conditions, they require that the prosecutor (the 'denouncer') be wholly identified with the ultimate values of the community, and be understood to speak in their name. For this to occur, the community must already share a common 'metaphysic', and a commitment to a 'legitimate order' from which the offender is to be estranged. More local conditions also influence the 'effectiveness' of the ceremony—'factors like the territorial arrangements and movements of persons at the scene of the denunciation, the numbers of persons involved as accused, degraders and witnesses, status claims of the contenders, prestige and power allocations among participants, all should influence the outcome'.[66]

It is hardly surprising then—though it is seldom noticed by the secondary literature—that Garfinkel's essay concludes on a subversive point rather than a functionalist one. His final sentence points out that the foregoing analysis 'tells us not only how to construct an effective denunciation but also how to render denunciation useless'.[67] Garfinkel reminds us of what should be obvious but is too easily forgotten: namely, that social rituals are by no means guaranteed to achieve their intended results. The efficacy of such occasions depends upon a fragile set of preconditions which may or may not be met, depending upon specific circumstances. As Mary Douglas remarks: 'religions do not always make believers more loyal to their rulers or more industrious in their gardens and boats, any more than magic always brings fishes to the nets. Sometimes it does, sometimes not.'[68] Durkheim's functional account of punishment is too ready to assume the very 'functionality' which it sets out to prove. His discussion proceeds as if the rituals of punishment always give rise to a single solidarity-enhancing effect upon a morally homogeneous and receptive community. Outside Durkheim's functionalism, there is no reason to assume that all or any of these presumptions hold good.

---

[65] Garfinkel, 'Conditions of Successful Degradation Ceremonies', p. 400.
[66] Ibid. 404.   [67] Ibid.
[68] Douglas, *How Institutions Think*, p. 35.

As a final example, I turn to Kai Erikson's study *Wayward Puritans* which is generally held up as a historical affirmation of Durkheim's claims about punishment and social solidarity.[69] Erikson's investigation of the early Puritan settlements in Massachusetts, and the ways in which criminal law and penal measures were used to establish the boundaries of social order and the identity of the group, has been accorded the status of an empirical proof of the Durkheimian 'hypothesis'. Of course the Puritan settlers' community represents an ideal case for confirming Durkheim's views rather than refuting them: being a tightly knit, religious group, sharing a common set of beliefs in a foreign and threatening environment, one would expect a degree of shared ritual and moral solidarity which may not be found elsewhere. But in fact, if we examine Erikson's study in detail we find that his analyses do not just 'confirm' Durkheim's—they also point to a crucial modification of the Durkheimian argument. Erikson's description of the Salem witchcraft trials shows very clearly how the public condemnation of this 'crime' (which was also a sin and a heresy) served as an occasion for the cathartic resolution of deep anxieties and a reaffirmation of the strength of God's people in the presence of the Devil. It shows the reality of group emotions—in this case, primarily hysteria—and the ways in which judicial procedures operate to 'express' these feelings, and also to channel and resolve them in relatively controlled and organized ways: as the author stresses, this major social convulsion was altogether over within the space of a year.

But Erikson's study is not just about a society and its individual deviants. For the most part, his book is a description of the deep social and religious tensions within this small community: the crises of religious authority, the sectarian in-fighting, the struggle to protect the Puritan orthodoxy against challenge by Quakers, 'Antinomians', and other heretical sects. In this context it becomes clear that the exercise of criminal punishments against individual 'witches'—who were viewed as human incarnations of devilish beliefs and thus as symbols of the heresies espoused by non-Puritan sects—was also the forceful imposition of a particular framework of politico-religious authority on to a society riven by factions and deep tensions.[70] Such an interpretation is very different from Durkheim's vision of a society at one with itself, dealing with individual deviants; and indeed it recalls the points made earlier concerning the constituted nature of any 'collective conscience' and the role of power in its construction.

In the light of the foregoing remarks, it seems necessary to reformulate the Durkheimian thesis in something like the following terms. The processes of punishment do not necessarily promote 'social solidarity' in the sense implied by Durkheim. Rather they should be regarded as a ritualized attempt to

---

[69] K. Erikson, *Wayward Puritans: A Study in the Sociology of Deviance* (New York, 1966).

[70] W. J. Chambliss makes a similar point in his essay 'Functional and Conflict Theories of Crime: The Heritage of Émile Durkheim and Karl Marx', in id. and M. Mankoff (eds.), *Whose Law? What Order?* (New York, 1976).

reconstitute and reinforce already existing authority relations. Where there are limits to that authority, or contests of authority, the effects of punishments upon these limits and contests will depend upon the rhetorical power of the occasion and the receptivity of the social audience. Like all rituals of power, punishments must be carefully staged and publicized if they are to have their intended results, and can only succeed when the surrounding field of forces makes this possible.[71]

This point leads on to a rather wider one. The revisions and qualifications which I have introduced suggest that we need to rethink entirely Durkheim's central argument that punishment is functional for society. Clearly punishment does perform certain 'functions'—it sanctions certain kinds of rules, restrains certain kinds of conduct, expresses certain felt emotions, and reaffirms specific forms of authority and belief. But these rules, conducts, emotions, beliefs, and authorities need not be coterminous with 'society' or be sanctioned in a way which necessarily promotes social harmony. One has to analyse punishment's effects in relation to specific interests, specific social relations, and particular outcomes—bearing in mind that what is 'functional' from one point of view may be dysfunctional from another.

Durkheim's work is deficient in a number of respects, not least in ignoring the role of power differentials in the maintenance of social order and underplaying penality's capacity to function as an amoral instrument of regulation. But for all these difficulties, Durkheim does succeed in opening up important dimensions of the social processes of punishment which are not otherwise apparent. He shifts our attention from the managerial, administrative aspects of punishment (which form penality's modern self-image) to the governmental, social, and emotive aspects of the process. Instead of seeing a utilitarian mechanism involved in the narrow technical business of crime control, we see an institution which also operates on a different, symbolic register and resonates at both the social level and at the psychological level of individual emotion. The sense he gives of the sacred, of the emotions which are stirred by crime and punishment, of the collective involvement of onlookers, of the role of penal rituals in organizing this, and finally, of the social and moral significance of penal practices—all these interpretative insights have been shown to be important and also relevant to an understanding of punishment today.

Above all, his claim that punishment can be at once politically necessary—for the maintenance of a particular form of authority—and penologically limited in its capacity to control crime, seems to touch upon a crucial characteristic of punishment which goes unnoticed elsewhere. This sense of being simultaneously necessary and also destined to a degree of futility is what I will term the *tragic* quality of punishment. Arguably, at least, this is an

---

[71] See G. Schattenburg, 'Social Control Functions of Mass Media Depictions of Crime', *Sociological Inquiry*, 51 (1981), 71–7, which suggests that in contemporary societies the mass media representations of crime and punishment have taken over the social functions which Durkheim ascribes to penal ritual.

intrinsic characteristic of juridical punishment which, for centuries now, has been largely obscured by the Enlightenment belief that penal institutions can perform a wholly positive, utilitarian role. As I will argue at more length later, this built-in limitation upon punishment's utility must be recognized if we are to develop more realistic expectations about the uses and possibilities of penality today.

4

The Political Economy of Punishment

Rusche and Kirchheimer and the Marxist Tradition

In this chapter and the next I want to approach the institutions of punishment from a quite different angle, turning to a whole range of issues which are largely untouched in the Durkheimian tradition. In particular I want to investigate the economic and political determinants of penal policy, the role of penal institutions in strategies of class rule, and the ways in which penality serves to articulate state power, both symbolically and materially. Questions such as these have already been raised in the preceding critique of Durkheim, and in fact a number of sociological traditions typically concern themselves with problems of this kind.[1] However, in modern social science the tradition which has best articulated such issues, and has done most to develop a vocabulary within which to express them, has been Marxist theory in its various versions. This is particularly true in the sociology of punishment where most enquiries of this kind have been launched from within a Marxist or neo-Marxist problematic—although as I will show, such concerns are by no means foreign to the work of Foucault, or Weber, or even Elias. In the light of this fact, my discussion in these two chapters will focus upon the various Marxist interpretations of punishment, using them as a means of highlighting the kinds of questions I have indicated, and at the same time examining Marxism's adequacy as a way of framing such issues.

Marxism's ability to provide a highly developed set of theoretical tools for certain kinds of social scientific enquiry has made it an important conceptual resource for much of the critical work in this field, and there has been much borrowing of concepts in work which is by no means fully Marxist in orientation. Indeed, some of the studies which most powerfully utilize Marxist concepts and interpretations do so without explicit acknowledgement, and in conjunction with concepts which derive from elsewhere.[2] There are many reasons why studies which use Marxist concepts might not wish to claim a full Marxist pedigree for their interpretations. In the case of Rusche and Kirchheimer's work—where Marxist ideas pervade the whole text but are rarely explicitly stated—this was probably a matter of presentational discretion rather than

---

[1] Especially the Weberian tradition: see M. Kennedy, 'Beyond Incrimination'; S. Spitzer and A. Scull, 'Social Control in Historical Perspective', in D. Greenberg (ed.), *Corrections and Punishments* (Beverly Hills, Ca., 1977); and J. Smith and S. Fried, *The Uses of the American Prison* (Lexington, Mass., 1974) for examples in the sociology of punishment.

[2] e.g. Hay, 'Property, Authority and the Criminal Law'; Ignatieff, *A Just Measure of Pain*; and Garland, *Punishment and Welfare*. Even the classic Marxist interpretation of punishment—Rusche and Kirchheimer's *Punishment and Social Structure*—does not explicitly describe itself in Marxist terms.

intellectual doubt.[3] However, for more recent work in this field, the tendency to use Marxist concepts without invoking the whole tradition has usually been an attempt to escape the stultifying effects of orthodoxy without losing the intellectual force and analytical power of the key Marxist concepts. Many of the writers influenced by this tradition have endeavoured to combine Marxist concepts with ideas and arguments drawn from the likes of Weber, or Foucault, or Freud, and to deal with issues—such as criminal law and penal institutions—which would not be central to a more orthodox rendition of Marxism.

This rather loose relationship between Marxist orthodoxy and what might be called 'neo-Marxist' studies of punishment has also been brought about by the fact that neither Karl Marx nor Friedrich Engels actually made any substantive contribution to the analysis of penal institutions. In contrast to other areas of Marxist study—such as political economy, law, the family, the state, and so on—there are no founding texts which set up a developed Marxist position on the question of punishment, so in that sense, there is no original orthodoxy to overcome.[4] Consequently, Marxist-inspired studies of punishment have turned not to specific, originating texts but instead to the broad theory of social structure and historical change which the Marxist tradition has generated, and they have used this theoretical framework as a foundation for their own specific analyses. And precisely because these penal studies develop out of an extended—and, it should be said, controversial—framework, rather than from a single point of origin in Marx or Engel's own writings, they display a variety of approaches and starting-points rather than a singular style of analysis. Unlike, for example, those working within the Durkheimian tradition, Marxist students of punishment have had to work out for themselves the place of punishment within the broader social theory, and to decide which explanatory concepts best capture penality's role and social meaning. The outcome has been a variety of analyses, each one linking punishment into the Marxist theory of society, but each one giving a slightly different emphasis to the nature of that link and to the interpretative account which follows from it.

A consequence of this for the present discussion is that we are obliged to examine a series of specific Marxist analyses, dealing with each one in turn, rather than setting out 'the' Marxist approach to punishment and discussing it as such. Before doing so, however, it will be useful to sketch out the central elements of the Marxist theory of society, in order to show the overall

---

[3] *Punishment and Social Structure* was published in 1939 by a group of German Marxist exiles for an American readership which was generally hostile to Marxist politics and ideas. On the reaction of the Frankfurt School Marxists to the demands of their new American location, see M. Jay, *The Dialectical Imagination* (London, 1973).

[4] For discussion of Karl Marx's brief writings on the question of punishment, see D. Melossi, 'The Penal Question in *Capital*', *Crime and Social Justice*, 5 (1976), and M. Cain and A. Hunt (eds.), *Marx and Engels on Law* (London, 1979), ch. 5.

framework which lies behind these interpretations and which holds them together as variations upon a complex Marxist theme.

1. THE FUNDAMENTALS OF A MARXIST APPROACH

Like Durkheimian sociology, Marxist theory offers an holistic approach to the explanation of social life. It argues that society has a definite structure and organization, as well as a central dynamic, which pattern social practices in specific, describable ways, and which connect together areas of social life—most famously 'politics' and 'economics'—which are often experienced as disparate. Within this structured social formation, the key determinant of social organization is provided by the mode of production, the argument being that the way in which economic activity is organized and controlled will tend to shape the rest of social life. In effect, the thesis is that 'the economy'—that sphere of activity which produces the material necessities of life—will always be the key locus of power in any society. Those groups which dominate in this realm will thus be able to impose their power—and the distinctive social relations which this economic power requires—on to the other spheres of social life. Consequently, the institutions of law, politics, morality, philosophy, religion, and so on will tend to be forceably adapted to fit the conditions of economic life, and will come to take on forms and values which are in keeping with the dominant mode of production. This structural organization of society, in which the mode of production is fundamental and determinative of non-economic relations, has often been expressed in terms of the metaphor of 'base and superstructure'. This architectural figure, first used by Marx himself, conveys very well the idea of the economic level as the crucial foundation upon which the 'superstructure' of political and ideological relations is built. It shows that although superstructural forms have a real effect in shaping social life and have distinctive features of their own, they are ultimately dependent upon an underlying framework of productive relations. These economic relations in turn provide the support upon which the superstructures are based and so broadly determine the forms which these social realms can take. It is also stressed that the form of determination implied by this metaphor—backed up by the detailed arguments which Marx provides—is not a direct, one-to-one determinism, but rather a broadly structuring form of causation, setting forms and limits upon social relations in the same way that foundations shape and limit the possibilities of any building.

Like all simple metaphors, this one has its limitations, and it fails to convey the full complexity of the Marxist theory of social formations. In particular, its spatial configuration implies too clear a separation between the 'economic' and the 'non-economic' dimensions of society, for, as the more sophisticated Marxists point out, the two spheres are always interactive and mutually constituting, even if 'the economic' is determinative 'in the last instance'. Thus to give an illustration, the historical development of capitalist forms of production may be said to have transformed legal relations and shaped the judicial sphere in ways which correspond with the needs of capital. But it is no less true that capitalist relations of production and economic forms are themselves partly dependent upon legal categories—such as contract, property, sale, ownership, corporation, etc.—so that the causal relationship is by no means unidirectional. Marxism, then, involves a 'materialism' or a commitment to economic determinism, but this principle is capable of being expressed in sophisticated and non-reductionist ways.

The concept of 'mode of production' serves to organize the Marxist vision of history as well as the theory of social structure, so that historical periods are characterized by the dominance of 'ancient' or 'feudal' or 'capitalist' modes of production, and historical sequence is fundamentally the transition from one mode to another. There is undoubtedly a measure of evolutionism involved in this account—particularly in its treatment of technological change and the argument that the developing means of production tend to outstrip social relations and form a pressure for social change.[5] But this stress upon technological evolution is balanced by Marxism's insistence that the key dynamic in history and in society is, in fact, that of class struggle, which implies a more dialectical and more open-ended understanding of the historical process. For all its concern with the laws of capital accumulation and the structural constraints which these impose, Marxism is also insistent that it is the struggles of class forces which are decisive in bringing about social change and giving specific shape to concrete institutions.

In the Marxist perspective, class struggle is seen as an endemic element and the driving force within any social formation other than communism. All non-communist modes of production are, on this account, based upon an antagonistic division between two fundamental classes—the subordinate class (of slaves, serfs, or wage-labourers) which labours, and the dominant class (of citizens, feudal lords, or bourgeoisie) which appropriates the fruits of that labour.[6] Precisely because the dominant class derives its wealth from the exploitation of the subordinate class, this antagonism is an objective aspect of productive relations, and, in time, these class divisions in the economic base will tend to penetrate all the other aspects of life and reproduce themselves there. Societies are thus deeply fractured by objective class divisions, and these divisions constitute the fault-lines and contradictions across which social conflicts will be fought out, particularly where the subordinate classes become conscious of their exploitation and organize to resist or overthrow it.

Within such societies, the ruling classes organize their power not just at the place of production but across the whole social terrain, so that all the institutions controlled by these classes tend to become more or less developed

---

[5] For a sophisticated defence of this position, see G. A. Cohen, *Karl Marx's Theory of History: A Defence* (Princeton, 1978).

[6] In any specific social formation these fundamental classes will be joined by other, secondary classes deriving from previous or subordinate modes of production.

instruments for the preservation of class rule. In particular, the institutions of the state play a key role in organizing ruling-class power, in subduing political opposition, and in promoting social policies which further the perceived interests of the dominant class. Legal relations, political structures, and ideological practices (such as education, religion, morality, and 'common sense') are also seen to be shaped by categories, beliefs, values, and relationships which derive from capitalist interests and which express the status quo. These institutions, in turn, function to legitimate the class divisions and inequalities which exist—whether by denying them through reference to formal equalities, obscuring them through the promotion of other social divisions such as race, status, or morality, or else justifying them as necessary and inevitable. Of course the relationship which exists between an economically dominant class and the institutions of state, law, education, religion, and so on can range from the open dominance of feudalism, to the more indirect influence which is a feature of democratically organized politics. But Marxist theory assumes that an economically dominant class will strive to extend its dominance into the other spheres of social life, and will normally have the power to do so more or less successfully, and more or less completely.

Given this conceptual framework, together with the commitment to radical change which has always been a feature of Marxist writing, it is not surprising that the major texts of this tradition have identified a number of highly strategic issues and deemed them to be the central topics of Marxist analysis. Nor is it surprising that these turn out to be issues such as the nature of productive relations, the character of ruling-class power, or the possibilities of working-class organization—in other words, questions concerning the 'basic' social relations, their conditions of existence, and the possibilities for structural change. However, since the end of the Second World War, there has also grown up a much wider field of Marxist studies dealing with issues which are less obviously or immediately tied to the orthodox forms of class struggle but which are deemed important nevertheless. This generalization of Marxist enquiry is partly a political response to the stabilization of capitalist regimes and the receding prospects of international revolution, and partly a sign of the domestication of Marxist thought and its new-found place in the universities and academic research. But, whatever the reasons, Marxist analyses have more and more moved away from a narrow focus upon modes of production and have come to investigate the wider supports of ruling-class power, particularly questions of state power, law, culture, and ideology. These 'superstructural' investigations have revealed the continuing importance of non-economic relations in the maintenance of economic power, and, in so doing, have tended to broaden the analytic concerns of the Marxist tradition, extending it into spheres of social life which were once regarded as unimportant or epiphenomenal.

2. MARXISM AND PUNISHMENT

The emergence of criminal law and punishment as objects of Marxist analysis has been very much a part of this process of rethinking and renewal within the Marxist tradition, and the analyses which exist are mostly the result of modern neo-Marxist work rather than of the classical literature. The first studies of punishment to employ a Marxist framework emerged, significantly, from within the Frankfurt school of social research which produced a revisionist reading of Marxist concerns and gave priority to research into the cultural spheres of capitalist society. Later, in the 1970s, the most important historical studies of criminal law and penal sanctions—by writers like Hay, Linebaugh, and Thompson—would be undertaken within a Marxist historiography which had moved far away from the rigours of classical orthodoxy towards a more humanist, more culturally oriented understanding of social life.

One important consequence of this late emergence of penality as a Marxist object of investigation has been a certain diversity in the accounts which have been constructed. The problem of locating 'punishment' within the Marxist conceptual framework has led some writers, such as Rusche and Kirchheimer or Melossi and Pavarini, to stress the interconnections between penal institutions and the economic requirements of modes of production, while other writers, such as Pashukanis or Hay or Ignatieff have preferred to stress the role of punishment in political and ideological class struggles and in the maintenance of state power or ruling-class hegemony. We thus find some Marxist accounts dealing with punishment as an economic phenomenon which is ancillary to the labour-market, others discussing its political role as a repressive state apparatus, and yet others conceiving it as an ideological institution which deals in symbols of legitimacy and the justification of class rule.

As we have seen, this diversity prevents us from talking of 'the' Marxist analysis of punishment and necessitates a sequential discussion of the various individual studies, but it should perhaps be stressed that these are, in fact, variant positions within a broadly shared framework, rather than competing and incompatible accounts. For all their difference of focus and emphasis, they share a common perspective on punishment which links it, above all, with a particular set of property relations and with the struggles of a ruling class to maintain its social and economic dominance over the subordinate classes in society. The distinctive starting-point in Marxist analysis—of punishment as of all else—is the perspective of class struggle: how does punishment function with respect to class relations? How is it shaped by them? How does it contribute to their reproduction? Each of the variants chooses to pursue this complex question in a different way—tracking it down into its different social dimensions, revealing the various ways in which class issues resonate in punishment. But they each move off from broadly similar premises and they each arrive at conclusions which are mutually compatible and complementary. And if one contrasts this class perspective—in all its possible ramifications—

with, for example, the 'society-as-a-whole' position of Durkheim, then it quickly becomes apparent that the Marxist literature asks questions and pursues issues which are distinctive and quite separate from other modes of enquiry in this area.[7]

3. THE THEORETICAL FRAMEWORK OF RUSCHE AND KIRCHHEIMER

The best-known and most influential example of a Marxist interpretation of punishment is to be found in the work of Rusche and Kirchheimer, specifically their joint 1939 text, *Punishment and Social Structure*, and George Rusche's earlier essay on 'Labor Market and Penal Sanction' (1933) which set out the main theses of this interpretation. While this body of work is by no means the most sophisticated example of Marxist analysis—and is sometimes lightly dismissed by critics as nothing more than crude reductionism—it nevertheless represents the most sustained and comprehensive account of punishment to have emerged from within the Marxist tradition, and the one which owes least to other traditions of interpretation. For this reason I have chosen to consider Rusche and Kirchheimer's work at some length, and to highlight the distinctive perspective which it represents. In doing so, I will seek to give a positive, 'best-case' reading of their work which emphasizes its interpretative possibilities and the strength of many of the sociological insights and connections which it develops.

Rusche and Kirchheimer's work was conceived and carried out within the overarching framework of the Frankfurt Institute of social research, which had as its hallmark the endeavour to provide a materialist reading of bourgeois culture by bringing Marxist concepts to bear upon the 'superstructures' of social life. As Max Horkheimer notes in his preface to *Punishment and Social Structure*, 'the formulation of the problem and the method of analysis are closely bound up with the field of investigation which the Institute has chosen, namely the inter-relationship among various social spheres'.[8] The book is thus an early instance of the wider neo-Marxist tradition which I described above, though it would be no less true to say that Rusche and Kirchheimer's work is rather more 'economistic' and less culturally sensitive than the work of other Frankfurt School authors such as Adorno, Benjamin, Marcuse, or Horkheimer himself.

Punishment and Social Structure is, for the most part, a narrative history of penal methods, charting their development from the Middle Ages to the middle years of the twentieth century. To a large extent, the book's theoretical apparatus is submerged beneath the surface of its historical account, and,

---

[7] It is this class vision which separates Marxist from Durkheimian accounts of punishment, not, as is sometimes thought, the issue of materialism. Durkheim is not 'idealist' in his view of punishment: on the contrary, he sees the institutions of moral life (punishment included) as being grounded in material relations and ways of life—above all, in the division of labour.

[8] Rusche and Kirchheimer, *Punishment and Social Structure*, p. ix.

where it does make theoretical pronouncements, these are all too briefly stated, usually in a language which discreetly avoids explicit Marxist terms or vocabulary. Nevertheless, if one reads this text closely, together with the more openly stated arguments of Rusche's 1933 essay, it becomes possible to reconstruct the theoretical structure which has guided the research and produced the historical narrative.

Rusche and Kirchheimer's approach sets out a few basic questions, and, by way of answers to them, a cluster of interlinked propositions about the nature of punishment and its social functioning. The fundamental research questions are quite simple, and are straightforwardly put: 'why are certain methods of punishment adopted or rejected in a given social situation?' and 'to what extent is the development of penal methods determined by the basic social relations?'[9] But even in their evident simplicity, such questions already imply a particular angle of enquiry, which is not shared by all investigators of penal phenomena. To enquire about the variation in penal forms or methods, and their links to specific social situations, is to begin with an emphasis which is very different from Durkheim's, to take one significant example. The central focus for Rusche and Kirchheimer is to be upon the determinants which bring about the selection and use of specific penal methods, rather than other possible issues, such as penality's general functioning or its promotion of moral effects. And of course the reference to 'basic social relations' and their determinative influence upon penal methods is an invocation of Marx's materialist arguments rather than an 'obvious' question to ask about punishment. Like all interpretative analyses, Rusche and Kirchheimer's is as distinctive in its point of departure as in its final formulations.

The theoretical propositions about punishment which are then enumerated are equally distinctive and equally Marxist in character. These can be summarized as follows:

1. Punishments are to be viewed as historically specific phenomena which only appear in particular, concrete forms. As they put it: 'punishment as such does not exist, only concrete systems of punishment and specific criminal practices exist. The object of our investigation, therefore, is punishment in its specific manifestations . . .'.[10] This principle of historical specificity is intended to distance Rusche and Kirchheimer's work from those historians and sociologists (Durkheim among them) who view punishment as something universal and largely immutable, and, at the same time, to insist upon the possibility of radical change through historical transformation. The historicity of punishment is thus central to the Marxist account, for both theoretical and practical-political reasons.

2. In keeping with the Marxist interpretation of history, this historical specificity of punishment is to be understood in a very definite sense. It is the emergence of a particular mode of production, its rise to dominance, and its

---

[9] Rusche and Kirchheimer, *Punishment and Social Structure*, p. 3.   [10] Ibid. 5.

ultimate supercession by a revolutionary new mode which punctuates the history of society and characterizes its basic processes. Consequently, it is the mode of production which is the key determinant of 'specific penal methods in specific historical periods' and 'only a specific development of the productive forces permits the introduction or rejection of corresponding penalties . . .'.[11] Rusche and Kirchheimer's formula in this respect neatly summarizes the Marxist view of human history and the place of punishment within it: 'every system of production tends to discover punishments which correspond to its productive relationships.'[12]

3. A striking theoretical principle which separates Rusche and Kirchheimer's analysis from the assumptions of common sense, and effectively justifies a study of punishment in its own right, is what might be termed the principle of punishment's independent significance. The point here is that although all systems of punishment are to some extent oriented towards the control of crime, specific penal methods are never determined by this objective alone, but always by wider social forces and determinants. Rusche and Kirchheimer thus set out an argument which I put forward in Chapter 1—to the effect that penal forms must be viewed as social artefacts, which cannot be understood by penological ends alone—and they do so in very forceful terms:

> the bond, transparent or not, that is supposed to exist between crime and punishment prevents any insight into the independent significance of the history of penal systems. It must be broken. Punishment is neither a simple consequence of crime, nor the reverse side of crime, nor a mere means which is determined by the end to be achieved. Punishment must be understood as a social phenomenon freed from both its juristic concept and its social ends. We do not deny that punishment has specific ends, but we do deny that it can be understood from its ends alone.[13]

Punishment, then, is to be viewed as a social phenomenon, which has a set of determinants and a social significance which go well beyond the technical requirements of crime control.

4. A theoretical point which is nowhere explicitly stated in Rusche and Kirchheimer's text, though it is in fact crucial to their analyses, is that penal institutions are to be viewed in their interrelationship with other institutions and with non-penal aspects of social policy. In effect, penal policy is taken to be one element within a wider strategy of controlling the poor, in which factories, workhouses, the poor law, and, of course, the labour-market, all play corresponding parts. In his 1933 essay, George Rusche remarked that '. . . the criminal law and the daily work of the criminal courts are directed almost exclusively against those people whose class background, poverty, neglected education, or demoralization drove them to crime',[14] and it is this perception

---

[11] Ibid. 5, and 6.   [12] Ibid. 5.   [13] Ibid.
[14] G. Rusche, 'Labor Market and Penal Sanction: Thoughts on the Sociology of Criminal Justice'. (orig. pub. 1939), trans. and repr. in T. Platt and P. Takagi (eds.), *Punishment and Penal Discipline* (Berkeley, Ca., 1980), p. 11.

of punishment as being aimed at the control of the lower orders which pervades the later work, and leads its authors to link penal sanctions with other social policies aimed at the same populations. Throughout the historical chapters in *Punishment and Social Structure* we learn how penal practice was co-ordinated with contemporary policies in respect of vagrants, or beggars, or factory workers' or the recipients of poor relief, and how principles and techniques came to be transferred from one set of institutions to another. Rusche and Kirchheimer thus anticipate Foucault's *Discipline and Punish* and my own *Punishment and Welfare*, in arguing that the similarities of regime, organization, and structure which seem to link factories, workhouses, and prisons are to be understood as the consequence of their strategic overlap and interrelated function.

5. It also follows from the point made above that punishment must be viewed not as a social response to the criminality of individuals, but, above all, as a mechanism which is deeply implicated within the class struggle between rich and poor, bourgeoisie and proletariat. As Rusche put it in 1933, 'the history of the penal system is . . . the history of the relations [between] the rich and the poor'.[15] Or, again, in the same essay: '. . . the task has been to study the historical relationship between criminal law and economics, the history of class struggle, and to utilize these inter-relationships to analyze the present prison system.'[16] For Rusche and Kirchheimer, this class struggle—and punishment's part within it—is mainly played out in and around the labour-market, so that the emphasis of their research was primarily economic rather than political or ideological.

6. It is a basic proposition of Marxist theory that social relations and institutions within a class society are misrepresented and distorted by the operation of ideology, so that their real significance is usually hidden from view. For Rusche and Kirchheimer, it is precisely this ideological distortion which allows punishment to be perceived as an institution which benefits 'society-as-a-whole', when, in fact, its real function is to support the interests of one class against another. Consequently, if punishment is to be properly understood, one has to put aside penality's official rhetoric and legal self-description and analyse instead its role in the economic class struggle: '. . . it is necessary to strip from the social institutions of punishment its ideological veils and juristic appearance and to describe it in its real relationships.'[17] By undertaking to analyse penality as a social phenomenon with a role in the class struggle, Rusche and Kirchheimer's basic project had already gone some way along this path. But they carry this principle further during their historical narrative when they insist upon treating the rhetoric of reformers and officials alike with deep scepticism, and looking beneath these 'surface appearances' to uncover the underlying (and usually disguised) purposes of penal innovations.

---

[15] T. Platt and P. Takagi (eds.), *Punishment and Penal Discipline*, p. 13.
[16] Ibid.   [17] Rusche and Kirchheimer, *Punishment and Social Structure*, p. 5.

As they express this at one point: 'reformers create the illusion that a specific penal practice is bound up with a specific penal theory. [But] we are actually turning things upside down, however, if we take at its face value the imaginary power of doctrine over reality, instead of understanding the theoretical innovation as the expression of a necessary or already accomplished change in social praxis.'[18] Invariably, these underlying purposes—punishment's 'real relations'—turn out to be integrally linked to the economic interests of the dominant class.

This then is the general theoretical framework out of which *Punishment and Social Structure* emerged, and its Marxist provenance is perfectly evident. However, this set of propositions, important as it is, serves only to locate the problem of punishment within the Marxist problematic and set the analysis in motion. Thereafter it was left to Rusche and Kirchheimer to develop more specific concepts and arguments which related directly to punishment, and to show precisely how the hypothesized relationships and economic determinations actually worked themselves out in the concrete field of penal practices. In point of fact, Rusche and Kirchheimer's specific arguments relate almost entirely to the ways in which the operation of the labour-market comes to influence the methods of punishment and the ways in which penal sanctions are used, though the relationship between 'labour-market and penal sanction' is recognized to be complex, multifaceted, and liable to change over time.

In very broad terms, the labour-market, together with the demography of population growth, tends to fix the social value of human life, or at least the lives of those displaced serfs, vagrants, and wage-labourers who come to be objects of social administration. During periods when labour is in abundant supply, penal policy can afford to be reckless with human lives, as it tended to be in the late Middle Ages when capital and corporal punishments were widespread. However, where demand for labour threatens to exceed supply—as it did in some parts of Europe in the mercantilist period—then the state and its penal institutions will be less ready to dispense with the valuable resources which their captives represent, and more likely to put offenders to work in some way or another. This relative value of penal labour has, according to Rusche and Kirchheimer, been a crucial determinant of several penal institutions, which have responded to economic imperatives and punished accordingly. Thus penal measures such as galley slavery, transportation, forced labour, the early modern houses of correction, and even some twentieth-century rehabilitative regimes, have been positively shaped by the concern to use convict labour, and are presented as clear instances where economic interest was the leading determinant of penological innovations.

Another, more immediate way in which the labour market influences penal sanctions relates to the issue of 'less eligibility' and relative standards of living. For the lower classes and the propertyless sectors of modern capitalist

---

[18] Ibid. 141–2.

societies, the fluctuations of the labour-market and the rise and fall of the demand for their labour effectively dictate their conditions of life and standards of living.[19] Such classes, it is argued, often have little commitment to the law and the dominant moral order, and their conduct is directed more by economic necessity than by moral affiliation.[20] In such alienated circumstances, criminality may present itself as a possible means of survival, particularly when times are hard and other opportunities are few. Consequently, the criminal law and its penal sanctions are required to ensure that individuals are unable to sustain a living by criminal means, and to threaten severe penalties for those who are tempted to try. This kind of punitive back-up to the disciplines of the labour-market—in the form of harsh vagrancy laws and houses of correction—was of particular importance during the early development of manufacture and factory labour, when workers were reluctant to undertake the new conditions of work and sought to escape from their masters and the demands of 'free' labour.

In order to function in this role as a coercive ancillary to the labour-market, it is vital that penal institutions (and indeed other ancillaries such as workhouses and poor law agencies) adopt regimes which are markedly more unpleasant than the conditions of life experienced by the lowest strata living in free society. In this way, the labour-market can be seen to structure not only the normal conditions of the labouring classes, but also the penal institutions which are used against them when they resort to crime or political resistance. Rusche and Kirchheimer argue that this regressive relationship between labour-market and penal institutions—summed up in the notion of 'less eligibility'—has proved to be 'the leitmotiv of all prison administration down to the present time'.[21] Thus the discipline, the diet, the labour requirements, the accommodation, and the general living conditions of penal institutions are seen to be carefully calibrated to ensure that the overall regime remains sufficiently unpleasant to serve as a deterrent to the lowest social classes. Punishments, on this argument, are seen as being shaped not so much by the nature of criminal offences, or their moral seriousness, but instead by the nature of the normal living conditions of certain social groups. As the authors argue in a chapter entitled 'Modern Prison Reform and Its Limits', this concern for relative deprivation in punishment is 'the inner contradiction which underlies every reform program to a greater or lesser degree'.[22] It ensures that: 'all efforts to reform the punishment of criminals are inevitably limited by the situation of the lowest socially significant proletarian class . . .'[23] Far from being an inevitable aspect of social progress, penal reform occurs only where economic exigencies are relaxed, or when 'humanitarian principles coincide . . . with the

---

[19] Note that the introduction of social security provision as a tax-funded safety net for the casualties of the labour-market necessarily complicates the Rusche and Kirchheimer thesis.

[20] Rusche, 'Labor Market and Penal Sanction', p. 11.

[21] Rusche and Kirchheimer, *Punishment and Social Structure*, p. 94.

[22] Ibid. 159. On this see H. Mannheim, *The Dilemma of Penal Reform* (London, 1939).

[23] Rusche, 'Labor Market and Penal Sanction', p. 12.

economic necessities of the time'.[24] And even where reformers do succeed in establishing humanitarian measures, these are always liable to be 'surrendered . . . to the mercy of every crisis in the market'.[25]

In addition to shaping the options of the work-force in general, modern punishments from the sixteenth century onwards are seen to shape the attitudes of the individual convict-worker. Rusche and Kirchheimer suggest that a constant theme within penal institutions has been their concern to imbue prisoners with the disciplines and attitudes necessary for adaptation to the workplace. The modern prison—like its forerunners the house of correction and the *hôpital général*—is, among other things 'a way of training new labour reserves'.[26] The designers and administrators of nineteenth-century prison regimes endeavoured to train prisoners into an 'unconditional submission to authority', teaching them to 'resign themselves to a quiet, regular and industrious life' so that when the time came for re-entry into society the convict would have learned 'to submit willingly to the fate of the lower classes'.[27] Penal institutions, then, are seen to have a positive, if relatively minor, role in constituting the work-force, as well as the more general negative function of ensuring that individuals know that honest labour, however burdensome, is preferable to its criminal alternatives. And these labour-market functions do more than just locate penality in a network of social institutions, making it 'an integral part of the whole social system'.[28] They also help define the interior of penal institutions, shaping their regimes in particular ways, introducing factory disciplines into the prisons, and setting stringent limits upon the possibilities of reform.

The labour-market, then, and its related imperatives and fluctuations, forms the basic determinant of punishment in Rusche and Kirchheimer's account. It is not, however, the only determinant. The authors argue that in certain circumstances—which I will describe in a moment—the economic sphere of production operates in a manner which effectively relinquishes the need for punitive measures to discipline the work-force, and also makes it impossible to use convict labour in an economically effective way. In such circumstances, the major determinant of penal measures becomes the concern to minimize expenditure, and to reduce the financial burden represented by punishment: 'insofar as the basic economic needs of a commodity-producing society do not directly determine the creation and shaping of punishments . . . the choice of methods is largely influenced by fiscal interests.'[29] This second-line fiscal determinant fits, of course, with the general concern to make punishments 'less eligible' but it also leads to the use of measures such as the fine, which in the twentieth century has come to be the most frequently

---

[24] Rusche and Kirchheimer, *Punishment and Social Structure*, p. 84.
[25] Ibid. 151.
[26] Ibid. 63.
[27] Ibid. 107.
[28] Ibid. 207.
[29] Ibid. 7.

deployed penal measure and 'the epitome of rationalized capitalist penal law'.[30]

In addition to these 'economic' and 'fiscal' determinants, Rusche and Kirchheimer accept that a range of other forces is also involved in the shaping of penal measures. The most explicit statement of this occurs in Rusche's essay of 1933 where he says '. . . the dependency of crime and crime control on economic and historical conditions does not, however, provide a total explanation . . . for example, the penal system and the ritual of criminal procedure are shaped by various forces, including religious and social phenomena'.[31] But one can also find points in the text of *Punishment and Social Structure* where we are told of the effective operation of 'religious attitudes', 'ideology', 'politics', administrative convenience, bureaucratic tendencies, criminological theories, and even emotional dispositions such as 'sadism' and humanitarianism.[32] These factors, however, are mentioned in the historical narrative without being fully integrated into the book's theoretical framework. Instead, we are left to assume that they operate, as it were, within the spaces which economic forces leave open to them.

4. RUSCHE AND KIRCHHEIMER'S PENAL HISTORY

Working with the concepts set out above, Rusche and Kirchheimer present a broad historical account which correlates the development of penal measures with the general pattern of economic change and particular variations in the supply, the demand, and the social use of labour power. This historical survey is pitched at a fairly high level of abstraction, and is very much dependent upon secondary literature and the historiography which was available in the 1930s. Moreover, it is presented as an exemplification or 'proof' of a thesis, rather than a balanced historical account, so that it tends to select material which suits its case, and disregard that which does not. As we shall see, subsequent research gives good reason to doubt several of the interpretations made in *Punishment and Social Structure* and to judge most of them as partial at best. But there is undoubtedly an element of truth in its account, even if this truth needs to be qualified by others, and many of its arguments are persuasive, at least in the broad terms in which they ought to be understood. As we found with Durkheim's work, it is perfectly possible to regard an author's purported substantiation of a thesis with some scepticism, while yet finding some merit in the thesis itself.

The central concern of Rusche and Kirchheimer's historical account is to identify the specific penal methods which have emerged during the early

---

[30] Rusche and Kirchheimer, *Punishment and Social Structure*, p. 206. For a sociological account of the use of the fine in modern society, see P. J. Young, *Punishment, Money and Legal Order* (Edinburgh, forthcoming).

[31] Rusche, 'Labor Market and Penal Sanction', p. 11.

[32] Rusche and Kirchheimer, *Punishment and Social Structure*, at pp. 37, 183, 185, 134, 156, 151, 121, and 84 respectively.

modern and modern periods and to show how these can be understood by reference to the economic and fiscal forces described above. I will confine myself to this central theme in presenting their account, leaving aside the rather sprawling social history which accompanied the original.

4.1 *Punishments in the Middle Ages*

The starting-point for their analysis is Europe in the early Middle Ages, prior to the emergence of capitalist relations and a centralized state power. In this period, criminal conduct was largely dealt with as a matter for private vengeance or settlement between the parties most immediately involved, with fines and penance being the most common means of settling such disputes. However, by the fourteenth and fifteenth centuries, a number of developments took place which 'militated against the private character of early medieval criminal law and . . . transformed it into an instrument of domination',[33] most notably the emergence of central powers seeking to impose their authority upon their subjects and to enjoy the fiscal benefits which could be derived from fining violators of the public peace. With this transfer of penal power from the local community to an increasingly authoritative central agency, the fine 'evolved from [being] a compensation to the offended party into a method of enriching the justiciaries' and came to be reserved only for the rich, while corporal punishments became the standard means of dealing with those offenders who could not pay financial penalties.[34]

During this same period a number of factors combined to create an increasingly impoverished and displaced population of peasants, who were forced into vagrancy, vagabondage, and crime by 'the shift from agriculture to grazing, the rise of a capitalistic pasturage system with its resulting pauperization of large sections of the countryside' and 'a general increase in the population'.[35] The threat posed to property and to public order by these roving bands of masterless men prompted the authorities everywhere to respond with repressive measures, and so the late Middle Ages came to be characterized by harsh, physical punishments, ranging from whipping and branding to brutal forms of mutilation, execution, and the exposure of corpses.[36]

According to Rusche and Kirchheimer, these barbarous penalties cannot be ascribed 'simply to the primitive cruelty of an epoch now vanished'.[37] There was, no doubt, an element of sadism involved in these punitive displays, allowing the public to satisfy 'a lust for cruelty' while also permitting the authorities to direct this mass hatred against individual criminals, outsiders, and witches, thereby 'diverting responsibility [for economic hardship] from themselves'.[38] But cruelty, and particularly its expression in judicial acts, is itself a social phenomenon with particular conditions of existence, and it needs

---

[33] Ibid. 10.   [34] Ibid. 17.   [35] Ibid. 12.
[36] On vagrancy in the early modern period, see A. L. Beier, *Masterless Men: The Vagrancy Problem in Britain, 1560–1640* (London, 1985).
[37] Rusche and Kirchheimer, *Punishment and Social Structure*, p. 23.   [38] Ibid. 21.

to be explained by reference to the social relations within which it exists. Rusche and Kirchheimer find that explanation in the fact that, during this period, there was a massive oversupply of labour, particularly in the growing urban centres, which led to the devaluing of human life, and created pressure for a penal policy which was little short of genocidal: 'As the price paid for labor decreased, the value set on human life became smaller and smaller. The hard struggle for existence moulded the penal system in such a way as to make it one of the means of preventing too great an increase of population.'[39]

4.2 *Punishment and the rise of capitalism*

Towards the end of the sixteenth century, the economic and demographic characteristics of several European countries began to alter, bringing about profound changes in their social policies and in the methods used to punish offenders. In effect, population growth had been checked by the Malthusian factors of wars, plagues, and famines, while, at the same time, an expansion of trade, of markets, and of manufacture was made possible by new naval trade routes, colonial conquests, the impact of precious metals, and an increased consumer demand from the wealthy populations in the towns and cities. In stark contrast to the previous century, the new mercantilist epoch was faced with a shortage of labour, high wage costs, and a difficulty in securing willing work-forces for the new forms of manufacture and production. This situation prompted governments to introduce a range of social policies aimed at the furtherance of industry and the protection of trade, including attempts to regulate wage levels, working hours, emigration, and the treatment of the poor. Propelled both by the Calvinist doctrines of the Reformation countries, and the new Catholicism of the Counter-Reformation, social policies laid great stress upon the need to labour, the criminality of idleness, and the importance of linking charity to a work ethic. In effect, labour power came to be viewed as one of the state's most vital resources, and policies aimed to enhance its force and harness its power. Accordingly, it was this economic rationale rather than any humanitarian concern which led to the gradual abandonment of extensive capital and corporal punishments and the emergence of new penal methods in this period.

Rusche and Kirchheimer point to three new forms of punishment introduced in this early modern era—galley slavery, transportation, and various forms of 'penal servitude at hard labour'.[40] Galley slavery was utilized in Europe— particularly in France and Spain—from the late fifteenth century until the eighteenth, as a punishment for major offenders as well as for beggars and vagabonds. According to their account, the rulers of the sea-going nations introduced this measure because they found difficulty in recruiting free men for the task, whereas convicts could be compelled to a lifetime's sentence of strenuous and hazardous work. The frequency of sentences of this kind rose

---

[39] Rusche and Kirchheimer, *Punishment and Social Structure*, p. 20.   [40] Ibid. 24.

and fell with the demand for oarsmen, convicts were specially selected for their strength and stamina, and galley slaves would be released from their service only when their health failed and they could no longer perform the necessary labour.[41] For Rusche and Kirchheimer, this is a clear instance of their general thesis: 'what is significant in the development of the galley as a method of punishment is the fact that economic considerations alone were involved, not penal. This is true for both the sentence and its execution. The introduction and regulation of galley servitude were determined solely by the desire to obtain necessary labour on the cheapest possible basis.'[42] It was only when technical improvements in the design of sailing ships made rowing largely obsolete in the first half of the eighteenth century that this penalty was abolished, whereupon it was replaced by forced labour in the *bagnes* (labour camps) at ports such as Toulon and Marseilles.[43]

The introduction of transportation as a penal sanction follows a similar pattern and is explained by the same imperatives. Colonial powers such as Spain and Portugal utilized the labour of convicts in their foreign colonies and military settlements as early as the fifteenth century, and transportation to America and later to Australia formed a central element of England's penal system from the sixteenth to the mid-nineteenth century. According to Rusche and Kirchheimer, the availability of huge tracts of unworked land in the colonies, together with a high demand for colonial products at home, brought about 'a constant shortage of labour' for which the transportation of convicts was an obvious response.[44] Transportation 'cost the government little' since contractors were found who could make a profit from the sale of convicts to colonists, and critics who argued that the export of labour power represented a loss to the wealth of the nation were answered by using transportation only for those who would otherwise be sentenced to death.[45] By the early eighteenth century, however, transportation was being used in England as a regular sentence for larceny and various other offences, and not just as a commutation of a capital sentence. Although the advocates of transportation frequently represented it as an opportunity for the correction of offenders—who were normally released after a period of forced labour and allowed to become settlers in the colony—Rusche and Kirchheimer are deeply sceptical about such humanitarian motives, and they point to the fact that bodily strength or special

---

[41] On galley slavery in Europe, see A. Zysberg, 'Galley and Hard Labor Convicts in France (1550–1800)', in P. Spierenburg (ed.), *The Emergence of Carceral Institutions: Prisons, Galleys and Lunatic Asylums, 1550–1900* (Rotterdam, 1984), and also T. Sellin, *Slavery and the Penal System* (New York, 1976).

[42] Rusche and Kirchheimer, *Punishment and Social Structure*, p. 55. In fact galley slavery clearly did perform penal functions—it was certainly painful enough to serve as a deterrent and a retribution. Rusche and Kirchheimer's point is that the choice of this method of inflicting pain was determined solely by economic (and military?) interests.

[43] On *bagnes* see A. Zysberg, 'Galley and Hard Labor Convicts in France (1550–1800)'.

[44] Rusche and Kirchheimer, *Punishment and Social Structure*, p. 58.

[45] Ibid. 60. For supporting evidence on this point see J. Beattie, *Crime and the Courts in England, 1660–1800*, pp. 479 ff., 504, 600 n.

labouring skills—rather than 'reformability'—were the chief considerations which shaped the decision as to who would be transported. They are similarly sceptical about the reasons why the American colonists came to oppose this practice and to regard the reception of convicts as a 'humiliating obligation'— since such objections were only heard once the development of the Negro slave-trade made available a cheaper and less restricted source of labour: 'once transportation ceased to pay, the colonists realized that it was a shameful business unworthy of them.'[46]

It was, of course, the American Revolution and the War of Independence in the 1770s which eventually put an end to transportation to America so that one might be led to ascribe its demise to political rather than economic factors, but Rusche and Kirchheimer offer a different interpretation: '. . . American conditions had already demonstrated the limited possibilities of absorbing convict labor. The colonial economic system made its continuance impossible long before political conditions finally put an end to transportation.'[47] Following the cessation of the American penal route, Britain resorted to a variety of public works which utilized convict labour—most notably the temporary expedient whereby prisoners were confined in disused naval vessels (the 'hulks') moored off shore, and were put to work building piers and harbour walls and dredging river estuaries. After 1787, however, transportation was resumed, this time to the new Australian colony where convict labour was put to use first by the military governors and later by large landowners. By the mid-nineteenth century, however, two economic tendencies conspired to undermine the policy and lead to its abolition. The first problem was that of less eligibility. After the early years in which transportation to the unknown, far-distant, and scarcely inhabited Australia inspired genuine terror in the lower classes a new perception of transportation emerged, at least among those who administered it. The possibilities of work, early freedom on ticket of leave, and eventual prosperity in the new land made the authorities fear that transportation was ceasing to be a serious deterrent to crime at home. By 1819 the British government felt compelled to instruct the colonial military officials to increase the severity of their regimes, and to counteract the sense that Australia offered an attractive rather than a deterrent prospect. According to Rusche and Kirchheimer, however, 'even the extreme terror and disciplinary system of [Governor] Arthur, which was limited by the economic needs of the colony, had little success in overcoming the attractiveness of transportation as compared with the miserable conditions of the lower classes in England'.[48] At the same time, a growing number of free immigrants were being attracted to the colony, and these new settlers, objecting to their wages being undercut by the cheap labour convicts and emancipists, began to oppose transportation. Despite the support of 'employers . . . who profited from cheap convict labour' the system was gradually discontinued, first in New South Wales, then

---

[46] Rusche and Kirchheimer, *Punishment and Social Structure*, p. 61.
[47] Ibid. 123.   [48] Ibid., 120–1.

subsequently elsewhere.[49] A similar sequence of transportation being introduced as an economic expedient and then abandoned when its economic advantages recede, is described in respect of France, and, to a lesser extent, Austria and Prussia, all of which attempted to make use of this system in the seventeenth and eighteenth centuries.

The most lasting penal innovation of the mercantilist era was not these attempts to use forced labour on board ship or in distant colonies, but rather a method of using it within the homeland itself, in the confines of specially adapted institutions. Rusche and Kirchheimer describe how countries such as England, Holland, Germany, and France—the leading regions of emergent capitalism—began to develop a variety of carceral institutions which had in common a concern to put their inmates to work and to train them in the disciplines of industry. The earliest example of such an institution was the London Bridewell, opened in 1555, which sought to rid the city of vagabonds and beggars and which developed a hiring-out system to allow local tradesmen to exploit its reservoir of labour. Similar institutions—such as the Zuchthaus and Spinnhaus in Amsterdam, or the Hôpital Général in Paris—were soon established elsewhere, each one unique in its specific inmate composition and organization, but all of them sharing the elements of confinement, forced labour, and reformative purpose. Out of these institutions developed the idea of the 'house of correction', which quickly became a feature of most European cities, particularly in the German-speaking countries. 'The essence of the house of correction', according to Rusche and Kirchheimer, 'was that it combined the principles of the poorhouse, workhouse and penal institution.' Its main aim was 'to make the labor power of unwilling people socially useful' by putting them to work under supervision within a closely disciplined and orderly regime.[50] 'By being forced to work within the institution, the prisoners would receive a vocational training at the same time. When released, it was hoped, they would voluntarily swell the labor market.'[51]

These early modern institutions were not without their opponents—particularly the trade guilds which resented violations of their monopolies and competition from unfree labour—and their maintenance often involved the city authorities in considerable expenditure for which taxes had to be raised or official lotteries organized. Moreover, Rusche and Kirchheimer accept that many houses of correction failed to achieve their economic or reformative aims and had, by the eighteenth century, fallen into decay and disorganization. But nevertheless they insist that '. . . it is certain that the possibility of profits was a

[49] Ibid. 118.
[50] Ibid. 42. Simon Schama describes how the notorious (and perhaps fictional?) 'drowning cell' in the Amsterdam house of correction presented inmates with the stark choice of working (at its handpump) or literally 'going under' as the cell was slowly flooded with water. As Schama points out, the precarious geography of The Netherlands made this a peculiarly apt symbol for depicting the necessity of work. S. Schama, *The Embarrassment of Riches: An Interpretation of Dutch Culture in the Golden Age* (London, 1987), part 1.
[51] Rusche and Kirchheimer, *Punishment and Social Structure*, p. 42.

decisive motive for the houses of correction' and their overall assessment is that 'it is equally certain that the houses of correction were very valuable for the national economy as a whole. Their low wages and their training of unskilled workers were important contributing factors in the rise of capitalist production.'[52]

As well as contributing to the emergence of modern capitalism, these institutions also served as the basis upon which the modern prison system was built. At first only minor delinquents were sentenced to these institutions, along with vagrants, beggars, orphans, and children deemed in need of reform, but eventually more serious criminals were also sent there, so that by the eighteenth century this penal function began to displace the institutions' wider uses. For Rusche and Kirchheimer, then, the earliest prisons were established, like their institutional forerunners, as methods of 'exploiting labor' and of 'training new labor reserves'.[53] New penitentiaries were built and old buildings refurbished to secure these economic ends (though, significantly, those jails which were not 'susceptible to commercial exploitation' remained unreformed and 'in very bad condition') until, by the end of the eighteenth century, imprisonment had taken the place of physical forms of punishment as the most frequently used response to crime.[54]

The modern prison, then, emerged towards the end of the mercantilist period during which labour was in short supply and social policies were designed to utilize and exploit whatever manpower was available. However, no sooner had the prison come to dominate penal policy, than these social circumstances were reversed and the prison's economic base 'ceased to exist'.[55] Rusche and Kirchheimer argue that by the 1790s, 'what the ruling classes had been seeking for over a century was now an accomplished fact— relative overpopulation'.[56] During the eighteenth century, Europe's population underwent a rapid expansion. Unable to support themselves on the land, thousands of agricultural workers began to stream into the towns, creating, by the first decades of the nineteenth century, a large unemployed population in the cities, which ensured low wages for those in work and immiseration for those who were not. This decline in the living conditions of the least favoured was reflected in the deteriorating state of those institutions—poorhouses, houses of correction, prisons—which catered for the poor, and Rusche and Kirchheimer point to John Howard's surveys as evidence of how far even the best institutions had declined in this period.[57]

4.3 *Punishment after the industrial revolution*

The industrial revolution of the early nineteenth century and its accompanying demands for free trade and *laissez-faire* policies constituted the final blow

---

[52] Rusche and Kirchheimer, *Punishment and Social Structure*, p. 50.   [53] Ibid. 63.
[54] Ibid. 69.   [55] Ibid. 84.   [56] Ibid. 86.
[57] J. Howard, *The State of the Prisons in England and Wales* (Warrington, 1777), and *An Account of the Principal Lazarettos of Europe* (Warrington, 1789).

against the old mercantilist social regime, which was speedily dismantled in one country after another. At the same time the introduction of industrial machinery and early forms of mass production made such work as was still being done by the inmates of institutions increasingly unprofitable and hard to sustain. In this context, the reformatory concerns of penal institutions, and the higher standards of convict life to which they had aspired, simply collapsed along with the economic basis upon which they had been built.

From this economic point of view, the new prisons were obsolete practically as soon as they had been established. However, the industrial crisis of the early nineteenth century, with its high unemployment, extensive pauperism, and volatile politics, also led to a massive increase in the rates of crime, so that the question of penal policy was forced on to the political agenda of every nation. According to Rusche and Kirchheimer, the immediate response of some sectors of the ruling class was to call for the reintroduction of the bloody methods of the sixteenth century and put aside the humane experiments of recent times. Torture, physical destruction, 'the ax, the whip, and starvation . . .' were invoked as the proper solutions to the heightening threats of crime and disorder.[58] However, a century of Enlightenment criticism of corporal punishments, together with the joint demands of conscience and political prudence, led the authorities to remodel the prison establishments rather than return to the methods which had preceded them. Imprisonment was now to become a rational system of deterrence based upon terror and degradation rather than economic labour and individual reform. '[W]hat European society with its industrial reserve army needed was a punishment which would strike fear into the hearts of the starving', and it found such a measure in the new regimes of solitary confinement.[59]

Despite the reformative rhetoric which accompanied these developments, Rusche and Kirchheimer view the introduction of such a system as a thinly disguised form of torture and intimidation, calculated to deter even the most immiserated sections of the working classes. Granted that the reformers 'would have rejected any suggestion of a return to medieval forms' and genuinely 'did not want prisoners to be tortured' the effect was very close to this none the less.[60] Prison work was transformed from a productive, profitable form of training into an extended torment of labour at tread-wheels and cranks and other forms of unproductive chore. Prisoners were left in silence and solitude for great lengths of time, which generally failed to have any reformative effect but succeeded in heightening the terror and deprivation which a prison sentence could represent. The new prisons were thus as wasteful of human life and of surplus labour in their way as medieval sanctions had been, though now this irrationality was disguised by a rhetoric of reform and religious ideology: 'solitary confinement, without work or with purely punitive labor, is symptomatic of a mentality which, as a result of surplus population, abandons the attempt

[58] Rusche and Kirchheimer, *Punishment and Social Structure*, p. 132.
[59] Ibid.   [60] Ibid. 133.

to find a rational policy of rehabilitation and conceals this fact with a moral ideology.'[61]

The experience of prison use in the USA during the nineteenth century forms a separate case in Rusche and Kirchheimer's account because in the northern states of the USA there was a persistent labour shortage which allowed penitentiaries to function as productive economic units in a way which was impossible elsewhere. Prisoners in these states were put to work, either manufacturing goods within the institution or else being contracted out to private entrepreneurs or public works, and there was no resort to the kinds of punitive, unproductive labour represented in Europe by the tread-wheel and the crank. Rusche and Kirchheimer acknowledge that here, too, a religious concern to reform prisoners and save their souls played a large part in the enthusiasm for the penitentiary system, but they insist that economic imperatives remained the primary determinant. The fact that the more productive Auburn system—which allowed convicts to work in association—was everywhere preferred to the strict solitary confinement of Pennsylvanian prisons, is deemed to be sufficient proof of this. Thus in certain parts of the USA, 'prisons became factories once again and began to produce goods on a profitable basis'.[62] And, as Beaumont and de Tocqueville's study of the 1830s suggests, '. . . the new prison regime was established at small expense, was self-supporting, and was even a source of revenue'.[63] Convict labour was curtailed only at the very end of the nineteenth century, when free workers and their unions began to object to competition from prison manufactories subsequent to which prison industries were subjected to certain restrictions. Even then, productive prison work continued to exist, producing goods for prison or governmental use rather than for the free market.[64]

By the beginning of the twentieth century, European punishments, and to a lesser extent those of the USA, had ceased to be directly implicated in the productive processes of capitalism because technological developments and the opposition of free labour had undermined their capacity to operate as economic units. Increasingly, therefore, penal policy came to be determined by fiscal forces and indirect economic forces (such as the living conditions of the working classes and the need for less eligibility) rather than by immediate productive concerns. The rise of the fine and its widespread use to deal with offences which were previously imprisonable was the most prominent instance of this tendency. And, as Rusche and Kirchheimer point out, the generalization of this sanction in the twentieth century itself implied the existence of certain economic conditions, notably a thoroughly monetarized economy and a

---

[61] Rusche and Kirchheimer, *Punishment and Social Structure*, p. 137.
[62] Ibid. 130.   [63] Ibid. 131.
[64] There is, in fact, much variation in the US experience, with many southern states placing much greater emphasis upon convict labour, and continuing to do so well into the 20th cent. See J. Conley, 'Prisons, Production and Profit: Reconsidering the Importance of Prison Industries', *The Journal of Social History*, 14 (1981), 257–75, and E. L. Ayers, *Vengeance and Justice: Crime and Punishment in the Nineteenth Century American South* (New York, 1984).

minimum level of disposable income available to much of the population. As they put it: 'the frequency of fines is not primarily the result of legislative or judicial measures or theories, but is rather an accurate reflection of the prevailing social and economic conditions.'[65]

These same economic conditions which ensured higher wages, social benefits, and rising standards of living for much of the working population before 1914, brought about a series of social and penal reforms which altered the nature of imprisonment and made more extensive use of re-education measures such as reform schools, probation, and after-care. In effect, the existence of 'relative prosperity' resulted in a 'general tendency toward leniency', an improvement in prisoners' living conditions, more frequent use of fines, greater efforts at rehabilitation, and the development of what Rusche and Kirchheimer take to be 'a more rational and more humane praxis'.[66] They insist, however, that these penal measures are premissed upon changeable economic forces—as shown, for example, by the penal trends visible in the Fascist regimes of the 1930s, where the economic crisis sparked by 'the transition from the system of competition to monopoly capitalism' had had far-reaching consequences, including the weakening of legal freedoms, an emphasis upon penal severity, and the reintroduction of capital punishment.[67]

Punishment and Social Structure ends its historical account by repeating the claim that penal policy and the crime rate are in fact causally independent of each other, although both are determined by the same network of social and economic conditions. Consequently, the only way to reduce crime and to achieve a rational and humane penal policy is to address the class system and economic conditions which underpin this and every other sphere of social life. As they put it, 'the crime rate can really be influenced only if society is in a position to offer its members a certain measure of security and to guarantee a reasonable standard of living. The shift from a repressive penal policy to a progressive program can then be raised out of the sphere of humanitarianism to constructive social activity.'[68] In the context of this project, with its Marxist concepts and concerns, it would be no more than reasonable to interpret this last phrase as linking true penal reform to the dismantling of the capitalist class system and the construction of a socialist society.

5. RE-EVALUATING *PUNISHMENT AND SOCIAL STRUCTURE*

Rusche and Kirchheimer's text was little read or referred to when first published in 1939. Apart from brief citations in the work of Sellin and Sutherland, both of whom had been advisers to the original publication, the

---

[65] Rusche and Kirchheimer, *Punishment and Social Structure*, p. 173.
[66] Ibid. 147, 163.
[67] See A. Scull, *Decarceration* (Englewood Cliffs, NJ, 1977) for a similar argument linking changes in US penal and mental health policies to economic change and a fiscal crisis of the state.
[68] Rusche and Kirchheimer, *Punishment and Social Structure*, p. 207.

book was largely ignored for 30 years. It was not until it was reissued in 1968—to an audience taken up with the themes of radical criminology and revisionist history—that its arguments came to be widely known, but ever since then the book has been accorded something like the status of a classic text within the sociology of punishment. *Punishment and Social Structure* has formed the inspiration for a growing research literature on economics, crime, and punishment; it has influenced other historical studies; and it has come to the central point of reference in Marxist discussions of punishment.[69] Indeed, Melossi and Pavarini's *The Prison and the Factory*—the best-known recent work in this area—is largely an elaboration of the Rusche and Kirchheimer thesis, showing how the early prisons in Europe and the USA functioned to discipline a proletarian workforce by instilling the factory-based virtues of obedience, hard work, and docile behaviour, and arguing that the state of the labour-market directly influences the shape of internal prison regimes, which tend to become rehabilitative only where labour is scarce, and become merely 'destructive' when it is not.

For all its new-found status though, Rusche and Kirchheimer's work has not escaped serious criticism. Indeed, the sociological and historical research which it has provoked has often shown the limitations of the original arguments, and the need to revise many of its specific judgments. As might be expected when such a single-minded interpretation is imposed upon a broad historical canvas, historians have been quick to show the many points at which the thesis needs to be qualified in the light of more detailed evidence. Research into the history of transportation from Britain has shown that, at least in its Australian phase, this system was devised as a response to a penological crisis at home rather than for economic advantage abroad, and that the costs of transporting, guarding, and maintaining the early convicts were a considerable burden upon the state.[70] Historians of the house of correction have argued that, although commercial motives may have played a part in the founding of these institutions, few of them could in fact sustain any financial benefits. Typically, they were funded by charitable donors or by means of local taxation, and ran at a substantial cost which was only ever partly offset by the sale of inmates' labour and produce. As for the training of docile workers, the evidence suggests that this was, like modern-day rehabilitation, more a matter of

[69] See the essays collected in T. Platt and P. Takagi (eds.), *Punishment and Penal Discipline* (Berkeley, Ca., 1980); D. Melossi and M. Pavarini, *The Prison and the Factory* (London, 1981); C. Adamson, 'Toward a Marxian Penology: Captive Criminal Populations as Economic Threats and Resources', *Social Problems*, 31 (1984); id., 'Punishment After Slavery: Southern State Penal Systems, 1865–1890', *Social Problems*, 30 (1983); G. Gardner, 'The Emergence of the New York State Prison System: A Critique of the Rusche and Kirchheimer Model', *Crime and Social Justice*, 29 (1987), 88–109; Conley, 'Prisons, Production and Profit'; S. Box, *Recession, Crime and Punishment* (London, 1987).
[70] See Beattie, *Crime and the Courts in England, 1660–1800*, ch. 9; R. Hughes, *The Fatal Shore: A History of the Transportation of Convicts to Australia, 1787–1868* (London, 1987); A. R. Ekirch, *Bound for America: The Transportation of British Convicts to the Colonies, 1718–1775* (Oxford, 1987).

reformers' intention than of realized effect, so that the long history of these institutions cannot be explained in terms of their role in this respect.[71]

In respect of the early nineteenth-century prisons, the story is rather similar. The building of penitentiaries and model prisons—many of which featured the monumental architecture and ornamentation of prestige buildings—was often a massive financial expenditure, undertaken with little prospect of reimbursement. As such, the new prisons bear witness to the growing capacities and revenues of the state rather than to any economic benefits to be had from imprisonment. Similarly, though prisoners' labour was always envisaged as part of the regime, its profitability was frequently subordinated to other considerations, such as prison discipline, general deterrence, or individual reformation. Certain institutions—such as Cherry Hill Penitentiary in Pennsylvania or Pentonville in England—deliberately adopted regimes which were expensive to establish and promised little in the way of economic return, and even the more cost-conscious establishments which were built on the lines of the Auburn system could rarely expect to offset their running costs, let alone the capital expenditure involved in their construction. Compared with the low financial costs of fines, corporal punishment, and executions, the use of imprisonment was never an economically attractive option.

More importantly, the intense debates and public concern which occurred around questions of prison design and the details of regimes cannot be understood if we confine ourselves to an economic vocabulary of motives. As Ignatieff and Rothman have clearly shown, the early prison reform movement was also taken up with social, political, and religious concerns which did much to shape the configuration of penal practices which was eventually established.[72] In the same way, it is equally limiting of understanding to talk of the physical punishments which were used in the later Middle Ages purely in terms of socially permitted sadism. In Rusche and Kirchheimer's view, the absence of economic constraints on the abuse of life simply left the field open to the play of unrestrained emotion. But as we will see when we discuss Michel Foucault's work, even the most shocking penal atrocities were generally undertaken within a positive framework of political intent and social symbolism.

Rusche and Kirchheimer's general thesis linking penal forms to modes of production and working-class living standards is also put in question by contemporary evidence which shows a wide variation in penal practice between societies which share similar economic conditions. Rates of imprisonment and lengths of prison sentences, the use of fines and alternatives to custody all vary greatly from one advanced capitalist society to another. On the other

---

[71] See J. Innes, 'Prisons for the Poor: English Bridewells, 1550–1800', in F. Snyder and D. Hay (eds.), *Labour, Law and Crime: An Historical Perspective* (London, 1987); P. Spierenburg, 'The Sociogenesis of Confinement and its Development in Early Modern Europe', in id. (ed.), *The Emergence of Carceral Institutions*; J. Sharpe, *Crime in Early Modern England, 1550–1750* (London, 1984), ch. 8; and Beattie, *Crime and the Courts in England, 1660–1800*, ch. 10.

[72] Ignatieff, *A Just Measure of Pain*; D. Rothman, *The Discovery of the Asylum: Social Order and Disorder in the New Republic* (Boston, 1971).

hand, the penal methods and institutions adopted by countries operating socialist or quasi-socialist economic forms do not seem to differ greatly from those used in capitalist states, though their penal ideologies, custodial regimes, and target populations do show some important differences.[73]

There are other specific points which could be made about Rusche and Kirchheimer's account, but I have covered enough of them to show the general tenor of these criticisms. What all these empirical revisions point to is actually an underlying problem in their theoretical approach so this ought to be discussed in these terms. As I noted above, Rusche's initial description of his project makes it clear that he did not intend to offer a comprehensive explanation of penal phenomena and their historical development. Moreover, the economic arguments of *Punishment and Social Structure* are also, at various points, supplemented by references to a range of non-economic forces which are acknowledged to operate in the penal realm. However, despite this suggestion that a plurality of forces may converge to shape penological outcomes, the authors insist at every stage that economic causes are always the primary ones involved. Usually, as with transportation, galley slavery, houses of correction, or fines, this is a matter of positive causation in which economic imperatives directly shape the penal sanction. Occasionally it takes the form of a negative argument which states that, because economic circumstances devalue labour power, penal sanctions are free to destroy it, either through physical punishments or else in destructive prison regimes. Whenever other forces such as religious enthusiasm, penal theory, social politics, or humanitarianism might be perceived as more immediately bound up with the development of the phenomenon, they are promptly reduced to secondary importance, like shadows cast by a more solid economic reality. Unlike many recent Marxist theorists who are careful to acknowledge the relative autonomy of political and ideological forces and their independent capacity for causal action, Rusche and Kirchheimer insist upon a materialist reductionism in which economic forces are 'real relations' and the rest of the social complex is largely epiphenomenal. This insistent emphasis upon the economic can be seen as a reaction to conventional penal history's virtual neglect of the issue, and in fact the book frequently reads like a thesis being dogmatically argued in the face of unnamed opponents. The effect of this polemical approach is to produce an unbalanced, one-sided history which altogether weakens its plausibility by overstating its argumentative case.

Punishment and Social Structure seriously overestimates the effective role of economic forces in shaping penal practice. It grossly understates the importance of ideological and political forces and has little to say about the internal dynamics of penal administration and their role in determining policy. It gives no account of the symbols and social messages conveyed by penal measures to

---

[73] See the articles and bibliography on China and the Soviet Union under the heading 'Comparative Criminal Law and Enforcement', in S. Kadish (ed.), *Encyclopedia of Crime and Justice*, i (New York, 1983), 182–214.

the law-abiding public and hence no sense of the ways in which these symbolic concerns help shape the fabric of penal institutions. Nor does it pay any regard to popular attitudes towards punishment and the troublesome evidence that suggests widespread lower-class support for punitive policies: an issue which certainly raises questions about any simple class conflict view of penal practice.[74] Official discourse and judicial rhetoric are likewise dismissed as a disguise to mask economic interest, thus preventing the analysis of these constitutive and effective areas of penal practice.

The crucial processes of legislation—which form the immediate and proximate causes of new penal measures—are left entirely unanalysed, as are the ideologies and interests of the various professionals and administrators whose decisions effectively operate the penal system. Similarly, there is little detailed attention paid to the role of political conjunctures in setting the direction of penal policy and bringing about political changes.[75] Instead, the analysis proceeds by producing correlations between what it takes to be economic interests on the one hand and penal outcomes on the other. In doing so, it simply takes it for granted that all the intermediary processes have automatically worked to realize this connection.[76] This last presumption is particularly implausible with regard to diversified, democratic societies, where penal decisions are undertaken by a personnel which may be quite remote from the sphere of economic activity. If it is to be argued that economic imperatives are conveyed into the penal realm, then the mechanisms of this indirect influence must be clearly specified and demonstrated, otherwise correlations can be seen as mere coincidence. It would, for example, be necessary to describe the ways in which penal decision-makers—especially sentencers, prison authorities, and state officials—come to recognize labour-market 'needs' and 'ruling class interests' and then make decisions in accordance with them: a complex research task which has recently been begun by the work of Steven Box.[77]

This catalogue of historical and theoretical criticisms forces us to draw back from Rusche and Kirchheimer's arguments in their strong form and to recognize limitations that affect even a qualified version of their economics-determines-punishment thesis. But to draw this conclusion is by no means to reject all the theoretical arguments which underpin their work. The problem

[74] On this question, see chs. 3 and 10.

[75] For a general discussion, see M. Ryan, *The Politics of Penal Reform* (London, 1983). For historical case-studies, see J. Davis, 'The London Garotting Panic of 1862: A Moral Panic and the Creation of a Criminal Class in mid-Victorian England', in V. A. C. Gatrell *et al.* (eds.), *Crime and the Law* (London, 1980); R. Tombs, 'Crime and the Security of the State: The "Dangerous Classes" and Insurrection in Nineteenth Century Paris', in Gatrell *et al.*, *Crime and the Law*; and S. Hall *et al.*, *Policing the Crisis: Mugging, the State, and Law and Order* (London, 1978).

[76] In their discussion of the mercantilist period, the link is fairly direct: the king instructs the judges of the need for galley slaves. But in the 18th cent. '. . . the courts became what they are today, relatively independent branches of the administration which have often represented the permanent interests of the bourgeois social order more consciously than the government did, and even sometimes in opposition to it' (*Punishment and Social Structure*, p. 81). This last point raises obvious problems about the recognition and representation of 'interests'.

[77] See Box, *Recession, Crime and Punishment*, esp. chs. 4 and 5.

with their account is that they present an important pattern of determination as being an exclusive one. Instead of investigating how economic pressures operate alongside other non-economic forces to shape penal practice, they simply assert the primacy of the former. In doing so, they omit from their account the complex processes whereby economic structures come to affect social policies, sometimes by imposing a direct imperative, sometimes by setting the broad limits within which policies will be deemed feasible, most often by imposing considerations of economic 'good sense' in a way which compromises or qualifies ideologically inspired initiatives.

The effect of these criticisms is not to produce a refutation of Rusche and Kirchheimer's arguments, but rather a scaling down of their claims and a qualification of their scope. Whatever failings their account might have, it does succeed in identifying the broad structural constraints which economic relations represent in respect of penal policy. It demonstrates an important link between the labour market and penal policy and shows how developments in one field can have repercussions upon the other. It also presents enough evidence to show that economic and financial considerations have featured prominently in penal policy decisions, and have strongly influenced specific practices and institutional features. Most importantly, it reveals some of the ways in which penal policy is caught up within the divisions of social class and shows convincingly that penal institutions need to be understood as part of much wider social strategies for managing the poor and the lower classes. One can perhaps best appreciate the advance in knowledge that their work represents by placing it alongside Durkheim's theory of punishment, which has nothing whatsoever to say on any of the above issues. Crude and unsubtle as it sometimes is, *Punishment and Social Structure* still succeeds in opening up a whole vista of understanding which simply did not exist before it was written.

5

Punishment as Ideology and Class Control
Variations on Marxist Themes

If the economism of Rusche and Kirchheimer's account ultimately restricts their interpretation of punishment, it also deforms their representation of Marxism and their attempt to realize its explanatory potential. As was stressed in the introductory pages of the last chapter, Marxism need not be interpreted as a form of economic determinism or social reductionism. As much of the modern literature in this tradition has shown, Marxism can be read in a more complex and sophisticated way as an account of interacting structures and processes, in which class relations are sustained (or transformed) by means of ideological and political struggles as well as by economic forces.

Interpreted in this non-reductionist way, a Marxist account of criminal law and punishment could avoid many of the limitations implicit in *Punishment and Social Structure* by locating penality within the field of ideological and political forces, instead of viewing it only in economic terms. Such an interpretation would continue to view penal institutions as being caught up in class relations and economic structures, but could offer a more nuanced and subtle account of the part played by penality in the negotiation of ruling-class hegemony and the maintenance of a stable social order. No such account presently exists, so to some extent this is merely conjecture, but its possibility is strongly suggested by a number of Marxist and neo-Marxist analyses which already exist and which have contributed substantially to our understanding of punishment. None of these works has attempted an integrated theory of punishment on the scale of *Punishment and Social Structure*; more usually they have touched upon penality as one element within a wider theory of law or in a substantive historical investigation. But it is possible to retrieve these specific insights and arguments about punishment and treat them as theoretical arguments which can be abstracted from their substantive contexts and used more generally. By doing so, one can perhaps build up a more adequate interpretation and use it to throw some light upon the functions of punishment in modern society. As with the discussion of Durkheim, my aim is not to find reasons for setting an approach aside, but rather to grasp what is important within a particular perspective and show how it might be developed.

1. PASHUKANIS AND THE FORM OF PENAL LAW

In elaborating his general theory of law and Marxism, the Russian jurist E. B. Pashukanis presents a series of arguments about punishment which can be developed in this way. The general thesis which he proposes is both a jurisprudential and a sociological one, showing how the juridical categories which constitute modern law are dialectically linked to capitalist economic relations. For Pashukanis, the central forms and categories of 'bourgeois' law are direct corollaries of forms which are embodied in capitalist commodity exchange. Law thus gives legal expression to a specific form of economic relations in a way which both legitimizes and facilitates the latter. Legal categories of the person define individuals as 'isolated egoistic subjects', 'the bearers of autonomous private interests', and 'ideal property owners' who relate to one another—and to the world—through the forms of contract, ownership, and exchange.[1] In taking this form, the law reproduces conceptions of the person and of social relations which are specifically capitalist—since these categories are merely a legal expression of bourgeois values and of the conditions necessary to market exchange—though it does so in a way which implicitly denies any such partiality. In effect, the law materializes and universalizes categories which are specific to a particular class-based mode of production.

Historically, this bourgeois form of law has been shaped by legal responses to economic development, so that one might say it is economically determined. But Pashukanis stresses that the reverse is also true: the legal form provides an important regulative structure which sanctions capitalist relationships and enforces the appropriate economic rules. At the same time, law provides a powerful ideology which helps legitimize these relations by phrasing particular economic interests in a vocabulary of universal right. The law is thus an institutional structure and a regulative discourse which has its own forms of existence and effectivity, but which is, at the same time, bound up with the sphere of capitalist economic life. Legal relations thus 'form a united whole with the material relations of which they are the expression'.[2]

In a chapter on 'Law and the Violation of Law', Pashukanis argues that this analysis can be extended beyond the laws of commerce and property to cover the sphere of criminal law and punishment as well, since the commodity form predominates there as elsewhere. Once they enter the drama of criminal court proceedings, real concrete persons and their disputes are transposed into 'a peculiar juridical reality, parallel with the real world'.[3] Within this strange world of the court-room, individuals come to be seen as legal subjects, bearing all the attributes of free will, responsibility, and hedonistic psychology which the standard bourgeois individual is deemed to possess, no matter how far the actualities of the case depart from this 'ideal'. The defendant's personality and actions are viewed through the prism of this ideological form which is at once mythical and socially effective, so that even the most destitute and desperate victims of market society are deemed to be free and equal and in control of their own destinies once they appear in a court of law.[4]

---

[1] E. B. Pashukanis, *Law and Marxism: A General Theory* (London, 1978), p. 188.
[2] Ibid. 184.   [3] Ibid. 167.
[4] In *Mythologies* (London, 1973) Roland Barthes discusses the way in which law invokes a 'particular psychology in the name of which you can very well today have your head cut off' (pp. 45–6).

In the same way, the practice of sentencing and the philosophy of punishment which underlies it are shown to be structured by the general form of law and its bourgeois underpinnings. According to Pashukanis, the essential idea in sentencing is that punishment should be an 'equivalent' of the offence, so that justice consists in a kind of equity or fair trading which exchanges one harmful action for another that equals it. This idea of an equivalent—which Pashukanis traces back to the commodity form—makes punishment itself into an exchange transaction, in which the offender 'pays his debt' and wherein crime becomes 'an involuntarily concluded contract'.[5] In dealing with offenders in this way, the courts help regenerate the basic cultural forms of capitalist society in the face of actualities such as inequality, unfreedom, and destitution, which could otherwise have a disturbing influence. By repeating the myths and the verities of the market system the courts help sustain that continuity of meaning and 'the dialectical connection between the various aspects of culture' upon which ideological authority depends.[6]

Pashukanis argues that the realities of crime and punishment are very different from those portrayed by the legal form and its ideological appearance. The criminal law is, like all law, an instrument of class domination and occasionally of 'class terror'.[7] It protects the property claims of the dominant classes, as well as the social and moral structures which support them, and is directed 'chiefly against those elements who have lost their position in society' or else against those who pose a political danger.[8] Pashukanis thus insists that '[e]very historically given penal policy bears the imprint of the class interests of that class which instigated it'.[9] Those theorists—like Durkheim—who fail to identify this class dimension are merely reproducing the ideological effect which the law seeks to promote: 'the would-be theories of criminal law which derive the principles of penal policy from the interests of society as a whole are conscious or unconscious distortions of reality. "Society as a whole" does not exist, except in the fantasies of the jurists. In reality we are faced only with classes, with contradictory, conflicting interests.'[10]

Penal practice, then, is a mechanism of class rule embodied in a legal form which seeks to disguise its class content. When this legal form succeeds in promoting its ideological effect, criminal law furthers the claims of 'the constitutional state' and its claim to be a neutral guarantor of individual freedoms. However, Pashukanis reminds us that 'the criminal court is not only an embodiment of the abstract legal form'—it is also 'a weapon in the immediate class struggle'.[11] Consequently, there will be occasions when the exigencies of the political situation lead the state authorities to dispense with the niceties of legal form and pursue their class objectives by more direct

[5] Pashukanis, *Law and Marxism*, p. 169. Nietzsche makes this same argument in *The Genealogy of Morals*, pp. 194–5.
[6] Pashukanis, *Law and Marxism*, p. 181. For detailed studies of this process, see R. V. Ericson and P. M. Baranek, *The Ordering of Justice* (Toronto, 1982) and P. Carlen, *Magistrates' Justice*.
[7] Pashukanis, *Law and Marxism*, p. 173.
[8] Ibid. 174.   [9] Ibid.   [10] Ibid.   [11] Ibid. 176.

means: 'the sharper and more bitter this struggle, the more difficult it will be for class rule to be realized within the legal form. When that happens, the "impartial" court and its legal guaranties will be ousted by an organization of unmediated class violence, with methods guided by considerations of political expediency alone.'[12] Thus when the protection of class interest demands it, the legal and cultural forms which normally encase penal practice will give way to a more direct deployment of penal violence. Penality is, in the last instance, a political instrument of repression, though it is more usually hemmed in by ideological concerns and legal procedures.

According to this analysis, the determination of punishment by economic forms and class interests sets definite limits upon the prospects for penal reform or for a rational penal policy. For Pashukanis, as for the other progressive penologists of the 1920s and the 1930s, a rational penal policy would concern itself not with retribution but with social defence or rehabilitation.[13] But to pursue a policy of this sort would involve depriving criminal proceedings of their 'juridical soul'—that 'irrational, mystified, absurd element' which insists upon an exchange conception of punishment, a responsible legal subject, and an extension of bourgeois legal forms into the heart of the penal process.[14] Such a reform would in effect detach penal practice from its ideological moorings—a change which would be deeply resisted by the state and the ruling classes. This is why the theoretical critiques of progressive criminologists are so often limited in their practical effects. The critics suppose that they are confronted with a system based upon mistaken views which can be countered 'by theoretical critique alone'. But Pashukanis insists that the irrational commitments of the penal system are overdetermined symptoms which have a reason for their existence and will not be removed by gentle criticism: 'in reality this absurd equivalent form results, not from the aberrations of individual criminologists, but from the material relations of the society based on commodity-production which nourish it.'[15]

The contradiction between punishment's social purpose and its legal form 'does not exist in books and theories alone'. It is a contradiction grounded 'in life itself,' in judicial practice, in the very structure of society' and only a revolution in social structures can bring about the conditions needed to dislodge it.[16] As Pashukanis declares at one point, 'the forms of bourgeois consciousness cannot be eliminated by a critique in terms of ideas alone for they form a united whole with the material relations of which they are the expression. The only way to dissipate these appearances which have become a reality is by overcoming the corresponding relations in practice, that is by realizing socialism . . .'[17]

Finally, Pashukanis extends his interpretation into the realm of actual penal sanctions, and argues that specific penal practices and institutional forms can also be understood by reference to the commodity form and its associated

---

[12] Pashukanis, *Law and Marxism*, p. 176.   [13] Ibid. 177, 179, 184.
[14] Ibid. 177.   [15] Ibid. 181–2.   [16] Ibid. 182.   [17] Ibid. 184.

consciousness. As we have seen, the tendency to develop sentencing tariffs which calibrate punishments in arithmetical terms is an effect of the exchange principle in the penal sphere, and of course the modern use of monetary fines fits perfectly within this structure. But Pashukanis argues that imprisonment must also be seen as a specifically bourgeois invention, utilizing conceptions of the person and of value which spring up from the capitalist mode of production and which reproduce bourgeois mentality in the process of punishing. 'Deprivation of freedom for a period stipulated by the court sentence, is the specific form in which . . . bourgeois-capitalist criminal law embodies the principle of equivalent recompense. This form is unconsciously yet deeply linked with the conception of man in the abstract, and abstract human labour measurable in time.'[18] Capitalist economic relations gave rise to the idea of man as the possessor of labour power and of liberty, both of which could be calibrated and measured in terms of time, and it was thus capitalism which gave rise to modern imprisonment, which is premissed upon precisely this mentality.[19] Echoing a famous passage of Marx, Pashukanis concludes that 'industrial capitalism, the declaration of human rights, the political economy of Ricardo, and the system of imprisonment for a stipulated term, are phenomena peculiar to one and the same historical epoch'.[20] Like Rusche and Kirchheimer, Pashukanis perceives a deep connection linking imprisonment to capitalism, but where the former suppose this to be an economic relation— to do with the management of the labour-market—the latter points to a cultural form which emerges from the sphere of production and comes to be reproduced and reinforced elsewhere.

Pashukanis concludes this analysis of the prison by making an important observation which restates his cultural-form-as-ideology argument and also opens up a significant insight concerning the prison. Outlining a position which would later be developed by Michel Foucault, he argues that although imprisonment appears as a 'deprivation of liberty' and is so represented in legal discourse, its reality is far more than that of a mere deprivation. It involves specific disciplinary, corrective, and punitive practices which are inflicted upon the prisoner without necessarily being declared in law. The law states that there can be no punishment which is not declared in law—*nulla poena sine lege*—but what, Pashukanis asks, is the real implication of this in practice? 'Is it necessary for every potential criminal to be informed in minute detail about the corrective methods which would be used on him? No, it is much simpler and more brutal. He must know what quantity of his freedom he will have to pay as a result of the transaction concluded before the court.'[21] The legal representation of imprisonment as merely the deprivation of freedom is

---

[18] Ibid. 181.
[19] See E. P. Thompson, 'Time, Work Discipline and Industrial Capitalism', *Past and Present*, 38 (1967), 56–97.
[20] Pashukanis, *Law and Marxism*, p. 181.
[21] Ibid. 184.

thus as distorted and incomplete as the law's customary representation of individual freedom itself.

Pashukanis's discussion of punishment has a number of important lessons to teach us. His identification of the formal similarities which link the appearance of penal practices to other realms of social practice shows how certain cultural forms tend to penetrate different spheres of social life, until these pervasive cultural figures, generated and regenerated in institutional practice, come to seem naturalistic and self-evident. The idea of equivalence, the autonomy of the legal subject, the idea of liberty and its calibrated deprivation, all these are facts of penal life which have their origin elsewhere but which have come to seem obvious through extension and repeated use. By showing their links to a historically specific economic process, Pashukanis uncovers a layer of significance in penal practice which was submerged beneath its very 'naturalness'.

His analysis is also useful in stressing that punishment is a form of social action which operates within a legal framework and is deeply affected by legal forms and procedures. Punishment may serve certain social purposes, such as crime control, social defence, or rehabilitation, just as it may, in Rusche and Kirchheimer's terms, serve certain economic or fiscal objectives. But it will do so only to the extent that these objectives can be pursued within the forms of legality and the categories of juridical discourse. This commitment to legality is precisely what criminological progressives found 'absurd' or 'irrational' in the penal process, since it entails a series of myths and fictions which do not square with the actualities of social life and individual conduct. But for Pashukanis, as we have seen, the legalism of penality is far from unreasoned: it is a necessary consequence of the fact that penal laws and institutions are located within the system of ideological forms which express and perpetuate capitalist power. To remove this 'absurd' legal element from punishment would involve unhinging penal practice from the network of power relations of which it forms a part.

As events have shown, however, Pashukanis tended to overstate the fixity of the legal forms within which penality was encased. During the twentieth century, capitalist societies throughout Europe and America have modified their commitment to juridical forms in the process of punishment. They have introduced indeterminate sentences, conceptions of irresponsibility, and categories of criminal psychology which differ markedly from the classical legal forms and conceptions of the subject. None of these changes has completely removed the older legal forms from penal practice, but they have modified their operation considerably, and have done so without any fundamental revolution in the economic sphere.[22] In retrospect, it seems apparent that Pashukanis has exaggerated the extent to which capitalist economic forms require a particular legal framework in which to survive. Extrapolating from

[22] On this, see my *Punishment and Welfare*. For a critical discussion of Pashukanis on law, see P. Q. Hirst, *On Law and Ideology* (London, 1979).

the orthodoxies of nineteenth-century capitalism at the highpoint of economic and social liberalism, he underestimates the flexibility of this economic system and the variety of social and legal forms with which it is compatible. It may well be true that capitalist commodity exchange necessitates a legal framework which specifies 'free' legal agents, forms of property, and an enforceable apparatus of contract, but the forms which this framework can take are more numerous and more varied than Pashukanis envisaged. In the same way, penal forms must be compatible with the economic and social relations within which they exist, but there are many forms in which this condition can be satisfied.

It might also be pointed out that Pashukanis presents a rather simple-minded conception of penality's class function, which in its way is merely the inverse of the Durkheimian view which he so vehemently opposed. For Durkheim, punishment expresses the interests of society as a whole, while for Pashukanis only the ruling class finds its interests expressed in penal practice— for the rest of society criminal justice in the bourgeois state is 'organized class terror'.[23] We have seen in earlier chapters why Durkheim's view is untenable, but the position which Pashukanis adopts against it is, in fact, equally implausible. The criminal law provides protection as well as 'terror' for the working classes, and there is undoubtedly a general social function involved in certain of its aspects such as the prohibition of violence and the punishment of predatory criminals. If penality serves a class purpose it does so in a way which enlists support among the subordinate classes and which protects interests which are experienced as being universal rather than specific. The key to understanding criminal law in class terms is to appreciate the ways in which particular interests are interwoven with general ones. Thus, to take an important example, the property of everyone may be equally protected, but the definition of property which the law upholds makes no distinction between 'individual property' and 'property in the means of production', so that the same law which protects everyone at one level, also legalizes the basis whereby one class exploits the other. Any adequate analysis of penality's class dimension must seek to understand these complexities and include them in its account rather than pretend they do not exist.

Ironically, Pashukanis himself provides all the elements for a sophisticated account of this kind, although he singularly fails to develop it. One could argue, using his analysis, that it is precisely the legal form which penality takes which simultaneously provides a degree of equality and protection for everyone, while also contributing to a system of inequality and class domination. By framing social regulation in legal terms, every individual in society becomes entitled to claim the protections of law for his or her person or property— whether as victim or as accused—and is accorded the status of a free and equal subject before the law. As a defence for the poor and the vulnerable against

[23] Pashukanis, *Law and Marxism*, p. 173.

attack or as a protection against state power when accused, these legal provisions are of genuine value to members of all classes. But precisely because the law deems all individuals to be free and equal and because it protects the rights of property without distinction, it silences the real inequalities of power, status, and freedom which separate the rich from the poor and the owners of the means of production from those groups whose real property is miniscule. The forms of law thus provide a real measure of social protection against crime and criminal assaults, but no protection whatsoever against the harms of economic domination and the social injuries of class.[24] This argument is, in effect, the Marxist critique of the form of law as applied to criminal law and penal practice and it can be used to produce important insights into the social effects of punishment. The surprise is that Pashukanis should so clearly have drawn it to our attention without having made use of it himself.

2. THE IDEOLOGICAL FUNCTIONS OF CRIMINAL LAW

The account of modern punishment developed by Pashukanis situates it as a politico-ideological instrument of the bourgeois state, structured by economically derived categories and deployed in the furtherance of ruling-class power. Without denying the economic analyses of Rusche and Kirchheimer, it brings to bear a different set of Marxist arguments and interprets penality in accordance with them, thereby adding an important new dimension to the Marxist account. This attempt to understand punishment in terms of its ideological and political uses is further developed by the historian Douglas Hay in his analysis of eighteenth-century English criminal law, although his conception of these processes differs in important respects from that of Pashukanis. Both theorists conceive of punishment as being concerned with ideological legitimation and with class coercion, but where Pashukanis stresses the effects of structural forces and cultural forms which operate 'behind the backs', and often outside the awareness, of social agents, Hay lays much more emphasis upon deliberate human actions and the strategic calculations of those in power. In effect, the historian seeks to understand in human terms the genesis of the structures, the cultural figures, and the systematic social patterns which give content to the philosopher's abstractions. His focus is primarily upon penal decision-making—upon legislative processes, sentencing choices, the organization of penal ceremonies, and the mentalities which inform these various processes, rather than upon the penal forms and cultural patterns which are their result.

Douglas Hay's theorization of punishment was developed as part of a specific historical enquiry into the workings of criminal justice in eighteenth-century England. The starting-point for his investigation is a pair of interrelated paradoxes which prompt him to ask certain questions about the unstated

---

[24] See R. Sennett and J. Cobb, *The Hidden Injuries of Class* (New York, 1972).

functions of penal practice in English society at that time. The first paradox is one which other historians have also noted but rarely satisfactorily resolved, and it concerns the problem of capital punishment.[25] The problem here is to explain the stubborn commitment of successive English governments and judiciaries to retaining—and indeed expanding—the range of capital statutes and their associated practices of pardon and commutation, at a time when fewer and fewer death sentences were actually carried out, and when reformers strenuously criticized the absurdity of this situation. How is one to account for the apparent irrationality which lay behind 'this determination of Parliament to retain all the capital statutes, even when obsolete, and to continue to create new ones even when they fell stillborn . . .'?[26]

The second problem is a more abstract one, which emerges when the Marxist understanding of class societies is brought to bear upon the facts of social organization in eighteenth-century England. How did the English ruling class maintain its ascendancy long after the social ties of feudalism had broken down, and in a period before a modern apparatus of rule had been constructed? What were the political arrangements and social institutions which 'made it possible to govern eighteenth-century England without a police force or without a large army' at a time when social divisions and dis-locations made England an 'unruly, disorderly, almost anarchic society . . .'?[27]

In unravelling these puzzles, Douglas Hay produces a compelling account of the informal levers of power and influence in English society and the ways in which these were orchestrated through the institutions of criminal justice. Implicit in this account is a theory of the ideological and political functions of the penal process which can, with a little care, be abstracted from its historical context and used in the analysis of punishment today.

Echoing Pashukanis on the 'absurdities' of legal formalism, Hay argues that the apparently irrational commitments of eighteenth-century legal policy were in fact deeply grounded 'in the mental and social structure' of English class society.[28] Anomalous as this system may seem, the governing classes were willing to live with it precisely because they perceived the unreformed law to be serving their best interests. As Hay puts it, 'the criminal law was critically important in maintaining bonds of obedience and deference, in legitimizing the status quo, in constantly recreating the structure of authority which arose from property and in turn protected its interests'.[29] The system of criminal justice performed these supportive functions, Hay argues, by means of a judicious combination of physical and symbolic persuasion which was calculated 'to

---

[25] On this see L. Radzinowicz and J. Langbein, each of whom proposes explanations which differ from that developed by Hay. L. Radzinowicz, *A History of English Criminal Law and its Administration from 1750*, i (London, 1948), and J. Langbein, 'Albion's Fatal Flaws', *Past and Present*, 98 (1983), 96–120.

[26] Hay, 'Property, Authority and the Criminal Law', p. 24.

[27] Ibid. 56. The second quotation in this sentence is from L. Stone, *The Past and the Present Revisited* (London, 1987), p. 250.

[28] Hay, 'Property, Authority and the Criminal Law', p. 26.   [29] Ibid. 25.

mould the consciousness by which the many submitted to the few'.[30] The criminal law and its associated penal practices functioned, in effect, as an ideological system, and, like all ideology, it conveyed 'a set of ideas designed to vindicate or disguise class interest'.[31] From this point of view, the inconsistencies and irrational weaknesses of the system were not in fact weaknesses at all— they were the points at which personal discretion could be exercised and ideological interests sustained.

Hay's analysis of criminal justice as ideology identifies three thematic dimensions through which its persuasiveness flowed. The first of these concerns the 'majesty' of the law and the powerful imagery and symbolism which legal ceremony sustained. Eighteenth-century English justice was staged as a series of dramatic spectacles: the ceremonial entry of the judiciary into the town, the elaborate proceedings of the trial, the sober rituals of confession and execution —each of which was performed with fastidious attention to detail and concern for dramatic effect. According to Hay there was 'an acute consciousness' that such ceremonies were 'platforms for addressing "the multitude"' and 'the judges' every action was governed by the importance of spectacle'.[32] The carefully worded rhetoric of these occasions invoked the voice of paternalistic authority, the passions of righteous vengeance, and the symbols of God's justice and mercy, in a style which was calculated to rouse the emotions of onlookers and secure their identification with the imperatives of the law. 'In its ritual, its judgments and its channelling of emotion the criminal law echoed many of the most powerful psychic components of religion', but the faith which these rituals nourished and sustained had a definite political content.[33] Criminal trials were, in effect, symbolic celebrations—and material realizations —of the power of the law and its grounding in property and social class.

The second thematic of legal ideology is its stress upon the idea of 'justice'. Despite their class connections, and their *de facto* enactment by a parliamentary élite, law and the legal process displayed a real commitment to juridical norms such as procedural fairness, 'punctilious attention to forms', strict observance of rules—in short, to 'legalism' and the ideals of legal justice.[34] The legal system's integrity in these respects was much vaunted and operated as a powerful element of law's ideological appeal. The law's careful concern for whatever little property the poor possessed, its willingness to be invoked by the poor victims (where they could afford the expense of a prosecution) as well as by the rich, its occasional conviction and execution of men of property such as the infamous Lord Ferrers, gave a real substance to the rhetoric of 'equality before the law', and its application to all alike. And, as Hay points out, this willingness to provide 'equal justice for murderers of all classes' was used to

---

[30] Hay, 'Property, Authority and the Criminal Law', p. 26.
[31] Ibid.   [32] Ibid. 28, 27.   [33] Ibid. 29.
[34] Ibid. 33. For a discussion of the different conceptions of 'justice' which came into contest in this period and later, see R. McGowan, 'The Image of Justice and Reform of the Criminal Law in Early Nineteenth Century England', *The Buffalo Law Review*, 32 (1983), 89–125.

represent *all* of the law as serving popular interests in the same way: 'the trick was to extend that communal sanction [the community support that some laws could inspire] to a criminal law that was nine-tenths concerned with upholding a radical division of property.'[35]

The third theme which Hay identifies as characterizing eighteenth-century English law is that of 'mercy'. In contrast to the more formalistic and professionalized rules and proceedings which came to replace it in the nineteenth century, the legal process of this period left extensive spaces for discretionary decision and personal influence. The importance of private prosecution, character-witnessing, pardon pleas, and jury decisions provided opportunities for powerful individuals to grant or withhold favours to their social inferiors and to each other—for instance by providing the funds to pursue a case, or a statement of a man's good character, or, most importantly, a plea for the commutation of a death sentence once it had been passed. These personal initiatives linked criminal justice into the wider social network of patronage and deference, and gave the local élite a powerful leverage upon the mechanisms of the law. In extreme cases—where an employer or landlord's plea for a pardon could mean the difference between life and death—this leverage was of decisive importance, but more generally it meant that the processes of law could be gently manipulated, the better to serve the interests of the social élite. Hay discusses the 'delicacy and circumspection' with which the authorities gauged public opinion before making decisions about the execution or the timing of death sentences, and he concludes that this discretionary use of mercy 'allowed the rulers of England to make the courts a selective instrument of class justice', while proclaiming the law to be 'incorruptible' and absolutely determinate.[36] Taken together, these various routes of influence allowed the criminal law to become a barely resistant object of 'private, extra-legal dealings' whereby 'the king, judges, magistrates and gentry' bent the statute and common law to purposes of their own.[37]

In their performative unity, the themes of majesty, justice, and mercy gave the law an ideological structure which was universally social in appearance and deeply class oriented in effect. According to Hay, this delicate ideological system was the product of 'countless short-term decisions' based upon 'intuition', 'trial and error', and a clear sense on the part of key actors of where the reigning interests ultimately lay.[38] It was not an automatic effect of class structures or juridical forms but rather an achievement of human action, and the cunning of a ruling class which knew how to rule.

As to the persuasiveness of this display, and its ability to win the allegiance— or at least the grudging submission—of the subordinate classes, Hay accepts that the evidence is equivocal. It is likely that popular attitudes were ambivalent, and that cynicism and disrespect for the law co-existed with belief in its justice—'[P]erhaps the ordinary Englishman played the role assigned to him,

---

[35] Hay, 'Property, Authority and the Criminal Law', p. 35.
[36] Ibid. 48.   [37] Ibid. 52.   [38] Ibid. 53.

and was never convinced by the play'.[39] And certainly there were groups among the ruling classes, especially the 'middling men', who felt that the unreformed law was neither conscionable in its severity nor particularly effective in serving their specific interests. But, for all this, Hay concludes that it was 'the criminal law, more than any other social institution' which allowed England to be governed by a small élite lacking extensive administrative or military capacity, and that the ideology of law 'was crucial in sustaining the hegemony of the English ruling class'.[40]

Since it first appeared in 1975, Hay's interpretation has attracted a good deal of attention and has become part of the received wisdom of radical criminology and sociological studies of punishment. However, it has also provoked a good deal of critical controversy among professional historians, and subsequent historical studies give us reason to qualify Hay's conclusions and rethink some of his arguments. In particular, historians such as John Langbein, P. J. R. King, and Lawrence Stone have argued that class interest was much less of a force in shaping legal decisions than Hay implies, and that the popular support for the legal system, such as it was, flowed from a recognition of the real protections which law afforded, and not from unfounded ideology or 'false consciousness'. Langbein, for example, stresses that in the property offences which made up the bulk of the courts' work, the victims who resorted to the law were themselves often drawn from the poorer classes and were typically little better off than the offenders they prosecuted. Moreover, he claims, there was a widespread moral consensus which found most property crimes to be blameworthy, and which regarded violent or recidivist offenders as deserving of severe punishment, so that 'men of the non-elite could predominate (as prosecutors and jurors) in convicting persons who committed property crimes'.[41] As for the intercession of private interests and the extra-legal manipulation of key decisions regarding sentencing, the research of P. J. R. King suggests the official handling of reprieve and pardon matters was rather more principled than Hay implies. King's study of the relevant case papers suggests that an informal set of considerations—such as good character, youth, poverty, respectability, the absence of violence—actually shaped decisions, so that cases were mostly settled on their own merits rather in deference to the wishes of a well-placed petitioner (though of course the credibility of claims about character, respectability, and so on might well depend upon the social standing of the individuals who gave evidence).[42]

[39] Hay, 'Property, Authority and the Criminal Law', p. 54.

[40] Ibid. 56. E. P. Thompson in *Whigs and Hunters* (Harmondsworth, 1975) endorses Hay's conclusion: 'The hegemony of the eighteenth century gentry and aristocracy was expressed, above all, not in military force, not in the mystifications of a priesthood or of the press, not even in economic coercion, but in the rituals of the study of the Justices of the Peace, in the quarter-sessions, in the pomp of Assizes and in the Theatre of Tyburn' (p. 262).

[41] Langbein, 'Albion's Fatal Flaws', p. 108.

[42] P. J. R. King, 'Decision-Makers and Decision-Making in the English Criminal Law, 1750–1800', *Historical Journal*, 27 (1984), 25–58.

Questions about the integrity or corruption of eighteenth-century law, while fascinating in themselves, are less relevant to our purposes than the points concerning punishment's role as a class instrument. Langbein's point about the poor's support for the law, and their willingness to use it against others is supported by the work of Brewer and Styles and by Beattie, and, increasingly, it is a point conceded even by radical and Marxist criminologists.[43] However, the fact that the criminal law can draw upon wide moral support for many of its actions does not undercut the argument made earlier, to the effect that this limited moral support tends to be converted into support for the law as such, and thus for the private forms of property and resulting social hierarchies which the law sustains.[44] Similarly, Langbein's argument that the criminal law is a marginal sphere of social power, when compared with the laws which define ownership and control of the means of production, can be granted—as it would be by any Marxist—without losing sight of the criminal law's ability to legitimize these property rules as well as its own, and intervene when necessary to protect them. As Lawrence Stone puts it, 'the criminal law—but not the civil law—was indeed in the last resort an instrument of the elite to protect their own and other people's lives and property by the use of selective terror. What else has the criminal law ever done?'[45]

As I argued earlier, both here and in Chapter 3, it is necessary to see criminal law and punishment as representing a complex combination of universal social interests on the one hand, and specific class interests on the other, the exact balance depending upon the specific laws concerned and the social setting in which they operate. The conclusion which I drew in that earlier discussion was that punishment aims to reinforce the claims of social and legal authority, however these are structured, and Douglas Hay's work stands as a forceful confirmation of this point. Penal law, at base, concerns itself with social authority and the governing claims of those in power. It reinforces these claims by means of coercive sanctions as well as symbolic displays, making punishment a form of power exercised as well as power expressed. Where social power and authority are structured upon definite class lines, as they were in eighteenth-century England, then punishment will reproduce the forms and the figures of class even when its actions appear to transcend class divisions and protect those on the wrong side of the class divide.

---

[43] J. Brewer and J. Styles (eds.), *An Ungovernable People: The English and their Law in the Seventeenth and Eighteenth Centuries* (New Brunswick, NJ, 1980); Beattie, *Crime and the Courts in England, 1660–1800*. For evidence from the 17th cent., see C. Herrup, 'Law and Morality in Seventeenth Century England', *Past and Present*, 106 (1985), 102–23. Among the many radical criminologists whose work addresses this more complex relationship between the lower classes and the criminal law are I. Taylor, *Law and Order: Arguments for Socialism* (London, 1981); J. Lea and J. Young, *What is to be Done About Law and Order?* (Harmondsworth, 1984); and E. Currie, *Confronting Crime: An American Challenge* (New York, 1985).

[44] For a detailed analysis of how this 'conversion' occurs, see Mead, 'The Psychology of Punitive Justice'.

[45] Stone, *The Past and the Present Revisited*, p. 250.

A related point concerns the theory of punishment's social significance which is implicit in Hay's historical account. One of the most striking features of this Marxist analysis is the close resemblance which it bears to the Durkheimian theory of punishment. This is not, of course, a resemblance of a substantive kind, since Durkheim sees only a *conscience collective* where the Marxist finds class interest and the legitimation of class rule. But in analytical terms both accounts insist that some of penality's major effects are sustained not against offenders or potential criminals, but on a wider moral register, which connects with popular mentalities and public attitudes towards social authority. Both Durkheim and Hay agree that penality works through the forms of ritual display and symbolic representation, and addresses itself to an audience of onlookers as much as to the offender in the dock. Both insist that such displays can be crucial to the generation and regeneration of a society's culture and the individual's commitment, whether by shoring up the claims of authority or else by dealing with social dangers. Despite radical disagreement over the interpretation of penal symbols and the nature of the societies which they depict, both accounts thus confirm the operation of punishments within this wider sphere of psychic and cultural life.

Whereas Rusche and Kirchheimer's materialist account of penal forms and their economic basis bears little relation to Durkheim's theory, dealing with a set of problems which falls outside Durkheim's range, the analyses of Hay (and to a lesser extent of Pashukanis) cover very similar ground and in very similar ways. They are each interpretations of the same social process. In fact if one understands the Marxist term 'ideology' to refer to the class content of cultural representations and practices—which is certainly the sense in which Hay and most neo-Marxists use the term—then it becomes clear that ideological analysis is effectively cultural analysis from a specifically political point of view. Despite Durkheim's failure to register the fact, one would expect that the social sentiments conveyed by penal practices will always contain a distinctively political content, since, as we saw before, representations of society and social order are always representations of a particular conception of society and particular ways of being orderly. Durkheim's own example of the religiosity of punishment in an absolutist regime suggests as much: whenever a punishment is enacted it is not just 'society' which is reaffirmed but 'absolutist' society. The Marxist analysis develops this point to show that this most universal of social functions can affirm narrow class interests while seeming to do the reverse.

3. PENAL FORMS AND SOCIAL FORMATIONS

So far I have discussed interpretations which have approached punishment from the point of view of economic relations, juridical–ideological forms, or political manipulation, each one developing a particular dimension of the punishment–society relationship. There is, however, another style of analysis, also much influenced by Marxism, which stresses what one might call the overdetermination of punishment within any social formation. This kind of account—which is usually concrete and historically detailed—stresses that penal policies and institutions are formed not by a monolithic process but instead by a whole range of forces which converge upon the issue in any particular conjuncture. Penality is thus the overdetermined resultant of a set of conflicting and connecting forces. But what makes these accounts Marxist or neo-Marxist, rather than merely multi-factorial, is their insistence that the forces which shape penal policy exist within the broader structures of a mode of production and a hierarchical society. So even when the historical actors in penal policy debates are motivated by religious or humanitarian or scientific concerns, the outcomes of their efforts will be constrained by the structures of social power and the invisible pressures of the dominant class culture.[46]

A good example of this style of analysis is Michael Ignatieff's *A Just Measure of Pain*, which examines' the origins of the penitentiary in the industrial revolution. Like David Rothman's parallel account of the *Discovery of the Asylum* in the USA, Ignatieff located the birth of the penitentiary in the search for a new form of social order in the early decades of the nineteenth century, following the breakdown of the traditional ties of localism, the growth of city populations, and the emergence of capitalist social relations. His account of the period is nuanced and subtle, paying particular attention to the range of forces which operated for reform, among them religious non-conformists, utilitarian social critics, progressive employers, city magistrates, rural justices, and Parliamentary reformers. Each of these groups had its own peculiar complex of motivations which led it to support the idea of the penitentiary as a general response to crime, and it was these converging motivations and ideologies which mobilized the movement for reform and eventually saw the institutions built.

But Ignatieff also insists that the details of reformers' intentions and manœuvres must be seen against the broader social canvas of a society which was actively restructuring itself to adapt to the new bases of social life. Consequently, his account of the penitentiary's emergence places it firmly within a new logic of class relations and a correspondingly new set of strategies and institutions for managing the poor. Productive relations, labour-market conditions, concerns about property, and the language of articulate class interests are all well back in the analysis, since penal policy was debated and constructed by other forces using different vocabularies. But these background factors nevertheless formed the horizons of possibility and the structural underpinnings of change, so that the key to the penitentiary's success was its ability to connect to these wider interests. The penitentiary had appeal

---

[46] '. . . the important issue is no longer how punishment can be utilized to "solve" the immediate problems of political control or state-building in a narrow sense, but rather how punishment is woven into the entire fabric of social relations which articulate and give substance to the relationship between economically distinctive classes.' S. Spitzer, 'Notes Toward a Theory of Punishment and Social Change', *Research in Law and Sociology*, 2 (1979), 223.

'because the reformers succeeded in presenting it as a response, not merely to crime, but to the whole social crisis of the period, and as part of a larger strategy of political, social and legal reform designed to re-establish order on a new foundation'. By the 1840s 'it was seen as an element of a larger vision of order' which commanded 'the reflexive assent of the propertied and the powerful'.[47]

Perhaps it is wrong to present Ignatieff's account alongside more specifically Marxist ones, since its social history makes no explicit reference to Marxist theory. My justification for this is that Ignatieff works with a conception of society based around class divisions, a capitalist mode of production, and a state apparatus which conserves the inequalities of this social order, but of course such conceptions are not the exclusive prerogative of the Marxist tradition.[48] But whether or not Ignatieff's text should be considered a Marxist one, it is certainly congruent with the Marxist model and it utilizes basic conceptions which most Marxists would share. Consequently, for my purposes, it can serve as an illustration of how a specific configuration of economic developments, class interests, and social crises can be seen to facilitate, if not fully determine, important developments in penal policy.

My own book, *Punishment and Welfare*, is also an account of how penal policies are forged by particular social movements within the constraints of larger social structures—the case in point being the development of new penal-welfare institutions in Britain in the late nineteenth and early twentieth centuries. Like Ignatieff's work, *Punishment and Welfare* borrows Marxist concepts and arguments without placing itself within the Marxist framework; in fact in its theoretical inspiration the book is closer to the work of Michel Foucault which has a complicated and often critical relationship with orthodox Marxism.[49] However, for all its detailed use of Foucauldian concepts, and its concern with issues which escape the Marxist framework, *Punishment and Welfare* is an analysis of how a changing mode of production gave rise to political and ideological developments which had direct consequences for social and penal policy. And, in the course of this analysis, it makes use of concepts such as 'ideology', 'hegemony', 'class', and 'state' in a way which owes much to Marxist writers such as Antonio Gramsci and Gareth Stedman Jones.

The book's argument makes it clear that penal institutions and crime-control policies have their own internal dynamics which cannot be regarded as expressions or reflections of events occurring elsewhere. Institutional regimes develop specific problems, reforming groups or professional agencies pursue particular programmatic goals, and the pragmatics of crime-control demand

---

[47] Ignatieff, *A Just Measure of Pain*, p. 210.

[48] See M. Ignatieff, 'Class Interests and the Penitentiary: A Reply to Rothman', *The Canadian Criminology Forum*, 5 (1982), which reiterates the importance of class, property, and (agricultural) capitalism in Ignatieff's interpretation of penal change.

[49] See B. Smart, *Foucault, Marxism and Critique* (London, 1983).

certain kinds of response, none of which is reducible to, or fully determined by, other social processes. Nevertheless, penality is also a state-directed practice, embedded in legal forms and ideological frameworks, which forms one element within a broader range of social policies directed against the poor. Consequently, it is also caught up in the wider dynamics of the social formation, and its contours will be determined by the complex interaction of its internal penal processes with these broader social structures and relations.

Moving from this conception, *Punishment and Welfare* begins with an account of British penality in the mid-Victorian era which traces the links between the details of penal practice and the wider structures of social life. It describes the system's reliance upon conceptions of the offender which stress the freedom, equality, and responsibility of the legal subject, the implicit individualism of its obsession with cellular isolation, the work-ethic ideology conveyed by its use of prison labour, the absence of state aid for offenders, and the operative conception of punishment as a kind of social contract response to the individual who freely chooses to break the law. The parallels which these penological conceptions have with the political ideology of *laissez-faire* individualism and their evident affinity with related conceptions of the minimalist state, the freedom of the individual in market society, and the need for deterrent, less-eligible, social policies, suggest that penality was, to a large extent, structured by its social context. They suggest a coherence—an ideological and strategic fit—which linked penality into the circuits of the dominant ideology and implicated it within the predominant structures of class relations. The criminological conceptions and prison regimes of the 1860s and 1870s were, in effect, part of a network of strategic links and structural homologies which had rendered Victorian penality congruent with the class relations and social policies of the time.

The transition from this Victorian mode of penality to the modern penal-welfare arrangements which emerged after 1895 is presented as a complex historical process in which a series of reforming movements and interest groups took a part. The proponents of a new scientific criminology, advocates of eugenics and social insurance, social workers, charity organizers, penal administrators, and New Liberal political reformers each contributed to the struggles and debates of these years, and much of the book is taken up with describing the interaction of the reformers' programmes and the conflicts and alliances which emerged. But these specifically penal movements did not occur in isolation. Their intellectual forms, ideological concerns, and political ambitions were part of a much wider restructuring movement which effectively reorganized British social, political, and economic institutions into a new social-democratic, welfarist form. One could trace this movement to the economic and political changes which Marxists describe as the transition from liberal to monopoly capitalism, but in fact the important issue is less one of causal priority than of causal interconnection. Economic changes had political and ideological corollaries, and vice versa, and the sphere of social and penal policy was deeply embroiled in these transformations. Questions of penal policy —such as the responsibility of individuals for their actions, the responsibility of the state for their reform, the style of institutional regimes for their treatment—were intimately linked to other issues of social policy, such as the proper running of the workhouses or the organization of the poor law, and these in turn raised general issues about the regulation of the labour-market, the proper role of the state, and the general strategy to be adopted towards the care and control of the poor.

The intersection of these various issues, and the consciousness of policy makers that they were in fact connected, is well evidenced by the many official reports and recommendations of the period between 1895 and 1914, in which similar ways of thinking and acting were applied to a whole range of otherwise disparate penal and social problems. Consequently when the new apparatus of penal-welfare was eventually constructed it was premissed upon a set of social principles and ideological commitments which marked it off from the liberalism of the nineteenth century and linked it into a new set of institutional strategies which came to be called the Welfare State. Its distinctively positive approach to the reform of deviants, its extensive use of interventionist agencies, its deployment of social work and psychiatric expertise, its concern to regulate, manage, and normalize rather than immediately to punish, and of course its new 'welfarist' self-representation—all these characteristics combine to link the new penality into the new set of social strategies, ideological forms, and class relations which emerged at this time.

The Marxist implications which one might draw from this study would point to the links between particular modes of production and modes of penality, the tendency of legal and penal categories to correspond to the dominant pattern of economic relations, and the supporting role which penal ideologies play in constructing a hegemonic form of social domination: the arguments of Rusche and Kirchheimer, Pashukanis, and Hay are all thus exemplified in a single concrete case. But the emphatic point of the study is not that these processes determine penal outcomes, but rather that penal outcomes are negotiated within the limits which these broader structures lay down. And, moreover, these structures do not work all by themselves, somehow managing to control all the outcomes by automatic means. Instead, it is a matter of decision-making agents—in this case reformers, administrators, and politicians —who consciously perceive the bounds of political possibility and adjust their actions within them, sometimes struggling to change the rules of the game, more often making compromises with the constraints which they face. This argument suggests that structures are made effective—or are made to change— through the medium of human action and the specific struggles and outcomes which such action will always involve. It is thus wrong to suggest that penal forms are 'determined' by a particular mode of production, or by a particular pattern of class relations. Like everything else, penal forms are produced by conjunctural politics and by specific struggles in the sphere of penality itself.

The wider structures of economy, law, and ideology—not to mention the institutional grid of social policies—will produce pressures towards specific kinds of penal practice, and will limit the range of possible outcomes. But this is best thought of in terms of an 'elective affinity' rather than as a necessary determination. The causal forces identified in the Marxist account—essentially those of economics and class—are by no means the exclusive or even the immediate determinants involved in penological developments. In order to give an account of actual penal changes, historical studies are obliged to deal with forces which have only a tangential or an indirect linkage to the determinants dealt with by the Marxist model, so that inevitably Marxist concepts remain in the background of analysis—as with Ignatieff—or else provide only a partial account, as in my own work. Indeed, the most obvious limitation of *Punishment and Welfare* as a *historical* account, is its tendency to view penal change only from the point of view of its implications for class domination and the control of the poor. In doing so, it replaces the analysis of *cultural* forces by an analysis of *ideological* forces; a perspective which highlights the political implications of penal measures but tends to silence any other significance which they might have.[50]

In this sense, *Punishment and Welfare* might be used to point up the limits of Marxism in the analysis of penality. Marxism, in fact, has little that is specific to say about the institutions of punishment: such detail as the book provides on this is developed from outside the Marxist framework. Unlike the work of Durkheim—or indeed of Foucault—Marxism offers no concepts or analyses which are peculiar to this set of institutions, and it has no particular theory of punishment as such. Instead, it describes how penality—like other social institutions—comes to be caught up by its location in class society and shaped by class-related determinations. This in itself is invaluable in its way—not least because most penal systems exist in class-divided contexts—but it is a theory of penality's 'outside' and the internal implications thereof, rather than a comprehensive theory of penality. Marxism provides us with an account of penality's relationship with its class-structured political and economic environment and the implications this has for penal forms and penal practices. In most societies, the impact of class divisions upon penality is pervasive and profound but in so far as penality has other determinants, or relationships or significance, the analyst needs to look beyond the Marxist framework.

One can summarize the theses which have emerged from the various Marxist studies in the following way:

1. As a state-controlled apparatus of repression and ideology, penality plays a role in more extended social conflicts and strategies of domination. Alongside its social functions in the control of crime it operates as an instrument of governance by one class against another.

---

[50] For a discussion of some of the cultural themes implicit in the penal reforms of this period, see M. Wiener, 'The March of Penal Progress?', *The Journal of British Studies*, 26 (1987), 83–96.

2. Conversely, these wider ideological, political and economic struggles play a part in shaping punishment and structuring its categories so that penal practices mesh with the political objectives and ideological commitments of the ruling bloc.

3. Penality is intimately linked with the legal sphere and is patterned by legal forms and principles. To the extent that the law is a system of ideological display, punishment contributes to its legitimatory functions and effects. Through the medium of penality, state power and state violence can be articulated in legal forms which enlist popular consent.

4. Punishment exists in an interrelationship with other social policies, particularly those policies which manage the poor and their conditions of life—such as the poor law, social work, social security, and labour-market regulation.

5. Above all, penal practices are shaped by the condition of the lower classes and the strategies adopted towards them by the governing élite. Punishment forms a key part of the policing and social policy measures which together regulate the poor and seek to manage problem populations. Thus penal measures will be shaped not just by patterns of criminality—themselves linked to the conditions of life of marginal groups and their relation to other classes—but primarily by ruling-class perceptions of the poor as a social problem and the preferred strategies for their treatment. These forms of treatment may involve aspects of caring and charity as well as coercion and control, but the embeddedness of these forms within wider strategies of rule is the point most crucial for their comprehension.

The striking thing about these five key points, expressed in this way, is that although they have emerged from Marxist or neo-Marxist analyses, they are by no means tied to that framework. Whether taken singly or jointly, they do not depend upon specifically Marxist arguments such as the theory of surplus value, the primacy of the economy, or the determination of social consciousness by social being, nor do they employ any uniquely Marxist terms or concepts. They do, of course, assume such things as the existence of class divisions, strategies of domination, and a state which is allied to the interests of a ruling bloc, but these premises are also shared by other sociological frameworks, notably those of Weber, Foucault, and Elias. If this is the case, and the most important points made about penality by the Marxist tradition are not essentially 'Marxist', then these key propositions should be viewed as rather more compatible with other perspectives than they at first sight appear.

6

Punishment and the Technologies of Power

The Work of Michel Foucault

1. AN INTRODUCTION TO FOUCAULT'S APPROACH

The work of Michel Foucault, and particularly his book *Discipline and Punish*, has recently become a central reference-point in the sociology of punishment. In fact Foucault's influence has been such as virtually to eclipse the other, more established, traditions which I have described, and to set a new agenda for contemporary research in this field. As one writer puts it 'to write today about punishment and classification without Foucault is like talking about the unconscious without Freud'.[1]

Amidst all the clamour and acclaim that currently surrounds Foucault's work, it is quite possible to overstate its originality and its distinctiveness, and indeed I will argue in a subsequent chapter that many of Foucault's main themes are already well developed in the work of Friedrich Nietzsche and Max Weber. But there is nevertheless a singularity about Foucault's analysis of punishment which marks it off from the Marxist or Durkheimian traditions and establishes it as an important perspective in this field. Instead of highlighting the social context or moral foundations of penality, Foucault's work takes us straight to the internal workings of the apparatus itself, focusing upon the actual technologies of penal power and their mode of operation. His studies analyse in detail the principles of surveillance and discipline which are inscribed in modern penal institutions, the grammar of modern penological discourse, and what one might describe as the 'penological rationalities' which operate in the penal realm. And although his analyses fasten on to the particularities of penal institutions and discourses, they are also concerned to show the detailed linkages and homologies which connect penal power with other areas of governance and discipline, just as his analyses of 'penological science' serve to reveal the regulatory and individualizing role of the human sciences more generally. Thus whatever else is distinctive about the Foucauldian approach to punishment and society, its chosen level of analysis and its tendency to move from institutional detail to broader social pattern—rather than vice versa—mark it off from other traditions in this field.

In this chapter, and in the two which follow, I aim to show how Foucault's arguments and analyses ought to be used in thinking about modern penality. To this end I will present an exposition and a constructive critique of his work, identifying the distinctive strengths and contribution of this approach, and suggesting how its 'power perspective' might be allied with other interpretations to form a more multidimensional framework of interpretation. As we will see,

---

[1] Cohen, *Visions of Social Control*, p. 10.

the precise contours of Foucault's account, and its lines of divergence from other traditions, need to be carefully specified in order to capture the subtleties of his approach, but by way of introduction a few thematic distinctions will serve here as a rough guide to the terrain that Foucault occupies.

Foucault's analysis of punishment is quite distinct from Durkheim's, appearing to contradict it at a number of points, and, for the most part, dealing with phenomena which hardly appear in Durkheim's work. *Discipline and Punish* stresses the instrumental and utilitarian nature of modern punishment and says virtually nothing about the moral or emotional components which play such a central part in Durkheim's account. Whereas for Durkheim punishment is deeply embedded within collective sentiments, and conveys the moral energy of the citizenry against its criminal enemies, for Foucault it is a system of power and regulation which is imposed upon a population, and his account has little to say about the sources of this power or the constituency of its popular support. There are, as we will see, points of convergence between the two perspectives—both of them make (unwarranted) functionalist assumptions about penality's effects, both provide analyses of discipline which are strikingly similar, both discuss the penal ceremonies of the *ancien régime* in parallel terms. But, in the main, Foucault's work constitutes a quite separate interpretation of punishment which stresses themes often diametrically opposed to those which appear in Durkheim's account.

Foucault's relation to Marxism is rather less clear-cut. Some writers have argued that the two interpretative perspectives—when applied to punishment —are complementary rather than in conflict, though, at a more general level, Foucault is clearly critical of many aspects of the Marxist tradition, particularly its claim to scientificity, its totalizing approach, and its emphasis upon the state to the neglect of other sites of power.[2] But the fact is that Foucault's investigations adopt a level of analysis which is quite different from that commonly used by Marxists, so that his findings have sometimes been used to extend Marxist accounts rather than to contest them. His explorations of themes such as power, domination, and subordination touch upon concerns which are shared by the Marxist tradition, even if they find a rather different inflection there, and his adoption of a hostile and deeply sceptical stance towards established institutions provides a measure of common ground with Marxism and other forms of critical theory. Nevertheless, one can point to important differences in perspective which distinguish the Foucauldian account of punishment from those developed within a marxist framework.

As we have seen, the Marxist account places punishment within a context of power relations—organized along class lines and grounded in an exploitative mode of production—and in some instances describes it as an instrument of state power, used for repressive or ideological purposes. But this Marxist

    [2] Melossi and Pavarini, *The Prison and the Factory* and my own *Punishment and Welfare* combine Marxist and Foucauldian arguments. On Foucault's relation to Marxism, see Smart, *Foucault, Marxism and Critique*, and also N. Poulantzas, *State, Power, Socialism* (London, 1978).

approach tends to address penality from the outside, as it were, showing the impact of this class context upon penal forms and upon the ways in which penal sanctions are used. Foucault, in contrast, focuses upon the power relations internal to the penal process, analysing these in detail along with the techniques and knowledges which they entail. He presents a phenomenological account of penal relations as power relations—an internal analytics of how penal institutions are structured, how they exercise control, and how they are informed by particular forms of knowledge and technique. His description of power in the penal sphere—and more especially in society—builds up from the examination of these details and avoids the explicit use of any preconceived scheme of class relations and social structures: indeed Foucault's whole mode of theorizing seeks to avoid any suggestion that society is a coherent totality which can be analysed by means of structural models or global conceptions.

Like the Marxists, Foucault sees punishment as fundamentally involving questions of power and of government, but he deals with these questions by examining the very fabric of penality, not just by invoking its context and determinants. He provides an analysis which is specifically about penal techniques and institutions and knowledges, showing a level of penological understanding and detail which easily surpasses that of Rusche and Kirchheimer or the others in that tradition. For some critics, this level of phenomenological description is achieved at the cost of neglecting penality's social grounding, its political context, and the important question of who or what directs the use of punishment.[3] But, as I will go on to suggest, this point might better be interpreted not as a criticism so much as an indication of the focus and limits of Foucault's account. It is an accurate index of the difference which separates Foucault's analytical concerns from those of the Marxist tradition and other critical approaches to penality.

Foucault's major contribution to this area may well be his phenomenology of penal control, but in constructing this interpretation Foucault has also provided an influential account of penal history and the political determinants of penal change. This genealogy of modern punishment differs in important respects from other accounts of penal history and implies a model of historical explanation which has been taken up by subsequent writers. In the pages which follow, I will be concerned to reconstruct Foucault's interpretation of penal change as well as his analytics of penal power and to subject them both to discussion and positive critique.

Foucault is perhaps best understood as a critical theorist whose philosophical and historical work seeks to question the forms of power and rationality which structure the modern world. Running through all his many studies—on madness, medicine, modern discourse, sexuality—there is a concern not just to describe the conventions through which we organize our knowledge of ourselves and our world, but also to show the costs of these conventions and

---

[3] See T. Platt and P. Takagi, 'Perspective and Overview', in id. (eds.), *Punishment and Penal Discipline*.

the forms of oppression they entail.[4] This critical upheaval is most vigorously applied to those historical developments which have done most to shape our modern world, among them the scientific revolution, the Enlightenment, the growth of democracy, the rise of the social sciences, and the development of social engineering. Above all, Foucault has undertaken a prolonged assault upon what he regards as the myths of the Enlightenment. 'Reason', 'science', 'freedom', 'justice', and 'democracy'—all these shibboleths of Western culture have been reassessed in the course of his effort to analyse the power effects of Reason and trace the oppressive shadows which it throws. In its way Foucault's work is reminiscent of Max Weber on rationalization or Sigmund Freud on civilization, each showing the price that has to be paid for ways of life that are cherished in the modern world—with the important difference that Foucault's tone is that of a subversive who questions the established values as well as their costs.

It is within this wider critical project that *Discipline and Punish* should best be understood. Despite being subtitled 'the birth of the prison' and presented, for the most part, in the form of a historical narrative, the book works less well as a history of punishment than as a structural analysis of power,[5] or to be more exact, of the peculiarly modern form of exercising power which Foucault calls 'discipline'. For Foucault, an investigation of the emergence of the prison in the early nineteenth century is actually a means of exploring the much wider (and more contemporary) theme of how domination is achieved and individuals are socially constructed in the modern world.

Foucault starts from a study of penal history which brings into focus the way in which violent, repressive forms of governance, such as corporal and capital punishment, gave way at a particular time to the milder regulative techniques represented by the prison. This focus is then broadened out to produce a general picture of the gentler forms of control—inspection, discipline, 'normalization',[6] etc.—which have come to take the place of repressive violence in modern strategies of law and government. In Foucault's account the prison is conceived as epitomizing these wider social forms—not because it is a 'typical' institution but rather because it is the place where modern techniques of control are revealed in their full unbridled operation. Consequently a close analysis of the

---

[4] M. Foucault, *Madness and Civilisation: A History of Insanity in the Age of Reason* (New York, 1965); id., *The Birth of the Clinic: An Archaeology of Medical Perception* (London, 1973); id., *The Order of Things: An Archaeology of the Human Sciences* (London, 1970); id., *The Archaeology of Knowledge* (London, 1972); id., *The History of Sexuality, i. An Introduction* (New York, 1978); id., *The History of Sexuality, ii. The Use of Pleasure* (New York, 1986).

[5] Foucault is not a structuralist in the sense of one who strictly follows the methodological rules of structuralist analysis (e.g. as set out in the work of Ferdinand de Saussure or Claude Levi-Strauss). He is, however, concerned to identify the structures that define the shape and limits of discourses and of institutional practices.

[6] The concept of normalization refers to that form of regulation which works by setting standards or norms for proper conduct and correcting deviations from the norm. In its positive, correctional orientation it is rather different from the simple prohibition and punishment of misconduct. See the discussion later in this chapter.

machinery of imprisonment, and of the knowledge on which it is based, can form the basis for a general anatomy of modern forms of power and control.[7]

2. The birth of the prison as a historical problem

Discipline and Punish is not a 'difficult' text in the sense of being overly technical or accessible only to the specialist, but its style of presentation does create certain difficulties. For the most part it adopts an allusive, suggestive, literary form, markedly different from the propositions, arguments, and evidence of most Anglo-American scholarship. To those with a taste for it, this stylized presentation can serve to enhance the pleasure of the text, but it also has the effect of submerging its theses below the surface, making them at times difficult to grasp. For all its literariness though, the exposition is in fact underpinned and organized by a very tightly structured argument which can be unearthed and presented as such.

The opening section of *Discipline and Punish* sets up the problem which the book will unravel by presenting the reader with a startling juxtaposition of two very different styles of punishment. The first is the execution of a regicide, conducted in a public square in Paris in 1757 before a crowd of spectators. Punishment here is enacted through an extended ritual of atrocities in which the body of the condemned man is utterly destroyed beneath a display of authorized violence.[8] The second is an institutional timetable, used in a Paris reformatory some 80 years later, setting out a minutely detailed regime to regulate the daily lives of its inmates. This time the punishment takes place in silence and in private, and proceeds without any overt ceremony or violence.

Foucault takes each of these measures to be definitive of the penal style of its period and—though here he is less explicit—to portray the forms in which power is exercised in modern society and in the 'classical' society which preceded it.[9] The historical problem which he sets himself is to explain the disappearance of punishment as a public spectacle of violence against the body, and to account for the emergence of the prison as the general form of modern punishment. Linked to this historical enquiry is a more structuralist concern to analyse the techniques and forms of power which these punishments

[7] For a similar kind of study, using an analysis of power in a maximum security prison to illuminate the operation (and the defects) of totalitarian political power, see Sykes, *The Society of Captives.*

[8] The example Foucault uses in the execution of Robert Damiens for an attack upon the person of Louis XV. Although Foucault does not mention it, the sovereign's punishment extended beyond Damiens himself: '. . . the close relatives of the traitor were deprived of their family name and banished, and the family house was razed to the ground.' J. McManners, *Death and the Enlightenment* (Oxford, 1981).

[9] Foucault uses the term 'classical age' to refer to what other historians might call the early modern period, i.e. the late 16th, 17th, and early 18th cents. He develops this periodization particularly in *The Order of Things* where he traces out 'the classical episteme', i.e. the structures of knowledge and discourse of the classical period.

involve, and to identify the wider framework of social relations in which they operate.

This change in penal styles, which, according to Foucault, took place throughout Europe and the USA between about 1750 and 1820, is to be understood as a qualitative shift rather than a mere decrease in the quantity or intensity of punishment. The target of punishment is shifted so that measures are now aimed to affect the 'soul' of the offender rather than just to strike his body.[10] At the same time the objective of punishment undergoes a change so that the concern is now less to avenge the crime than to transform the criminal who stands behind it.

This change in penal technology—from the scaffold to the penitentiary—signifies for Foucault a deeper change in the character of justice itself. In particular the new concern—which the prison introduced—to know the criminal, to understand the sources of his criminality, and to intervene to correct them wherever possible, had profound implications for the whole system of criminal justice. In this modern system the focus of judgment shifts away from the offence itself towards questions of character, of family background, and of the individual's history and environment. This will ultimately involve the introduction of experts—psychiatrists, criminologists, social workers, etc.—into the judicial process, with the aim of forming a knowledge of the individual, identifying his or her abnormalities and bringing about a reformation. The result of these changes is a system of dealing with offenders that is not so much punitive as corrective, more intent upon producing normal, conforming individuals than upon dispensing punishments: a penal system that the Americans named best when they called it, simply, 'corrections'.

On a wider scale, these developments represent illustrative models of how power operates in modern society. Open physical force, the apparatus of violence, and the ceremonies of might are more and more replaced by a mode of power based upon detailed knowledge, routine intervention, and gentle correction. The idea now is to regulate thoroughly and at all times rather than to repress in fits and starts, and by this means to improve troublesome individuals rather than to destroy them.

It is because it contains this wider indicative significance that punishment comes to be of importance for Foucault's work, permitting him to present a general genealogy of power based upon the particulars of penal history.[11] This

---

[10] As we will see, the body is still addressed by the disciplines, but as an instrument for transforming the soul rather than as a surface on which to inflict pain. A similar contrast is developed by de Tocqueville in *Democracy in America*, pp. 255–6: 'Under the absolute government of a single man, despotism, to reach the soul, struck at the body . . . but in democratic republics that is not at all how tyranny behaves; it leaves the body alone and goes straight to the soul.' Quoted in Dumm, *Democracy and Punishment*, p. 134.

[11] Foucault uses 'genealogy' in the Nietzschean sense to describe his method of writing a 'history of the present'. The point of his history is to cast light on a contemporary issue or institution by investigating those historical conditions that brought it about. It shares this orientation towards the present with what are often (disparagingly) termed 'Whig' histories, but

analysis of power-through-punishment is, of course, a very specific interpretative framework for writing penal history and enables Foucault to adopt a quite distinctive approach to his material. According to the rules of study which he sets out, punishment is to be understood as 'a political tactic', situated within the general field of power relations.[12] It is to be studied with a view to its positive effects, however marginal or indirect, and not simply as a repressive mechanism. It is to be thought of as intimately and internally linked with the development of 'the human sciences' (psychology, sociology, criminology, etc.) and the specific ways of knowing which they represent, and not merely influenced by them from the outside. And, finally, the new concern with the individuality of the offender—with his 'soul'—is to be conceived as the most recent aspect in a longer history of ways in which 'the body' has been dealt with by political policies.

3. THE FUNDAMENTAL CONCEPTS: POWER, KNOWLEDGE, AND THE BODY

Foucault's rules for studying punishment are in turn founded upon three major and interrelated concepts which he uses to analyse the fundamentals of any structure of domination: namely power, knowledge, and the body. For Foucault, as for Nietzsche and more recent authors such as Deleuze and Guattari, the human body is the ultimate material which is seized and shaped by all political, economic, and penal institutions.[13] Systems of production, of domination, and of socialization fundamentally depend upon the successful subjugation of bodies. More specifically, they require that bodies be mastered and subjected to training so as to render them docile, obedient, and useful to a greater or lesser degree. Some institutions—such as forced labour—master the body from the outside, as it were, using physical force and restraint to make the individual do their bidding. Others, however, aim to have their commands internalized, producing an individual who habitually does what is required without need of further external force. This 'self-controlled' body is brought about by exerting an influence upon what Foucault calls 'the soul' which in turn directs behaviour.[14] In this sense, strategies[15] of power have their real,

where they seek to celebrate contemporary achievements by depicting them as the 'end' of history, Foucault's genealogy uses history to problematize and destabilize the present.

[12] Foucault, *Discipline and Punish*, pp. 23–4.

[13] See Nietzsche, *The Genealogy of Morals*, and G. Deleuze and F. Guattari, *Anti-Oedipus: Capitalism and Schizophrenia* (New York, 1977).

[14] Foucault uses the notion of 'the soul' to refer to what psychologists variously term the psyche, the self, subjectivity, consciousness, or the personality. He appears to use it for its metaphoric resonance—'the soul is the prison of the body'—but also to avoid using a more theoretical term of art that might seem to commit him to a particular psychology of one kind or another. For Foucault it is the soul that is 'the seat of the habits' and thus the target of disciplinary techniques.

[15] Foucault stresses that his concept of 'strategy' is not to be understood as the game plan of any particular strategist. Rather it is a term that refers to a discernible pattern of institutional practices or political actions which operate across a number of sites. These practices or actions are structured and to some extent calculated, but they are not necessarily co-ordinated by any single decision-maker or agency.

operative impact at the point where they come in contact with the bodies of their subjects: there is 'a micro-physics of power' where power has its bodily materiality and effects. As Foucault puts it at one point, '. . . in thinking of the mechanisms of power, I am thinking rather of its capillary forms of existence, the point where power reaches into the very grain of individuals, touches their bodies, and inserts itself into their actions and attitudes, their discourses, learning processes, and everyday lives'.[16] The discovery of this 'micro-physics', and the claim that it reveals the essence of power more clearly than conventional political analysis, together amount to one of Foucault's most important and original contributions.

'Power', for Foucault, is not to be thought of as the property of particular classes or individuals who 'have' it, nor as an instrument which they can somehow 'use' at will. Power refers instead to the various forms of domination and subordination and the asymmetrical balance of forces which operate whenever and wherever social relations exist. These power relationships, like the social relations which they invest, display no simple pattern since, for Foucault, social life is to be thought of as taking place not within a single overarching 'society', but instead across a multiplicity of fields of forces which are sometimes connected and sometimes not. His special focus is always upon the way these power relations are organized, the forms they take and the techniques they depend upon, rather than upon the groups and individuals who dominate or are dominated as a consequence. His concern is thus with power and its materialized forms—a matter of structural relationships, institutions, strategies, and techniques—rather than with concrete politics and the actual people they involve. In this conception power is a pervasive aspect of social life and is not limited to the sphere of formal politics or of open conflict. It is also to be thought of as productive in effect rather than repressive in so far as power shapes the actions of individuals and harnesses their bodily powers to its ends. In this sense power operates 'through' individuals rather than 'against' them and helps constitute the individual who is at the same time its vehicle.[17]

This relationship between forms of power and the bodies which are caught up in them involves a third element, that of 'knowledge'. Foucault uses this again rather abstract noun to describe the 'know-how' upon which techniques and strategies depend and to point to the cognitive aspects which are inherent in all policies or programmes of action. Any exercise of power relies, to some extent, upon a knowledge of the 'target' or field of operation which is being addressed. The successful control of an object—whether it is an object in nature or a human object—requires a degree of understanding of its forces, its

[16] M. Foucault, 'Prison Talk', in id., *Power/Knowledge*, ed. C. Gordon (New York, 1980), p. 39.

[17] '[Individuals] are always in the position of simultaneously undergoing and exercising power. They are not only its inert or consenting target; they are always also the elements of its articulation. . . . The individual is an effect of power, and at the same time, or precisely to the extent to which it is the effect, it is an element of its articulation.' M. Foucault, 'Two Lectures', in id., *Power/Knowledge*, p. 98.

reactions, its strengths and weaknesses, its possibilities for change. Consequently, the more it is known, the more controllable it becomes. For Foucault the relationship between knowledge and power is thus an intimate and internal relationship in which each implies and increases the other, and his use of the term 'power–knowledge' is a kind of conceptual shorthand used to emphasize these interconnections. One major implication of this which is given a prominent place in *Discipline and Punish* is that the 'sciences of man' (the social or human sciences) which developed in the eighteenth and nineteenth centuries, must be thought of not as independent intellectual developments but rather as knowledge forms and techniques of enquiry which are deeply embedded in the history of power–knowledge and its relations with the body.

Taking these concepts as a framework of study, the history of punishment (and behind it, the history of government) is thus conceived of, at base, as a set of developing relationships between power, knowledge, and the body. In fact, although Foucault never discusses the status of this analytical framework, the implicit claim seems to be that power–knowledge–body relations constitute the irreducible basis of society and the historical process: bodies caught up in power–knowledge relations form a kind of physical substratum whch serves as a foundation for social relations and institutions. As for the intellectual developments which take place in legal theory or in the programmes of penal reformers, and even the wider changes which we see as the growth of individualism and the 'humanization' of sensibility—all these provide only a surface history, as far as Foucault is concerned. Rather than being the causes of penal and political change, these are merely the effects of more profound developments at the level of power–knowledge–body relations. In rendering the history of punishment as 'a chapter of political anatomy', Foucault is not offering one interpretation to be added to others; he is claiming to unearth the elementary structures upon which all else is based.[18]

4. THE MEANING OF THE SCAFFOLD

The narrative proper of *Discipline and Punish* begins with a discussion of 'the spectacle of the scaffold' in which Foucault traces the meanings implicit in the *ancien régime*'s practice of public torture and execution, setting out the legal and political frameworks within which it operated, and the reasons why it was abandoned towards the end of the eighteenth century. In the course of this exposition he stresses the political rationale which lay behind these penal measures, presenting them as important elements within a coherent strategy of domination. Far from being the arbitrary outburst of unrestrained cruelty which its critics described, torture is shown to be a carefully regulated affair, tied to a set of legal doctrines and ceremonies which controlled its use and gave it a practical meaning.[19]

[18] Foucault, *Discipline and Punish*, p. 28.
[19] For a fuller account of the legal use of torture in the Europe of the *ancien régime*, see Langbein, *Torture and the Law of Proof.*

First of all it formed part of the process of judicial investigation, being used to elicit the confession of the accused and thus give the mark of truth and 'self-evidence' to the findings of the prosecution. The use of judicial torture to elicit evidence from the accused was carefully regulated and allowed only where sufficient written evidence already existed to imply a prima-facie degree of guilt. In most European countries, with the notable exception of England, the entire criminal procedure remained secret so that throughout the investigation even the accused was unaware of the evidence against him: as Foucault puts it 'knowledge was an absolute privilege of the prosecution'.[20] In this context the ceremony of public punishment which followed a finding of guilt was also an act of revelation, revealing to the public what had been achieved in secret, repeating the torture of the condemned man and his confession of its justice.

Secondly, the public execution must also be understood within a specific political framework which accorded it a precise function and significance. According to the political theology of the classical age, any crime signified an attack upon the sovereign, since the law represented and embodied the sovereign's will. Punishment is thus an act of vengeance, justified by the sovereign's right to make war on his or her enemies and conducted in appropriately warlike terms. In keeping with the military sources of this sovereign power, justice is a manifestation of armed violence, an exercise in terror intended to remind the populace of the unrestrained power behind the law. The body of the condemned here becomes a screen upon which sovereign power is projected, or, more precisely, a flesh upon which the marks of power can be visibly engraved.[21] The execution itself is a ritual display of strength and an affirmation of power, conducted like any other great ritual, with the pomp and fastidiousness of public ceremony. It is, as Nietzsche suggests, an invocation of victory in warfare—a 'triumph'—'the violating and deriding of an enemy finally subdued'.[22] At the centre of this ceremony stands the personal power of the Sovereign rather than any impersonal conception of justice, a fact which is dramatically reinforced by the practice of last-minute pardons or suspensions of sentence over which the sovereign retained full personal control.

Foucault acknowledges that the use and acceptance of public tortures and executions depended upon certain external cultural and demographic conditions which produced a particular historical attitude towards the body. The low cost of labour power, the Christian contempt for the body, the high mortality rate, all helped to make death familiar and gave rise to rituals which taught people to cope with it. But he insists that it was, in the end, more specifically political

---

[20] Foucault, *Discipline and Punish*, p. 35.

[21] Deserting soldiers in the army of Louis XIV were sentenced by court martial 'to have their noses and ears cut off, their heads shaven, their cheeks branded with two fleur-de-lis and to be put in chains . . . at the head of the troops they had deserted', before being sent to the galleys (Zysberg, 'Galley and Hard Labor Convicts in France'). See too Franz Kafka's chilling account of 'the engraver' in his short story, *In the Penal Settlement* (London, 1973).

[22] Nietzsche, *The Genealogy of Morals*, p. 213.

considerations which, in eighteenth-century France at least, kept this system in place. In the face of uprisings, the threat of civil war, and the rise of the *parlements*, the political symbolism and real force displayed at the scaffold made it a central prop of sovereign power.

5. THE EIGHTEENTH-CENTURY CRITIQUE OF CRIMINAL JUSTICE

Why then, at the end of the eighteenth century, was this system replaced by one which claimed for itself the virtue of being 'humane', a system which suppressed those very elements of open power and violence which had previously formed the heart of punishment? Here again Foucault insists upon an answer in terms of politics and the organization of power. He describes how executions could sometimes degenerate into disorderly scenes when, instead of bearing respectful witness, the crowds came to mock the authorities and to transform the condemned man into a popular hero. This tendency is said to have become more pronounced towards the end of the century when on more and more occasions the crowd revolted against what it saw to be injustice, class law, or the execution of one of its own. The result of these disorders, Foucault claims, was to bring about 'on the part of state power, a political fear of the effects of these ambiguous rituals'.[23]

This theme is continued when Foucault turns to the critiques of criminal justice which emerged in the pamphlets, tracts, and petitions which were produced in the period prior to the revolution in France. The terms in which the critics put their case proclaimed the principles of 'humanity' and the rights of man—principles which were to extend even to the wretched criminal, so as to bring a measure of leniency and restraint to penal law. But for Foucault, as for several other historians of this period, the real force which mobilized this reform movement cannot be attributed to a philosophical system or even to a humane concern for the fate of others.[24] It was rather the baser and more familiar principle of self-interest which led to a recognition of political exigency and the need for appropriate change.

In this period there appears to have been a change in the predominant pattern of criminal behaviour which became more property oriented and professionalized, and hence more threatening, at a time when the growth of ports, warehouses, and large workshops put more and more moveable property at risk. More generally the development of a capitalist economy brought about new and stricter attitudes on the part of the rising middle classes towards the non-observance of law and the illegalities of the popular classes. Those various illegalities—such as tax and rent avoidance, smuggling, poaching, and gleaning

---

[23] Foucault, *Discipline and Punish*, p. 65.

[24] Foucault's analysis of 18th-cent. criminal justice draws explicitly on the French historiographical work of P. Chaunu and E. Le Roy Ladurie, but it is also striking how closely it parallels the arguments of D. Hay *et al.*, *Albion's Fatal Tree*, and E. P. Thompson, *Whigs and Hunters*, which were published in the same year. Foucault's interpretation of the political meaning of public executions is also similar to that set out in Durkheim's 'Two Laws of Penal Evolution'.

—which had been widespread and customarily accepted in the landed economy of the *ancien régime*, now took on the less tolerable appearance of property violations. In the face of these concerns, the irregular terrorism of eighteenth-century criminal justice—with its multiplicity of courts, its competing jurisdictions, its lack of a systematic police, and its innumerable loopholes— appeared at once over-severe and ineffective. What the critics demanded was a more rational and more certain system of justice: one based upon an extensive and detailed policing, a uniform and systematic penal procedure, and punishments which were carefully moderated to fit the crime. What was wanted was neither excess nor leniency but instead a certainty and comprehensiveness of application which would operate 'down to the finest grain of the social body'.[25] This framework was thus designed to deter the incipient criminality of the lower classes in a new and efficient manner, but also to limit the arbitrary power of the sovereign at the same time. When the great criminal law reforms swept Europe at the start of the nineteenth century, setting up codes, defining offences and scales of penalties, reorganizing procedure and jurisdiction, it was to these dual ends that they were orientated. Penality was being adapted to the emerging structures of modernity.

6. THE PENAL THEORIES OF THE REFORMERS

Against this background of political change and criminal law reform, *Discipline and Punish* then turns to the particulars of the penal reforms that were proposed by Beccaria and the 'Ideologues' in the late eighteenth century. These reformers advocated what Foucault calls 'the gentle way in punishment'—a whole system of sanctions which was starkly opposed to the excesses of the *ancien régime*. They declared that punishment must not be arbitrary, the capricious expression of a sovereign's will, but instead should be a reflection of the crime itself, as when work is used against idleness, shame against vanity, pain against violence, and so on. This kind of 'analogical' punishment, where penalties echo the crimes they punish, would establish an apparently 'natural' link, thus representing punishment as an effect of the law of nature instead of a display of political power. At the same time, these derivative penalties would attack the source of crime by punishing precisely those interests and desires which prompted the offence in the first place.

The reformers also insisted that these punishments and their implicit messages should be publicly displayed for all to see, since punishment was at once an example to everyone and in the interests of everyone. But if punishment still aimed to influence others, it was now addressed to the calculating, reasoning mind of the citizen and not to the trembling bodies of cowed onlookers—a matter of gentle didacticism, and not of terror. Punishment was now to be a lesson, a sign, a representation of public morality which was to be

---

[25] Foucault, *Discipline and Punish*, p. 80.

openly displayed to all: 'In the penalty, rather than seeing the presence of the Sovereign, one will read the laws themselves.'[26]

For this to happen, a whole diverse repertoire of suitable public punishments would have been necessary, reflecting the different crimes, reversing the various interests, revealing their warning signs for all to see. It is therefore a central historical paradox that what in fact developed at this time was not the diversified public theatre of punishment which the reformers had outlined, but instead a system of imprisonment in which the prison became the standard sanction for virtually the whole range of offences. As Foucault makes clear, the generalized use of the prison, with its characteristic secrecy, isolation, and monotony, was largely at odds with the theories of the reformers. And this development is all the more surprising when Foucault tells us that, prior to this time, imprisonment had only a limited and marginal position within most penal systems, functioning merely as a place to secure offenders awaiting trial or punishment, rather than as a standard penalty in itself. This being the case, how could imprisonment so quickly become the general mode of legal punishment?

7. The 'disciplinary' origins of the prison

The usual explanation for the rise of the prison points to the prior existence of several great models of punitive confinement—the Rasphuis of Amsterdam, the *Maison de Force* at Ghent, the Gloucester Penitentiary in England, and the Walnut Street Prison in Philadelphia. These institutions, with their emphasis upon work and reformation, had developed regimes which to some extent converged with the reformers' programmes, in so far as they were correctionalist rather than punitive in design. But if prison regimes and the reformers' programme both aimed to reform the individual, they went about this in quite different ways, each using a quite different technology to get hold of the individual and transform him, each developing its own specific techniques for addressing 'the body' and gaining access to 'the soul'. The reformers approached the matter at the level of ideas—proposing signs, lessons, and representations as forms of persuasion or aids to calculation. In contrast to this the prison seizes the body of the inmate, exercising it, training it, organizing its time and movement in order ultimately to transform the soul, 'the seat of the habits'. It takes hold of the individual, manipulating and moulding him or her in a behaviouristic mode, rather than just attempting to influence his or her moral thinking from the outside. There is thus a major difference between the reformers' model and the prison-based system which came to be established— a difference which is primarily technological rather than legal or theoretical.

The major problem, then, around which the whole of *Discipline and Punish* actually turns, is why did the prison succeed in displacing the demands of the reformers and the logic of penal theory? Where did it come from and how did it

---

[26] Ibid. 110.

come to be so quickly and universally accepted? At this point the text undergoes a sudden and rather disconcerting shift of focus, moving away from penal ideas and legal theory to examine a much wider, non-discursive, series of developments: the evolution of what Foucault calls the disciplinary techniques. This turns out to be the most original and interesting aspect of Foucault's historical argument. Where conventional accounts of penal history—and even the 'revisionist' accounts of Rothman and Ignatieff—give a central place to the 'ideological' genesis of modern punishment, locating it within the history of ideas and intellectual movements, Foucault shifts attention to the role of political technology in penal development. In doing so he allows us to come to terms with the physical materiality of the prison—and its political significance —to an extent which has never previously been achieved.[27]

Setting aside the historical narrative pursued in the first section of the book, the three central chapters of *Discipline and Punish* adopt a more structuralist mode in order to map out the techniques and principles of disciplinary power. They aim to produce a diagram of disciplinary technology reduced to its ideal form, the idea being to show its logic and operating principles rather than to give a history of its actual development and use.

7.1 *Training the body*

Discipline, for Foucault, is 'an art of the human body' and a method of mastering the body and rendering it both obedient and useful, and as such has a very long history.[28] However, it was in the classical age that the body came to be conceived as an object and target of power which could be controlled and improved without the costly use of violence. The techniques that provided these means of control and improvement were first generated in a variety of institutions—in the army, the monasteries, and in schools, hospitals, and workshops—but from the sixteenth century onwards these began to be consolidated and reproduced whenever and wherever they seemed applicable.

Foucault sets out a kind of blueprint of the general methods and principles of discipline, abstracting these from the practices and texts of the period. In his description, discipline is above all a 'political anatomy of detail'.[29] It operates on the smallest scale of control, paying attention not primarily to the whole body but to its individual movements and gestures. It aims to increase the efficiency of each movement and develop its co-ordination with others, exercising different forces and building them up together. It does this by bringing to bear a constant, uninterrupted supervision which is alert to the slightest deviation, thereby allowing a meticulous control of the body which is being disciplined.

---

[27] Rothman, *The Discovery of the Asylum*; Ignatieff, *A Just Measure of Pain*. For a discussion of how these 'revisionist' texts revised the orthodoxies of penal history, see S. Cohen and A. Scull (eds.), *Social Control and the State* (Oxford, 1983), chs. 3 and 4. On power as it operates in prisons and other 'total institutions', see Sykes, *The Society of Captives*, and Goffman, *Asylums*.
[28] Foucault's *Discipline and Punish*, p. 137.   [29] Ibid. 139.

In order to facilitate this kind of control, certain organizational principles were developed, adapted to particular institutions at first, but later generalized to suit other circumstances. Thus it was the army which did most to develop the art of distributing individuals in space—its ranks and files introducing a set orderliness into a mass of individuals, separating them one by one so that they could be individually viewed, supervised, and assessed. This same form of distribution was quickly adopted in the schoolroom, the workshops, the hospital, and so on. Similarly the monastery developed the timetable—a means of imposing set rhythms to organize time and movement, specify a series of occupations, and regulate the cycle of repetition. On a smaller scale, the concept of 'the manœuvre' derives from both the barracks and the workshop. In this repeated routine the exact posture of the body, the positioning of the limbs, and the smallest of bodily movements were programmed to increase their efficiency and link them to the use of a weapon or the operation of a machine. By these means, bodies were to be put through their paces until they became docile, efficient, useful machines, programmed to carry out the functions to which they had been trained.

7.2 *Normalizing deviance*

Of course individuals are by nature recalcitrant, and so dealing with disobedience is a central problem for any method of control. Significantly, these disciplinary methods do not simply punish troublesome cases, but develop a whole new method of sanctioning which Foucault calls 'normalization'. This method is essentially corrective rather than punitive in orientation, concerned to induce conformity rather than to exact retribution or expiation. It involves, first of all, a means of assessing the individual in relation to a desired standard of conduct: a means of knowing how the individual performs, watching his movements, assessing his behaviour, and measuring it against the rule. Surveillance arrangements and examination procedures provide this knowledge, allowing incidents of non-conformity or departures from set standards to be recognized and dealt with, at the same time 'individualizing' the different subjects who fall under this gaze. And since the object is to correct rather than punish, the actual sanctions used tend to involve exercises and training, measures which in themselves help bring conduct 'into line' and help make individuals more self-controlled.

'The examination' is, for this system, a central method of control, allowing close observation, differentiation, assessment of standards, and the identification of any failure to conform. So too is the dossier or case record, which allows the characteristics of the individual to be assessed over time and in comparison with others. From this time onwards, writing about individuals ceases to be a form of worship fit only for notables, kings, and heroes, and becomes instead a form of domination to which the powerless are more and more subjected. Out of these practices emerges a detailed and systematic knowledge of individuals, a knowledge which gave rise, in turn, to the various 'human sciences' of criminology, psychology, sociology, and so on. And, as Foucault is at pains to point out, the procedures of observation, examination, and measurement which allow this knowledge to develop are, at the same time, exercising power and control over the individuals who are isolated—and in a sense, constituted—within their gaze.

7.3 Bentham's Panopticon

The 'Panopticon' or 'Inspection House' which Jeremy Bentham designed in 1791 is seen by Foucault as the very epitome of these power–knowledge principles. It takes the form of a circular building, with individual cells around its perimeter whose windows and lighting are arranged so as to make their occupants clearly visible to the central inspection tower, though it remains opaque to them. It is thus an architectural form designed to individualize bodies and to render these individuals constantly subject to the knowledge and power of the authorities who occupy its centre. In time, this constant visibility and vulnerability induces self-control on the part of the inmates of the cells. Power no longer needs to unleash its sanctions and instead its objects take it upon themselves to behave in the desired manner. Any remnant of physical repression is thus gradually replaced by a gentle but effective structure of domination. Moreover, the power relations involved are, in a sense, automated and objective. They are an effect of the distribution of places and visibility and do not depend upon the strength or intentions of those who occupy these positions: 'the perfection of power should tend to render its actual exercise unnecessary . . . this architectural apparatus should be a machine for creating and sustaining a power relation independent of the person who exercises it; in short, . . . the inmates should be caught up in a power situation of which they are themselves the bearers.'[30]

According to Foucault, the usefulness of these panoptic, disciplinary principles was such that they were soon imitated in society's major institutions and eventually came to be generalized throughout the entire social body. However, the actual nature of this 'generalized panopticism' is not precisely detailed in Foucault's text. Sometimes the claim is relatively modest—that all modern forms of power have been affected by the development of disciplinary principles. At other times a more inflated rhetoric takes over and describes modern society as 'the disciplinary society'—a 'society of surveillance' in which we are all subjected to 'infinite examination' in 'the panoptic machine'.[31]

7.4 Discipline and democracy

Whatever the exact extent of these large claims, a number of points are clearly made regarding the genesis of the disciplines and their subsequent effects. First of all, although it was within the context of early European capitalism that the disciplines achieved their rapid development, their techniques and

---

[30] Foucault's *Discipline and Punish*, p. 201.   [31] Ibid. 209, 217, 189, 217 respectively.

principles are transferable and may be operated elsewhere and under different regimes. However, they do have a special and interesting relationship to the development of democracy in the West, summed up in the aphorism that 'the "Enlightenment" which discovered the liberties, also invented the disciplines'.[32] According to Foucault, it was ultimately the generalization of discipline which underpinned and made possible the generalization of democratic constitutions and the expansion of liberal forms of freedom. Without this vast infrastructure of power relations which subjected the masses to an orderly, disciplined existence, the extension of 'liberty' could never have taken place. This echoes the Hobbesian argument that freedom under the law implies a prior process of subjugation, and it constitutes the meaning of Foucault's suggestion that discipline is 'the dark side' of democracy and its egalitarian laws.[33] Foucault argues that the effect of disciplinary relations is to undercut the fairness of exchange and the equalities of status provided for in law and legal doctrine, an effect which operates in an invisible and extra-legal fashion. The disciplines ensure that real constraints and controls are introduced into relationships which the law deems to be voluntary or contractual, thus permitting the coexistence of legal freedom and habitual domination. It is in this sense that the disciplines are said to be 'a sort of counter-law'.[34]

Returning now, after this long but crucial detour, to the problem of penal history, we are able to view the rise of the prison in a rather different light. Given the context in which Foucault has located it, the prison now appears as an aspect of that wider historical phenomenon, the development and generalization of the disciplines. And indeed, if one thinks of the specifically modern developments in penology which have been associated with the prison—the investigation of 'the criminal' behind the crime, the concern with correction and adjustment, the involvement of experts whose task it is to observe, to assess, and to cure—then one can see the extent to which disciplinary and normalizing concerns have indeed penetrated the judicial framework of the criminal justice system.

This genealogical argument—that the disciplines are the ancestors of the prison—is presented by Foucault in its strongest version when he argues that the 'general form' of the prison institution was prefigured in these wider disciplinary developments, and simply imported into the legal system from outside. To this extent, nineteenth-century penal history should not be seen as part of the history of moral ideas but rather as a chapter in the history of the body and its investment by power–knowledge techniques. Within these terms, the great model prisons of Ghent, Gloucester, Walnut Street, etc. must be seen

---

[32] Ibid. 222.

[33] Ibid. 222. Here Foucault's argument closely parallels Marx's famous distinction between 'the two spheres' of capitalist society—the sphere of consumption or exchange, which is the realm of freedom and equality, contrasted with the sphere of production where despotism and exploitation are the order of the day. K. Marx, *Capital*, i (London, 1976), p. 280. See on this B. Fine *et al.* (eds.), *Capitalism and the Rule of Law* (London, 1979).

[34] Foucault, *Discipline and Punish*, p. 222.

as the first points of transition or imitation, not as innovations as such. This genealogy also serves as an explanation for the rapid acceptance of the prison as an 'obvious' or 'natural' institution. In a society which was already becoming inured to the operation of disciplinary mechanisms, the prison could appear to be self-evident right from the beginning.

A further consequence of this genealogical argument is that it changes the way we must think about the character and function of the prison. If it is conceived, from the start, as being a disciplinary institution, then its function of confinement and deprivation of liberty must always have been supplemented by a second, disciplinary function, namely the transformation of individuals. Foucault asserts that this is in fact the case: that the 'penitentiary techniques' of isolation, work, individualized treatment, and the adjustment of sentence to reflect reformatory progress are all hallmarks of the disciplinary process. Indeed he points out that one ironic consequence of the prison's disciplinary function is that it involves giving the prison authorities a degree of autonomy and discretion to carry out this task, thus re-creating in a new form all the arbitrariness and despotism which was so much criticized in the old penal systems.

7.5 'The criminal' and 'criminology'

The operation of the disciplinary prison also gave rise to a new body of information and knowledge about the criminal which was not previously available. Prison practices of isolation, observation, and individual assessment ensured that offenders were no longer thought of in the abstract, but were instead studied as individuals with their own characteristics, peculiarities, and differences. Whereas the law viewed offenders as being no different from anyone else, except in so far as they happened to have committed an offence, the prison aimed to individualize offenders, to find out what kind of people they were, and to determine the relationship between their character and their criminality. In this sense, the prison led to the discovery of 'the delinquent'— of the criminal type whose biography, character, and environment mark him or her off as different from the non-delinquent. And from this point one can trace the rise of a science of criminology which takes up the task of investigating this criminal entity, and describing it in all its aspects.

In respect of this 'delinquent' and the 'criminology' to which it gives rise, Foucault makes a point of major importance. He argues that the prison did not 'discover' delinquents, but rather it *fabricated* them, and it did so in two distinct senses. First of all, it 'made' delinquents in a literal sense by creating the conditions for recidivism: offenders were so stigmatized, demoralized, and deskilled in prison that after their release they tended to re-offend, to be reconvicted and eventually be transformed into career criminals. Secondly, the prison produced the delinquent in a categorical or epistemological sense, by creating in the course of its practices, the category of 'the individual criminal': it was in the prison that the individual criminal first became a visible, isolated object of intense study and control. One implication of this is that criminology—that systematic knowledge of the delinquent suggested by and developed within the prison—owes its existence to a system of power and to that system's hold over individual bodies. Criminology is founded on a particular power–knowledge regime, not an undeniable truth.[35]

8. THE 'FAILURE' OF THE PRISON

The final sections of *Discipline and Punish* return to the historical narrative and trace, rather too hurriedly, the actual impact of the prison and its position within the contemporary network of social control. In many ways this is the least satisfactory part of the book, but it does state a thesis which is clear and of considerable interest: namely, that the prison has always been a failure in penological terms, but that it successfully achieves important political effects at a wider social level, which is why it has never been abandoned.

Foucault shows that the defects of the prison—its failure to reduce crime, its tendency to produce recidivists, to organize a criminal milieu, to render prisoners' families destitute, etc.—have all been recognized and criticized from as early as the 1820s up to the present day. Moreover, each time this critique is restated, the official response has been to reassert the maxims of good penitentiary practice rather than to dispense with the institution itself. This historical pattern of constant failure and constant resistance to change leads Foucault to raise forcefully a question which is in many ways central to contemporary penal politics, namely: why does the prison persist? As usual the answer he gives to this familiar question is not at all the familiar one. Instead he offers explanations which are what one might call 'depth explanations' in so far as they refer to decisions and rationales which are neither apparent nor easily demonstrable. He suggests two such reasons; the first is that the prison is 'deeply rooted', by which he means that it is embedded in the wider disciplinary practices which he deems to be characteristic of modern society.[36] This, of course, refers back to his wider genealogical argument. The second is that the prison persists because it carries out 'certain very precise functions'.[37] This functional argument is pursued by reversing the problem of failure and asking if it can instead be understood as a covert form of success. In other words, he asks what interests could be served by the production of delinquency, recidivism, and a criminal milieu and could these 'interests' so act as to perpetuate these apparent defects?

The answer which he outlines here is placed not on a penological level but in the wider, political sphere and against the background of French politics in the 1840s and 1850s. What it amounts to is an argument that the creation of

---

[35] For an analysis of criminology conceived in similar terms see D. Garland, 'The Criminal and His Science', *The British Journal of Criminology*, 25 (1985), 109–37, and id., 'British Criminology Before 1935', *The British Journal of Criminology*, 28 (1988), 131–47.
[36] Foucault, *Discipline and Punish*, p. 271.   [37] Ibid.

delinquency is useful in a strategy of political domination because it works to separate crime from politics, to divide the working classes against themselves, to enhance the fear of prison, and to guarantee the authority and powers of the police. He argues that in a system of domination which depends upon respect for law and for property it is essential to ensure that illegalities and law-breaking attitudes do not become widespread or popular, and, above all, that they do not become linked with political objectives. In this context, the unintended creation of a delinquent class may be turned to advantage in a number of ways. Delinquency in itself is no great political danger—its attacks on property or authority are individualized and often petty, moreover its victims are usually from the lower classes—and it can therefore be tolerated by the authorities, at least within certain limits. And by creating a well-defined delinquent class, the prison ensures that habitual criminals are known to the authorities and can more easily be managed or kept under surveillance by the police.

What is more, the existence of a delinquent class can be used to curb other kinds of illegalities in a number of ways. First of all, the police measures and supervision which it necessitates can be used for wider political purposes. Secondly, the predatory nature of delinquency makes it unpopular with other members of the working classes, who tend to call upon the law as a protection and increasingly to shun law-breaking in itself. The myths of dangerousness which grow up around the criminal element add to this process of distancing and division. Finally, an awareness that imprisonment tends to bring about a subsequent identification with the criminal ranks gives people added reason to avoid taking any risks with the law and to distrust those who do. On this account then, the prison does not control the criminal so much as control the working class by creating the criminal, and, for Foucault, this is the unspoken rationale for its persistence. Clearly this is not a policy which is ever declared as such in public, but Foucault insists that it does in fact amount to a deliberate strategy. Consequences of imprisonment, which were unintended and thought of as detrimental at first, were subsequently recognized to be of some use. Consequently they were reinforced and deliberately employed in what might be termed a regrouped strategy.[38] The prison is thus retained for its failures and not in spite of them.

9. THE CARCERAL CONTINUUM

The closing section of the book is entitled, simply, 'the carceral'. It describes how the frontiers between judicial punishment and the other institutions of social life, such as the school, the family, the workshop, and the poor law came

---

[38] A contemporary example of the unintended consequences of the prison being used in just this way is the 'Sacred Straight' juvenile program developed in New Jersey, USA, in the early 1980s. Here the facts of intra-prisoner violence, rape, and brutality were explicitly used by the authorities to try to deter young offenders from becoming involved in crimes that might lead to imprisonment.

increasingly to be blurred by the development of similar disciplinary techniques in all of them, and the frequent transfers which take place from one institution to another. (Foucault cites the example of a reformatory for youth, which receives problem cases from families, schools, and prisons, and deals in the same disciplinary way with offenders and non-offenders alike.) According to Foucault, there exists a kind of carceral continuum which covers the whole social body, linked by the pervasive concern to identify deviance, anomalies, and departures from the relevant norms. This framework of surveillance and correction stretches from the least irregularity to the greatest crime and brings the same principles to bear upon each. The idea of the 'continuum' is important here, not just to describe the relations of one institution to another, but also to suggest the similarities that exist between societies. Foucault's description of Western liberal democracy as a society of surveillance, disciplined from end to end, is deliberately reminiscent of a totalitarianism which is usually ascribed to others. And in case anyone should miss this implied reference to the Gulag and its confinements, he coins the phrase 'carceral archipelago' to describe the chain of institutions which stretches out from the prison.

To return, finally, to punishment once more, all this has some very specific consequences for the way we think about penal practice. Within this overall framework, the process of punishing is not essentially different from that of educating or curing and it tends to be represented as merely an extension of these less coercive processes. This has two important results. First of all legal punishments come to be regarded as more legitimate and less in need of justification than when they were previously seen as forms of harm or coercion. Secondly, the legal restriction and limitations which once surrounded the power to punish—tying it to specific crimes, determining its duration, guaranteeing the rights of those accused, etc.—tend to disappear. Penal law in effect becomes a hybrid system combining the principles of legality with the principles of normalization. Its jurisdiction is thus extended so that it now sanctions not just 'violations of the law' but also 'deviations from the norm'. In this system there are many areas where the traditional protections of 'the rule of law' and 'due process' are no longer operative, or even appropriate, but so far no new framework of review and limitation has been developed to deal with these new forms through which modern administrative power actually operates.

10. FOUCAULT'S CONTRIBUTION

The arguments of *Discipline and Punish* have had an enormous impact in and across a whole range of intellectual specialisms. Indeed to try to trace this in any detail would require a fairly extensive history of contemporary intellectual culture. Its theses about the nature and location of power have been taken up as a corrective to the orthodoxies of Liberalism and Marxism alike, helping to shift them both away from the grand conceptions inherited from nineteenth-century political culture (the state vs. the individual; capital vs. labour, etc.). At a time when 'politics' is increasingly conducted in terms of marginal, small-scale, and single-issue struggles, Foucault's more dispersed and localized conception of power has made his work attractive to many. In particular, his idea of power as positive and productive has made it easier to develop political analyses of the various agencies of health, insurance, social security, education, psychiatry, etc., which increasingly regulate our lives, though they do so in a way which can hardly be described as 'repressive'. Similarly, his demonstration of how the conceptual systems of an age define its patterns of domination—summed up in the power–knowledge formula—has led to a more sophisticated understanding of the various human sciences and also of those 'normalizing' institutions in which these knowledges operate.[39] For present purposes, though, the major effect of the book has been to present a new perspective in the sociology of punishment, a perspective which has tended to displace the older traditions of interpretation in this area and to define a new approach to the study of penality.

Foucault's account of punishment and penal history is intentionally 'perspectival'. It views penal phenomena from the point of view of power–knowledge and the body, setting aside all other angles of interpretation and points of view. As well as shaping his historical account, this perspective leads Foucault to deal in some depth with certain dimensions of penality—especially its technical and discursive dimensions—which are generally neglected by other sociologists of punishment, whether Marxist or Durkheimian. He argues that power operates—and is literally 'materialized'—at the crucial level of techniques, apparatuses, and institutions, and therefore can best be understood by a detailed examination of this technology in action. As we have seen, this position leads him to an investigation of these technical elements which eventually issues in a penetrating and revealing account of what is, after all, the very stuff of penal institutions. The principles of surveillance, observation, and inspection, and of disciplinary training, examination, and normalization —together with the physical, architectural, and organizational forms in which they are embodied—are presented to us so clearly and in such detail that we can begin to understand the material practices upon which modern penal institutions depend.

This focus upon the materiality of penal practices and their effects is paralleled in Foucault's account by an analysis of the forms of thought and categories of action which have emerged as a corollary of this disciplinary fabric. This description of modern penal discourse succeeds in identifying some of the key characteristics of contemporary penology and grounding them

[39] See J. Donzelot, *The Policing of Families* (London, 1980); R. Castel, *The Regulation of Madness: The Origins of Incarceration in France* (Berkeley, 1988); F. Castel et al., *The Psychiatric Society* (New York, 1982); N. Rose, *The Psychological Complex* (London, 1985); P. Miller and N. Rose (eds.), *The Power of Psychiatry* (Cambridge, 1986); J. Minson, *The Genealogy of Morals: Nietzsche, Foucault, Donzelot and the Eccentricity of Ethics* (London, 1985). See also the journal *Ideology and Consciousness* (subsequently, *I. & C.*).

within the overall structure of which they form a part. Familiar ideological themes such as the emphasis upon reform and correction, the concern to improve rather than destroy, the representation of punitive measures as educational or therapeutic, and the sense of embarrassment where open violence or punitiveness occur, now emerge as products of an operational logic which has been laid bare by Foucault's work. Similarly, the adoption of 'managerial' rather than punitive attitudes by penal administrators, the displacement of juridical forms by administrative categories, and the scientific frame of mind which drives out moral condemnation and puts criminological diagnosis in its place all come to seem more comprehensible given Foucault's account of penal modernity and its distinctive operational forms.

The distinctiveness of this Foucauldian account—and the basis of its widespread appeal among criminologists and penologists—does not lie precisely in its concern with 'power'. After all, the intrinsic power of penal measures (whether seen as 'repressive' or 'ideological') and their articulation with the power of the ruling class, is a standard of Marxist interpretations, and even Durkheim conceives of penal sanctions as relaying (and realizing) the power of collective beliefs. Instead, Foucault's singularity lies in his identification of power relations in the intimate details of penal measures—at the points where specific forms of power and knowledge actually make contact with the offender—and his analysis of the different practical forms which these can take. This level of analysis opened up an area of study which had previously been the preserve of conventional penology and which had been left more or less untouched by sociologists and historians working in the Marxist or Durkheimian moulds. In contrast to the rather abstract, external, and 'non-penological' accounts offered by these other sociological traditions, Foucault addresses himself to the minutiae of penal practice and the intricacies of institutional life in a way which recalls—and goes beyond—the classic studies of prison life offered by Clemmer, Sykes, and Goffman.[40] Moreover, what he finds there is a complex of forces and relations which he deems to be symptomatic of much more general social patterns, thus giving penology a significance which it has rarely had before. In the light of *Discipline and Punish*, the 'technical' and avowedly 'apolitical' concerns of conventional penology now become precisely the areas of most interest to anyone wishing to discover how power operates (and disguises itself) within modern society. Penality is thus revealed as having an internal and intimate relationship with power, rather than being simply its occasional instrument or ally.

This new perspective on penality appeared at a time when practical events were leading in a similar direction. In the 1970s, when the book was first published, the policies of 'treatment' and 'rehabilitation' were being subjected to a sustained political attack throughout Europe, Scandinavia, and North America, as were the individualizing, 'positivistic' criminologies upon which

[40] See Clemmer, *The Prison Community*, Sykes, *The Society of Captives*, and Goffman, *Asylums*. Foucault's study shares much with this tradition although none of these texts is cited in his work.

these policies were based.[41] In this context, *Discipline and Punish* seemed to offer a trenchant theoretical critique of structures and institutions which were being directly experienced as oppressive by those who were caught up in them. Despite its sometimes abstruse character, Foucault's analysis helped make sense of the frustrations and resistances which lay behind the prison riots of the 1970s, making us more fully conscious of the power–knowledge machinery which prisoners were collectively resisting.[42]

In the period following the publication of *Discipline and Punish*, a whole body of research has appeared which analyses penality in terms derived from Foucault's work. Terms such as 'power', 'knowledge', 'normalization', and 'discipline'—as well as a more amorphous notion of 'social control'—have come to hold a central place in this literature, much of which is dedicated to the analysis of 'the power to punish' in its various forms. Foucault's theses about the nature of modern penal power have been scrutinized and to some extent refined. The disciplinary and normalizing aspects of contemporary penal systems have been identified and criticized, as have the financial controls, classical legal penalties, and purely repressive measures which continue to operate alongside them. Criminologists—and indeed criminal justice practitioners—have become more conscious of the ways in which regimes achieve their disciplinary effects and are alert to the ways in which community corrections may involve a dispersal of discipline. Consequently, new penal measures are nowadays subjected to a new kind of scrutiny which assesses their 'net-widening' effects and pays close attention to the transfers of power and knowledge which they entail.[43] As a result of Foucault's work there is now a much greater sensitivity to the nuances of penal measures and to what they can tell us about the regulatory means through which we are governed and the forms of subjectivity (or objectivity) into which offenders are pressed. Analysts have learned to take seriously the criminological conceptions and other forms of knowledge upon which penal strategies are based and to explore the consequences of these ways of thinking and acting—both in the field of penality and in respect of wider issues of governance. In short, the principles of

---

[41] For critiques of treatment and rehabilitation, see the American Friends Service Committee, *Struggle for Justice* (Philadelphia, 1971); N. Kittrie, *The Right to be Different* (Baltimore, 1972); and Allen, *The Decline of the Rehabilitative Ideal*. On the critique of positivist, correctionalist criminology, see D. Matza, *Delinquency and Drift* (New York, 1964), and I. Taylor *et al.*, *The New Criminology* (London, 1975).

[42] See M. Foucault, 'On Attica', *Telos*, 19 (1974), 154–61.

[43] On the various modalities of penal power, see D. Garland and P. Young, 'Towards a Social Analysis of Penality', in id. (eds.), *The Power to Punish*. On disciplinary regimes, see P. Carlen, *Women's Imprisonment: A Study in Social Control* (London, 1983). On the 'dispersal of discipline', see S. Cohen, 'The Punitive City: Notes on the Dispersal of Social Control', *Contemporary Crises*, 3 (1979), 339–63; T. Mathiesen, 'The Future of Control Systems—The Case of Norway', in Garland and Young (eds.), *The Power to Punish*; and A. E. Bottoms, 'Neglected Features of Contemporary Penal Systems' in *The Power to Punish*. On the community corrections movement and its net-widening effects, the *locus classicus* is Cohen, *Visions of Social Control*. On changing patterns of penal control, see J. Lowman *et al.*, *Transcarceration: Essays in the Sociology of Social Control* (Aldershot, 1987).

penal control and the internal workings of penal institutions are now better understood than ever before.

Unfortunately, however, the perspective which *Discipline and Punish* constructs has often been taken up in a manner which tends to displace other interpretative accounts, rather than supplement them or add a new dimension to their explanations. Foucault's power perspective has come to be seen as providing a general theory of punishment which excludes other forms of theorization rather than invites them. To some extent, this runs counter to the status that Foucault himself claims for his work. The idea of a general theory of punishment—or of anything else for that matter—is something which he is careful to disavow, claiming to be concerned with specific practices and concrete details rather than any grand theory. But, as was suggested earlier, behind this modest denial lies the very clear affirmation that the power perspective which he develops is in fact a fundamental one, undermining and enveloping all competing explanations. This, in effect, is what has happened—the grand claims displacing the lesser ones—so that a deliberately partial account (in both senses of 'partial') is now taken for a general one which explains all there is to explain in the field of penality. The discussion which follows in the next chapter will try to show how Foucault's account, for all its strengths, needs to be supplemented and corrected by other interpretations if the characteristics of modern penality are to be fully understood.

7

Beyond the Power Perspective
A Critique of Foucault on Punishment

In my discussion of Foucault's work in this and the subsequent chapter I aim to do two things. The first of these aims is to subject the specific arguments of *Discipline and Punish* to detailed criticism, and to suggest ways in which these critical points reflect upon broader issues within Foucault's work. The second is to deal directly with the broad themes which run through Foucault's work, particularly the themes of 'power' and 'rationality', and to show how these might be developed in order to further our understanding of modern punishment. The general tenor of the discussion will be positive, since I consider Foucault's perspective to be of great value in analysis. But I want to insist that Foucault's work—like that of Durkheim and the Marxists—provides only a partial and limited basis upon which to study punishment or any other social institution. In particular I will argue that neither punishment nor penal history can be wholly understood in terms of power or rationality and that the attempt to analyse them in these terms has led to a number of serious errors in *Discipline and Punish*. The critique which I will develop will not deny the validity of the perspective which Foucault sets out, but will challenge its capacity to stand on its own as an explanatory framework for the analysis of punishment and penal change. Against the singularity of this analysis in terms of power, I will argue that a wider, more pluralistic vision is necessary.

1. FOUCAULT'S HISTORICAL CLAIMS

Before taking up this critique, it is useful to note how historians have dealt with *Discipline and Punish* and the numerous historical claims which it makes. Although my main concern will be to question Foucault's general perspective rather than the historical details of his account, in the end the theoretical generalities and the historical particulars of *Discipline and Punish* are heavily interdependent. As with all historical work, it is the implicit theory which supplies the criteria upon which evidence is selected, given its significance, and fitted into the overall picture, so any criticism of Foucault's 'sociology' will have implications for this 'history' and vice versa.

Characteristically, while sociologists have tended to generalize from Foucault's work, taking up its concepts, developing its logic, and applying it to other materials, historians have been much more hesitant and circumspect.[1] Those who have addressed his substantive work rather than his philosophy or

---

[1] For discussions of Foucault by historians, see M. Perrot (ed.), *L'Impossible Prison* (Paris, 1980); G. Wright, *Between the Guillotine and Liberty* (New York, 1983); P. O'Brien, *The Promise of Punishment* (Princeton, 1982); Spierenburg, *The Spectacle of Suffering*; R. A. Nye, *Crime, Madness and Politics in Modern France* (Princeton, 1984); Stone, *The Past and the Present Revisited*.

method have tended to modify his theses, presenting alternative, less general interpretations which they claim are more in keeping with the evidence. One thesis which has come under sustained attack has been Foucault's interpretation of when and why the practice of public torture and execution was abandoned in Europe. As we saw, *Discipline and Punish* locates this historical development between about 1750 and 1820 and accounts for it primarily in terms of a strategic shift in the mode of exercising power. This explanation has been challenged on a number of counts by the work of Pieter Spierenburg, which argues that the abolition of the public execution should not be viewed as an independent event but instead as one stage in an extended process of change which brought about the privatization of punishment and a reduction in the display of suffering.[2] This series of events began about 1600 when there was a sharp decline in the judicial use of mutilation and maiming in the European countries and proceeded in gradual stages (the removal of permanent scaffolds, the ending of the routine exposure of corpses, etc.) until by the nineteenth and twentieth centuries most of these nations had altogether abandoned corporal and capital punishments. Viewed in these terms, the changes Foucault describes were already well under way during the *ancien régime*, and appear to have been bound up with developments which were not entirely to do with power or politics. In this respect, Spierenburg sets out a strong case, arguing that the decline in penal suffering and publicity was linked to general changes in sensibility and attitudes towards violence which can be traced over the same extended period—these cultural changes being in turn linked to the formation of states and their internal pacification. More recent work by John Beattie on criminal justice in England between 1660 and 1800 also questions the periodization set out by Foucault in this respect and goes on to show that imprisonment was in fairly widespread use as a punishment for minor offenders in the early decades of the eighteenth century.[3]

Foucault's identification of political exigencies as the primary cause of change is also cast into doubt by alternative accounts. John Langbein's research suggests that changes in the law of evidence probably formed the proximate cause of the abandonment of torture,[4] while Robert Brown argues that the whole confessional system in which torture was grounded depended upon a set of religious and psychological beliefs which had to be altered before

---

[2] Spierenburg, *The Spectacle of Suffering*, and id., *The Emergence of Carceral Institutions*.

[3] Beattie, *Crime and the Courts*. On the use of imprisonment in medieval Europe, see Langbein, *Torture and the Law of Proof*; R. W. Ireland, 'Theory and Practice within the Medieval English Prison', *The American Journal of Legal History*, 31 (1987), 56–67; and R. B. Pugh, *Imprisonment in Medieval England* (Cambridge, 1970).

[4] Langbein, *Torture and the Law of Proof*. Langbein argues that judicial torture could be abolished in the 18th cent. because prior changes in the law of proof had rendered it unnecessary. It was the growing authority of the legal profession within increasingly stabilized nation states, together with the availability of new punishments other than blood sanctions, which made it possible from the 17th cent. onwards for jurists to develop a new system relying upon the judicial evaluation of evidence, which gradually replaced the old Roman–canon law of statutory proofs.

any change in penal practice was able to take place.[5] There were thus determinants of penal reform which had distinctively legal and cultural roots and which need to be considered alongside the political forces which Foucault describes: they cannot be ignored or simply reduced to questions of power. Equally relevant is Spierenburg's observation that the evidence of scaffold riots and disorders is much less widespread than Foucault suggests, and that, in any case, the risk of disorder had always accompanied executions and could not, in itself, have been sufficient reason to abandon the practice.[6]

Historians have also taken exception to Foucault's account of the role of the reformers in the development of the prison in the late eighteenth century. According to *Discipline and Punish* the reformers were, for all their talk of 'humanity' and the 'rights of man', primarily concerned to 'insert the power to punish more deeply into the social body'.[7] Indeed, it was only their desire for more efficient control and not their detailed programmes which was ever really taken up in practice—ironically enough in the shape of an institution which they had never particularly favoured. In contrast to this version of events, writers such as David Rothman and Michael Ignatieff give a more central place to the efforts of reformers in shaping the precise details of prison regimes. Many of the reformers they discuss were strong advocates of the prison and were instrumental in designing and legislating for the new institutions, and their concerns extended to matters of sanitation and health, the introduction of religious instruction, the proper feeding and clothing of prisoners, and the ending of their brutal exploitation by warders and other inmates.[8] Whereas for Foucault leniency in punishment is understood as a ruse of power, allowing a more extensive form of control to take hold, in these other accounts it is viewed as a genuine end which was sought after, along with others, for reasons of authentic benevolence or religious conviction. That such intentions sometimes resulted in the kind of outcomes that Foucault describes is not denied by these accounts. Indeed it is precisely this problem of distorted, unintended outcomes that they focus upon, showing how the dictates of 'conscience' can in practice become routines of 'convenience' for other purposes. But they stress none the less that these motivational patterns and ideologies did have real effects and are therefore an important factor in understanding penal institutions and the process of penal change. Moreover, as Spierenburg points out, it is perfectly possible to combine a desire for more humane treatment with a demand for greater control, and there is no reason why one should be reduced to the other.[9]

---

[5] R. Brown, 'The Idea of Imprisonment', *The Times Literary Supplement* (16 June 1978).

[6] Spierenburg, *The Spectacle of Suffering*, p. 108.

[7] Foucault, *Discipline and Punish*, p. 82.

[8] Rothman, *The Discovery of the Asylum*, and id., *Conscience and Convenience* (Boston, 1980), and Ignatieff, *A Just Measure of Pain*, and id., 'State, Civil Society and Total Institutions', in S. Cohen and A. Scull (eds.), *Social Control and the States* (Oxford, 1983).

[9] Spierenburg, *The Spectacle of Suffering*, p. 184.

Foucault's historical account can also be criticized for failing to supply the kind of evidence which is required for the arguments it makes. This is particularly true of the period at the turn of the nineteenth century when imprisonment first became a general policy, and also at the unspecified point later in the century when the penal strategy was revised in order to turn the failures of the prison to good political use. In the first case we are told that the 'prison form' found its way into legislation as a result of a society-wide disciplinary strategy, rather than as an outcome of particular penal theories. However, as Paul Patton points out, one would expect a thesis such as this to be supported by evidence drawn from the actual legislative process, showing how 'disciplinary' considerations entered the discussions and shaped policy decisions.[10] No such evidence is offered.

The same point can be made with even greater force against the second argument, since we are asked to accept that the creation of a criminal class became a deliberate feature in a political strategy. The terms used by Foucault to characterize this development—terms like 'strategy' and 'efforts'—imply that definite elements of intention and calculation lie behind it. He is not claiming merely that events turned out as they did in some unintended functional process; it is rather a matter of strategic calculation, a policy designed and operated in order to work that way.[11] Now there has been much discussion of what exactly Foucault means by the term 'strategy' and it can be accepted that it does not necessarily imply some kind of omniscient strategist who directs operations in line with a plan of operation. But, whether he has in mind an individual, an institution, or even a dispersed pattern of decisions which somehow add up, he needs to produce evidence of these strategic decisions actually taking place. Again no evidence of this kind is presented.

As we saw, Foucault uses this covert strategy argument to explain why the prison has survived despite its failures and the clear implication is that it is this strategy which keeps the prison in place today. However, his account shows only that such a strategy may have made political sense in the particular circumstances of France in the 1840s and 1850s. It says nothing about the basis for its existence in the late twentieth century unless Foucault believes that the same political circumstances prevail today. Whether or not there is evidence to support any part of Foucault's claim, it should be clear that a quite different argument would be necessary to explain the use of the prison in two quite different periods, a century apart.[12]

---

[10] P. Patton, 'Of Power and Prisons', in M. Morris and P. Patton, *Michel Foucault: Power, Truth, Strategy* (Sydney, 1979).

[11] See Foucault, *Discipline and Punish*, pp. 272 ff., and esp. Foucault, 'Prison Talk', *Power/Knowledge*, pp. 40–2.

[12] Brown in 'The Idea of Imprisonment' makes a related point when he points out that in the 19th cent. societies with widely different traditions, levels of industrialization, and types of political system all adopted the prison. This would seem to cast doubt upon the generalizability of the specific links between the prison and class domination which Foucault identifies in 19th-cent. France.

Finally, *Discipline and Punish* claims that a new, normalizing, disciplinary approach became dominant in the penal system with the emergence of generalized imprisonment in the nineteenth century. However, aside from a few examples and illustrations (the Paris Reformatory, Mettray, etc.), Foucault presents no extensive or quantitative evidence which would substantiate this characterization of modern penal practice. Instead he simply lists what he takes to be the individualizing, disciplinary characteristics of 'modern punishment' and implies that these have all been in place, more or less, since the beginning of 'the carceral era' nearly 200 years ago. Subsequent research has shown, however, that the spread of these individualized normalizing methods only really took off in the early twentieth century and that even now they have not yet succeeded in displacing other non-disciplinary sanctions—such as the fine—from the central position in penal practice.[13] More importantly for Foucault's argument, this trend towards normalizing, disciplinary sanctions and an administrative mode of dispensing them has never successfully banished the punitive, emotive character of the penal process. Throughout the twentieth century, the condemnatory rituals of criminal courts and the humiliating routines of penal institutions have retained a clear concern with expressing punitive passions and moral censure, even in the years when the treatment ethos was at its zenith. This is clearly true in the adult courts, where the figure of the 'rational criminal' was never fully displaced. But even in the sphere of juvenile justice, where the rehabilitative ideal has most clearly taken hold and where the language of punitiveness is now largely absent, normalizing techniques have continued to exist in tension with a measure of punitiveness which has compromised and limited their effects.[14] Accordingly, if the development of discipline was actually slower and more limited in penal practice than *Discipline and Punish* makes out, then this must in turn throw doubt upon its more general claims about the extension of disciplinary mechanisms 'throughout the social body'. If we are not altogether justified in characterizing modern penal systems as 'disciplinary' or 'panoptic', where does this leave the notion of 'the disciplinary society'?

There are other points of detail which could be taken up in this way, as well as more general ones such as Clifford Geertz's observation that *Discipline and Punish* is rather like a Whig history in reverse, tracing the Rise of Unfreedom and the inexorable regress of liberty.[15] But the major critical theme which

[13] See Garland, *Punishment and Welfare*, which argues that although disciplinary measures and reformative aims were a feature of modern imprisonment from the late 18th cent. onwards, the 19th-cent. prison relied upon mass regimes and uniform treatment. Only at the end of the 19th cent. were measures introduced which were designed to individualize and normalize offenders on a basis of detailed knowledge and differentiated treatment. On the place of the fine in modern penal practice, see P. J. Young, *Punishment, Money and Legal Order*, and Bottoms, 'Neglected Features of Contemporary Penal Systems'.

[14] On tensions in juvenile justice, see J. Sutton, *Stubborn Children: Controlling Delinquency in the USA, 1640–1981* (Berkeley, 1989); and R. Webb and D. Harris, *Welfare, Power and Juvenile Justice* (London, 1987).

[15] C. Geertz, 'Stir Crazy', *The New York Review of Books* (26 Jan. 1978).

emerges, and is independently made by many different critics, concerns Foucault's overestimation of the political dimension. *Discipline and Punish* consistently proposes an explanation in terms of strategies of power—sometimes in the absence of any supporting evidence—where other historians would see a need for other factors and considerations to be brought into account. In the remainder of this chapter, I will argue that the reason for this one-sided history is in fact a similarly one-sided understanding of punishment and penal institutions, and that neither do justice to the phenomena they describe.

2.. FOUCAULT'S CONCEPTION OF PUNISHMENT

Despite its extensive use of historical sources and materials, it is arguable that *Discipline and Punish* is not primarily a historical text. Rather it should be viewed as a work of social theory and cultural criticism which proposes a new way of thinking about social institutions and illustrates this by means of an historical account. The real core of *Discipline and Punish* is in fact the power perspective which it sets out and it is this perspective rather than any specific historical claims which has been most influential.

As we have seen, *Discipline and Punish* interprets punishment in terms of power: as a form of power in itself—'a political technology'—and also as one instrument among others in a wider field of power relations—'a political tactic'.[16] What is meant by 'power' here is the idea of controlling—or rather 'producing'—behaviour, whether directly through the disciplinary training of offenders or, more indirectly, by way of deterrent threat and example to the general population. Punishment is thus thought of as a means of control which administers the bodies of individuals and, through them, the body politic.

It is important to realize that this relationship between punishment and power is not proposed as a hypothesis to be investigated, nor as one aspect among others, but rather as the basis upon which punishment is to be understood. We are invited to approach the study of penal institutions on the assumption that everything that occurs there is fundamentally oriented to the enhancement of control and the maximization of regulatory power. Moreover this punishment-as-control conception refers not just to the intentions of reformers or the aims of administrators; it is taken to be the way in which the system actually works. We are first of all to assume that penal practice is explicable in terms of power and then to explore in what sense this is true.

The force of this theoretical preconception is such that Foucault refuses to accept that there are elements of the penal system which either malfunction and so are not effective as forms of control or else are simply not designed to function as control measures in the first place. In contrast to Durkheim or Mead, who argue that the dynamics of punishment involve deeply irrational and emotive elements—with the result that penalties are often badly adapted

---

[16] Foucault, *Discipline and Punish*, pp. 24, 23.

to control purposes—Foucault proceeds as if penality affords no place to non-rational phenomena. When such phenomena do seem to occur, Foucault's reaction is to look more closely, to examine them from every angle, to keep searching until he uncovers their hidden utility for power. The most startling example of this is when the apparent failures of the prison are reconceptualized to emerge as successful moves within a wider strategy of political control, but it is a tendency which is general in his work.

This radical perspective is often revealing and insightful as I have tried to show above, and when used with the inventiveness and subtlety of its author, it can lead to brilliant results. However, like any thoroughgoing scepticism it operates best as a heuristic device, producing questions and interpretations which can later be balanced against the weight of evidence and alternative explanations. It does not work well as a general theory or interpretation. Unfortunately, it has been in this more general and dogmatic mode that the power perspective has been used, both in *Discipline and Punish* itself and in much of the subsequent work which has been written in this style.[17]

Foucault's emphatic depiction of punishment as a technology of power-knowledge and his primarily political account of its historical development have produced an instrumental and functionalist conception of punishment in which penal practice is always shaped exclusively by the requirements of social control and in which its design is always calculated to maximize control effects. This notion of punishment, devoid of irrational or counter-productive features, and directed exclusively to the task of regulating conduct, seems to come very close to the utilitarian ideal set out by Jeremy Bentham in *An Introduction to the Principles of Morals and Legislation*.[18] There is, however, a curious difference between the two. Whereas Bentham set out his rationalistic control framework as an ideal to aim for, and deplored the ritualistic, non-utilitarian actualities of punishment which he observed in practice, Foucault seems to assert that 'Benthamism' is, in fact, a deep description of the actual nature of modern punishment. Bentham's vision turns out to be a reflection of the very nature of things—we live in a thoroughly calculated, controlled, panoptic world—and Foucault's approach is to analyse social institutions in these terms.

There can, of course, be no doubt that penal policy is the subject of strategic planning and rational administration, nor that the control of the behaviour of offenders and potential offenders is one of its central aims. But as even Bentham was forced to acknowledge, these are by no means the only factors involved. Then, as now, penal policy was shaped by a variety of ends—such as justice, economy, vengeance, forgiveness, charity, evangelism, and so on—and had to find a way of combining rational strategies with the demands of

[17] Foucault does say at one point that other interpretations are possible and 'legitimate' (ibid. 25), but he makes no effort to assess the limits of his power-based analysis, and he is dismissive of accounts which are phrased in terms of changing ideologies or sensibilities.

[18] J. Bentham, *An Introduction to the Principles of Morals and Legislation* (London, 1789).

legal culture, popular sentiment, and ritualistic tradition. For these reasons, punishment always ends up being rather different from control, pure and simple. Moreover, as Spierenburg's work makes clear, the instrumental use of penal measures for control purposes is always in tension with social and psychological forces which place clear limits upon the types and extent of punishment which will be acceptable in any specific situation. The principles of discipline and power–knowledge techniques may provide a technology of control with a given logic and potential but the extent to which it is used, and the purposes to which it is put, will depend upon wider social and cultural forces.

Cultural traits and sensibilities can be seen to influence the penal system in a variety of ways. Most obviously modern sensibilities and notions of justice place strict limits upon the forms of punishment which are tolerable, thus prohibiting forms of penal control which could be highly effective—such as intensive forms of behaviour modification or brain-washing, not to mention old-fashioned blood sanctions.[19] But contemporary mores also contain more punitive elements which find expression in penal systems to some degree, whether in the symbolic denunciations of the sentencing process or in the petty degradations of institutional regimes. These punitive aspects are often seen as reinforcing the control elements of the system, but they can also have the opposite effect. There is, for example, psychological and penological evidence to show that punitiveness is actually a very inefficient and temporary form of control.[20] It may even be that part of the reason why our penal institutions are poor at exerting control and modifying the conduct of offenders is precisely because they are punitive in form. Advocates of rehabilitation have long argued this position, but have found it difficult to replace traditional punitiveness by more 'rational' forms of control.

3.   THE PRISON'S PERSISTENCE AND THE SPREAD OF DISCIPLINE

If one returns to the analyses of *Discipline and Punish* bearing this point in mind, some quite different interpretations suggest themselves. Take, for example, the argument that the prison has been retained, despite its apparent defects, because its 'failures' are useful in exerting political control. As we have seen, Foucault is led to make this argument because he has presupposed that imprisonment is to be understood as 'a political tactic'. According to his functionalist logic, an institution which is truly counter-productive could not survive for long, and certainly not for two centuries, so there must be some hidden sense in which it succeeds as an instrument of control. Having put the question thus, he produces an answer of sorts—the prison does not control the

---

[19] See ch. 10.
[20] See R. H. Walters, J. A. Cheyne, and R. K. Banks (eds.), *Punishment* (Harmondsworth, 1972), for a discussion of the psychological evidence.

criminal, it controls the working class by creating criminals—and this, he claims, is its real function and the reason for its retention.

This answer seems implausible and is not supported by much in the way of evidence, although it or something like it is necessitated by the logic of Foucault's approach. It may well be that the prison's tendency to produce demoralized, recidivist delinquents has some effect in leading others to avoid law-breaking or any contact with law-breakers (though deterrence research leads one to doubt even this).[21] But any value which this might have for the authorities must be weighed against the constant source of embarrassment, criticism, and expense caused by high recidivism rates and the escalating costs of imprisonment. In the absence of any hard evidence that a strategy with these objectives does really exist, it would appear that Foucault is simply taking the (unintended) consequences of the prison to be its (intended) *raison d'être*—a form of invalid reasoning which is often associated with functionalist accounts.

In considering the status of the modern prison we should show more hesitation than did Foucault in accepting the conventional wisdom that the prison has 'failed'. This complaint has become so established that there is little questioning of its basis, but it is important to ask by what standards the prison's performance is being measured when this judgment of failure is made. If the scale is set by the Utopian ambitions of early prison reformers, then clearly a failure has been sustained, but these expectations (of reform, crime reduction, and redemption) were always unrealistic and seem a poor basis of evaluation to use today. If, on the other hand, the prison is measured against the performance of other complex institutions, such as the school, or the hospital, or the social work and social security systems, for example, then its failure is by no means so obvious. All institutions entail social costs and succeed only partially in pursuing their multiple objectives: our judgment of their performance depends upon our understanding of their aims and the expectations which attach to them. To take one important example, no one is surprised when hospitals experience high levels of chronic illness and death alongside a smaller number of successful cures, even though scientific and medical developments have grossly inflated public expectations in this sphere. This is because the proper measure of an effective hospital is not the incidence of cure but rather the efficiency with which appropriate treatments are delivered to patients. (The health of the population and the curative powers of modern medicine are effectively given facts, as far as the institution is concerned.) In the same way, the prison might be evaluated in terms of its ability to deprive offenders of their liberty in accordance with a court order, to

---

[21] The deterrent potential of imprisonment—as measured against alternative penalties—is not clearly proven. To the extent that the threat of imprisonment does deter, the length of sentence or the consequences of being an ex-prisoner are in some cases less relevant factors than the shame of being imprisoned in the first place. See the review of research by Beyleveld, *A Bibliography on General Deterrence Research*.

exclude them from society for a period of time, or to inflict mental suffering in ways which satisfy a punitive public—in which case its only failures would be occasional escapes and unwonted leniencies.[22]

Viewed in this way, the prison becomes much less of a failure than Foucault and a long tradition of critic–reformers would have us believe. To make this point is not to defend the institution—whether conceived as reformative failures or punitive successes, the majority of prisons still fall below the minimum standards of decency which we should require of civilized institutions. But what we should expect of prisons, and what in fact *is* expected by those who support the institution, are two different things. And the point here is that when seen against its real social background of popular concerns and political demands the prison is much less anachronistic and much less of a 'failure' than Foucault assumes.

If we leave aside Foucault's assumptions, there are plenty of better explanations which can be found to account for the prison's survival. It may be, as Durkheim suggests, that it satisfies a popular (or a judicial) desire to inflict punishment upon law-breakers and to have them dismissed from normal social life, whatever the long-term costs or consequences.[23] It also may be that any penal system needs an ultimate sanction which can forcibly incapacitate the recalcitrant and take dangerous individuals out of circulation. Following the decline of the death penalty and transportation, the prison represents the only available and culturally accepted means of doing this. Equally, it may simply be that once it was actually built the massive infrastructure of imprisonment represents an investment (in terms of buildings, administrative structures, and professional careers) which is too costly to give up but is sufficiently flexible to adapt itself to the various penal policies which have come into vogue. The prison may thus be retained for all sorts of reasons—punitiveness, economy, or a plain lack of any functional alternative—which have little to do with any latent success as effective control or political strategy.

This example suggests that, contrary to *Discipline and Punish*, there is no reason to suppose that either 'control' or 'power' is the exclusive motivation of penal practice, nor that penal policy is always organized according to instrumental, strategic considerations. Indeed if we think of the practicalities of the criminal justice system, it is clear that no matter how hard administrators strive to develop rational control-oriented policies, they are always in the end the servants of other, independent decision-makers (the judiciary, the legislature,

---

[22] It is notable that sentencers do not seem to consider the prison a failure, in so far as they use imprisonment time and again for the same individual. It appears that, for sentencers, imprisonment 'works', to some extent at least, because it is intended as a punitive measure. In contrast, many sentencers consider that sanctions such as probation or community service have failed whenever an individual re-offends after having undergone such a sentence. Non-custodial sanctions are often thought of as reformative or 'second-chance' measures which may or may not 'work'. If they 'fail', sentencers are frequently reluctant to reuse them and instead move up the tariff to what they consider 'real' punishment—i.e. a term of imprisonment.

[23] See Durkheim, 'Two Laws of Penal Evolution'. On the ambivalent place of vengeance in contemporary culture, see Jacoby, *Wild Justice*.

the public) whose demands are often at cross purposes. Within this complex system, control is likely to be a major goal, but one which is always compromised by other considerations, just as power is likely to be divided and internally contested by the different agencies involved. Rather than approaching punishment from the point of view of power alone, our framework of study should also be geared towards the interpretation of the conflicting social forces, values, and sentiments which find expression in penal practice.

Foucault's reluctance to acknowledge the role of any values other than power and control in the development of punishment has other consequences in *Discipline and Punish*. In particular, it leads him to neglect the political and ideological forces which put up a principled opposition to the introduction and extension of disciplinary practices. As was noted above, disciplinary strategies have only ever been partly implemented in most modern penal systems and, in practice, they exist within what is still a predominantly legalistic, judicial framework. These limits of implementation—which make disciplinary practice far less extensive than Foucault implies—are largely the result of a sustained opposition on the part of the liberal political establishment, and particularly by the legal profession and the judiciary. And this resistance stems, at least in part, from a refusal to accept the violations of legal and liberal principles which a full-scale disciplinary programme would entail. These principles—of due process, the rule of law, the rights of the individual, equality of treatment, and so on—have formed a historical counterpoint to the demands of power, and have been used to oppose 'discipline' not just by its working-class targets, but also by important sections of the dominant class. No doubt part of what is at issue in these conflicts is a disagreement on how best to exercise power—just as it was in the debates of the eighteenth-century reformers. But other values also play a part, sometimes as absolute ends in themselves, and they act to limit power, rather than to conceal or extend it.[24]

Foucault's tendency to discuss the spread of discipline as if it were politically unopposed is a serious deficiency in his account. Although he never states this explicitly, his use of terms like 'the disciplinary society' or 'the society of surveillance' give the definite impression that the disciplinary programme has become a reality in a process of unopposed and uncompromised implementation. Having reconstructed a kind of blueprint or ideal type, showing what a totalized discipline would look like, one would have expected him to go on to show the divergences between the real world and this heuristic figure of the 'ideal'. Instead he writes as if the two were identical. This produces a thoroughly alarming depiction of the social world precisely because it ignores all the forces which operate to restrain the disciplinary impulse and to protect

[24] A case in point would be the refusal of the ecclesiastical courts of the Middle Ages to utilize blood sanctions, since these were deemed inconsistent with the clerical station. Instead, the Church authorities developed the use of imprisonment, and in exceptional cases—such as heresy—' "relaxed" the condemned heretic to the secular authorities for the imposition of capital punishment' (Langbein, *Torture and the Law of Proof*, p. 29).

liberties. What is in fact a description of the control *potential* possessed by modern power–knowledge technologies is presented as if it were the reality of their present-day *operation*. It is a worst-case scenario which ignores the strength of countervailing forces.

A good illustration of this might be the modern deployment of 'welfare sanctions' such as probation, community supervision, psychiatric orders, and so on. Such sanctions are potentially very authoritarian—as *Discipline and Punish* and my own *Punishment and Welfare* have shown. But counter-powers, safeguards, and limitations may be built into the context in which the sanction is deployed in ways which qualify its power potential and render it less intrusive. Thus the orientation of the agents involved, their ideologies, their resources or lack of them, the legal limits placed upon their powers, the rights of clients, and the resistance that they offer, can all moderate the extent to which the sanction's power is actualized. Foucault's work has the useful effect of highlighting the dangers that such sanctions contain, but it fails to balance this by describing their actual meaning-in-use and the constraints which they encounter.[25]

4. Powers and Values

These criticisms of Foucault's conception of punishment can be extended to refer to the more general conception of power which runs through *Discipline and Punish*. As we have seen, the scepticism of Foucault's power perspective points to the persistent 'will to power' which is alleged to lie behind the language of penal reform and the events of penal history, producing a kind of penological rendering of Nietzsche's *Genealogy of Morals*. In Foucault's work, as in Nietzsche's before him, systems of morality, ethics, and sensibility are broken down to reveal the more basic questions of power which motivate them and give them their real meaning. This critique of morals in the name of power does more than simply set *Discipline and Punish* apart from more conventional histories of punishment. In so far as these other histories are written in terms of changing morality and social sentiment, it actually subverts them, criticizing their terms as superficial and unanalysed. The ethical values, religious beliefs, and humane sensibilities that others present as contributory causes of penal change are, for Foucault, at best the 'incidental music'[26] which accompanies change, at worst, a euphemistic covering-device for new forms of power.

It is certainly necessary to investigate the circumstances in which social values exist and are transformed, rather than accepting them as basic,

---

[25] See also Sykes on the defects of total power in the prison setting: 'The lack of a sense of duty among those who are held captive, the obvious fallacies of coercion, the pathetic collection of rewards and punishments to induce compliance, the strong pressures toward the corruption of the guard in the form of friendship, reciprocity, and the transfer of duties into the hands of trusted inmates—all are structural defects in the prison's system of power rather than individual inadequacies' (*The Society of Captives*, p. 61).

[26] The phrase is from Geertz, 'Stir Crazy'.

unconditioned facts. And *Discipline and Punish* gives a classic demonstration of how effective such an approach can be. But it is, however, a mistake to suppose that values and ethics are somehow reducible to the will to power. It is a mistake not because people are necessarily principled moral agents who will uphold ethical values and renounce the pursuit of power. Rather it is a mistake because it is simply untenable to suppose that 'power' can be so completely separated from 'value': powers and values always in practice coexist in an integral relationship—rather like that which links power and knowledge.

Power is not a thing in itself, despite Foucault's tendency to use the term 'power' as if it were a proper noun. Power is instead a relational concept. It is the name we give to the capacity to realize a desired goal in a particular situation, and in human cultures the goals which may be valued and sought after are many and varied. If we wish to abstract our analysis away from real situations, it is possible to discuss technologies of power without reference to values. In that case we are discussing power as a set of means or capacities which may be put to a variety of uses, and so it is reasonable to leave aside questions of value or objective. But once we move on from there to analyse the actual operation of forms of power in society, then a crucial question will always be: what values does this power serve? When he engages in this form of analysis, Foucault writes as if the only possible ends of power are power and more power, control and more control. Yet, as we have seen, this view is untenable even with respect to punishment which is perhaps the nearest thing we have to a control institution: it would hardly make sense in other fields such as health care, education, or welfare where similar technologies of power are put to use.

By focusing his study upon the prison and penal institutions, Foucault gives the impression that the aims of power—the norms which the disciplines impose—are always those of conformity, obedience, and behaviour control. By extension, power in the wider 'disciplinary society' appears to be concerned solely with this kind of domination, albeit in ways which make bodies useful as well as docile. It is true that in subsequent writings Foucault did much to extend and develop this vision of power, emphasizing its capacity to induce pleasure, discourse, action, and subjectivity.[27] But the story which *Discipline and Punish* tells—and the one which most influences current work in the sociology of punishment—is one of meticulous domination and thoroughgoing control, so that we are left with the distinct impression that society's practices of normalization—its imposition of standards upon conduct—are oppressive in all their aspects. Despite Foucault's later stress upon 'subjectification', *Discipline and Punish* tells a story of the *objectification* of human beings through the use of power–knowledge, and its critique of power and society is

---

[27] See Foucault, *The History of Sexuality*, i, and id., 'The Subject and Power', in H. L. Dreyfus and P. Rabinow, *Michel Foucault: Beyond Structuralism and Hermeneutics* (2nd edn., Chicago, 1983), 208–26.

largely an extension of this imagery of dehumanizing domination.[28] But this sweeping cultural critique is only rhetorically possible because *Discipline and Punish* focuses upon the norm of obedience. Had it focused upon some of the other norms which social and even penal agencies try to inculcate—such as literacy, cleanliness, health, responsibility, independence, stability, etc.—its critique would not have been so easily made. I mention these other norms—which are sometimes enforced using a measure of force or even oppression—because they will probably strike the reader as intrinsically more acceptable than the kind of thought-control that Foucault dwells upon. My point here is that even the forceable imposition of norms is not always reprehensible—it depends on the circumstances and one's evaluative judgment of the norms in question. The essential point of political analysis must be to distinguish and evaluate separately the various objectives which our institutions seek and the means which they use to achieve them. Foucault's work refuses to make discerning judgments about the different purposes to which 'power' can be put, and, in so doing, implies that one is no better than any other.

5. POWER AND POLITICS

If *Discipline and Punish* fails to investigate the objectives of power, it is no better at describing its agents. Of course Foucault rejects the idea that power is a thing that is 'held' by someone, but even if we accept his structural or relational approach to power we still need to know who are the people in positions of power and how they came to be there. On these crucial questions, Foucault is notoriously reticent. Sometimes he uses the abstractions of Marxist terminology ('the dominant class', 'the state', 'the bourgeoisie'), occasionally he mentions 'the judges', 'psychiatric experts', or 'the administration', but more often he simply avoids the issue altogether by using passive grammatical constructions which do not name subjects. This failure to identify agents and decision-makers—or even any recognizable process of policy-making—makes it difficult to accept his use of terms like 'strategy' and 'tactics', even though these terms are often crucial to his argument.

In the absence of any identifying data or descriptions, what emerges is a rather vaguely defined conflict between a dominating class and those who are dominated and next to nothing about the forces which are operative in day-to-day penal politics. Ideological conflicts amongst ruling groups and their implications for penal policy, institutionalized tensions between different agencies in the penal process, popular support for certain measures, and the cross-class alliances that they produce—these feature hardly at all in *Discipline and Punish*. In this sense, Foucault's conception of power is strangely apolitical. It appears as a kind of empty structure, stripped of any agents, interests, or

[28] See Dreyfus and Rabinow, *Michel Foucault: Beyond Structuralism and Hermeneutics*, chs. 7 and 8, which distinguishes between Foucault's 'Genealogy of the Modern Individual as Object' and his 'Genealogy of the Modern Individual as Subject'.

grounding, reduced to a bare technological scaffolding. It is thus no accident that so much attention is given to the *design* of Bentham's Panopticon, and so little to the actual fate of this project, which in fact fell victim to the struggles amongst political factions and interest groups which dominate government policy-making.[29]

Foucault's use of the Panopticon image to sum up modernity is no doubt intended to evoke echoes of the 'iron cage' of rationality that Max Weber described.[30] But it is also particularly appropriate as a Foucauldian metaphor, because, despite his disclaimers, Foucault understands power as an apparatus of constraint. In the end, power is a kind of total confinement which envelops the individual, moulding the body and soul into patterns of conformity. Power is at once socialization and social control.[31] It constructs the individual as a subject, but it is always an individual who is 'subjected' or subjugated in the same process.

Beneath this oppressive burden it is 'the body' which somehow represents the individual's instinctive source of freedom. It is the body which resists, the body which has to be dominated, and ultimately the body which comes to be 'the prisoner of the soul' (once the soul has been fabricated by society's discipline). This time the theoretical echoes stretch back to Freud and to Nietzsche, and suggest that at the bottom of things lies the old opposition between nature (the body) and culture (the power of social discipline). But we receive nothing more than hints in this regard and so the basis of Foucault's theory remains unargued.

In fact the resistance of prisoners to the disciplinary process, and the failure of the prison to effect their reform, raise serious theoretical problems for Foucault's account which are merely passed over here in silence. First of all, if the prison is a concentrated, totalized form of discipline and it none the less fails in its disciplinary endeavours, how effective are other forms of discipline which lack the prison's coercive advantages?[32] This important problem might be resolved by pointing to the effects of developmental psychology: the disciplines may operate most effectively upon young, immature subjects whose characters have not yet been formed, so families and schools may succeed where prisons usually fail. Or, more interestingly, one could point out the limitations upon the disciplinary process which a punitive context entails; as Durkheim suggests, punitive disciplines may be ineffective precisely because the process of punishment robs the offender of the sense of

---

[29] On the fate of Bentham's scheme, see G. Himmelfarb, 'The Haunted House of Jeremy Bentham', in id., *Victorian Minds* (New York, 1968). On the influence of Panoptic principles in the history of prison architecture, see Evans, *The Fabrication of Virtue*.

[30] M. Weber, *The Protestant Ethic and the Spirit of Capitalism* (London, 1985), p. 181.

[31] For a discussion on this point, see Stone, *The Past and the Present Revisited*, ch. 15.

[32] It is of interest that this unresolved issue in Foucault's work reflects a parallel tension in Nietzsche. In *The Genealogy of Morals*, Nietzsche says that pain and punishment were used, over millenia, to create man as a calculating, responsible entity. But he also argues that punishment tends to provoke resistance rather than improvement (pp. 189–94, and p. 214).

pride and moral self-respect which self-discipline requires. This Durkheimian point leads on to the important question of the individual's orientation and relationship to disciplinary power. In many disciplinary situations, such as the monastery, the school, or the factory, the individual co-operates in his training because, at least to some extent, he shares the goals of the disciplinary process (to overcome the flesh, to become educated, to earn a wage). The key problem for the prison as a form of discipline is that individual prisoners may have no inclination and no need to take an active part in the process.

Each of these points seems to offer plausible reasons why prison discipline is often ineffective, but in highlighting the role of subjective or psychological factors they seem to lead away from the rather more automatic conception of discipline which Foucault implies. The same problem can be seen if we consider the question of resistance. To the extent that he discusses prisoner resistance—in *Discipline and Punish* and in his subsequent commentaries upon it—Foucault suggests an unreasoned bodily force which hardens itself to resist the demands of disciplinary routines.[33] But in fact the crucial element within this process may have less to do with bodily forces than with the response of the subject to his or her situation. Ian Hacking has argued that in the production of persons—disciplinary or otherwise—a crucial element in the process is always the subjective orientation of the person concerned which may embrace the imposed role or may instead resist it.[34] Neither Hacking nor Foucault has much to say about this crucial vector of responsive conduct but one would expect that the factors which normally have a bearing upon subjective orientation—such as the sense of identity, relationships with others, cultural affiliations, and so on—would play a part in grounding any resistance which occurs. Turning to more empirical research on the issue, one finds that the forms of inmate resistance with which we are familiar do indeed suggest that the social psychology of cultural identification is one key to understanding this process. Resistance to official authority occurs most frequently and most effectively in those prisons where an alternative inmate culture offers oppositional identifications, roles, and forms of support for those who adopt them. The work of Patricia O'Brien, for example, shows that the resistance which figured in the French prisons of the nineteenth century was facilitated not by resistant bodies but by the availability of alternative languages, forms of conduct, and identities which amounted to an inmate subculture.[35]

[33] See Foucault, *Discipline and Punish*, p. 30, where he discusses the nature of prisoner revolts and the history of resistance to the prison: 'In fact, they were revolts, at the level of the body, against the very body of the prison.' Also in the essay 'Body/Power' he states that 'Power, after investing itself in the body, finds itself exposed to a counter-attack in the same body' (in id., *Power/Knowledge*, ed. Gordon, p. 56.

[34] I. Hacking, 'Making Up People', in T. C. Heller *et al.* (eds.), *Reconstructing Individualism* (Stanford, 1986).

[35] O'Brien, *The Promise of Punishment*, ch. 3. On inmate subcultures more generally, see Clemmer, *The Prison Community*; Sykes, *The Society of Captives*; J. B. Jacobs, *New Perspectives on Prisons and Imprisonment* (Ithaca, NY, 1983); Cloward *et al.*, *Theoretical Studies in Social Organization of the Prison*.

Interestingly, had Foucault investigated these processes, he could have described an irony which would have helped him explain the production of 'the delinquent' in a more convincing manner. In effect, the inmate may embrace the prison subculture in order to avoid becoming a slave of the official system and to maintain a measure of autonomy and self-respect in the face of its disciplinary machine. But the existence of this inmate subculture tends—in the kind of dialectic described by Sartre in his biography of Jean Genet[36]—to increase the stigma of the ex-convict and deepen his criminal identifications: someone who has been inside is not just an offender but is also an 'ex-con': probably schooled in a culture of homosexuality, corruption, violence, and deception. Thus by struggling to avoid an institutional identity which was despised ('the good inmate') prisoners often took on another one (the 'con') which the public had reason to fear and despise. By studying more closely the nature of resistance, Foucault would have done something to balance his account of power, but, as these remarks suggest, he might also have been led to revise this account in some important respects. In particular he might have been led to describe the operation of power upon individuals as being less of an 'automatic' process and more a matter of micro-political conflict in which the individual subject may draw upon alternative sources of power and subjectivity to resist that imposed by the institution.[37]

Foucault's vision of power may be a positive conception in the sense that power moulds, trains, builds up, and creates subjects, but it also involves a thoroughly negative evaluation. Foucault writes as someone who is absolutely 'against' power. His critique is not of one form of power in favour of another but is rather an attack upon power itself. This is why the critical tone of *Discipline and Punish* is never transformed into a truly critical argument which points to alternative forms of regulation which are possible and might be preferable to those which it decries.[38] It never even declares from what position it mounts its critique, since to do so would be to accept the necessity of power and choose between its forms. Instead it is written as if its author were 'outside' of power and therefore outside of society as well.

---

[36] J.-P. Sartre, *Saint Genet: Actor and Martyr* (London, 1988).

[37] The work of Erving Goffman is an important antidote here. In *Asylums* Goffman outlines a conception of the individual as an entity which defines itself not in conformity with institutional pressures but in tension with them. On this reading, inmates always 'take up a stance' towards the institution, and the individual should be seen as '. . . a something that takes up a position somewhere between identification with an organization and opposition to it, and is ready at the slightest pressure to regain its balance by shifting its involvement in either direction. It is thus *against something* that the self can emerge' (p. 280).

[38] T. Mathiesen, *The Politics of Abolition* (London, 1974), explicitly adopts this kind of critical strategy, refusing to propose alternative penal measures to replace those which it criticizes. For a critical discussion, see D. Downes, 'Abolition: Possibilities and Pitfalls', in Bottoms and Preston (eds.), *The Coming Penal Crisis*. On 'abolitionism' as a strategy for change in criminal justice, see, more generally, Bianchi and van Swaaningen (eds.), *Abolitionism*, and the special 'Abolitionist' issue of the journal *Contemporary Crises*, 10 (1986). The essay by R. De Folter in the latter collection argues that Foucault should be understood as an 'abolitionist'.

There is an important sense in which discipline can create freedom as well as control. As Foucault's own subsequent work shows, discipline is necessary to the development of self-control and therefore to subjectivity.[39] Equally it can form the basis for a regulatory network through which the norms of health, security, and welfare can be systematically provided for whole populations—providing a degree of freedom from want, illness, and ignorance which would otherwise be impossible. The ultimate questions which need to be faced, whether in penal policy or in social policy, are not about power or no-power but rather about the ways in which power should be exercised, the values which should inform it, and the objectives which it should pursue. These points are well understood by Émile Durkheim, whose discussion of discipline is in other respects very similar to that of Foucault. Like Foucault, Durkheim sees discipline as a set of forces which act upon individuals, constructing them as centred subjects and subjugating them to social norms.[40] But, for Durkheim, this process is not only a necessary one—for the sanity of the individual, and for the stability of society—it is also a *moral* one, occurring within a sanctioned moral framework which renders it authoritative rather than merely coercive. Durkheim thus distinguishes between disciplinary forces which have an authoritative moral status and those which do not, arguing that the former are essential to social health while only the latter are oppressive in the sense that Foucault implies. It is precisely because the disciplines of the penal realm rarely carry real moral conviction for the offenders concerned that they so signally fail to have a lasting disciplinary effect. On this analysis, the realm of punishment may well have adopted disciplinary techniques as Foucault says, but it is the last place that one would expect them to succeed—unless offenders can be persuaded of the moral as well as the physical force of the rules they have breached. However, the idea that penal measures may contain a genuine moral charge, which commands some degree of social support, takes us outside the framework that Foucault employs.

Foucault's analyses of penal institutions and penal techniques provide us with an invaluable phenomenology of the forms of power and knowledge which are activated in the penal sphere. More than any other theorist, he gives us an account of the micro-physics of penal power and the ways in which penal measures lay hold of individuals and subject them to processes of discipline, normalization, and punishment. But as the preceding arguments have tried to show, it is a mistake to move from an analysis of how power is organized in the penal sphere to the argument that penality is nothing but this power. Punishment is more than just a political instrument of control, and it is a reductionist conception which sees penal history purely in terms of power–knowledge and

[39] Foucault's *History of Sexuality*, i, develops an important conception of a form of power or governance which he terms 'bio-politics'. This refers to those strategies of governing that concern themselves with the life, health, efficiency, and security of whole populations. Bio-political regulation operates at the level of social groups and populations and is seen as a form of modern power that accompanies and complements the individually oriented 'disciplines'.

[40] See Durkheim, *Moral Education*, esp. p. 46.

its transformations. To say—correctly—that punishment is a form of power immediately raises the question: 'what kind of power?' Is it authorized? Does it command popular support? What values does it convey? Which objectives does it seek? How is it shaped by sensibilities and in what kind of culture and morality is it grounded? But even to ask such questions is already to go beyond the limits which Foucault's critical theory sets for itself.

8

The Rationalization of Punishment
Weberian Themes and Modern Penality

1. FOUCAULT AND WEBER

Before leaving aside the themes raised by Foucault's work, I want to show how several of Foucault's concerns can be understood as a reworking of more familiar Weberian analyses and arguments. Such a discussion is undertaken not to diminish any claims which Foucault may have to originality but rather to open up some important Weberian issues, and, in particular, to explore how processes such as rationalization, professionalization, and bureaucratization have been manifested in the development and functioning of modern penality. As well as this, I will attempt to sketch out some of the effects which these developments have had, both upon the form of modern punishment and upon the ways in which it is generally perceived.

Foucault is a philosopher and social analyst writing self-consciously in the tradition of Nietzsche and Weber. From Nietzsche he adopts a sceptical perspective which scutinizes everything for signs of a will to power; a genealogical method, which searches for the meaning of the present via the paths of its construction; an emphasis upon the body as a kind of analytical grounding; and certain suggestive arguments about punishment which see it as a means of constructing self-disciplined individuals, subjected to a superior power. The philosophical animus of his work is thus decidedly Nietzschean, as are its aphoristic style, its occasional excesses, and its lack of concern for balance or circumspection. However the detailed analytics which he presents—particularly when he deals with the disciplines—and his implicit conception of modernity as an increasingly rationalized organization of powers and capacities, owes much more to the influence of the sociologist Max Weber. In part this is a matter of methodology—as is made clear by Foucault's careful positivism and his use of what are, in effect, 'ideal types'—but the more important continuity between these two writers relates to their shared concern with the forces of discipline, bureaucracy, and rationalization, and the impact of these forces upon the social world and human relations.

That Foucault should have leaned so heavily upon Weber's historical sociology is not surprising. Weber's sociological concepts, and particularly his account of modernity, have become taken-for-granted elements within modern social thought, to the extent that most accounts of modern institutions speak a Weberian language without feeling the need to acknowledge it as such. Moreover, because Weber's work offers specific analyses and descriptions rather than a holistic system of thought, it is possible to use his arguments without being bound into a closed circle of formulations and doctrinal views. Unlike Marxist or even Durkheimian models, Weberian concepts do not link up into a systematic theory of social structure or a determinate account of social dynamics. Weber, quite as much as Foucault, insists upon analysing social relations and social institutions without positing any essential or unified conception of the social whole.

In the sociology of punishment as it currently exists there is no explicitly Weberian theory which characterizes penality in a particular way, or offers an interpretative perspective from 'Weber's point of view'. But if one studies the literature closely, it becomes clear that Weberian arguments and analyses feature again and again. This is most obvious in the vast literature which deals with the courts, the police, and the prisons from an organizational point of view, discussing the peculiar dynamics and goal displacements which bureaucratization has introduced into the criminal justice sphere, but there are other ways in which Weberian concepts are put to work. To take just one striking example, the history of US prison reform described by David Rothman in his books *The Discovery of the Asylum* and *Conscience and Convenience* is organized around a cyclical pattern of brief inspirational reforms, led by dedicated, zealous individuals, followed by a slower process of petrification, ossification, and the displacement of the originating ideals by more mundane organizational objectives.[1] Rothman coins a new set of terms for this process, calling it the dialectic of 'conscience' and 'convenience', but in fact his argument repeats almost to the letter the Weberian scheme of charismatic change followed by the routinization of charisma.[2] To the extent that Rothman's narrative has an analytical, explanatory content, it is almost entirely Weberian.

In the same way, we might say that Foucault's account of the disciplines is fundamentally an elaboration of the insights provided by Weber in his chapter on 'The Meaning of Discipline' in *Economy and Society* where Weber describes how first the army and then the factory train men so that they are 'completely adjusted to the demands of the outer world, the tools, the machines—in short, to an individual "function"'. In this disciplinary process, 'the individual is shorn of his natural rhythm as determined by the structure of his organism; his psycho-physical apparatus is attuned to a new rhythm through a methodical specialization of separately functioning muscles, and an optimum economy of forces is established corresponding to the conditions of work'.[3] Foucault may have provided us with the most detailed analysis of the disciplines and their operational logic, but he was by no means the first to point to their principles or their social importance.[4]

The development of the disciplines is a key theme in Foucault's account of modern punishment and of Weber's account of modern society, but for both

[1] Rothman, *The Discovery of the Asylum*, and id., *Conscience and Convenience*.

[2] See the chapter entitled 'Charisma and its Transformations' in M. Weber, *Economy and Society*, eds. G. Roth and C. Wittich (Berkeley, 1978), ii. 1111–57.

[3] H. H. Gerth and C. Wright Mills (eds.), *From Max Weber* (London, 1948), pp. 261–2.

[4] In his essay 'On the Characteristics of Total Institutions', Erving Goffman also anticipates many of the analytical points that Foucault makes regarding the operative principles of disciplinary regimes. See Goffman, *Asylums*, esp. pp. 13–22.

writers disciplinary practices are only one element within a much broader developmental process in which social practices come to be 'rationalized', and 'instrumentalized', in a utilitarian fashion. According to Weber, rationalized social practices are those rule-governed forms of social action which are calculated and calculable, based upon a self-reflexive knowledge of their aims and conditions, and oriented to achieving these ends by the most instrumentally appropriate means. Historically, and conceptually, these practices are counterposed to affective, customary, or traditional forms of social action, since these non-rational or quasi-rational forms are dictated by emotion, habit, or other irrational factors. The move from traditional or affective practices to rationalized forms of action is seen by Weber (and by Foucault) as a distinctively modernizing development, in which social practices become better informed, more efficient, and more self-consciously adapted towards specific objectives.[5] In the course of this development, 'science' (including social science) comes to replace belief, calculation replaces commitment, and technical knowledges replace traditions and sentiments as the leading determinants of action. In consequence, social practices and institutions become more instrumentally effective, but at the same time they become less emotionally compelling or meaningful for their human agents. For Weber—and in large part for Foucault too—the human consequences of this ever-more rationalized social world involve not only 'disenchantment' and the loss of spiritual faith and value commitment: they also entail a heavy measure of constraint and oppression which is psychologically burdensome for the individual. Weber's image of the iron cage of modern rationalism, and Foucault's vision of the disciplinary society, each attempt to capture and convey this ironic sense of modernity and its discontents.

The great interest of Foucault's (partly-Weberian) analysis of punishment is that he shows how this broader rationalization process has transformed an institution from being a morally-charged and emotive set of ritual practices into an increasingly passionless and professionalized instrumental process. In the pages which follow, I will explore this 'rationalization' of punishment in an attempt to spell out precisely what these changes have amounted to, and how they fit with this more general thesis. Having drawn up the evidence for the proposition that punishment has become, to some extent at least, a rationalized form of social practice, I will then try to place this development within its wider context. Recalling the earlier discussion of Durkheim, it will be seen that this Weberian–Foucauldian theme of rationalization appears to run directly counter to the Durkheimian insistence that penality—even modern penality— is fundamentally a passionate reaction grounded in non-rational motivations and rituals. But instead of rejecting one or the other thesis out of hand, I will

---

[5] Even Durkheim accepts that modern punishment has been rationalized in this respect: 'Today, since we better understand the end to be attained, we better know how to utilize the means at our disposal. . . . [Punishment] now produces its effects with a much greater understanding of what it does' (*The Division of Labor*, pp. 87–8).

argue that both themes are in fact characteristic of modern punishment—although they are functionally separated to some extent within the specialized division of labour of the modern penal process. My argument will be that there are two contrasting visions at work in contemporary criminal justice—the passionate, morally toned desire to punish and the administrative, rationalistic, normalizing concern to manage. These visions clash in many important respects, but both are deeply embedded within the social process of punishing. It is in the conflict and tension between them that we will find one of the key determinants of contemporary penal practice.

2. THE RATIONALIZATION OF PUNISHMENT

The rationalization and bureaucratization of the penal process has undoubtedly been the most important development to have taken place in penality in the nineteenth and twentieth centuries.[6] Over the course of the last 200 years, the localized, *ad hoc*, and frequently makeshift penal arrangements of previous periods[7] have given way to a professionalized, administrative infrastructure which commands significant tax-funded budgets, large numbers of career personnel, an extensive network of institutions and agencies, and a range of technical knowledges and social science discourses. These fundamental developments in the social organization of penality—much more than any change of law or of penal sanction—have had profound implications for modern punishment, not only for the way in which sanctions are delivered but also for the social meanings which attach to them and for the ways in which they are experienced by the public and offenders alike.

Discipline and Punish is by no means the only study to draw attention to these administrative developments in the penal field. There is a large historical literature devoted to tracing the course of institutional change in this area, and the theme of administrative rationalization—often conceived as an index of penal 'progress'—is one of the underlying principles which holds together many narrative histories of punishment.[8] In Foucault's account, the focus of attention is upon the prison and how it gave rise to new rationalities and new

---

[6] Spierenburg shows that this process had already begun in the 17th cent., with clerks and secretaries attending executions and making written records of the proceedings. Spierenburg, *The Spectacle of Suffering*, p. 80.

[7] For examples see J. Sharpe, *Crime in Early Modern England*, p. 178.

[8] On British penal history, see S. Webb and B. Webb, *English Prisons Under Local Government* (London, 1922); S. McConville, *A History of English Prison Administration*, i (London, 1981); and Radzinowicz, *English Criminal Law and Its Administration*. On institutional change in the USA, see B. McKelvey, *American Prisons: A History of Good Intentions* (Montclair, NJ, 1977); O. F. Lewis, *The Development of American Prisons and Prison Customs, 1776–1845* (Albany, 1922); H. E. Barnes, *The Evolution of Penology in Pennsylvania* (Montclair, NJ, 1968); W. D. Lewis, *From Newgate to Dannemora: The Rise of the Penitentiary in New York, 1796–1848* (Ithaca, NY, 1965). For an interesting account of how the Californian parole system emerged not so much from rehabilitative ideologies as from the rationalization of penal decision-making—specifically the transfer of discretionary release decisions from the governor to a bureaucratic staff—see S. L. Messinger *et al.*, 'The Foundations of Parole in California', *Law and Society Review*, 19 (1985), 69–106.

techniques of managing conduct, but in the pages which follow I want to pursue this Weberian theme on a rather broader canvas, identifying the range of 'rationalization processes' and their consequences for the way we think about and utilize punishments today. In doing so, I am conscious that I am simplifying a very complex historical process, and reducing it to a few fundamental lines of development. But for all its vicissitudes, the historical record of penal change does amount to a broad developmental pattern in this particular respect, and my purpose here is merely to indicate the kinds of sociological and penological ramifications which these developments have had.

From the late eighteenth century onwards, the processes of punishment have come to be increasingly monopolized and administered by central governmental agencies. This tendency towards centralization—which has occurred everywhere—was prompted by the rise of penal measures such as transportation and imprisonment which required administrative capacities and funding unavailable to local authorities, but it is also of a piece with the much broader processes of state expansion and consolidation which have occurred in the modern period.[9] Throughout the nineteenth century in Britain, and for an even longer period in some US states, central and local authorities were in conflict over this question, and a variety of devices such as inspection, regulation, and grants-in-aid were used to wrest control over penal processes away from the local jurisdictions in which they were traditionally lodged. Eventually, centralized administrative structures were established which proceeded to rationalize the penal process in a number of important respects. The funding of penal measures ceased to be part-dependent upon private sources of finance—such as jailors or contractors' fees, charities, churches, etc.—and became a public burden, based upon tax revenues and governmental direction. Hierarchical chains of command were established linking the local staffs of prison institutions or probation agencies into a state-wide or national structure, allowing a degree of centralized policy-making and enforcement which had not previously been possible. A measure of uniformity was introduced into previously disparate establishments; separate institutions were co-ordinated to a greater degree; general regulations became effective; and the autonomy of individual institutions and agencies was considerably reduced. At the same time, there was a substantial growth in the scale of the penal infrastructure—partly due to the abandonment of corporal and capital sanctions (which had required little in the way of an administrative apparatus), partly due to the expansion of the population and rising rates of criminalization.[10]

[9] For an analytical history which lays stress upon the processes of state formation as a central dynamic in penal development, see Spierenburg, *The Spectacle of Suffering*; id., *The Emergence of Carceral Institutions*; and id., 'From Amsterdam to Auburn: An Explanation for the Rise of the Prison in Seventeenth Century Holland and Nineteenth Century America', *The Journal of Social History*, 4 (1987).

[10] For an account of a parallel development, the centralization and professionalization of policing, see V. A. C. Gatrell, 'Crime, Authority and the Policeman-State, 1750–1950', in

This expanded administrative network came increasingly to be staffed by paid, trained officials so that the penal system became the site of a number of professional groupings—prison governors, wardens, medical officers, social workers, probation officers, and, later, criminologists, psychiatrists, and psychologists—each with its own jurisdiction, career structure, interests, and ideologies.[11] As might be expected, the emergence of various professional groups within the penal process has had a series of sociological consequences. An elaborate division of labour has grown up in which specialized agencies and functionaries carve up the various tasks of penological work, often coming into conflict with one another in the process. What we refer to, broadly speaking, as juridical 'punishment', thus came to be a complex, differentiated process, involving a series of agencies, each displaying a distinctive set of concerns and objectives, and often drawing upon different sources of social support. Each separate aspect of this increasingly balkanized penal system has come to be characterized by bureaucratic structures and procedures, so that even the non-institutional processes (such as probation, social work, after-care, etc.) which began as voluntary, charitable initiatives, are now routinized and administered by much the same organizational structures as the custodial tasks of the system. Thus even the most personalized and individualized aspects of this 'people-processing' system are now managed from within bureaucratic agencies—with all that this implies.[12]

Most of these new occupational groups have developed professional aspirations of one sort or another. Reformatory managers, prison medical officers and psychiatrists, probation officers, correctional executives, parole agents, juvenile justice professionals—all of them have pursued their own claims to specialized expertise and have tried to influence penal policy in accordance with these claims. These groups vary between themselves as to the forms of knowledge, clinical skills, or technical capacity to which they lay claim and they diverge considerably on matters of penal policy and politics. However, all of them, as professional penal agents, tend to represent themselves in a positive, utilitarian way, as offering a particular service, or carrying out a useful social task. Characteristically, they avoid the bad conscience and cultural infamy that used to attach to the executioner or the jailer by claiming to be more than merely instruments of punishment.[13] Instead of being the vehicles of punitive

F. M. L. Thompson (ed.), *The Cambridge Social History of Britain, 1750–1950*, 3 vols. (Cambridge, forthcoming). See also S. Spitzer, 'The Rationalization of Crime Control in Capitalist Society', in Cohen and Scull (eds.), *Social Control and the State*.

[11] For an analysis of these penal professionals, their characteristic concerns, and the languages they employ, see Cohen, *Visions of Social Control*, ch. 5.

[12] One of the unintended consequences of the prisoners' rights movement in the USA and elsewhere has been to accelerate this process of bureaucratization within the prison system. As James Jacobs has pointed out, prisoners' rights litigation has given rise to a new generation of trained administrators, capable of responding to the courts' demands for rational, rule-governed procedures within the institutions and records to show their implementation. See Jacobs, *New Perspectives on Prisons and Imprisonment*, ch. 2.

[13] On the cultural status of executioners, see Spierenburg, *The Spectacle of Suffering*, ch. 2.

reaction—a status which even rank and file prison guards seek to avoid—these groups tend to represent themselves positively, as technicians of reform, as social work professionals, or as institutional managers.[14] It is thus no coincidence that the period in which these professional bureaucracies have emerged is also the period in which punitive sentiments have been increasingly marginalized in official penal discourse and replaced by more utilitarian objectives and expectations. If we nowadays expect 'results' from punishing, it is in large part the doing of these groups and their self-descriptions.

The most evident result of these convergent processes of centralization, bureaucratization, and professionalization has been that modern penal systems have been able to cope, reasonably effectively, with very large numbers of offenders. To the extent that modern punishment is exercised more or less uniformly, by trained personnel, in conditions which are sanitary, regulated, and organized (at least in comparison with the period prior to the nineteenth century) it does so by virtue of its rationalized administrative forms, without which the field would be hopelessly chaotic. As Weber says, 'precision, speed, unambiguity, knowledge of the files, continuity, unity, strict subordination, reduction of friction, and of material and personal costs' are the benefits of bureaucratic organization and, to this extent, the conventional histories of penal 'progress' contain an important element of truth in their congratulatory account.[15] But these administrative developments have done more than simply enhance the efficiency with which penal sanctions are delivered. They have also done much to alter the cultural meaning of these sanctions and transform the way in which punishment is generally perceived.

It is a characteristic of bureaucratic organizations that they operate in a passionless, routinized, matter-of-fact kind of way. No matter in what field of social life they operate—whether in health care or social work or punishment—bureaucracies strive to act *sine ira ac studio* (without anger or enthusiasm), performing their tasks with studied neutrality and objectivity. As Weber puts it, such organizations become deliberately 'dehumanized' and, to the extent that they approach this ideal, they succeed 'in eliminating from official business love, hatred and all . . . irrational and emotional elements'.[16] We can see this very clearly if we consider the way in which penal administrators regard the offenders with whom they have to deal. Prison officials, in so far as they are being professional, tend to suspend moral judgment and treat prisoners in purely neutral terms. Typically, the evaluative terms which are used relate to administrative criteria rather than moral worth, so that prisoners will be treated not as evil or wicked persons on account of their offence, but as good or bad inmates on account of their institutional conduct.[17] (Hence the much quoted formula that offenders come to prison *as* punishment and not *for* punishment.) Probation officers, forensic psychiatrists, and fine-enforcement

---

[14] See Cohen, *Visions of Social Control*, and Christie, *Limits to Pain.*
[15] Gerth and Mills (eds.), *From Max Weber*, p. 214.   [16] Ibid. 216.
[17] See DiIulio, *Governing Prisons*, pp. 167 ff., and Sykes, *The Society of Captives*, p. 31.

officials regard their 'clients' in this same professional manner, bringing to bear diagnostic and risk-management considerations rather than moral judgments.[18] In effect, penal professionals tend to orientate themselves towards institutionally defined managerial goals rather than socially derived punitive ones. Instead of seeking to convey moral outrage, punitive passions, or vengeful sentiments, these agencies tend to neutralize the affect of the penal process, to do their job in a professional manner, leaving the tones of moral opprobrium to the court and the public.

To some extent, no doubt, this has always been the case wherever penal sanctions have been administered by paid officials rather than by the aggrieved parties or the public. Even the medieval executioner would seek to perform his task according to the standards of his trade, its technical demands, and the precise instructions of the law: he was never a mere instrument of popular feeling. But 'professionalism' and 'objectivity' are a matter of degree. And these traits tend to become more pronounced the more the organization of punishment approximates to the bureaucratic. Thus Jacobs' study of a twentieth-century US prison describes in detail how its administrative structure gradually evolved from a personalistic, charismatic regime towards a rational–bureaucratic one, and this process brought with it a new conception of the prison officials' task: 'Brierton [the prison warden who introduced professional management techniques into the Stateville penitentiary] has brought a new definition of administration to the prison. He stresses efficient and emotionally detached management. He has attempted to remove the affect attached to handling inmates.'[19] Within this bureaucratic framework, considerations such as moral deserts or the sanctity of rules take a back seat to the smooth running of the institution: as Jacobs tells us, this new warden 'has de-emphasized the need to punish prisoners for violations of rules, while focusing on the need to restrain those who can be seen to be a threat to institutional security. He is not committed to a particular standard of living that the prisoners "deserve": that is a matter for the courts and the legislature.'[20]

This interpolation of a bureaucratic process between the reactive emotions of society and the actual punishment of the offender is often deemed to be an index of the refinement and civility attained by criminal justice. The rule of law requires that its penalties be executed in a rule-governed, routine, and impassive fashion, which in turn requires a good deal of social distance and professional objectivity. Bureaucratization is thus a component of measured and impartial justice. This, no doubt, is true so far as it goes. But the point I wish to make here is that the professionalization of the punitive process has, in the twentieth century, reached a point where penal professionals have been able to redefine the social meaning of punishment. To the extent that penal

---

[18] See R. F. Sparks, 'The Enforcement of Fines: The Process from Sentence to Committal', *The British Journal of Criminology*, 13 (1973), 92–107, on how the logic of debt-management tends to displace that of retribution in the enforcement of monetary sanctions.

[19] Jacobs, *Stateville*, p. 104.   [20] Ibid.

measures have become professionalized they have also been removed from direct public participation and involvement and have been cast in a form which de-emphasizes their moral content. Once penalties ceased to be executed in public, or in ways which sought to express public sentiments, the direct expression of outrage or emotion was increasingly cordoned off—limited to the public galleries of the court-room or the letters columns of the press.

From the mid-nineteenth century onwards, many of the official ways in which punishment was discussed and represented came to reflect the 'rational' and 'scientific' conceptions of professional penal administrators and criminologists, who endeavoured to define penality in ways which were not emotionally or morally charged. The management of reformatories, penitentiaries, or even of probationers was redefined as a scientific task, demanding knowledge, skill, and expertise and a cast of mind which could only be disrupted by considerations of an emotional or sentimental kind. These 'managerial' concerns gradually came to dominate penological discourse, turning it into a 'penitentiary science' rather than a moral philosophy. Issues such as reformatory method and institutional regime which would once have been seen as side issues, subordinate to the main task of punishing, came to be vaunted as leading issues which were often pitted against punitive considerations rather than allied to them. By the end of the nineteenth century, a scientific criminology and penology had emerged in Europe and North America which amounted to a kind of 'rationalization' of penal discourse. As Raymond Saleilles put it, this new criminology attempted to replace the value rationality of traditional penal morality with a new purposive-rationality, which would adopt whatever technical methods were best suited for the control of crime.[21] Criminology was, in effect, an expression of the Enlightenment ambition to cure social ills by the application of Reason, and its emergence both expressed and reinforced the developing administrative logic of nineteenth-century penal systems.

Within these new ways of conceiving punishment, the problem of punishment was reformulated in technical terms as a question of social engineering and adjustment, and of course the role of the expert was deemed central to its solution.[22] Not surprisingly, this new 'scientific' approach was enthusiastically adopted by prison administrators, wardens, medical officers, and probation officers who saw themselves as the new criminological technicians—just as it was vigorously rejected by others (including many magistrates, politicians, judges, police officers, and members of the public) who felt that this vocabulary failed to convey the social condemnation that crimes should properly receive. From the turn of the century onwards this 'progressive' vision of a scientific penology based upon therapy and risk-management—rather than moral censure and punishment—has formed the working ideology of significant sections of the penal professions. To the extent that this ideology influenced penal legislation and penal policy—and it did so to a considerable extent—

---

[21] R. Saleilles, *The Individualization of Punishment* (London, 1913), pp. 8–9.

[22] See generally Garland, *Punishment and Welfare*.

these professional groups succeeded in transforming the culture of punishment. They introduced the rationality of value-neutral science, a technical 'non-judgmental' vocabulary, a 'passion for classification', and a horror of emotional forces, into a sphere which was previously dominated by candid morality and openly expressed sentiment.[23] Of course one might argue, as many did, that this new technical discourse merely suppressed its affects and moral commitments, disguising them behind the bloodless language of social science. 'Rehabilitation', 'treatment', and 'correctionalism' all involve characteristic values and emotional attitudes (such as care, compassion, forgiveness, mercy) but the idiom which these policies preferred was one which talked not of moral values but of technical values, so that correctionalist policies tended to be argued for as expedient or effective rather than morally correct. Thus penality came more and more to be conceived, and talked about, and practised, in these rational, passionless terms wherein moral evaluation is displaced by scientific understanding. As Foucault says at one point, penality's fate was 'to be redefined by knowledge'.[24]

An ironic consequence of this avoidance of explicit moral argument (and thus of moral education) has been that the values and attitudes which underpinned the rehabilitative ethos have been undermined by the technical failures of correctionalism. When, in the 1970s and 1980s, it became common wisdom that rehabilitation did not 'work'—or at least worked no better than traditional punishment—it became apparent in the back-to-punishment movement that the values of compassion and welfarism had not, after all, become solidly entrenched in public attitudes or in penal policy. It is also significant, as Stanley Cohen has shown, that the eclipse of the rehabilitative ethos has done nothing to diminish the extensive network of investigative, classifying, and normalizing practices which were initially introduced under the rubric of 'helping the offender', but which now form an essential part of the power–knowledge network of penal control.[25]

The professionalization and bureaucratization of the penal process, together with the 'scientization' of penal ideology, has, in part at least, redefined the place and meaning of 'punishment' in modern society. As we have seen, the modern institutions of punishment are much less accessible to the public, much more secretive and socially invisible than the punishments of former times. The social tasks involved in punishment have been delegated to specialized agencies on the margins of social life, with the effect that they have, to some extent, become hidden. Punishment 'leaves the domain of everyday perception and enters that of abstract consciousness'.[26] What was once represented as an open, ritualized dialogue between the offender and the community is now a much more oblique communication carried out in institutions which give little

[23] On these tendencies, esp. 'the passion for classification', see Cohen, *Visions of Social Control*.
[24] Foucault, *Discipline and Punish*, p. 72.
[25] Cohen, *Visions of Social Control*.
[26] Foucault, *Discipline and Punish*, p. 9.

expression to the public voice.[27] Our practices of punishment have ceased to be social in the full sense and have become increasingly technical and professional. To the extent that the role of the public—or even of those who claim to represent them—has been diminished, the role of the expert has been correspondingly increased and, in the same movement, technical knowledge and diagnoses have displaced (or else disguised) moral evaluation and condemnatory judgment. The classifications and typologies which now proliferate in professional penal discourse represent themselves as morally neutral, rational means of fitting offenders to appropriate regimes rather than simple expressions of moral worth or community judgment.[28]

In general, these developments have had the effect of reducing the immediacy with which popular sentiment or political concern can be expressed within the act of punishing—as well as decreasing the direct knowledge and experience that most citizens have of this process. While legislators and judges make some claim to be expressing community feeling, and will adjust their penal actions accordingly, the penal administration is not accountable in the same way. Its primary concern is not to express public sentiment but to operate the penal system and harness its resources in the manner which it considers most rational and efficient. In consequence, correctional managers and administrators often seek to minimize the impact of political intervention and resist the 'irrational' forces of public sentiment, since these can lead to uncontrolled inputs into the system which may disturb managerial goals. To the extent that public opinion is volatile and uninformed, this may be deemed a desirable characteristic—a means of reducing 'noise' or disruption in the system. But it also has a reverse side, which may appear detrimental by the same criteria. In being kept at a distance from the penal process, and being unfamiliar—and often unconcerned —with its detailed operation, clientele, and effects, the public may become susceptible to misinformation about punishment. Sensational headlines, emotive political appeals, or particularly heinous cases may lead to outbreaks of popular emotion which lack the counterweight of extensive knowledge and moral commitment. In such circumstances, the public is still capable of acting upon penal institutions by means of political pressure, and it may do so to bad effect. Thus the professionalization of penality and its removal from the public sphere can go hand in hand with a failure to educate the public systematically in the actualities of punishment, leaving the 'liberal', 'civilized' professionals

---

[27] See Zeman, 'Order, Crime and Punishment: The American Criminological Tradition', Beattie, *Crime and the Courts* and Sharpe, *Crime in Early Modern England*, for descriptions of early modern punishments which highlight this ritualized dialogue.

[28] For a critique of these developments and an argument for the remoralization (and minimalization) of what he calls 'pain delivery', see Christie, *Limits to Pain*, and also his earlier essay, 'Conflicts as Property', *The British Journal of Criminology*, 17 (1977), 1–15. Louk Hulsman has also been an influential critic of formalized, legal methods of dealing with deviance. See L. Hulsman, 'Critical Criminology and the Concept of Crime', *Contemporary Crises*, 10 (1986), 63–80 and L. Hulsman and J. Bernat de Celis, *Peines perdues: le système pénal en question* (Paris, 1982). Cohen's *Visions of Social Control* discusses the oppositional, 'destructuring' movements which have developed since the 1960s in response to the institutional build-up of criminal justice.

complaining about the 'punitive' public and the unreasonable demands which it makes.

Increasingly, in the 1980s, correctional executives are using sophisticated modelling procedures which depict the penal process as an input–output system with limited resources, which must be managed in the most rational way. Their conclusions about the capacity of the system and resource implications of particular levels of sentencing or of specific legislative reforms are then fed back to the judiciaries and state legislatures in an attempt to 'rationalize' judicial or political actions in accordance with good systems management. These developments—which represent the current high point of a long-term trend—have been greatly encouraged by the resource problems of many penal systems in the 1980s, where very high rates of imprisonment and the costs associated with these have made such rationalization all the more imperative. Thus the increasing tendency to resort to sentencing commissions and legislative guidelines in recent years is one important instance of this trend—these commissions being concerned to rationalize resource use, as well as redefine the principles of justice which should guide sentencing decisions.

Instead of being merely the executors of judicial decisions and public sentiments, the penal bureaucracies and their staffs form a resistant institutional structure with its own powers to influence decisions and to define the actual character of punishments. Of course, the legal obligation to obey court orders and to follow statutory directions limits these powers in important ways and imposes certain inescapable tasks and directions upon this administrative network. But organizations develop interests and powers of their own, and the emergence of a powerful penal bureaucracy has done much to remake modern punishment in its own image. Thus, as Foucault's work showed very clearly (and as my own *Punishment and Welfare* helped to confirm), this emergent executive power has, from the early nineteenth century onwards, sought a measure of independence from the judiciary.[29] Increasingly, the key decisions in the penal process—such as the form and place of custody, the conditions of probation, the dates of release, the availability of after-care, and so on—have been monopolized by penal administrators, and have been made in accordance with an administrative logic, rather than a legal or judicial one. These executive powers to specify penal regimes, and to allocate particular offenders to one or the other, together with the administration's growing influence over penal policy and official penal discourse, have ensured that 'punishment' has become increasingly rationalized in the various ways which I have described. In the modern network of penal institutions and bureaucracies, 'punishment' has come to approximate a rational form of action, conducted in routine, matter-of-fact sorts of ways, and represented in morally neutral, managerial terms. Of course, underlying these 'objective' practices and discourses, there is

[29] See Foucault, *Discipline and Punish*, p. 10: 'Those who carry out the penalty tend to become an autonomous sector; justice is relieved of the responsibility for it by a bureaucratic concealment of the penalty itself.'

a range of values and beyond these a series of emotional forces and moral judgments. Resentment, outrage, hatred—as well as mercy, justice, and forgiveness—continue to feature within these rationalized measures. But they do so in an unexpressed, sublimated fashion, overlaid by a utilitarian concern with institutional discipline and individual management, so that even the most transparently punitive actions are often represented in more 'positive', instrumental terms.

Foucault's *Discipline and Punish* is very much an account of this rationalization process. It stresses that, in the modern era, punitive sentiments have come to be seen as shameful, negative, irrational, and that, more and more, punishment has been redefined in positive, administrative terms as a form of correction and normalization. For Foucault, the combined outcome of the growth of discipline, the influence of human science, and the extended power of the administrative networks has been to restructure penal practice in a new way. His own description of this new form of penality centres upon its intrinsic forms of power and knowledge and its relationship to the offender's body, but, as we have seen, one can also understand this in broader, Weberian terms, as the tendency towards rationalization in the penal realm. As the previous pages have made clear, Foucault's description captures a crucial characteristic of twentieth-century penality and indicates the basic features which constitute its 'modernity'. In certain aspects of punishment, as elsewhere in modern society, technical relations have tended to displace moral ones, therapies have replaced judgments, and the social sciences have occupied a space that used to be definitively moral and religious.

3. THE LIMITS OF RATIONALIZATION

Having stressed the importance of rationalization in certain areas of the penal system, and tried to suggest its characteristic effects, it is necessary now to point to the limits of this process and the persistence of non-rational and irrational forces in penality. The 'triumph of the therapeutic' is only ever a partial one, especially in the penal realm.[30] Rationalized forms, for all their importance and consequences, have never fully monopolized the realm of penality. As I will try to show in this final section—and as I have already implied in my discussion of 'power and value'—the development of rationalized bureaucratic forms does not abolish the place of (non-rational) values or morality—it merely disguises their operation and limits their scope. Rational, instrumental conduct always assumes some kind of end to which it is a means, which is to say some kind of value orientation and set of commitments. Values—and the non-rational choices and emotional attitudes which lie behind them—may be muted and displaced by bureaucratic institutions, but they do not disappear. Furthermore, the instrumental emphasis of some penal

[30] P. Rieff, *The Triumph of the Therapeutic: Uses of Faith After Freud* (Chicago, 1966).

institutions has always had to coexist with the more expressive, emotionally charged moral tones of other aspects of the system. Consequently, a true Weberian analysis is not one which concentrates solely upon 'rationalization' in punishment but instead one which traces out the interplay between rational, non-rational, and irrational forms of action in the penal realm. Like the disciplines (which are a special case of the general process), rationalization in penality has its limits and its countervailing forces.

On the face of things, all this talk of rationalization runs directly counter to the position that Durkheim adopts in his description of modern punishment. It will be recalled that Durkheim insists that punishment today continues to be a passionate, vengeful reaction, motivated by outraged moral sentiments. Under his description, punishment is far from 'rational' or morally and affectively neutral—it is an emotional response of great intensity. How, then, are we to square this description with the conceptions of Foucault's work, or with our Weberian account of the rationalization of punishment? It is tempting simply to dismiss one of these contradictory accounts, and argue that Durkheim is patently wrong in his characterization, having missed all that is important about modern punishment. But such a response would be altogether too hasty, for, as I suggested earlier, these two interpretations are not as incompatible as they at first sight appear. For one thing, Durkheim does acknowledge that modern punishment is undertaken in a self-conscious and purposively rational manner, and for another he accepts that the 'organs' of punishment—his term for penal institutions—operate to 'moderate' and to 'graduate' the emotional forces which motivate punitive measures. He may also have been aware that the social division of labour, which he so extensively analysed, was taking hold in the penal process as elsewhere, so that many of the points I have made about the compartmentalization of the penal process would fit in with his interpretation of modern society. Nevertheless, Durkheim still insists that modern punishment remains an irrational, emotional, and essentially 'punitive' affair.

Foucault, on the other hand, appears to be arguing that punishment is no longer 'punitive' or emotionally and morally charged: hence the contradiction. But in fact this latter statement misrepresents the scope of Foucault's argument. His analysis, unlike that of Durkheim, does not cover the whole social process of punishment, from prosecution through court trial to penal disposition. Instead he focuses primarily upon the practices of prisons and penal institutions and the rationalities which they employ. He deals with the prior aspects of criminal justice—such as the court-room process and sentencing decisions— only to the extent that these have been influenced by the new correctional technologies and the new criminological discourses. His is an account of penal administration and technology—that is to say, of one crucial aspect of the penal process, rather than of the whole process from beginning to end. And precisely because his purpose in analysing the prison was to understand the mechanisms of positive, disciplinary power—rather than to understand 'punishment' as such—his work makes no attempt to discuss the extent to which emotions and moral sentiments continue to structure the punitive process. In fact, like many analysts of modernity (though not, as it happens, Max Weber) Foucault focuses all his attention upon the new modernist aspects of social life and so neglects to deal with the continued operation of the old, and the subtle interactions between them.

I have already noted that the modern penal process is largely compartmentalized—broken up into specialized agencies and sequential stages. As we saw in Chapter 3, the court-room now forms the main arena in which punitive rituals are performed and moral sentiments expressed, while actual penal institutions are increasingly administered in a more instrumental, managerial mode. It is thus highly significant that Foucault, who seeks to understand the rationality of modern power, puts penal institutions into the foreground of his analysis, while Durkheim, with his concern to understand social morality, bases his account upon the court-room ritual and the legislation of criminal law. Seen in this way, as interpretations grounded in different aspects of a differentiated process, the question should no longer be: which one is correct, Foucault or Durkheim? Instead, we should enquire how the different tendencies which they describe interact with one another, how their conflicts are managed, and what effects these tensions have upon the modern process of punishment.

The disciplinary measures and rational institutions of the modern penal system may be morally neutral and unemotive in their operational style, but they exist within a context which has been socially and authoritatively defined as a punitive one. Prisons, reformatories, probation orders, fines, and so on operate within a symbolism of the punitive because they are invoked as sanctions within a condemnatory ritual and they derive their social meaning from this use. The social significance of these institutions, as well as the subjective meaning which they hold for those who occupy them, is largely fixed by this punitive usage, even though the institutions tend to deny or play down their punitive intent. The punitive, condemnatory sign thus throws a long shadow over everything the penal system does. In his account of the prison, Foucault seeks to bracket off this social usage, and treat the institution as a technical apparatus like any other. But when he says that the prison is 'just like' the factory, or the school, or the monastery, he is referring only to its internal practices, and not to the social meanings through which it is publicly understood. And while there are clearly technical homologies linking what is done within these various institutions, their social usage and significance are altogether different. To Foucault's analysis of penal technology one must therefore add an account of that technology's meaning-in-use, if the full significance of modern penality is to be understood.

In the end, it is the social context of meaning which defines the 'punitive' and not just the actual practices of penal institutions. The sign of condemnation, the act of censure, and the infamous characterization as 'criminal' are the essential aspects of punishing—and all these still attach to modern penal sanctions, however rational or disciplinary. Any comprehensive account of punishment must thus describe the signifying practices which censure and condemn—thus imparting value and meaning to penal measures—as well as the institutional practices which cash out these sentences of punishment. It is for this reason that much of the remainder of this book is devoted to the cultural aspects of punishment, and to an analysis of the signifiers and symbolic forms which give penal measures their social meaning.

The courts, as well as large sections of the public and many politicians, continue to address the issue of punishment using an expressive moral idiom, declaring substantive values and openly conveying emotive attitudes. Not infrequently—though not always—this is a punitive idiom, relaying outrage, condemnation, and the demand for retributive punishment. Penal institutions such as prisons, probation agencies, and community corrections groups—charged with the realization of these sentiments—are inevitably affected by the values thus expressed. They are affected by them directly when these values are translated into political decisions regarding budgets, permissible regimes, lengths of sentence, parole, and so on, and also indirectly, because these expressed values create a climate of opinion in which the institutions must work.[31] The cultivation of a neutral, managerial style within these institutions operates to modify these forces, both by bringing into play other values which the institutions tend to promote (such as cost efficiency, crime-control effectiveness, and administrative convenience), and by creating a kind of buffer between the public and the individual who is being punished, flattening out the highs and lows of popular sentiment, and ensuring that sanctions are delivered in a uniform and 'rational' manner.

The emergence of a penal bureaucracy as the organizational form through which penal sanctions are administered has meant that an instrumental, formal–rational style has been imposed upon a punitive process which embodies non-rational sentiments and non-instrumental aims. Actual punishments are thus always a compromise formation, being the outcome of these conflicting considerations and objectives. The urge to punish 'for its own sake'—as a matter of 'right' rather than as a means to an end—continues to exist in society, and punitive orientations are embedded in certain sectors of the criminal justice process. But this punitive force is ultimately exercised through an administrative apparatus, which, as we have seen, also tends to moderate and compromise its punitiveness. This conflict between the urge to punish and the forces of expediency and management runs through all aspects of the penal system, and, in an important sense, reflects the range of concerns and the deep ambivalence which the question of punishment evokes in the wider society. To some extent, institutional divisions (between court and prison, police and prosecution, probation and parole, etc.) help contain these conflicts, quarantining the different objectives into different segments of the system. But these boundaries merely structure these conflicts and make them manageable, rather than resolving them in any permanent way.

---

[31] Sykes suggests that penal administrators may sometimes turn this 'punitive' environment to their own ends, e.g. by using it to justify the kinds of stringent controls which help maintain a quiet, orderly prison. (*The Society of Captives*, p. 33).

9

Punishment and Culture

Cultural Forms and Penal Practices

1. THE QUESTION OF CULTURE

In this chapter, and in the two that follow, I want to move away a little from the theoretical perspectives which are most commonly used in the sociology of punishment in order to highlight an issue which is currently underemphasized: the question of culture. Although there are exceptions to this, the tendency of most sociologies in this area is to argue that penal systems have some kind of hidden social rationality rather than—or as well as—a purely penological one. Given this approach, the interpretative task is to show how penal processes in fact display the logic of power–knowledge techniques, of economic relations, or of modes of social organization, and thus reveal their external determinations and social functioning. Attention to values, sentiments, and non-rational commitments forms part of these analyses, but as we have seen—particularly in respect of Foucault's or Rusche and Kirchheimer's work—these issues are often in the background of analysis. Similarly, the tendency of most authors to adopt a functionalist style of explanation—showing how penality functions to promote control, or class, or solidarity—leads them to underemphasize questions of meaning. The 'significance' of penality for the actors involved gets translated into the 'significance' of penality for the functioning of the system—which is not at all the same thing.

In contrast to this, I want now to focus on the ways in which particular values and commitments enter into the penal process and become embodied there, and, more broadly, how cultural mentalities and sensibilities influence penal institutions. In part this will be an argument about the cultural determinations of punishment, but since the lines of causality run in both directions, and penality—like all institutions—contributes to the formation of culture, it might be better presented as an attempt to describe punishment as a cultural artefact, embodying and expressing society's cultural forms.

In one sense, this is what I have been doing all along, because political, economic, or organizational forms are themselves aspects of culture, at least if one takes this term in its widest sense as referring to the frameworks of meaning within which social action takes place.[1] The work of Foucault, of the Marxists, of Durkheim, and of Weber, each takes up a particular cultural trait or characteristic of modern society—its individualism, its rationality, its secularism, or its 'bourgeois' values—and explicates it in terms of a particular theory of social structure or of social change. So we have already encountered arguments which link cultural phenomena and penal institutions in a systematic,

[1] For a discussion of this 'semiotic' conception of culture, see Geertz, 'Thick Description: Toward an Interpretive Theory of Culture', in id., *The Interpretation of Cultures*, ch. 1.

if less than comprehensive, way. The problem is that each of these social theories gives a very selective account of culture, emphasizing cultural elements which fit into its general concerns while ignoring those which do not. Moreover, each of these traditions of social thought deals with cultural phenomena in its own particular way: sometimes—as with Weber and Durkheim—affording them a central place in accounts of social development; on other occasions— notably within the Marxist tradition—presenting them as the epiphenomenal effects of more solid, underlying structures. For the purposes of understanding the formation and social meaning of penality—a project which is quite distinct from these others—it is therefore necessary to construct a rather different cultural analysis, concentrating upon those elements which most influence punishment and showing how it is that they are expressed in the penal sphere.

However, there is one crucial point that we can take from these general social theories which has to do with the status of cultural phenomena. Each of the central traditions shows very clearly that the frameworks of meaning which we call culture cannot be separated off as a distinct realm of social life, independent of other social activity. Instead, culture must be viewed as inextricably bound up with material forms of action, ways of life, and situational conditions. The intricate, interwoven webs of significance which make up the fabric of a culture develop in a kind of dialectical relationship with social patterns of action, each supporting and facilitating the other, in much the same way that linguistic meaning is determined by social usage while simultaneously forming the framework in which that usage occurs. (Clifford Geertz captures this point well when he argues that culture and social structure are merely two aspects of the same 'thing'—meaningful social practice.)[2] We can thus talk about culture as a dimension of social life and a shaping context of social (and penal) action only if we do so in this related, grounded way.[3]

[2] Geertz, 'Thick Description: Toward an Interpretive Theory of Culture', in id., *The Interpretation of Cultures*, ch. 1.

[3] Some sociologists and historians have responded to this problem by talking of the different 'levels' or 'instances' or 'ensembles' which together make up the social formation. Thus the *Annales* school of historical writing identifies the 3 levels of *économies, sociétiés et civilizations* (economy and demography, social structure and culture), while Louis Althusser's structuralist Marxism revises this scheme to talk of the economic, political, and ideological instances. Each of these 'levels' is deemed to have its own characteristic institutions, dynamics, and forms of social practice; each develops at its own characteristic pace, leading or being led by the other levels; and each contributes to the complex, articulated structure which we call 'society'. Despite the attractions of this device—which for the *Annales* writers provided a way of doing 'regional' studies within a conception of total history, and for the Althusserians allowed a serious engagement with politics and culture within a framework not too far removed from the base–superstructure orthodoxy— this neat analytical division seems much too artificial and rather too tidy to form a useful way of carving up the world. Close investigation of any institution or symbol or site of social practice soon leads one back and forth across these supposed boundaries, blurring the distinctions and confounding the attempt to separate social realms in this way. Moreover, the fact that these 'levels' are always presented in the same ascending order, with economics first (and foundational) and the others coming afterwards, can be taken to suggest a hierarchy of causal priority which leaves cultural phenomena looking a little like ornamental icing upon a more substantial social cake.

Having suggested that we must attend to 'cultural' phenomena, and that 'culture' somehow accounts for patterns of penal behaviour, it is perhaps time to be a little more specific about what is meant by this term. The notion of 'culture', like other generic terms covering a diverse and complex field of phenomena, is the subject of much definitional debate and controversy. Indeed, in the field of anthropology, where it forms a leading concept, there are almost as many definitions of the term as there are anthropologists. In this discussion, I intend to use a wide definition which will cover those phenomena of cognition known as 'mentalities' and also those of affect or emotion usually termed 'sensibilities'. In its cognitive aspect, culture refers to all those conceptions and values, categories and distinctions, frameworks of ideas and systems of belief which human beings use to construe their world and render it orderly and meaningful. It thus covers the whole range of mental phenomena, high and low, elaborated and inarticulated, so that philosophies, sciences, and theologies are included alongside traditional cosmologies, folk prejudices, and 'plain common sense'. Likewise, normative schemes of taste, fashion, manners, and etiquette are no less a part of culture than are the developed systems of ethics, justice, and morality. These 'mentalities' or ways of thinking are, in turn, closely linked to ways of feeling and sensibilities, so that the cognitive aspects of culture become inseparable from its affective dimensions.[4] Thus, for example, scientific and rationalistic mentalities tend to foster a dispassionate, self-controlled 'objectivity' of feeling, while some religious thought-forms evoke a different structure of affect which may be passionate, stoical, or even, at times, ecstatic. The fact that thought and feeling are closely intertwined in this way means that when we talk of 'culture' we refer not just to intellectual systems and forms of consciousness but also to structures of affect and what might be called emotional configurations or 'sensibilities'.

The argument that will be adopted here is that these (socially constructed) sensibilities and mentalities have major implications for the ways in which we punish offenders. These cultural patterns structure the ways in which we think about criminals, providing the intellectual frameworks (whether scientific or religious or commonsensical) through which we see these individuals, understand their motivations, and dispose of them as cases. Cultural patterns also structure the ways in which we feel about offenders, not only through the evocative ritual processes which were discussed in Chapter 3, but also through the shaping of our sensibilities which I have begun to discuss here. The intensity of punishments, the means which are used to inflict pain, and the forms of suffering which are allowed in penal institutions are determined not just by considerations of expediency but also by reference to current mores and sensibilities. Our sense of what constitutes a conscionable, tolerable, or

---

[4] This conception of culture is considerably wider than that used by Durkheim in his early work and in his theory of punishment, where his discussion is focused upon 'morality'. His later work on religion and the social basis of epistemological categories is considerably closer to the present discussion.

'civilized' form of punishment is very much determined by those cultural patterns, as is our sense of what is intolerable or, as we say, 'inhumane'. Thus culture determines the contours and outer limits of penality as well as shaping the detailed distinctions, hierarchies, and categories which operate within the penal field. In the discussion which follows I will try to show just how these cultural patterns get reproduced in the penal sphere and with what effects.

The writer who has done more than anyone else to explicate the interaction between social relations and the psychological dynamics of 'sensibility' is Norbert Elias, and my discussion (like Pieter Spierenburg's work) will try to extend Elias's arguments into the sociology of punishment. As we shall see, Elias's study of 'The Civilizing Process' describes and analyses the long-term historical processes which resulted in the emergence of those distinctive cultural and psychic patterns which we call 'Western civilization', so I will be locating modern penality within an analytical account of 'civilization' and discussing it in these terms. For some sociologists of punishment, this may seem a surprising and rather retrograde step to take. After all, to talk of punishment and penal history in the same breath as 'civilization', echoes the complacency of modern common sense and all those Whiggish penal histories which present modern punishment as an outcome of unblemished progress— as a victory of humane values expressing the cultural supremacy of the present. In recent years sociologists and 'revisionist' historians have set themselves resolutely against this depiction of punishment as an expression of increasingly civilized humanity.[5] Treating modern punishment as an index of 'civilization' may, they suggest, make good reforming rhetoric, but it makes for bad history and uncritical sociology. In consequence, the most important advances in our interpretation of penal history have come about by applying an analytical scepticism to the reforming ideals and Enlightenment ethos which were traditionally credited with having brought about penal change. Revisionist historians have refused to accept the suggestion that penal changes represented (and were the product of) an improvement in the moral standards and humanity of society's guardians. And theorists such as Rusche and Kirchheimer, Michel Foucault, and Friedrich Nietzsche have brought to bear a 'hermeneutics of suspicion' which has relentlessly reduced penal philosophies, ethical ideals, and humanitarian sensibilities to the harder currencies of economic interest or the will to power.

As a reaction to uncritical moral histories of penal progress, this sceptical revision was probably necessary, and it has certainly been illuminating. It has succeeded in bringing to the surface important social and political aspects of punishment which had previously been hidden, and in challenging the complacent assumption that took modern penality to be more or less virtuous and beyond reproach. But this rejection of sensibilities and moral convictions from the explanatory framework of the sociology of punishment has been

---

[5] On revisionist histories of punishment, see Cohen and Scull (eds.), *Social Control and the State*.

altogether too vehement. The revisionist emphasis upon the implicit strategies of social control and domination which operate through punishment has hidden the important role which cultural values and sensibilities play in giving shape and limits to the penal measures which may be deployed.[6] It may be that hanging in chains, flogging bodies, or exposing offenders to crowd violence on scaffold or pillory no longer meshes with the strategies of rule and the political relations of our time and so their disappearance can be understood in political terms. But it is also the case that these measures would now be an affront to the normal sensibilities of individuals who have grown up in modern Western societies, and the reality and force of these sensibilities and moral commitments would soon be felt by any ruler who tried to reintroduce such 'barbaric' methods within that cultural context.[7]

What is needed now, in the sociology of punishment, is an analytical account of the cultural forces which influence punishment, and, in particular, an account of the patterns imposed upon punishment by the character of contemporary sensibilities. Such an account must acknowledge the reality and determinative capacity of feelings, sensibilities, behavioural proprieties, and cultural values, in order to trace their influence upon the organization of punishment. But there is no need for this analysis to be purely descriptive or uncritical. It should, for example, analyse the peculiar structure of these affects, examining how modern sensibilities are influenced by some events and not by others, how our emotional responses are attuned to recoil from open, physical violence but to tolerate coercion taking a different form, or to sympathize with some individuals while feeling indifferent towards the fate of others. Such an approach to sensibilities and their effects does not in the least preclude an understanding of interests and ulterior motives, although it does raise the difficult problem of their relationship. But then every attempt to fathom motivation must consider the interaction of conscience and convenience —of high feeling and low interest. As we will see, sentiments and sensibilities sometimes neatly coincide with interests of a political, economic, or ideological kind, as, for example, when humane measures also produce greater control and enhanced legitimacy. But sometimes the two pull in opposite directions, and this is where the reality of sensibilities is best revealed: where they show themselves to be a genuine social force and not just 'incidental music'.

Nor does this approach require us to desert sociology and turn to an abstracted psychology, since these sensibilities can be grounded in a developmental history which shows that cultural and psychic formations are themselves the outcome of changing patterns of social interdependency which provide

---

[6] Michael Ignatieff makes a related point when he insists that social relations (and therefore penal relations) can be based upon sympathy as well as domination. Ignatieff, 'State, Civil Society and Total Institutions: A Critique of Recent Histories of Punishment', in Cohen and Scull (eds.), *Social Control and the State*.

[7] As I will discuss in ch. 10, there are (all too many) occasions when the socially constructed inhibitions of civilized sensibility are overcome, or else evaded, but my point here is that such inhibitions do tend to operate in normal circumstances.

material supports and exert a situational pressure for these kinds of cultural development. Culture can thus be dealt with 'in its own terms'—as meaningful symbolic forms and authentic sensibilities—and yet located within the materiality of social and psychic structures. Mentalities, sensibilities, cultural and psychic forms have a life and a history of their own which can be traced and described from contemporary and historical sources. But like any aspect or 'level' of social existence, this form of life is dependent upon other forms, in particular upon social relations and institutions. Values and emotions may be individually experienced and nuanced, but they are patterned by cultural frameworks and supported by social structures. The trick, once again, is to view them in both their integrity and their relatedness.

An account of punishment, conceived in these terms, has the huge advantage of being able to take seriously the rhetoric and motivational formulations of penal reformers, which are so often framed in the language of sensibility, refined feeling, and humanitarianism. In doing so, the sociology of punishment would admit into its explanatory field those complex moral, religious, and emotional forces which historians have time and again identified as part of the motivational dynamic of penal reform.[8] But at the same time it would see these cultural forces against the background of social relations and historical change which has made it possible for people (often refined, privileged people of the upper or middling classes) to think and feel in these ways and to promote policies in accordance with their feelings. Morals and sensibilities are thus located within the grid of social interests and positions in a way which reflects the complex realities of cultural life.

By dealing in this way with the immediacies of culture rather than seeking to reduce them to something else, we deal directly with the medium in which punishments are conceived and developed. Penal laws and institutions are always proposed, discussed, legislated, and operated within definite cultural codes. They are framed in languages, discourses, and sign systems which embody specific cultural meanings, distinctions, and sentiments, and which must be interpreted and understood if the social meaning and motivations of punishment are to become intelligible. Indeed, even if one wishes to argue that economic or political interests form the basic determinants of penal policy, these 'interests' must necessarily operate through the medium of the laws, institutional languages, and penal categories which frame penal actions and organize their operation.[9]

Punishment, then, can be viewed as a complex cultural artefact, encoding the signs and symbols of the wider culture in its own practices. As such it forms one local element within the interlocking circuits of meaning which compose a society's cultural framework and can be analysed to trace its patterns of

---

[8] On this, see M. Wiener (ed.), *Humanitarianism or Control? A Symposium on Aspects of Nineteenth Century Social Reform in Britain and America, Rice University Studies*, 67 (1981).

[9] See my *Punishment and Welfare* for an extended analysis of how 'interests' and 'ideologies' come to be represented in criminological and penal discourses.

cultural expression. But we should be clear that this way of looking at punishment is simply that—a 'way of looking'—which helps us gain access to the social meanings which are implicit within the penal process. Any 'cultural' or 'discursive' approach to the phenomena should never lose sight of the fact that punishment is also, and simultaneously, a network of material social practices in which symbolic forms are sanctioned by brute force as well as by chains of reference and cultural agreement. Penal institutions form a functioning part of a structure of social action and a system of power, as well as being a signifying element within a symbolic realm, and in reality neither aspect ever exists without the other.

Penal practices are shaped by the symbolic grammar of cultural forms as well as by the more instrumental dynamics of social action, so that, in analysing punishment, we should look for patterns of cultural expression as well as for logics of material interest or social control. But in putting matters this way I do not mean to imply some kind of two-tier system in which a solid material base is merely overlaid with a cultural gloss, like the addition of a final coat of paint. All too often, in sociological analysis, the temptation is to split the thing analysed into two parts: an instrumental part and a symbolic part. The first is easily recognizable because it is composed of material practices which get things done while the second is merely decorative or 'discursive' and appears to have no substantive function.[10] This in turn implies a definite ranking of the two forms of analysis, and one tends to proceed to symbolic analysis as a kind of afterthought, particularly if an instrumental rationale has not been found.[11] I do not know if this kind of approach is ever very useful, but it certainly is not helpful as a way of dividing up punishment. As I have already tried to show, instrumental practices are always conceived within a context of cultural mentalities and sensibilities, so that instrumental and cultural forms are one and the same thing. Moreover, one can never separate out the instruments of punishment on the one hand and the symbols on the other: in this sphere (as in every other) symbols have a practical effect—the signs and symbols of condemnation are, as we have seen, central to and constitutive of punishment, while the instruments of penal practice have, as we will see, an inescapable cultural meaning.

2. CULTURAL FORMS AND PENAL PRACTICES

In their textbook account of the sociology of punishment, Sutherland and Cressey present what they describe as a cultural affinity theory of punishment.[12] This theory puts forward the proposition that the penal practices which a society adopts will tend to imitate or reflect the wider cultural forms which are

---

[10] For a discussion and critique of this tendency, see Geertz, *Negara: The Theatre State in Nineteenth Century Bali*, ch. 4.

[11] On this, see D. Sperber, *Rethinking Symbolism* (Cambridge, 1975).

[12] E. H. Sutherland and D. R. Cressey, *Criminology* (Philadelphia, 1970), chs. 14 and 15.

current within that society. Resemblances, parallels, and affinities thus link punishments to the wider culture and the specific forms of penality can be understood as an expression or even an effect of the general forms of culture. The problem with this 'theory' is that, as it stands, it is hopelessly banal. It tells us merely that the frameworks of meaning through which we generally lead our lives are likely to guide the ways in which we design our penal institutions—an insight of no great value or sophistication. However, the fault here lies not in Sutherland and Cressey's attempt to link punishment and culture but rather in the level at which they discuss the connection. In fact any attempt to discuss 'culture' in this generic way is likely to run into the same problems. This is because a culture is not a monolithic kind of thing which can feature as a simple variable in an explanatory formula. It is, instead, a rich composite of densely interwoven meanings which loses all its content wherever it is discussed in generic terms. Cultures are bric-à-brac ensembles of specifics, local details, and peculiarities and we are obliged to deal with them in these terms, which is why cultural history and anthropology—the cultural disciplines *par excellence*—rely so heavily upon ethnography and have so little time for grand theory and sweeping generalization. It may be useful to talk generically about culture when one is justifying its study and distinguishing it from other forms of life—as I have been doing in this chapter—but as soon as one embarks upon that analysis, general terms need to be replaced by particulars and matters of detail need to be brought into sharp focus.

That 'the ethnographic' is the appropriate mode for the discussion of culture and cultural effects creates a difficulty for me at this point. I want to discuss the ways in which cultural forms have a bearing upon penal forms, but I am precluded from dealing with this issue in the broad, theoretical terms which I have employed in previous chapters. On the other hand, I can hardly attempt to give an ethnographic account which would comprehend the myriad ways in which contemporary punishments are shaped by cultural characteristics and patterns—such work is the task of monographs, and it would require many of these to build up anything resembling an adequate picture of the whole. Instead what I propose to do is to give some brief illustrative examples, intended to show how particular mentalities and cultural conceptions have left their mark upon the history of penal practices. Thereafter I will turn to the question of sensibilities which will be dealt with more extensively and in more detail.

It is a characteristic of cultural forms that they tend to proliferate around differences which occur in the natural and social worlds.[13] Differences which appear to exist in the order of things are taken up, elaborated, and given cultural meanings which make sense of the distinctions involved, in a process which reworks the natural or the established in cultural terms, thereby

---

[13] See M. Douglas, *Natural Symbols: Explorations in Cosmology* (Harmondsworth, 1973), and id., *Purity and Danger: An Analysis of the Concepts of Pollution and Taboo* (London, 1966).

defining its significance 'for us'. Thus, for example, all cultures surround the events of birth and death with an elaborate patchwork of myths and meanings which function to domesticate these crucial happenings and allow us to cope with them in terms which appear to make some kind of sense. In precisely the same way, differences of age, of status, of gender, or of race find an important place in most cultures, and are elaborated in distinctive ways, so that to be 'young' or 'old', 'high' or 'low', 'male' or 'female', or 'black' or 'white' in a particular culture is to occupy a category which is defined in specific ways and surrounded by certain expectations, capacities, and understandings generated by the culture in question.

If we examine the history and practices of punishment it becomes clear that these same cultural distinctions and meanings have become operative in the penal sphere and have structured penal practice in accordance with their terms. To take an obvious example, all modern penal systems distinguish between adult offenders on the one hand, and juvenile or child offenders on the other, and the processes of 'juvenile justice' set in motion a whole series of cultural assumptions about the special characteristics of young people. So long as we remain within the mind-set of our contemporary culture, such distinctions appear obvious and necessary, seeming merely to reflect the true nature of things. But if we step outside these present-day assumptions, and view the issue historically, it becomes clear that the 'natural' distinctions of age have been understood very differently in other times by other cultures. Our particular conceptions of childhood and adolescence—and the assumptions of innocence, malleability, dependency, and incapacity which these conceptions entail—are relatively modern developments, having emerged in the eighteenth and nineteenth centuries.[14] Prior to this, the distinctions between adult and child were differently understood, involved less psychological distance and centred around a much earlier point in the individual's development. Accordingly, it was quite common in the seventeenth and eighteenth centuries for young persons aged 12 or 14 to be whipped, imprisoned, transported, or even executed. Indeed it was only from the mid-nineteenth century onwards that our modern conceptions of youth and childhood began to restructure the laws and practices of punishment in the ways that we now take for granted.[15]

The important point here, for our purposes, is that cultural patterns change over time, and that these cultural developments tend to exert a direct influence upon patterns of punishment. For the 'child savers' of the mid- to late nineteenth century in the USA and in Britain, the conviction and imprisonment of young people alongside adults was deeply shocking because it flew in the face of cultural conceptions of childhood which they and others held. It represented a scandal, a blatant contradiction between law and culture which became the

---

[14] See L. Stone, *The Family, Sex and Marriage in England, 1500–1800* (Harmondsworth, 1979); P. Aries, *Centuries of Childhood: A Social History of Family Life* (New York, 1965); J. Gillis, *Youth and History: Tradition and Change in European Age Relations* (New York, 1974).

[15] On the history of juvenile justice, see Sutton, *Stubborn Children*.

object of reforming campaigns and was eventually resolved by legislation setting up special reformatories, juvenile courts, and a more welfare-orientated approach to young offenders. Of course these reforming movements had other dimensions as well, involving professional interests, status conflicts, and political concerns, but there can be little doubt that genuinely felt cultural convictions played a crucial role in bringing about penal change.[16]

Distinctions based upon gender differences also play an important part in structuring penal practice. Historians such as Beattie and Spierenburg point out that in the seventeenth and eighteenth centuries female offenders were treated rather differently from their male equivalents, sometimes being dealt with more leniently on account of their sex, at other times being subjected to distinctive forms of sanction, such as garotting—which was the preferred form of execution for women in seventeenth-century Europe—or burning, which was the fate of women condemned for witchcraft. In our own time, female offenders are also dealt with in gender-specific ways which reflect traditional conceptions of the female role and its pathologies. In recent years a growing literature has developed which has documented these 'gendered' aspects of criminal justice, showing how conceptions of 'a woman's place' have influenced criminological understandings of female crime, the practices of prosecution and sentencing, and, most clearly of all, the special regimes and attitudes adopted in women's prisons and reformatory institutions.[17] At every stage in the penal process, cultural understandings of what women are like, and how they ought to behave, operate to define the appropriate response to their misconduct and to structure the punishment of women and girls. Of course precisely the same is true in respect of male offenders, who are understood and punished within the cultural framework of 'masculinity', no less than are female offenders in terms of 'femininity'. But precisely because the whole culture of femininity is currently subject to the massive challenge of the women's movement—a movement which, whatever its economic and political dimensions, is primarily a *cultural* movement—we are nowadays able to see more clearly than ever before just how much society's penal practice regarding women has been shaped by the arbitrary conventions of culture.

As recently as the eighteenth and even the nineteenth century, the differences of rank and social status which formed part of society's hierarchical culture were translated into differentiations in penal law and practice, so that nobles could expect to be punished differently from commoners (e.g. by being fined instead of whipped, beheaded instead of hanged, or by undergoing different

---

[16] For an account of juvenile justice history which stresses political and professional interests, see A. M. Platt, *The Child Savers: The Invention of Delinquency* (Chicago, 1977).

[17] See Carlen, *Women's Imprisonment*; E. Freedman, *Their Sisters' Keepers: Women's Prison Reform in America, 1830–1930* (Ann Arbor, 1981); H. Allen, *Justice Unbalanced* (Milton Keynes, 1987); C. Smart, *Women, Crime and Criminology* (London, 1976); P. Carlen and A. Worrall (eds.), *Gender, Crime and Justice* (Milton Keynes, 1987); A. M. Morris, *Women, Crime and Criminal Justice* (Oxford, 1987).

conditions of captivity).[18] And as we saw in our discussion of Hay's work on eighteenth-century England, matters of status and community standing were assumed to be a legitimate basis for differentiation in penal treatment (and this would apply to the distinctions between insider and outsider, local and stranger as well as between high and low). Even more recently, the racial distinctions which were current in British and US culture functioned to differentiate the treatment that blacks received in the penal system from that of whites.[19] Such distinctions are no longer respectable in the avowedly egalitarian, democratic legal cultures of twentieth-century Britain or the USA, nor do they exist in the legislation which regulates penal practices, though class and race distinctions continue to operate in more subtle and less visible ways. If the women's movement and feminist criminologists succeed in erasing the formal distinctions which currently structure penal practices along gender-specific lines—and there are already signs that this is happening—then this will, among other things, provide a striking example of how cultural movements shape the forms of punishment in accordance with their terms. On the other hand, the difficulties encountered in trying to eradicate the informal operation of prejudices which affect the penal treatment of racial, ethnic, and status groups long after such discrimination has become illegal, is testimony to the deep-seated nature of cultural patterns and their resistance to rapid change.

3. RELIGION, HUMANITARIANISM, AND OTHER CULTURAL FORMS

When historians talk of the cultural forces which have influenced penal policy, the forces which they have in mind are most often religion and humanitarianism. This is especially true where they are referring to the work of penal reformers in the eighteenth and nineteenth centuries, since religious conviction and humanitarian sensibility tended to play a crucial part in the motivation of those groups and in their understanding of the reformative process. Leaving aside the question of sensibilities—which will be discussed in the next chapter—it is clear that throughout the history of penal practice religion has been a major force in shaping the ways in which offenders are dealt with. My discussion of Durkheim's work has already shown how the religious mentalities of ancient societies and 'primitive' social groups often invested the penal process with a wholly religious meaning, so that punishment was understood as a necessary sacrifice to an aggrieved deity. In such cultures, crime is associated with sin, impurity, and danger and the act of punishment involves a process of expiation as well as a ritual cleansing of polluting elements in society. Of course, from the medieval period onwards, Western legal systems

[18] Thorsten Sellin's study of *Slavery and the Penal System* argues that long-term changes in the stratification of Western societies allowed punishments that were once reserved for slaves to be inflicted first upon low-class freemen and ultimately upon all offenders, regardless of social status.

[19] On the treatment of blacks in the American South during the 19th cent., see Ayers, *Vengeance and Justice*. On the question of racial integration in contemporary prisons, see Jacobs, *New Perspectives on Prisons and Imprisonment*, ch. 4.

have increasingly separated themselves from religious authorities and conceptions, but something of that earlier, religious culture still remains, and, from the Middle Ages right up to the present, religious belief has been an important force in shaping the practice and evolution of punishment.

To take only the best-documented instances, it is clear that the medieval Roman Catholic Church did much to develop the penal techniques which were later borrowed by secular states. As we have seen, the incompatibility of blood sanctions with clerical status and beliefs led the ecclesiastical courts to develop their own institutions of imprisonment, while the spiritual exercises of the monastic orders gave rise to the practices of cellular confinement and penitential discipline. Indeed, as late as the end of the eighteenth century, the Vatican prison served as a model for prison design in both Europe and America. In much the same way, the Protestant Reformation played a part in the development of secular imprisonment, first of all in the Dutch houses of correction of the sixteenth century, then later in the Quaker penitentiaries of the early nineteenth century, helping to formulate a combination of solitary cellular confinement and productive work which was supposed to produce spiritual redemption as well as painful bodily punishment. One can also see the traces of this religious inheritance marked in the fabric of many of the older prison buildings, especially those penitentiaries which employed a vernacular of spiritual regeneration and religiously inspired reform. The chapel-in-miniature design of the cells at New Jersey's Trenton prison, with their vaulted ceilings, their small windows high up on the wall, and their stoop-to-enter doorways, still stand today as an architectural reminder of this religious vision and its impact upon prison design, as do many other buildings which followed this penitential model of imprisonment.

This religious influence upon prison reform and penal policy remained a powerful one throughout the nineteenth century, as the work of Ignatieff and others has shown.[20] Evangelicals were in the vanguard of reforming movements both in Britain and in the USA, helping to ameliorate conditions of captivity or to aid prisoners upon their release, and later developing alternatives to imprisonment such as probation, which began as a form of missionary work funded by church-based temperance societies. Even today, Churches and religious groups are still in the forefront of those who agitate for penal reform or provide resources for needy offenders, and prison chaplains continue to play a small part in the life of the prisons even if their spiritual and pastoral mission is nowadays limited in its influence and often indistinguishable from the social worker role.

One of the reasons why the influence of religion upon punishment is so evident to the observer is that religious cultural systems are clearly articulated. Religions have creeds, theologies, and languages of their own, as well as churches, office-bearers, and a community of believers who identify themselves

---

[20] Ignatieff, *A Just Measure of Pain.*

in these terms. Particularly as we look back from a more secular age, it is easy to trace the impact of religious belief in this field, and there are distinguishing terms to hand—such as 'Protestant', 'Catholic', 'Quaker', 'Methodist', 'evangelical', and so on—which are readily available for our analytical purposes. But there are also other cultural forms which are important in this area and which should be given a place in our analysis. Such forms may be less easy to distinguish, never having been articulated in quite the same self-conscious way, and their influence upon punishment may be rather more difficult to discern; but if we are to understand the specific forms which penal practices take, and their relationship to the wider culture, then it is important to track these down.

One important example of a cultural form which has changed over time and has influenced penal practice accordingly is the conception of 'justice'. Historically, this term has usually been understood—especially by those historical actors who have used it to guide their conduct—as a timeless, unchanging category, so that the demands of justice, properly recognised, will always be the same. The notion of justice has thus been perceived as being beyond culture and outside of history; a kind of absolute which is unaffected by change or by convention. However, even if past generations believed that their invocation of justice was an appeal to an absolute value, it is clear that the conceptions of what this value demanded, and of what justice implied, have changed over time in important ways. Precisely because justice was understood as unchanging, any changes in the conventions whereby justice was enacted have tended to be gradual and unannounced.[21] Nevertheless, historians of criminal justice have begun to uncover important changes in the mentalities through which justice was conceived and enacted at different times, and these changing conceptions have been an important determinant of penal practice and its evolution.

John Beattie's detailed study of criminal courts and penal practice in England in the seventeenth and eighteenth centuries clearly reveals a process of change whereby one conception of justice slowly gave way to a rather different one, causing consequential changes in penal practice. Having described the personalistic, heavily discretionary decision-making processes which were characteristic of grand juries in the seventeenth century, and the virtual khadi-justice dispensed by officials who decided upon crucial questions such as sentences and pardons, Beattie argues that these procedures, far from being abuses or irregularities, were in fact a faithful enactment of the conceptions of justice which were then current. Thus, for example, the fact that jury members knew the accused, had formed views about his character, or even had a personal interest in the case, was no reason for bar or disqualification since 'the jury was not engaged in administering the law in the interests of a narrow and

---

[21] Revolutionary social groups sometimes explicitly reject pre-revolutionary conceptions of justice, calling them a sham and putting a self-consciously different conception of justice in their place (e.g. 'socialist' substantive justice in place of 'bourgeois' formal justice).

abstract ideal of justice, but rather in pursuit of the more general aim of preserving order and harmony in society by a variable and personal application of the State's coercive powers'.[22] Similarly, the tendency to treat some offenders more lightly than others on the grounds of gender or of character did not reflect a failure of justice so much as 'the absence of a conviction that what is meted out to one ought in justice to be done to all'.[23]

By the beginning of the nineteenth century, however, following the rise of Enlightenment ideals and the socio-political transformations which had engendered them, these older conceptions of justice were being replaced by rather different ones. The old substantive concerns and personalistic style gradually gave way to a more formal–rational approach to doing justice in which uniformity, proportionality, equality in law, and the strict application of rules came to dominate criminal law procedures. What had once been seen as the proper way of enacting the principles of justice now came to seem scandalous and unjust, at least to certain increasingly important groups within society and to the reformers who articulated their discontents.[24] In effect, the dominant culture and mental habits of one period were being slowly replaced by those of another, and the widespread influence of these newer mentalities—at least among the intelligentsia and middle classes—formed an important lever for practical change. This 'mental sea-change' is summed up by Beattie as follows, 'by 1800 a significant body of opinion was ready to . . . support penal measures that more nearly reflected a sense of the equality of men, of the worth of the individual and the rights of all men to fair and equal treatment before the courts'.[25]

Nor was this the last change that conceptions of justice were to undergo. At the turn of the twentieth century, the strict classicism and formal justice of the Enlightenment began to be challenged by new conceptions which placed less stress upon formal equality, proportionality, and strictly applied general rules and which emphasized instead the importance of substantive results, the need for individualized consideration, and the value of professional flexibility. This new, more substantive conception of justice (which was linked to the politics of social democracy and welfarism in the same way that classicist conceptions were linked to a conception of liberalism and the market economy) has existed ever since as an important strand in our cultural fabric—a strand which runs alongside the still resilient liberal tradition in a continuous process of dialogue and interplay. Moreover, as I have described in detail elsewhere, these welfarist conceptions of justice have been sufficiently powerful to bring about a series of practical changes in twentieth-century penal policy which have been of immense importance for the day-to-day running of the system.[26] In point of

---

[22] Beattie, *Crime and the Courts*, p. 403.   [23] Ibid. 439.

[24] On the links between competing social groups and competing conceptions of justice in 19th-cent. England, see R. McGowan, 'The Image of Justice and Reform of the Criminal Law in Early Nineteenth Century England'.

[25] Beattie, *Crime and the Courts*, p. 631.   [26] Garland, *Punishment and Welfare*.

fact, many of the intractable conflicts and dilemmas which emerge in contemporary penal practice—such as the clash between individualized sentences and the requirements of equality, or between the judge's desire to punish and the social worker's concern to help—are actually expressions of contradictory conceptions of justice which exist side by side within modern culture. Our inability to resolve these antinomies, or to render penal practice fully consistent, is not the fault of penal policy-makers—it is a consequence of modern society's cultural pluralism and the multiple conceptions of justice which find endorsement in the political community at large.

In the same way that cultural conceptions of justice have changed over time and have influenced penal practice accordingly, so too have conceptions of the criminal and of the nature of criminality. A history of criminological ideas would show important changes over time in the terms used to describe and to understand offenders, and of course these cultural conceptions of what the criminal is have influenced the ways in which societies have dealt with this shifting category of persons. A few examples drawn from historical studies can serve to illustrate this point.

Thomas Zeman's description of criminal justice in seventeenth-century Puritan Massachusetts describes how, in that community, criminals were understood and addressed through the mental categories provided by Protestant theology.[27] Individual offenders were viewed as sinners whose evil actions bore witness to an individual failure of will but also to the wretchedness of the human condition. Consequently, the appropriate social response to this sin was at once punitive and redemptive: the offender had to be punished in the name of the Law and also for the salvation of his or her soul. Puritan penal rituals—in theory at least—were not intended to isolate offenders and show them to be alien. Instead the arrangements of the ceremony, and the proclamations, sermons, and confessions which accompanied it, were intended to demonstrate an intimate link between the offender and the community of believers. Onlookers were made to feel that they too could be tempted into sin, particularly if they failed each other in their duty of mutual support and moral exhortation. In other words the sinner-offender was not conceived as 'Other' but rather as a kind of Protestant Everyman, a living example of the potential for evil which lies in every heart and against which every soul must be vigilant. In keeping with this conception, the dénouement of each public ceremony was aimed not at the vanquishing of the enemy, but instead at the reinclusion of the atoned and repentant sinner.[28]

---

[27] Zeman, 'Order, Crime and Punishment: The American Criminological Tradition'.

[28] For similar accounts of the relation between sin and crime in early modern England, see Sharpe, *Crime in Early Modern England, 1550–1750*, p. 6, and esp. Faller, *Turned to Account*, which states that 'whenever the question of the criminal's nature and motives arose, it was not his essential difference from the law-abiding majority that tended to be emphasized but his essential similarity. The root cause of crime, one reads again and again, is human depravity. And as all men are equally tainted from birth by original sin, criminals are not different in kind from other people,

The conception of the criminal which Beattie's research identifies in seventeenth-century England still bears some traces of a religious tradition but is increasingly phrased in secular moral terms. Here the criminal is also seen as morally corrupt, but this wickedness and corruption has more to do with a way of life than with a failure of will or a sinful soul. Men became corrupt because they strayed from the paths of respectability, neglecting their work and their families, drinking and gambling, and falling into evil habits. Criminals, it was widely believed, had served 'a kind of apprenticeship in wickedness in which they proceeded from minor wrongs to the very greatest crimes and eventually reached a point when they were beyond redemption'.[29] Accordingly, the primary concern of the courts was to adjudge the offender's character, his or her dangerousness and standing in the community, deciding on that basis whether he or she was an habitual who should be hanged or an otherwise worthy person who should be given a second chance.[30] This conception of the criminal as a being formed by habit was very clearly reiterated in the philosophical and psychological writings of the seventeenth and eighteenth centuries. Locke's mechanistic conception of the person formed by sense impressions, and Hartley's materialist psychology—both of which influenced the design of early prison regimes—were thus to some extent scientific reworkings of common-sense ideas which already had a place in judicial practice.[31]

By the middle of the nineteenth century, the writings of Beccaria, Bentham, and Mill had brought into cultural circulation a slightly different conception of the offender—one which emphasized the person's reasoning faculties and his ability to calculate interests and utilities. This hedonistic conception of the criminal, alongside the earlier Lockian one, played an important part in shaping the penal codes of this period, giving pride of place to deterrent measures and emphasizing the freedom of all rational individuals to obey the law. Later still, at the beginning of the twentieth century, the new scientific criminologies put forward a conception of the criminal as an abnormal human type, shaped by genetic, psychological, or social factors and, to some extent, unable to resist an inherent tendency towards criminal conduct. Once again, these new conceptions helped bring about a restructuring of penal practice, so that a formal process of character assessment became an important ancillary to sentencing, and specialist institutions and regimes were developed to deal with character types such as 'habituals', 'inebriates', 'psychopaths', and 'delinquents'.

---

only in degree' (p. 54). Cynthia Herrup suggests that it was 'the eventual erosion of the religious subtext in law [which] allowed offenders to be redefined as criminals and all criminals to be seen as alien' ('Law and Morality in Seventeenth Century England').

[29] Beattie, *Crime and the Courts*, p. 421.
[30] Ibid. 436.
[31] On this, see Ignatieff, *A Just Measure of Pain*; Bender, *Imagining the Penitentiary*, and Evans, *The Fabrication of Virtue*.

This last example shows how, in modern society, certain cultural themes—such as the nature of crime and criminals—have come to be articulated in what is thought of as a 'scientific' mode, that is to say, as 'knowledges' or discourses which claim a special relationship to truth. Increasingly, from the nineteenth century onwards, penal practice has been influenced by a variety of such knowledges, in the shape of scientific criminology, penology, psychology, medicine, and so on, which is what Foucault has in mind when he talks of penality being 'redefined by knowledge'. For my purposes here, it is useful to think of such knowledges not as revealed truths standing outside of time and place, but instead as specific cultural forms, to be considered alongside conceptions of justice, religious traditions, and all the other cultural themes I have mentioned.[32]

Precisely because 'sciences' (like organized religions) tend to be the most clearly specified of cultural forms, with their own specialized vocabularies, rationalities, and discursive structures, it has been possible to trace in some detail the influence of some of these discourses upon modern penality. This, indeed, is the project begun by Foucault when he traced the impact of disciplinary discourses upon penal institutions, but others such as Robert Nye, John Bender, and myself have followed this lead and have mapped out the influence upon the penal realm of discourses such as the medical theory of degeneracy, eugenics, scientific criminology, and certain philosophical conceptions of selfhood which also feature in the eighteenth-century novel. The story which each of these studies tells is a complex and very particular one, and I make no attempt to summarize them here, but it is worth emphasizing a point which is repeated throughout all such work, and it is this: to the extent that the distinctiveness of 'scientific' ideas allows their influence to be traced in any detail, these studies all tend to show the incorrigible complexity and overdetermination of the cultural realm as it relates to practice. In every case, a specific cultural form comes to influence or act upon penal practice only through a process of struggle, compromise, and alliance with a range of competing cultural forms, and tends to be reworked in its context-of-use to fit with the institutional patterns of the penal realm. Thus while it may be an easy matter to show in broad terms the influence of a particular knowledge, value system, or cultural form upon penal practice, the actual route by which one comes to influence the other, and the exact nature of that influence, are often much less easy to specify.

4. PENAL CULTURE AND ITS SOCIAL SETTING

One might summarize the concerns of this chapter by describing the problem in the following way. The diverse practices, routines, and procedures which make

---

[32] To say this is not at all to diminish the truth claims made by these discourses, but merely to identify them as self-consciously crafted and elaborated cultural forms which have been produced within that sphere of cultural life which we term 'science'.

up the penal realm are always undertaken within an immediate framework of meaning which one might term 'penal culture'. This penal culture is the loose amalgam of penological theory, stored-up experience, institutional wisdom, and professional common sense which frames the actions of penal agents and which lends meaning to what they do. It is a local, institutional culture—a specific form of life—which has its own terms, categories, and symbols and which forms the immediate meaningful context in which penal practices exist. As I argued above, any external force or determinant which seeks to transform penal practice—whether it be a law, a policy directive, or some economic or cultural rationality—must first transform this penal culture if it is to become effective.

The primary 'bearers' of this penal culture, and the agents who do most to transform cultural conceptions into penal actions, are, of course, the 'operatives' of the penal system—the personnel who staff the courts, the prisons, the probation offices, and the state departments. In consequence, a key determinant of penal practice will always be the training, education, and social upbringing received by decision-makers such as judges, prison guards, and state officials. But these professionals always receive their education and carry out their tasks within a broader cultural context, and are thus affected by the climate of public opinion and the tone of governmental direction. Consequently, the specific culture of punishment in any society will always have its roots in the broader context of prevailing (or recently prevailing) social attitudes and traditions.[33]

My concern here has been to delineate the relationships which link this penal culture to the wider social setting in which it exists, and, in particular, to show how certain cultural themes flow through both 'punishment' and 'society'. Part of this task has already been achieved in earlier chapters where particular aspects of penal culture were explained as the products of external social forces. Thus in discussing terms such as 'less eligibility', 'equality, uniformity, proportionality', or the 'principles of surveillance and discipline', and linking them to the wider networks of power and economy, theorists such as Rusche and Kirchheimer and Foucault were in fact explicating penal culture and grounding it in the structures of social life. However, in linking penal culture directly to social structure in this way, these accounts tend to leave out of account large stretches of the mediating cultural framework in which penality exists—particularly those forms of cultural life such as religious sentiment or humane sensibility which do not fit with their theoretical approach. This chapter and the next try to show how one can make good that omission.

---

[33] On the importance of the educational training of penal professionals, esp. sentencers, and on the relation between criminal justice élites and the wider climate of public opinion, see Downes, *Contrasts in Tolerance*. On the occupational culture of American prison guards, see Jacobs, *New Perspectives on Prisons and Imprisonment*, ch. 6. On the cultural framework within which Scottish criminal justice operates, see Carlen, *Women's Imprisonment* and Young, *Punishment, Money and Legal Order*.

The general position that is outlined, then, is that penal practices exist within a specific penal culture which is itself supported and made meaningful by wider cultural forms, these, in turn, being grounded in society's patterns of material life and social action. It hardly needs to be said that the major cultural themes which appear in penality—conceptions of justice, of crime, religious forms, attitudes towards age, race, class, gender, and so on—did not develop independently there, nor do they stand on their own as isolated beliefs. Like all cultural elements they are enmeshed with wider belief-systems and mentalities, deriving their sense and credibility from their ability to resonate with established ways of thinking and understanding. Nor does it need to be stressed again that these cultural themes are bound up with the parameters of material life and the grounded structures of social action. But to say that cultural forms are 'bound up with' or 'supported by' material practices is not to imply that they are merely a reflection of something else, or that their intrinsic characteristics are fully determined elsewhere. The discourses, symbolic forms, and mental representations of the cultural sphere have their own *sui generis* reality and their own internal dynamics. The mentalities of common sense, the arguments of theology, the principles of justice, the demands of feminist ideology, or the discourses of criminology—to mention just a few of the cultural forms we have encountered—all display a logic of their own, and are developed through mental work and creative, intellectual labour. Consequently, to say that penal culture exists in a social setting and is supported and constrained by wider cultural and structural forces, is not to deny the creative work that goes on in the penal realm itself.

This point is most forcibly made if one pays attention to the distinctive cultural artefacts that have been developed within the penal realm. Things such as prison buildings and bread-and-water diets, cranks and tread-wheels and picking oakum, lock-step marching and the gallows procession, scaffolds and pillories and electric chairs—not to mention inmate subcultures and the languages, roles, and relations they create—however much they owe to external forces, are, in the first place, artefacts which were created within the penal realm and which embody penal culture. Each specific item which has been developed for penological use will have been shaped, first of all, by the needs and the meanings of its penal context and by the usages of penal actors and authorities. Contained in the concrete details of each penal fact is a story of penal place and penal purpose and of the penological culture from which it derives. But precisely because penal institutions never exist in a vacuum, these specific forms and meanings can also be traced out, beyond the penal sphere, to reveal the linkages which tie penal culture into the frameworks and categories of the world outside. The analysis of penality's meanings—like the cultural analysis of any other form of life—will thus be a matter of tacking back and forth between a detailed ethnographic description of the specific meanings which clothe penal practice, and a more generalized conception of those mentalities which are dominant elsewhere in social life.

10

Punishment and Sensibilities

A Genealogy of 'Civilized' Sanctions

1. THE SOCIAL CONSTRUCTION OF SENSIBILITY

In the previous chapter, I dealt mainly with the cognitive aspects of culture, focusing upon the intellectual forms and systems of belief through which particular ways of punishing have been formulated and understood. But, as I noted earlier, an adequate account of culture must refer not just to mentalities and forms of thought, but also to what are known as sensibilities and ways of feeling. Cultures are differentiated not just by the mental equipment with which they endow their members but also by the particular psychic structures and personality types to which they give rise. Emotions, sensibilities, and structures of affect do, of course, have their roots in the basic psychological dynamics of human beings—the human organism is not an empty vessel into which culture simply pours its contents. But, as historians and anthropologists have shown, the basic drives and emotions of human beings are differentially developed by various forms of socialization and social relations, leading us to think of 'human nature' not as a universal disposition but instead as a historical result of culture acting upon nature in various ways.[1] All cultures promote certain forms of emotional expression and forbid others, thus contributing to a characteristic structure of affects and a particular sensibility on the part of their members. The range and refinement of the feelings experienced by individuals, their sensitivities and insensitivities, the extent of their emotional capacities, and their characteristic forms of gratification and inhibition show considerable variation across cultures. They display the very different ways in which specific cultural forms and practices interact with the structure of the human psyche and its development.[2]

The question of how sensibilities are structured and how they change over time is important here because it has a direct bearing upon punishment. We have seen already that crime and punishment are issues which provoke an emotional response on the part of the public and those involved. Feelings of

---

[1] On the way in which culture 'completes' the unfinished human organism, and is thus inextricably involved in the creation of 'human nature' in both the evolution of the species and the formation of individuals, see Geertz, 'The Impact of the Concept of Culture on the Concept of Man', and 'The Growth of Culture and the Evolution of Mind', both of which are reprinted in id. *The Interpretation of Cultures.*

[2] For discussions and case-studies illustrating this variation, see R. Harré (ed.), *The Social Construction of Emotions* (Oxford, 1986), and P. Hirst and P. Woolley, *Social Relations and Human Attributes* (London, 1982). The essays in the Harré collection argue that emotions are more or less entirely social constructions, being forms of learned conduct adapted to contexts of social action and social role. Hirst and Woolley—like Norbert Elias and Sigmund Freud—give more weight to innate psychic forces which, despite being overlaid by social training and only expressed in social codes, are never fully determined by social relations.

fear, hostility, aggression, and hatred compete with pity, compassion, and forgiveness to define the proper response to the law-breaker. Moreover, to the extent that punishment implies the use of violence or the infliction of pain and suffering, its deployment will be affected by the ways in which prevailing sensibilities differentiate between permissible and impermissible forms of violence, and by cultural attitudes towards the sight of pain.

I have argued earlier that penal policy tends to be considered today in administrative, means–end ways, rather than as a moral or fully social issue. But penal measures will only be considered at all if they conform to our conceptions of what is emotionally tolerable. The matter-of-fact administration of most penal policy is possible because it relies upon measures which have already been deemed tolerable and the morality of which can be taken for granted. By and large, the prior question of 'acceptability' has been settled—and in part forgotten—but it is a prior question nevertheless. I do not mean by this that governments and penal authorities always take care to search their consciences, or put morality before expediency in their use of punishments—clearly they do not. But political decisions are always taken against a background of mores and sensibilities which, normally at least, will set limits to what will be tolerated by the public or implemented by the penal system's personnel. Such sensibilities force issues of 'propriety' upon even the most immoral of governments, dictating what is and is not too shameful or offensive for serious consideration.

There is thus a whole range of possible punishments (tortures, maimings, stonings, public whippings, etc.) which are simply ruled out as 'unthinkable' because they strike us as impossibly cruel and 'barbaric'—as wholly out of keeping with the sensibilities of modern, civilized human beings. This is often experienced as a kind of visceral judgment—one which expresses emotional repugnance rather than rational objection. Such judgments, based upon the prevailing sensibilities, define the outer contours of possibility in the area of penal policy. Usually this boundary line has the unspoken, barely visible character of something which everyone takes for granted. It becomes visible, and obvious, only when some outrageous proposal crosses the line, or else when evidence from other times or other places shows how differently that line has been drawn elsewhere. It is therefore stating the obvious—but also reminding ourselves of something we can easily forget—to say that punishments are, in part, determined by the specific structure of our sensibilities, and that these sensibilities are themselves subject to change and development. In the remainder of this chapter I intend to investigate the precise nature of these modern sensibilities, to ask how they came to have their specific forms and with what consequences, and to explore their implications for the ways in which we now choose to punish.

In the vocabulary which is used to evaluate punishments there are a number of terms and distinctions which express the voice of sensibility. We talk of some punishments (usually those of other nations or other times) as being 'offensive', 'repugnant', 'barbaric', 'savage', or, in the language of the Eighth Amendment, 'cruel and unusual'.[3] In the same way we counterpose 'humane' penalties to 'inhumane' ones and insist that 'severe' measures, which may be tolerable, must not be confused with 'cruelty', which is not. There is, however, a single master-term which specifically captures the idea of refined sensibility and is frequently used as a touchstone in discussions of this kind; this is the notion of 'the civilized'. To say that a penalty is or is not 'civilized' is to measure it against the sensibilities which modern Westerners recognize as their own. 'Civilization' is a generic term conveying a fundamental distinction between the self-conscious refinement of feeling to which modern Western society lays claim, and the harsher, more primitive ways attributed to other peoples. As such, it is a powerfully evocative concept which has extensive connotations within our culture.

The link between the broad notion of 'civilization' and the particularities of a reformed penal system was first made by the Enlightenment critics of the eighteenth century, who protested that the European legal systems of their day still employed methods of punishment which should have been intolerable to any society which claimed to be civilized. Ever since then, the standards of 'the civilized' have been used to evaluate penality by critics and apologists alike, as in Winston Churchill's much quoted declaration that a society's penal methods are an index and measure of its civilization, or again, in Dostoevsky's remark that 'the standards of a nation's civilization can be judged by opening the doors of its prisons'.[4]

In its rhetorical use, the notion of 'the civilized' can, of course, be a bland and ethnocentric way of distinguishing others from ourselves, thus linking it into the worst forms of class or race prejudice and national chauvinism. But, as we will see, it can also be taken in a much more neutral, non-evaluative, *analytical* sense to describe a particular configuration of sensibilities and attitudes which is peculiar to Western societies in the modern period and which represents the outcome of a long developmental process of cultural and psychic change. Taken in this latter sense, the concept of a 'civilized' punishment is brimming with cultural and historical significance, and an analysis of its distinguishing characteristics offers us a way of identifying the contours of those modern sensibilities which operate in the penal sphere.

The indispensable guide for any such enquiry is the work of Norbert Elias and, in particular, his two-volume account of *The Civilizing Process*, first published in 1939.[5] In the course of this historical study, Elias sets out a detailed description of the ways in which Western sensibilities have changed since the late medieval period, identifying a number of broad developmental

---

[3] See L. C. Berkson, *The Concept of Cruel and Unusual Punishment* (Lexington, Mass., 1975).

[4] F. M. Dostoevsky, *The House of the Dead* (Harmondsworth, 1985). Churchill's declaration was that 'the mood and temper of the public in regard to the treatment of crime and criminals is one of the most unfailing tests of the civilization of any country' (Hansard, col. 1354, 20 July 1910).

[5] N. Elias, *The Civilizing Process*, i. *The History of Manners* (Oxford, 1978), and ii. *State Formation and Civilization* (Oxford, 1982).

patterns which seem to underlie the multitude of tiny, specific, and very gradual changes of attitude and conduct which the historical sources reveal. Having described this pattern of change, and the typical directions which it has taken, Elias then sets out an explanatory account which links changes of sensibility and individual psychology with wider changes in social organization and modes of interaction. Unfortunately, Elias has little to say about the way in which the history of punishment fits into the broad developments which he describes. He offers some brief remarks about the place of the gallows in the medieval world of the knight (it stands in 'the background of his life. It may not be very important but at any rate, it is not a particularly painful sight'),[6] and he notes, on the very first page, that 'the form of judicial punishment' is one of the social facts to which 'civilization' typically refers.[7] But beyond this, nothing specific is said. Nevertheless, it seems perfectly clear that Elias's analysis of the development and characteristics of modern sensibilities has a profound importance for the study of punishment, which, as I have argued, is a sphere of social life deeply affected by conceptions of what is and is not 'civilized'.

In the pages which follow I will set out the major themes of Elias's work and show how they can help us understand the historical development of penal sanctions and institutions. In doing so I will focus mainly upon his account of modern sensibilities and the characteristic structure of fears, anxieties, and inhibitions produced by the controls and rituals of contemporary culture. (It should be noted, however, that this psychic–cultural dimension forms only one aspect of Elias's general theory of social organization and development—a project conceived on the grand scale of Weber and Durkheim and synthesizing many of the arguments of these two writers. As one might expect, Elias refuses to abstract 'culture' or even 'psychology' from their roots in social life and organization.) Thereafter I will seek to analyse—and criticize—the interaction between contemporary sensibilities and contemporary forms of punishment. By means of such an analysis it may be possible not only to understand punishment better, but also to identify some important levers of penal change which other sociological accounts tend to overlook.

2. NORBERT ELIAS AND THE CIVILIZING PROCESS

In Elias's work, the concept of civilization refers to 'a specific transformation of human behaviour'.[8] The 'behaviour' which he describes includes the individual conduct of men and women as well as the kinds of collective behaviour which are manifested in cultural practices, rituals, and institutions. In each case he is concerned not only with the behaviours themselves and the detailed characteristics which they display, but also with the underlying psychic and social structures which such behaviours presuppose, and the ways in which these

---

[6] Elias, *The History of Manners*, p. 207.   [7] Ibid. 3.   [8] Ibid. 51.

structures interact to sustain one another. Indeed, despite the empirical emphasis of the work, and its ethnographic concern to provide detailed accounts of manners and behaviour, its real object of study is structural rather than empirical—it is above all an analysis of changing psychical structures and their relationship to changing structures of social interaction.

The 'specific transformation' implicit in Elias's concept of civilization refers to the long-term processes of change which have affected the behaviour and emotional life of Western peoples from the Middle Ages to the present. It is, of course, well known that there have been broad changes in modes of conduct, differentiating the characteristic behaviour of medieval society from that of our own: the very notion of civilization derives its standard sense from this contrast in mores and manners. But Elias's contribution has been to detail the shifts and stages of this transformation by making brilliant use of a body of historical documents which give very precise descriptions of the norms of conduct and the patterns of affect which existed in previous eras. By means of a close reading of etiquette manuals, pedagogical texts, fictional works, paintings, and various other documents of instruction or description, Elias is able to reconstruct the forms of conduct which prevailed among various groups from the Middle Ages onwards. By tracing through time the changing content of these 'manners books' and showing, for example, that new editions of a text would take for granted manners which earlier editions had explicitly to demand, or that norms which were once taught to adults later came to be the stuff of children's instruction, Elias is able to show how behaviour was gradually altered and refined by the insistent and increasing demands of cultural norms. Similarly, by tracing the distribution of such texts and norms throughout the population, Elias is able to show how a diffusion of manners gradually took place from one social group to another. This central body of source material is also further supplemented by more directly descriptive evidence, such as the diaries of contemporaries, novels, law suits, travelogues, and paintings, all of which are scrutinized for clues about social expectations and actual human conduct.

Transformations of behavioural norms—and, eventually, of behaviour— are traced by Elias in several different spheres of social and personal life. Table manners, attitudes towards bodily functions, the proper methods of spitting or blowing one's nose, behaviour in the bedroom, habits of washing and cleanliness, the expression of aggression, relationships between adults and children, the conduct of men in the presence of women, proper ways of addressing superiors or strangers—all these undergo important changes which Elias describes in rich and often fascinating detail. Moreover, he finds in this multitude of changes a number of recurring patterns and principles of development which give the whole movement a certain orderliness and direction. Typically, the civilizing process in culture involves a tightening and a differentiation of the controls imposed by society upon individuals, a refinement of conduct, and an increased level of psychological inhibition as the standards of proper conduct become ever more demanding. Thus the idea of 'civilization' can be taken to represent a *process*, which like any other process, has both causes and effects which the historian must try to understand.

In volume ii of *The Civilizing Process*, Elias shows how these developmental tendencies are linked to the expansion of social interdependencies—first in court society then in bourgeois market society—and are brought about by the heightening of calculation, self-control, and consideration of others which such societies both require and inculcate in their members. With the gradual historical movement from the knightly warrior societies of the Middle Ages to the relatively pacified court societies of the sixteenth and seventeenth centuries, violence comes to be monopolized by the central authorities, thereby reducing the levels of aggression manifest in normal social relations and heightening the levels of peace and security in which social life takes place. At the same time, social status and class distinction come increasingly to depend upon cultural achievement, language, and manners, particularly at the court where courtiers compete for the grace and favour of superiors by means of elaborate displays of civility and sophistication—displays which also serve to mark them off from their social inferiors.[9]

Later, with the development of market societies and the raising of cultural standards in the eighteenth and nineteenth centuries, the manners of the aristocratic élite spread outwards into the rising bourgeois classes, whose psychological capacities for self-restraint and instinctual renunciation were already well developed by the disciplines of the market and the asceticism of bourgeois life and religion. By the twentieth century, with its extensive markets and chains of interdependence, its differentiated social functions, and its mass-based political life—and with its increased standards of living and education among the general population—the cultural diffusion of 'civilized' norms and reserved behaviour has penetrated to most sectors of society, though of course detailed variations in standards and in manners remain a feature within and between societies. 'Civilization' is thus explained as a cultural configuration produced in Western societies by a specific history of social development and organization. It is the specific and fragile outcome of an evolutionary process which was socially determined though by no means inexorable, and which may at any time be reversed if wars, revolutions, or catastrophes undermine the forms of social organization and interdependence upon which it depends.[10]

---

[9] See Elias, *The History of Manners*, p. 217. On the use of speech, manners, and etiquette to express social class distinctions, see the classic studies by T. Veblen, *The Theory of the Leisure Class* (London, 1971), and P. Bourdieu, *Distinction: A Social Critique of the Judgement of Taste* (London, 1985).

[10] See Elias, *The History of Manners*, p. 125. See also p. 140 where he explains 20th-cent. 'permissiveness' and relaxations of social conventions as being possible because 'civilized' standards of conduct are now well consolidated and can be taken for granted. 'It is a relaxation within the framework of an already established standard.'

2.1 *The psychological concomitants of civilization*

Despite their intrinsic interest, Elias's sociological arguments are of less concern to us here than his social–psychological ones. In a bold and innovative attempt to historicize Freud's theory of the psyche, Elias argues that changes in cultural demands and social relations eventually have an effect upon the psychic organization of the individuals involved and, in particular, upon the structure of their drives and emotions. As he puts it, '. . . the social code of conduct so imprints itself in one form or another on the human being that it becomes a constituent element of his individual self. And this element, like the personality structure of the individual as a whole, necessarily changes constantly with the social code of behaviour and the structure of society'.[11] Human beings gradually internalize the fears, anxieties, and inhibitions imposed on them by their parents and their social environment, developing a super-ego which more or less effectively inhibits the expression of instinctual drives in accordance with the demands of cultural life.[12] There is thus a psychic corollary of cultural change—'the *psychical* process of civilization'[13]—which involves changes in the personality structure of individuals, especially the development of self-controls, internalized restraints, and inhibiting anxieties such as fear, shame, delicacy, and embarrassment. As I hope to show in a moment, the facts of this psychological transformation have important consequences for the ways in which we punish in modern society, so it will be useful at this point to discuss Elias's account of this change in some detail.

The psychological changes undergone by human beings in the long-term process of civilization—like the transformations undergone by the child in the process of growing up—affect the whole organization of personality and behaviour. In the course of this process, individuals come to develop new ways of relating to themselves, new ways of relating to other human beings, and new ways of relating to the physical and social environment. Following the emergence of a central power in society which monopolizes the use of violence and imposes its rule upon its subjects, and with the development of codes of conduct which require more refined social manners and more involvement with other social actors, it becomes necessary for the individual to impose increasing measures of self-restraint upon his or her own conduct. Open displays of aggression, or indeed spontaneous emotion of any kind, are increasingly forbidden by force of law or by social prudence. Through a

---

[11] Ibid. 190.

[12] At certain points in Elias's account he seems to emphasize the social restraint of biologically given emotion. This is a serious simplification which he in fact avoids elsewhere. It would probably be more accurate to talk of the ways in which social contexts of action and relationship tend to elicit, restrain, and regulate emotional states in individuals. The ways in which these coded social instructions interact with basic psychic and physiological processes (drives? instincts?) remain a matter of speculation and controversy. The Freudian account of the problem, upon which I rely at points in my argument, is as much subject to doubt as any other.

[13] Elias, *The History of Manners*, p. xii.

process of social learning (which becomes, in part, a matter of unconscious conditioning) individuals develop an ability to distance themselves from their instinctive drives and emotions, and to impose a measure of control upon their expression. To some extent this control is conscious, as where the courtier or the entrepreneur 'conceals his passions' or 'acts against his feelings', but in time a structure of internalized anxieties—the super-ego—makes this self-restraint more or less unthinking and automatic. Under pressure of increasing cultural demands (and, of course, the threat of force by governmental or parental authorities), the instinctual pleasures to be derived from the frank enjoyment of violence, smells, bodily functions, polymorphous sexuality, and so forth are largely repressed into the individual's unconscious. This act of repression sets up 'an invisible wall of affects' within the individual psyche, which is thereby split into a conflictual interplay of instinctual drives and internalized controls. To the extent that this repression is successful, the emotions and behaviour of the individual become more evenly ordered, less spontaneous, and less given to wild oscillation between extremes. Individuals are thus trained and psychologically equipped to sustain social conventions, and over time these conventions tend to become more demanding, calling for greater levels of restraint and forbearance and producing ever-increasing thresholds of delicacy and sensitivity.[14]

Social manners are primarily about the ways in which individuals relate to one another, and so the psychological structures underpinning human relations are also subjected to important changes by the process of civilization. During the course of this long-term change individuals have tended to become more willing—and better able—to adjust their conduct to take into account that of others, and generally more given to identifying other individuals as human beings like themselves who are worthy of respect and consideration. This refinement of manners and sensitivity to the feelings of others is at first a mark of respect for social superiors, and is undertaken consciously and instrumentally as an act of deference to a superior power, in the same way that violence is first renounced by knights in recognition of the prince's superior force of arms. However, as they are passed from generation to generation, these ways of behaving towards others gradually lose their instrumental aspect and become ways of behaving which individuals feel are right in themselves. Eventually, such manners are adopted towards social equals and even towards social inferiors as expressing the proper way to behave in the company of others. Ultimately, the individual may cease to be aware of these norms as social conventions and may even obey them in the absence of other people, so strong are the social conditioning and forces of habit which regulate such conduct.

Elias stresses that it is among the élite groups of court society that control of one's own emotions and sensitivity to the feelings and intentions of others undergo their most rapid development. The elaborate skills of calculation and

[14] Here, as at many other points, Elias's account of the civilizing process overlaps with Foucault's account of discipline and its effects.

self-control needed to manipulate one's way through the *affaires* and intrigues of the social situation of the court brought about a heightening in individuals' understanding of one another and of themselves, so much so that Elias credits this era with the development of the first truly 'psychological' approach to human conduct. The instrumental uses of this intense scrutiny of one's self and others can be clearly seen if one thinks of Machiavelli's writings, which are a lucid expression of the psychological orientation of court society. On the other hand, if one thinks of the humanist writings of this period, and the long line of writers from Erasmus and Montaigne to Voltaire who stress the fundamental identity of human beings with each other, one can also see the values—such as respect for the uniqueness and individuality of persons—to which these norms of civility eventually led. In the medieval world of the knight, with its mutually warring factions, '. . . there is no identification of man with man. Not even on the horizon of this life is there an idea that all men are "equal".'[15] With the development of court society, however, 'as the behaviour and personality structure of the individual change, so does his manner of considering others. His image of them becomes richer in nuances, freer of spontaneous emotions.'[16] Mutual identifications and understanding between individuals gradually emerge in this way, opening the way to the democratic movements of the Enlightenment and the practical humanism and utilitarianism that followed.[17]

Finally, and as part of the same civilizing process, the individual's psychological orientation towards the world at large undergoes a transformation which would eventually result in the scientific revolution of the seventeenth century and the continuous development of science and technology which has occurred ever since. The renunciation of short-term affects and the heightening of self-controls allows a more 'objective', unemotive, impartial approach to the world, just as the enhanced need for complex calculation develops skills of enquiry and a more 'scientific' attitude: 'Like conduct generally, the perception of things and people becomes affectively neutral in the course of the civilizing process. The "world picture" gradually becomes less directly determined by human wishes and fears, and more strongly oriented to what we call "experience" or "the empirical", to sequences with their own imminent regularities.'[18] This

---

[15] Elias, *The History of Manners*, p. 209.

[16] Elias, *State Formation and Civilization*, p. 273.

[17] For an important account of the social basis of humanitarian sensibility—which complements and in some respects refines that of Elias—see T. L. Haskell, 'Capitalism and the Origins of Humanitarian Sensibility', *The American Historical Review*, 90 (1985), 339–61, 547–66. Haskell argues that market society promoted a form of perception that was better able to identify long chains of cause and effect, which in turn extended the sense of responsibility which one individual could reasonably feel for the plight of others. This resulted in a widening of the effective range of moral action. At the same time, 'the market altered character by heaping tangible rewards on people who displayed a certain calculating, moderately assertive style of conduct, while humbling others whose manner was more unbuttoned or who pitched their affairs at a level of aggressiveness either higher or lower than the prevailing standard' (p. 550).

[18] Elias, *State Formation and Civilization*, p. 273. For an analysis of how this new cognitive style helped bring about a change in moral sensibilities, see Haskell, 'Capitalism and the Origins of Humanitarian Sensibility', pp. 342 ff.

scientific attitude, like the processes of 'rationalization' which Elias identifies from the sixteenth century onwards,[19] are, in effect, specific offshoots of the general processes of psychological and cultural change to which the concept of civilization refers. In these various ways then, the civilizing process produces individuals of heightened sensibilities whose psychological structures are heavily loaded with restraints, self-controls, and inhibitions. At the same time, however, the other side of this process is a liberating one, as individuals cease to be the slaves of instant emotion and become better able to adopt controlled, orderly attitudes towards the world and other people.

2.2 *The privatization of disturbing events*

In the development of manners and cultural rituals, a key feature which Elias identifies is the process of privatization whereby certain aspects of life disappear from the public arena to become hidden behind the scenes of social life. Sex, violence, bodily functions, illness, suffering, and death gradually become a source of embarrassment and distaste and are more and more removed to various private domains such as the domesticated nuclear family, private lavatories and bedrooms, prison cells, and hospital wards. Lying behind this process is the tendency to suppress the more animalistic aspects of human conduct, as being signs of the crude and the uncultivated. Such conduct comes to be defined as distasteful and unmannerly and individuals are taught to avoid shocking their superiors by displaying such behaviour in their presence. Eventually this cultural suppression becomes more general and more profound; the sight of other people openly suffering, or defecating, or displaying their bodily functions, becomes thoroughly distasteful and is banned from public places. Gradually, new and more private enclaves are developed 'behind the scenes' in which such activities can be undertaken more discreetly, withdrawn from the sight of others and often surrounded by an aura of shame and embarrassment. Thus, to take a specific example, the family bedroom has emerged as one such privatized space. According to Elias,

the bedroom has become one of the most 'private' and 'intimate' areas of human life. Like most other bodily functions, sleeping has been increasingly shifted behind the scenes of social life. The nuclear family remains as the only legitimate, socially sanctioned enclave for this and many other human functions. Its visible and invisible walls withdraw the most 'private', 'intimate', irrepressibly 'animal' aspects of human existence from the sight of others.[20]

Although Elias does not say so, this cultural tendency to force conduct behind the scenes is clearly a corollary of the psychic process of repression whereby instinctual wishes are forced back into the unconscious, to be enjoyed privately —and guiltily—in dream and phantasy. Both processes develop together, and both are the result of ever-more-demanding cultural standards which continu-

---

[19] Elias, *State Formation and Civilization*, p. 276.
[20] Elias, *The History of Manners*, p. 163.

ally increase the thresholds of delicacy, sensibility, and repugnance. Nor is it only in the area of 'intimate' behaviour that this process takes place. One of the key characteristics of modern, state-governed societies is that violence is no longer a tolerated aspect of everyday, public life. However, as Elias points out, violence in society does not disappear. Instead it is stored up 'behind the scenes'—in the barracks and armouries and prison houses of the state—ready to be used in case of emergency, and exerting an ever-present threat to possible violators of state norms and prohibitions. Thus '. . . a continuous, uniform pressure is exerted on individual life by the physical violence stored behind the scenes of everyday life, a pressure totally familiar and hardly perceived, conduct and drive economy having been adjusted from earliest youth to this social structure'.[21] It is therefore not in the least paradoxical that those societies which are in every respect the most civilized are none the less capable of unleashing the massive violence of world wars, nuclear attacks, and genocide should the restraints of civility be for any reason abandoned.[22]

As with other signs of brutishness, the sight of violence, pain, or physical suffering has become highly disturbing and distasteful to modern sensibilities. Consequently it is minimized wherever possible, though ironically this 'suppression' of violence is actually premissed upon the build-up of a state capacity for violence so great that it discourages unauthorized violence on the part of others. And where violence does continue to be used it is usually removed from the public arena, and sanitized or disguised in various ways, often becoming the monopoly of specialist groups such as the army, the police, or the prison staff which conduct themselves in an impersonal, professional manner, avoiding the emotional intensity which such behaviour threatens to arouse.

Elias's notion of 'civilization', then, has nothing in common with Whiggish narratives of moral improvement, nor does it imply some kind of secular decline in the quantity of bad conduct and human evil to be found in the world. Rather, it is reminiscent of Foucault's account of 'humanitarian penal reform' which insisted that the new prisons were not 'more lenient' or 'morally superior', but represented instead a new configuration of power, knowledge, and bodies. In much the same way, Elias's account of civilization is an analysis of how certain social and psychic changes have transformed the configurations and character of cultural life. In this new configuration, the place (and indeed the nature) of certain key elements—such as 'self' and 'other', 'love' and 'violence', 'public' and 'private'—are altogether different, and it is this

---

[21] Ibid. 239. On state violence and its place in everyday consciousness, see Poulantzas, *State, Power, Socialism*.

[22] Elias is well aware that civilized inhibitions can be swept aside in certain circumstances— e.g. where war or natural disasters disrupt normal social relations, or else where 'threats to state security' are said to create a state of emergency and the suspension of normal codes of conduct. In such circumstances, the 'defence' of 'civilization' can involve the abandonment of civilized conduct. His work also shows how the 'dehumanization' of the enemy is an important preliminary to the uncivilized treatment of opposing social groups.

sociological and historical difference which is the focus of his concern. Whether this change is for better or for worse is not a question which Elias sets himself.

This development of sensibilities, inhibitions, and cultural rituals which we equate with 'civilization' took place over a long period of time and with all the unevenness and vicissitudes of any long-term process. However, Elias identifies what he calls a 'typical civilization curve' which effectively summarizes the characteristic stages in this gradual development. I will end this section by quoting in full an example of this developmental curve, taken from his discussion of table manners and the socially sanctioned methods of carving animal meat:

[T]he increasingly strong tendency to remove the distasteful from the sight of society clearly applies, with few exceptions, to the carving of the whole animal. This carving . . . was formerly a direct part of social life in the upper class. Then the spectacle is felt more and more to be distasteful. Carving itself does not disappear, since the animal must, of course, be cut when being eaten. But the distasteful is removed behind the scenes of social life. Specialists take care of it in the shop or the kitchen. It will be seen again and again how characteristic of the whole process that we call civilization is this movement of segregation, this hiding 'behind the scenes' of what has become distasteful. The curve running from the carving of a large part of the animal or even the whole animal at table, through the advance in the threshold of repugnance at the sight of dead animals, to the removal of carving to specialized enclaves behind the scenes is a typical civilization curve.[23]

This quotation neatly summarizes much of Elias's discussion and illustrates several important points. But it also serves to suggest just how closely the history of punishment conforms to the general developmental pattern which Elias identifies. If one reads this passage bearing in mind the broad sweep of penal history then a number of very significant parallels quickly emerge. Over the same period of time—from the sixteenth century to the twentieth—punitive manners have undergone a very similar series of changes. In the early modern period, as we have already seen, capital and corporal executions were conducted in public, and both the ritual of judicial killing and the offender's display of suffering formed an open part of social life. Later, in the seventeenth and eighteenth centuries, the sight of this spectacle becomes redefined as distasteful, particularly among the social elite, and executions are gradually removed 'behind the scenes'—usually behind the walls of prisons. Subsequently, the idea of doing violence to offenders becomes repugnant in itself, and corporal and capital punishments are largely abolished, to be replaced by other sanctions such as imprisonment. By the late twentieth century, punishment has become a rather shameful social activity, undertaken by specialists and professionals in enclaves (such as prisons and reformatories) which are, by and large, removed from the sight of the public.

This example serves to demonstrate that the cultural and psychic transformations which Elias identifies as the origins of our civilized sensibilities may also have played an important part in shaping our institutions of punishment. If we accept the reality of the specific phenomena identified by this work—in particular the intensification of 'conscience', the increased restraints on violent behaviour, the growth of inter-human identification, the heightening of sensitivity to pain and suffering, and the broad cultural tendencies towards privatization and sanitization—then we are obliged to include such variables in any account of penal history or the sociology of punishment. Of course, the role of sensibilities in determining punishments is in no sense an exclusive one: as Elias himself shows, these psychic and cultural phenomena are always bound up with social structures, class struggles, and organizational forms, all of which might be expected to contribute to the shaping of penal practices. But once we grant them a reality and an effectivity, the cultural phenomena which Elias identifies must be included as an operative element in any social theory of punishment. In the pages which follow I will explore some of the interconnections which link changing sensibilities to changing forms of punishment, and conclude with a discussion of modern penality and the structure of sensibility which underlies it. This investigation begins by examining the work of Pieter Spierenburg and his use of Elias's thesis to explain certain aspects of the history of punishment.

3. SPIERENBURG'S HISTORY OF PUNISHMENT

Spierenburg's book, *The Spectacle of Suffering*, presents a specific (Eliasian) thesis relating the decline of public executions to a long-term transformation of sensibilities. In keeping with the broader contours of Elias's work, Spierenburg situates both the disappearance of the scaffold and the heightening of sensibility within a wider argument about the establishment of state power and the growing capacity of nation states to pacify their subjects and impose a settled form of law and order over their terrain. Spierenburg agrees with other writers—such as Foucault—that at a particular point in history public executions and their threatening display of state power ceased to be a necessary element in the maintenance of government. However, and in contrast to Foucault, Spierenburg concentrates his account upon the changing sensibilities which, in a crucial sense, mediated the link between state development and penal history. His argument is that although functional changes in the organization of society form the backdrop and basic conditions for penal development, it was the fact of changing sensibilities and the attitudes they inspired which formed the immediate context of penal reforms and the felt motivation for penal change.

Spierenburg presents a detailed description of the penal measures which were deployed in Amsterdam between 1650 and 1750 and a more general account of those in use in Europe at that time. For serious offenders the standard scaffold sentences included non-capital penalties (such as whipping, branding, and symbolic exposure with a rope around the neck); capital penalties (such as hanging, which was typically the most infamous form of death; garotting, which was often the fate of female offenders; and beheading, which was the usual end of homicides and offenders who had some claim to social rank); and also prolonged capital penalties (breaking on the wheel, burning, drowning . . .). Maimings such as tongue-piercing, blinding, or the cutting off of ears and hands were also known, but these were never standard penalties and their infrequent use declined sharply during the seventeenth century. In addition to these modes of execution—which served as a vivid reminder of the might of the authorities and their claim to monopolize the use of violence—there were further torments inflicted upon the offender which deliberately went beyond the point of death. The mutilation of dead bodies, the punishment of suicides, the exposure of corpses, all of these were regularly employed to signify the imperative character of the royal law or the laws of the new urban authorities. The standing gallows, built in stone and situated at the outskirts of towns, functioned in the same way to signal to town residents and travellers alike that here was a 'city of law', with soldiers being obliged to salute as they passed, and besieging armies often attacking it as part of their assault upon the city's authority.

The public ceremonies in which these atrocities were inflicted were presided over by town magistrates and, at least in the early stages, by the burgomasters as well. Large crowds, including rich and poor, parents and children, eagerly turned out to watch these executions, and, given the frequency of 'justice days' (the middle-size town of Breda had 224 between 1700 and 1795) the execution was a sight with which most people would be familiar.[24] Not surprisingly, the scaffold inspired its own peculiar myths and superstitions among the common people, but revulsion at its violence does not appear to have been an important element. Even the sight of exposed, rotting corpses in the fields at the edge of town appears to have made for a measure of indifference on the part of those who lived near them, if the evidence of contemporary paintings is to be believed.[25] All this, says Spierenburg, 'presupposes a society which tolerates the open infliction of pain' and manifests a 'positive attitude or indifference towards the suffering of convicts'.[26]

The argument is that during the sixteenth and seventeenth centuries, in a society where the level of public safety was low, where individuals were usually armed and quick to anger, and where traces of the feudal warrior-ethos and codes of honour still held sway, there was no general or deep-seated repugnance in the face of violence. 'Quick, head off, away with it, in order that the earth

---

[24] Radzinowicz reports that at one execution in England in 1776 some 30,000 people attended to watch the hanging, and he suggests that as many as 80,000 may have turned out at a Moorfields execution in 1767 (*A History of English Criminal Law*, i. 175, n. 45).

[25] Elias also notes the ability of late medieval people to tolerate the rotting corpses of criminals with comparative indifference. See the chapter, 'Scenes from the Life of a Knight', in *The History of Manners*, pp. 204 ff.

[26] Spierenburg, *The Spectacle of Suffering*, p. 54 and p. 13.

does not become full with the ungodly.'[27] The vehemence and savage force of this remark are distinctly Martin Luther's—he viewed the authorities as 'God's hangmen'—but according to Spierenburg it reflects the common mentality in its matter-of-fact acceptance of violence.

Of course sentiments of pity, sympathy, anger, or disgust were elicited by the fate of certain victims of the executioner. A more tender concern was expressed when someone was considered particularly unfortunate or innocent of the charge, and especially for rioters from the locality, with whom the crowd would personally identify. But there was no marked sympathy for common property offenders or the like on the part of the élite or the masses. Spierenburg argues that 'delinquents such as burglars, counterfeiters, procurers did not bring pity to the hearts of the spectators because the latter had no empathy for them as human beings' but this may overstate the point.[28] Rather, as Beattie, Zeman, and Masur suggest, those offenders who were generally executed were either outsiders, unknown to the townspeople, or else known thieves and recidivists regarded by all classes as dangerous and undeserving.[29] In such cases, where punishment was deemed to be necessary or deserved, the fact of its gross violence did not particularly disturb the equanimity of those who watched.

From the early seventeenth century onwards, in a process that would last for several centuries, the sensibilities and social relations tolerating violence began slowly to change. A fundamental change of attitudes seems to have occurred in The Netherlands and elsewhere by about the middle of the eighteenth century, and after 1800 the shift accelerated to form what is recognizably our own sensibility towards violence, suffering, and the fate of others. Spierenburg traces these changes and the growing appearance of 'verifiable expressions of repugnance and anxiety' in regard to violent public punishments, using the evidence of eyewitness reports, literary accounts, and documents relating to executions.[30] This developing sensitivity, growing from a mild ambivalence in the seventeenth century to the self-declared humanitarianism and sentimentalism of the eighteenth and nineteenth, was first and foremost a characteristic of élites. 'Conscience formation' and the refinement of manners were features of 'polite society', of the upper and middle classes who came to pride themselves on their delicacy and to despise those beneath them for their lack of culture and civilization. It was considered a mark of their uncivilized character that the lower-class crowds 'continued to be attracted to the event until the end' long after the rulers had withdrawn from such scenes, having ceased to take pleasure in the brutal execution of justice.[31] Only gradually did this cultivated sensitivity move out from the élite to take a hold on the attitudes of the popular classes.

---

[27] Martin Luther, quoted in Spierenburg, *The Spectacle of Suffering*, p. 33.   [28] Ibid. 101.
[29] Beattie, *Crime and the Courts*; Zeman, 'Order, Crime and Punishment: The American Criminological Tradition', and Masur, *Rites of Execution*.
[30] Spierenburg, *The Spectacle of Suffering*, p. 184.   [31] Ibid. 196.

According to Spierenburg, as the sense of repugnance or embarrassment at the sight of violence developed among the ruling groups, they gradually brought about the privatization of punishment and a reduction in the display of suffering. After 1600 there was a sharp decline in the use of maiming and mutilation. In the seventeenth century a growing revulsion at the sight of the scaffold led to stone scaffolds being replaced by temporary wooden structures that could be removed from view after use. By the middle of the eighteenth century the traditional use of torture in prosecution was caught up in this change of attitude so that even its defenders now felt obliged to display feelings of repugnance for the procedure they defended (in much the same way that Louis XV was moved to tears by the account of Damien's execution).[32] When half a dozen states abandoned the use of torture between 1754 and 1798 this was a consequence not so much of Enlightenment ideas (which repeated arguments that had been around for centuries) but of a changed sensibility which gave these critiques added force. The exposure of corpses was also abolished in the eighteenth century after having been a more or less routine accompaniment of executions (of 390 death sentences in Amsterdam between 1650 and 1750, 214 involved exposure of the corpse). In 1770 the magistrates of Amersfoort considered the decaying bodies of criminals to be a sight which 'cannot be but horrible for travelling persons' and stopped displaying corpses by the roadside, thereby showing greater concern for the sensibilities of strangers than for the deterrence of potential law-breakers.[33]

By the beginning of the nineteenth century, most of the old atrocities had disappeared, but this did not prevent sensitivity towards public executions becoming more widespread and outspoken. According to Spierenburg '. . . the élites had reached a new stage and identified to a certain degree with convicts on the scaffold. These delicate persons disliked the sight of physical suffering: even that of the guilty.'[34] When eventually, by 1870, most of Europe had abolished public executions (France was altogether exceptional, retaining them until 1939) this amounted to the 'political conclusion' of a cultural process which had begun centuries before. And though one might argue, as does Foucault, that public executions had by that time lost their functional utility within the dominant strategies of governance, part of the reason for this was that public displays of physical violence had also come to represent a shocking affront to the sensibilities of important sectors of the population. Cultural changes thus acted in concert with political change to bring about a transformation of punitive measures.

The importance of Spierenburg's work for the sociology of punishment is that it claims to identify phenomena which play an effective part in the shaping of penal practices and institutions. If he proves to be correct in this identification, then a focus upon these phenomena will constitute an important broadening of

---

[32] See McManners, *Death and the Enlightenment*, p. 383.
[33] Spierenburg, *The Spectacle of Suffering*, p. 191.
[34] Ibid. 204.

the field of enquiry. In particular it would counter the tendency recently established by Foucault's work to regard punishment as being shaped almost exclusively by strategic considerations of a political order. As I have already suggested, Foucault's emphatic depiction of punishment as a technology of power–knowledge, and his primarily political account of its development, has produced an over-rational, over-calculated conception of punishment in which its primary determinants are the requirements of social control. Elias and Spierenburg's work shows how security considerations and the instrumental use of punishment are always in tension with cultural and psychic forces which place clear limits upon the types and extent of punishment which will be acceptable. In that sense, their work deepens our conception of penality and renders it more complex.

4. THE HISTORY OF SENSIBILITY

It is necessary, though, to show some caution in discussing this question of sensibilities. Emotional attitudes and underlying sentiments are, in themselves, unobservable, and—at least outside the psychological laboratory—we can only infer sensibilities from the analysis of statements and actions. The danger in such inference is that misreadings are always possible, so for instance a rhetoric of feeling, used to disguise lower and more instrumental motivations, may be taken for the thing itself—which of course is the criticism which revisionist historians have made of conventional historiography in this field. Alternatively, changes in sensibility may be inferred from changes in social practice, which produces a problem of circularity if one then goes on to explain the latter in terms of the former (as, for instance, where Spierenburg cites the decline of public executions as evidence of increased sensitivity). Arguments about motives and feelings are always inconclusive and difficult to substantiate, particularly in historical research, and in discussing sensibilities we are dealing with deep structures of affect and motivation which can only be known through their social effects. Consequently, any claim that changing sensibilities were a causal agent in the restructuring of punishment must be supported by evidence above and beyond the expressed sentiments and rhetoric of penal reformers and 'enlightened' observers.

There is also a need to be circumspect in adopting Elias's thesis, since like any large-scale interpretation, it is open to detailed criticism and qualification. Thus Elias may well be correct about the structure of modern sensibilities, but he tends to overstate the contrast between the personality types of the medieval and modern ages. In his historical account of how modern sensibilities were formed he might be said to place too much emphasis upon the 'configurations of social interaction' and the force of cultural conventions, and to underplay the importance of the kinds of disciplinary, economic, and bureaucratic institutions stressed by Foucault, Marx, and Weber. Moreover, his reading of historical texts may be open to question, particularly since many of the documents he relies upon are in fact polemics, written by those concerned to reform manners and therefore prone to overstatement and distortion. But even accepting the force of those points—and others besides—it seems to me that Elias's major arguments about modernity can survive this criticism, and that in particular his claims regarding the development and character of modern sensibilities deserve to be taken seriously.[35]

One way of testing the strength of such claims is to look at corroborating evidence drawn from other fields of enquiry and spheres of social life. One would expect that any change in something as basic as the structure of human emotions and inhibitions would produce consequences not just in penal institutions but in a wide range of social practices. In fact, Spierenburg's work does not supply much wider evidence of this sort, and tends to rely too much upon the authority of Elias, but the work of other social historians in different fields provides a body of supporting evidence which makes the broad thesis of a civilizing process—influencing punishment and much else—seem largely persuasive.

Thus, for instance, a survey of historical research carried out by T. R. Gurr provides strong evidence to suggest a long-term and very substantial decline in levels of violent crime in English society from the thirteenth to the twentieth centuries, and Gurr points to 'the growing sensitization to violence' and 'the development of increased internal and external controls on aggressive behavior' as key factors in accounting for this decline.[36] Similarly, the more detailed investigations of early modern England carried out by Lawrence Stone, Keith Thomas, and John Beattie all point to high levels of violence in the everyday life of the sixteenth and seventeenth centuries slowly giving way to less aggressive social relations and a heightened aversion to cruelty and brutality during the eighteenth and nineteenth centuries.

In an important essay on the subject Beattie argues that 'damaging physical violence has diminished strikingly in daily life in England (and by inference in Europe and North America) over the past three centuries' and that, while men in the early modern period were not indifferent to the consequences of brutal behaviour, 'there was a much greater willingness to regard such behaviour as an acceptable means of maintaining authority or settling disputes in both

---

[35] The critical literature on Elias's work is now becoming quite extensive. For a summary, see R. van Krieken, 'Violence, Self-Discipline and Modernity: Beyond the Civilizing Process', *The Sociological Review*, 37 (1989), 193–218, and esp. its discussion of Benjo Maso's critique of Elias's reading of textual evidence. For a criticism of Elias's use of Freudian concepts, see C. Lasch, 'Historical Sociology and the Myth of Maturity: Norbert Elias' Very Simple Formula', *Theory and Society*, 14 (1985), 705–20. For a criticism of Elias's implicit evolutionism, see A. Giddens, *The Constitution of Society* (Oxford, 1984), and for an anthropological argument that there is no necessary relation between 'civilized' conduct and state formation, see the work of H. U. van Velzen, cited in Krieken. Other useful discussions include D. Smith, 'Norbert Elias—Established or Outsider?', *Sociological Review*, 32 (1984), 367–89 and the articles collected in *Theory, Culture and Society*, 4: 2, 3 (1987) ('Special Double Issue on Norbert Elias and Figurational Sociology').

[36] T. R. Gurr, 'Historical Trends in Violent Crime: A Critical Review of the Evidence', in N. Tonry and N. Morris (eds.), *Crime and Justice*, iii (Chicago, 1981), 295–353.

public and private arenas'.[37] Summarizing his own research, and that of other historians in different fields, Beattie shows how in the sixteenth and seventeenth centuries '[d]iscipline in the family and the workplace, in schools and in the army, was maintained . . . by a degree of physical coercion that would be shocking to modern sensibilities'.[38] He also shows how animals, criminals, servants, apprentices, children, and even wives were treated in this period with a casual cruelty that was 'largely unremarked on and unchallenged'.[39] The strongest evidence that early modern sensibilities could tolerate high levels of violence derives from the fact that seventeenth- and eighteenth-century penal systems relied very heavily upon gross forms of physical punishment and mutilation, and that such violence was clearly accepted by both the organizing élite and the mass of the public. As Beattie points out, a key feature of the scaffold, the stocks, the whipping-post, and the pillory was that they depended for their efficacy upon the active participation of the public, and no such involvement would have been possible if people had experienced a deep revulsion at the sight of such suffering. In fact the energy and zeal with which crowds of onlookers occasionally fell upon offenders locked in the pillory—sometimes beating or stoning them to death in full view of officials—suggests a singular lack of inhibition and sensitivity in this regard.[40]

Beattie goes on to argue that 'violence as an instrument of policy' was probably dependent upon the 'experience and acceptance of violence closer to home' and he produces evidence to suggest that popular attitudes may well have been shaped by the experience of violence in the home, the family, the school, and the workplace, where physical abuse and mistreatment were 'hardly restrained by either law or opinion'.[41] This suggestion is given further weight by Lawrence Stone's account of the extensive use of flogging and other physical punishments in the child-rearing and educational practices of the sixteenth and seventeenth centuries and by court records suggesting the prevalence of wife-beating and child abuse.[42] Other important evidence of a pervasive insensibility to cruelty comes from research into the nature of customary sports and recreations, and from Thomas's work on early modern attitudes towards animals, which reveal the extent to which physical violence, the shedding of blood, and the infliction of suffering were enjoyed for the sport and pleasure that they could provide.[43]

---

[37] J. M. Beattie, 'Violence and Society in Early Modern England', in A. Doob and E. Greenspan (eds.), *Perspectives in Criminal Law* (Aurora, 1984).

[38] Ibid. 36.   [39] Ibid.   [40] Ibid. 39.   [41] Ibid. 41–3.

[42] Stone, *The Family, Sex and Marriage*, p. 120: '. . . whipping was the normal method of discipline in a sixteenth or seventeenth century home, mitigated and compensated for, no doubt, by a good deal of fondling when the child was docile and obedient. Both rewards and punishments took physical rather than psychological forms.' On the evidence of wife-beating and child abuse, see Beattie, 'Violence and Society'.

[43] K. Thomas, *Man and the Natural World: Changing Attitudes in England 1500–1800* (Harmondsworth, 1984), pp. 143–50. See also R. W. Malcolmson, *Popular Recreations in English Society, 1700–1850* (Cambridge, 1973).

The historical work which has charted these violent cultural and psychic traits has also traced their transformation during the eighteenth and nineteenth centuries in a way which broadly supports Elias's thesis about the 'civilizing' of sensibilities. At present there is a measure of agreement—though not unanimity—among historians that the period between 1700 and the present has seen a change in sentiments with respect to violence, a growing antipathy towards cruelty of all kinds, and the emergence of a new structure of feeling which has changed the nature of human relationships and behaviour.[44] External evidence of such changes can be derived from alterations of legal and social practices which seem to suggest an underlying change of attitude. Thus, during the eighteenth century, criminal courts began to prosecute and punish violent conduct (assaults, reckless injuries, street-brawling, and so on) which would previously have been ignored, thus suggesting a growing sensitivity towards violence and an unwillingness to tolerate its use in public.[45] In the same way the rules and conventional opinions regarding physical chastisement in the family or the school underwent a significant shift in the period after 1750, and a husband's right to use physical punishment gradually came to be questioned and eventually denied. In education, too, there is evidence of a softening of views and a movement away from the idea that the will of the child needed to be broken by relentless physical punishment.[46] By the end of the eighteenth century the objections to corporal punishment were sufficiently well developed 'to excite the sympathy for those most despised of men, the common soldiers' and to produce a powerful campaign to oppose flogging in the army.[47] These same conscientious objections—sometimes mingled with other motives and interests, sometimes not—led to a whole series of reform movements during the nineteenth century, seeking to prohibit such things as blood sports, cruelty to animals, the ill-treatment of children, apprentices, criminals, and the insane, the slave-trade, and various other affronts to civilized sensibilities. In many cases they succeeded in securing changes in the law, in public opinion, even in actual practice. And when legal institutions failed to keep pace with changes in public attitude—as they frequently did throughout the nineteenth century—then conflicts inevitably ensued, leading to a clash between legal rules and individual conscience. Well-attested instances of this include those 'London shopkeepers and merchants and artisans' who 'were reluctant to prosecute property offenders when there was any danger of their being hanged' or the judges and jurors who proved to be similarly disinclined to see offenders executed and brought in 'verdicts of conscience' instead of the verdicts required by law.[48]

[44] For an opposing view, see A. Macfarlane, *The Justice and the Mare's Ale: Law and Disorder in Seventeenth Century England* (Cambridge, 1981), pp. 1–26, 173–98.

[45] See Beattie, 'Violence and Society', pp. 48 ff.

[46] Ibid. 51. See also J. H. Plumb, 'The New World of Children in Eighteenth Century England', *Past and Present*, 67 (1975).   [47] Beattie, 'Violence and Society', p. 51.

[48] Ibid. 56 and T. A. Green, *Verdict According to Conscience: Perspectives on the English Criminal Trial Jury, 1200–1800* (Chicago, 1985).

It seems clear, too, that members of the upper and middling classes living through these changes were sometimes conscious of this transformation of manners and sensibilities. Beattie points to the autobiography of Francis Place in which the author claims to have witnessed a cultural transition from 'the grossness and immorality' of the late eighteenth century to the 'civility' and 'refinement of manners' which he saw in the London society of the 1820s.[49] And during the course of the eighteenth century the 'man of feeling' emerged as a new cultural ideal, to be emulated by the literary and social élite: '[B]y the 1720s, "benevolence" and "charity" had become the most favoured words in literary vocabulary. There was something in human nature, said William Wollaston, which made the pains of others obnoxious to us. "It is grievous to see or hear (and almost to hear of) any man, or even any animal whatever, in torment." '[50] According to Thomas, Stone, and other historians of the period, the mid-eighteenth century saw 'a cult of tender-heartedness', an 'upsurge of new attitudes and emotions', and a self-conscious sentimentalism which expressed itself not just in literary effusions and outbursts of weeping but also in more tough-minded determination to 'ameliorate the human lot and to reduce the amount of sheer physical cruelty in the world'.[51] Reviewing a whole body of recent research literature, Lawrence Stone concludes that 'everything points to a transformation of attitudes to cruelty and violence during the eighteenth century'.[52] In a similar vein, with respect to the last half of the nineteenth century, and the decline in crimes of violence, V. A. C. Gatrell concludes that 'we are forced . . . to explain the decline in terms of heavy generalisations about the "civilizing" effects of religion, education and environmental reform'.[53]

There is thus a substantial body of historical evidence which would support the contention that something very like a civilizing process has indeed taken place, bringing about changes in sensibility and ultimately changes in social practice. Moreover, Spierenburg's specific claim that this transformative process must form part of the explanation for the long-term decline of scaffold punishments is given strong support by the findings of John Beattie who has carried out the most extensive and detailed work in this field. Concluding his long account of the changes which took place in the English penal system during the eighteenth century Beattie finds that:

the withering of support for a penal system that depended fundamentally on the threat of execution is to be explained by the merging of several strands of opinion and sentiment. To some degree it resulted from a broader movement of opinion in Europe and in England that came increasingly to abhor physical violence and cruelty to men and animals, and that can be seen at work in campaigns to abolish blood sports and other violent customary recreations, as well as in the movement against physical

---

[49] Beattie, 'Violence and Society', pp. 53–4.
[50] Thomas, *Man and the Natural World*, p. 175.
[51] Ibid. and Stone, *The Family, Sex and Marriage*, pp. 163–4.
[52] Stone, *The Past and the Present Revisited*, pp. 303–4.
[53] V. A. C. Gatrell, 'The Decline of Theft and Violence in Victorian and Edwardian England', in id. *et al.* (eds.), *Crime and the Law*, p. 300.

punishments of all kinds. That is perhaps the mental sea-change lying behind the opposition to capital punishment. . . . By 1800 a significant body of opinion was ready to condemn cruelty and disproportion in punishment as fundamentally unjust and unacceptable in a civilized society.[54]

5. THE CIVILIZATION OF PUNISHMENT

On the strength of this evidence, then, we have reason to take seriously the fact of sensibilities, their historical transformation in something like the direction Elias describes, and the proposition that these phenomena have direct consequences for the structure and development of penal systems. And in tracing the decline of scaffold punishments and linking it to changing sensibilities, Pieter Spierenburg has shown how an approach of this kind can deepen our historical understanding. However, there are also other aspects of Elias's interpretation of the civilizing process which seem particularly valuable for an understanding of modern punishment, and which ought to be developed by further research.

To begin with, the social process of privatization which Elias describes seems to illuminate a very important tendency in the history of punishment.[55] As I have noted above, punishment has certainly been one of those social activities which has increasingly been put 'behind the scenes' of social life. Instead of forming an aspect of everyday life, located in public space and openly visible to everyone—as was largely the case in the medieval and early modern periods—the punishment of offenders is nowadays undertaken in special enclaves removed from public view. Over a lengthy period of time, the visibility of punishments has been drastically reduced, as can be seen not only in the removal of the gallows from the public square to behind prison walls, but also in the movement away from public works which began in the early nineteenth century, in the blackened windows of the carriages which conveyed offenders to and from court, and in the care which is taken in the twentieth century to conceal even the smallest signs of punishment—whether it be handcuffs, prison uniforms, or electronic tags—from the public eye.[56] As replacements for these public spectacles, a whole network of closed institutions such as prisons, reformatories, and police cells have developed which are literally 'behind the scenes', allowing the punishment of offenders to be delegated to specialists whose activities are concealed behind high walls. Even in respect of 'non-institutional' sanctions, such as fines, probation, parole, and community service, the administration of punishment is essentially a private

---

[54] Beattie, *Crime and the Courts*, p. 631.

[55] To avoid confusion, it should be noted that the term 'privatization', as used here, has nothing to do with the kind of 'privatization' that involves the transfer of the administration or financing of penal institutions from state agencies to commercial corporations.

[56] On the changing forms of state executions, see J. Lofland, 'The Dramaturgy of State Executions', in H. Bleakley and J. Lofland, *State Executions Viewed Historically and Sociologically* (Montclair, NJ, 1977).

affair conducted by professional or semi-professional agents out of sight of the public.

Along with many other groups of deviant individuals, offenders are now routinely sequestrated from the sphere of normal social life, and the 'problem' that they represent is managed 'off-stage', in a discrete institutional setting which carefully controls its impact upon the public consciousness. Like the slaughter and carving of animals for human consumption, the business of inflicting pain or deprivation upon offenders has come to seem rather shameful and unpalatable. It is not a sight which is felt to be edifying for the modern public though it is an activity which is deemed to be necessary none the less, so our sensibilities are preserved by removing this painful undertaking to scarcely visible sites on the margins of society and social consciousness.[57]

The civilizing process in punishment is also apparent in the sanitization of penal practice and penal language. Pain is no longer delivered in brutal, physical forms. Corporal punishment has virtually disappeared, to be replaced by more abstract forms of suffering, such as the deprivation of liberty or the removal of financial resources. As we have seen, the aggression and hostility implicit in punishment are concealed and denied by the administrative routines of dispassionate professionals, who see themselves as 'running institutions' rather than delivering pain and suffering. Similarly, the language of punishment has been stripped of its plain brutality of meaning and reformulated in euphemistic terms, so that prisons become 'correctional facilities', guards become 'officers', and prisoners become 'inmates' or even 'residents', all of which tends to sublimate a rather distasteful activity and render it more tolerable to public and professional sensibilities.[58]

There may, of course, be other forces at work in bringing about these changes—we have already seen how political, economic, and organizational developments pushed punishment in similar kinds of directions during the nineteenth and twentieth centuries. But it seems undeniable that these outcomes were also in some part an adaptation to new facts of a psychic and cultural nature. Indeed, the appeal of Elias's very broad conception of 'the civilizing process' is that it seeks to capture the interdependence of processes of change occurring in quite different areas and 'levels' of society. In his work one can see how the processes of 'rationalization' which Weber discusses correspond

[57] This is not, however, an absolute rule, and community-based sanctions in particular do involve a degree of public visibility, in so far as they involve community volunteers, public works projects, and integration with regular community activities. But unlike the public works of the late 18th cent., offenders are not marked out by uniforms or balls and chains. They, and their punishments, are scarcely visible and much effort is devoted to maintaining this low profile.

[58] 'Pain delivery . . . in our time has developed into a calm, efficient, hygienic operation. Seen from the perspective of those delivering the service, it is not first and foremost drama, tragedy, intense sufferings. Infliction of pain is in dissonance with some major ideals, but can be carried out in an innocent, somnambulistic insulation from the value-conflict. The pains of punishments are left to the receivers. Through the choice of words, working routines, division of labour and repetition, the whole thing has become the delivery of a commodity' (Christie, *Limits to Pain*, p. 19). For a glossary of penological euphemisms, see Cohen, *Visions of Social Control*, pp. 276–8.

to changes in the structure of social organization as described by Durkheim, and to the structure of human personality as described by Freud. Society, its institutions, and its individual members are always historical and configurational outcomes—never the product of any single determinant or any necessary law.

The most obvious sense in which the civilizing process may be seen to have affected the penal system is in the extension of sympathy (or 'inter-human identification' as Spierenburg rather inelegantly puts it) to the offender, a development which has gradually ameliorated the lot of the offender and lessened the intensity of the punishment brought to bear. In much the same way that Durkheim talks of the growing recognition of the offender as an individual to be valued like any other, and hence to be treated mercifully, Elias points to the increasing capacity of modern sensibilities to take the part of the other and to extend consideration even to social inferiors and enemies. To the civilized conscience, so strong is the prohibition on violence and the repugnance in the face of suffering, that it is 'grievous to hear of any man in torment' even when that man is a criminal who has himself done harm. Thus the gradual but undeniable lowering in the intensity of punishment, the extension of charity to prisoners and offenders, the provision of social welfare measures in the twentieth century, the amelioration of prison conditions in most states and even the legal recognition of prisoners' rights in some of them, might all be understood as aspects of this more general movement in sensibilities—though as revisionist historians have stressed, it has often been possible to reform penality in ways which meet the demands of sentiment *and* the objectives of enhanced control or secure confinement.

Of all the 'civilizing' changes in punishment, however, the enhancement of sympathy for offenders and the amelioration of penal conditions is perhaps the least well developed. Despite 200 years of penal reform and demands for more humane methods, many prisons continue to be squalid, brutal places relative to general standards of life in the world outside. The average length of prison sentences is in many places increasing; thousands of offenders are still sent to prison for minor crimes; and capital punishments are still carried out in several states of the USA. One part of the reason for this is that other aspects of the civilizing process—such as the privatization and the institutionalization of punishment—tend to undermine the operation of sympathy by cutting off offenders from contact with the general public, and thereby heightening the alienation and marginalization of offenders, limiting public knowledge about their circumstances, and inhibiting the extension of sympathy and identification. But more importantly, the amelioration of punishment runs up against strong competing concerns for the maintenance of security, the need for deterrence, the concern for less eligibility, and, not least, the widespread punitive hostility towards offenders which continues even in the most 'civilized' societies. Of all the groups which make a claim upon public sympathy and fellow feeling, criminal offenders often seem to have the weakest claim, and this is particularly the case if they are represented as a wilful danger to the public, rather than as inadequate, or maladjusted, or as themselves victims of social injustice. There are thus other, instrumental considerations at work which have severely limited the extent to which punishments have been mitigated by a process of 'civilization'.

It would be a research task of great complexity to try to unravel the social basis of the varying attitudes which are adopted towards punishment in modern societies. There are, undoubtedly, conflicts of a rational kind which suggest that attempts to mitigate the rigours of punishment must be limited by the need to maintain proper levels of deterrence, security, and reprobation. No matter how refined our sensibilities, they will rarely be allowed to undermine what are seen as fundamental social needs. Moreover, any rational basis for public opinion is usually distorted by the tendency of political groupings to represent crime and punishment in ideological terms, harnessing these issues to metaphors of social danger or the need for authority, and misrepresenting the facts for the purpose of political persuasion.[59] There is also the important fact that sensibilities are likely to be unevenly developed in any particular society, revealing variations of attitude between different social groups. Elias's general model of a process of refinement which begins with the social élite and percolates downwards towards the masses would suggest a broad correlation between high social class and developed sensitivity—and one might find some evidence for this in the fact that most penal reformers have been drawn from upper- and middle-class backgrounds, that opinion polls in the USA and Britain show a tendency to evince more punitive attitudes the further down the social scale one goes, or even in the fact that the labour and trade-union movements have generally done little to improve the conditions of offenders and have sometimes been the most vocal proponents of less-eligibility attitudes. But such a correlation is by no means general or constant and it is certainly not the case that the social élite of Europe or North America are prevented in their reforming efforts by the common people.[60] Indeed, the leading proponents of 'popular authoritarian' attitudes, stressing severe punishment and harsh regimes, have usually been politicians of a conservative disposition and those sections of the ruling class which support them.

6. PUNITIVE AMBIVALENCE AND THE ROLE OF THE UNCONSCIOUS

There is, however, another reason why the civilizing process has brought about only a limited amelioration of punishment. This has less to do with rational considerations regarding security or the need for deterrence, and more to do with the irrationalities which can underpin public thinking on such

[59] For a study of the ideological uses of 'law and order' issues, see Hall *et al.*, *Policing the Crisis*.

[60] For a discussion of evidence on US and British public opinion about penal issues, see Jacobs, *New Perspectives on Prisons and Imprisonment*, ch. 5, and M. Hough and H. Lewis, 'Penal Hawks and Penal Doves: Attitudes to Punishment in the British Crime Survey', in Home Office Research and Planning Unit, *Research Bulletin*, 21 (1986). For a wider survey, see N. Walker and M. Hough (eds.), *Public Attitudes to Sentencing: Surveys from Five Countries* (Aldershot, 1988).

matters, producing an emotionally laden fascination with crime and punishment and sometimes a deep susceptibility for the rhetorical appeals of authoritarian penal policies. I am referring here to the psychological ambivalence concerning the punishment of others which might be said to be a characteristic of even 'civilized' sensibilities, and which has been alluded to already in Chapter 3. Neither Elias nor Spierenburg discuss this explicitly, or at least not in respect of punishment, but the fact of ambivalence and some of its penal implications can be derived from their theoretical arguments and from the Freudian analysis upon which these are based.

In the course of the civilizing process—at both the social and individual levels—human beings are led to repress (or to sublimate) their instinctual drives and particularly their aggressions. This process of repression, however, does not lead to the total disappearance of such drives—civilization does not succeed in abolishing the instincts or legislating them out of existence, as the wars and holocausts of the twentieth century show all too clearly. Instead, they are banned from the sphere of proper conduct and consciousness and forced down into the realm of the unconscious. Both Freud and Elias insist that repressed instincts and unconscious wishes continue to exist and to express themselves—either in the dreams and phantasy life of the individual, or else in the form of psychic conflicts and irrational behaviours. Civilization thus sets up a fundamental conflict within the individual between instinctual desires and internalized super-ego controls, a conflict which has profound consequences for psychological and social life. Thus while social prohibitions may demand the renunciation of certain pleasures—such as aggression or sadism—this may be only ever a partial renunciation, since the unconscious wish remains. Elias describes how society 'suppress[es] the positive pleasure component in certain functions more and more strongly by the arousal of anxiety; or, more exactly, it is rendering this pleasure "private" and "secret" (i.e. suppressing it within the individual), while fostering the negatively charged affects—displeasures, revulsion, distaste—as the only feelings customary in our society'.[61] Civilization thus makes unconscious hypocrites of us all, and ensures that certain issues will often arouse highly charged emotions which are rooted in unconscious conflict, rather than single-minded, rationally considered attitudes.

An indication of the undertow of repressed emotions which lies behind 'civilized' social attitudes is given by Elias when he discusses the aggressive tone which frequently accompanies the uttering of moral injunctions. In this example, Elias is particularly concerned with the adult's response to the child who has done something distasteful, but we might think in the same way about the response of the 'righteous citizen' to the criminal:

In this situation, the adult does not explain the demand he makes on behaviour. He is unable to do so adequately. He is so conditioned that he conforms to the social standard more or less automatically. And any other behaviour, any breach of the prohibitions or

[61] Elias, *The History of Manners*, p. 142.

restraints prevailing in his society means danger, and a devaluation of the restraints imposed upon himself.[62]

Here Elias, leaning on Freud's theory of repression, suggests a much fuller psychological account of the phenomenon that Durkheim describes as the 'passionate reaction' provoked by deviance. According to Elias,

the peculiarly emotional undertone so often associated with moral demands, the aggressive and threatening severity with which they are frequently upheld, reflects the danger in which any breach of the prohibitions places the unstable balance of all those for whom the standard behaviour of society has become more or less 'second nature'. These attitudes are symptoms of the anxiety aroused in adults whenever the structure of their own instinctual life, and with it their own social existence and the social order in which it is anchored, is even remotely threatened.[63]

The 'threat' posed by the criminal—and the fear and hostility which this threat provokes—thus have a deep, unconscious dimension, beyond the actual danger to security which the criminal represents. 'Fear of crime' can thus exhibit irrational roots, and often leads to disproportionate (or 'counter-phobic') demands for punishment. (Ironically, our psychological capacity to *enjoy* crime—at least in the form of crime stories—leads the media to highlight the most vicious, horror-laden tales, which in turn serve to enhance the fears which crime evokes. The linked emotions of fascination and fear thus reinforce each other through the medium of crime news and crime-thrillers.)

The behaviour of criminals, particularly where it expresses desires which others have spent much energy and undergone much internal conflict in order to renounce, can thus provoke a resentful and hostile reaction out of proportion to the real danger which it represents. Moreover, as I noted in Chapter 3, the fact that criminals sometimes act out wishes which are present in the unconscious of law-abiding citizens may account for the deep fascination which crime holds for many, and for the widespread appeal of crime literature, crime news, and the gruesome interest provoked by figures such as Jack the Ripper, Charles Manson, the Moors Murderers, Gary Gilmore, and so on.

It may also be the case that the punishment of others can provide a measure of gratification and secret pleasure for individuals who have submitted to the cultural suppression of their own drives, and for whom the penal system represents a socially sanctioned outlet for unconscious aggression. Freud stresses that the super-ego is developed in the child under a perceived threat of punishment (during the Oedipal conflict), and Elias makes it clear that the same threat of punishment (now from other social authorities) keeps up the anxiety needed to maintain high levels of self-restraint.[64] These internalized controls operate by creating what Freud calls 'a sense of guilt' in the individual, who is made to feel guilty whenever his instinctual wishes clash with his socially imbued conscience. This sense of guilt, according to Freud, 'expresses

---

[62] Ibid. 167.   [63] Ibid.
[64] See S. Freud, *Civilization and Its Discontents* (New York, 1962), p. 71.

itself as a need for punishment', thus setting up a kind of sado-masochistic tension between the harsh super-ego and the guilt-laden ego.[65] Freud himself translated this psychoanalytical insight into the criminological sphere when he argued in 1915 that there are 'criminals from a sense of guilt'—i.e., individuals who experience a need to be punished resulting from unconscious wishes and an over-severe super-ego.[66] This particular suggestion has been treated with some scepticism by criminologists, and would seem to be a plausible motivation for only a tiny minority of offenders. However, it might be more important to talk instead of 'punishers from a sense of guilt', since an unconsciously punitive attitude towards one's own anti-social wishes may carry over into a projected punitive attitude towards those who have actually acted out such prohibited desires. Likewise, the tendency of 'civilized' societies to 'lock away' offenders, thus putting them 'out of sight and out of mind' might be interpreted as a kind of 'motivated forgetting'—the social equivalent of the individual's repression of unconscionable wishes and anti-social desires.

If this is the case—and it is, of course, very difficult to prove either way— then the development of civilized sensibilities and heightened self-controls carries with it a counter-tendency towards punitiveness. In a society where instinctual aggressions are strictly controlled and individuals are often self-punishing, the legal punishment of offenders offers a channel for the open expression of aggressions and sanctions a measure of pleasure in the suffering of others. This view should not be exaggerated, however, and needs to be placed in a wider cultural and historical context. The view of James Fitzjames Stephens that it was the duty of the citizen to hate the criminal is nowadays considered reactionary and distasteful, and is normally cited to show how far we have come since the late nineteenth century. Similarly, the sight of a cheering crowd gathered outside a US prison to applaud a murderer's execution is viewed by many in that society as an embarrassing and distasteful expression of social pathology. Nevertheless, there remains an underlying emotional ambivalence which shapes our attitudes towards punishment and which has so far prevented the civilizing effects of transformed sensibilities from being fully registered within the penal sphere.[67]

---

[65] *Civilization and its Discontents*, p. 71. See also Freud's essay, 'The Economic Problem of Masochism', where he states: '. . . the sadism of the super-ego and the masochism of the ego supplement each other and unite to produce the same effects. It is only in this way, I think, that we can understand how the suppression of an instinct can—frequently or quite generally—result in a sense of guilt and how a person's conscience becomes more severe and more sensitive the more he refrains from aggression against others.' Repr. in S. Freud, *On Metapsychology*, vol. xi of the Pelican Freud Library (Harmondsworth, 1984), p. 425.

[66] S. Freud, 'Criminality from a Sense of Guilt', in 'Some Character-Types Met with in Psychoanalytic Work', in id., *Collected Papers*, iv, ed. J. Riviere (New York, 1959; 1st pub. in *Imago*, 4(1915–16)).

[67] Unfortunately such psychoanalytical literature as there is on this topic is often analytically crude and unpersuasive. See K. Menninger, *The Crime of Punishment* (New York, 1968); G. Zilboorg, *The Psychology of the Criminal Act and Punishment* (London, 1955); A. A. Ehrenzweig, *Psychoanalytic Jurisprudence: On Ethics, Aesthetics and 'Law'* (Leiden, 1971); and Alexander and Staub, *The Criminal, the Judge and the Public*. More subtle characterizations of the psychology of crime and punishment

7. CONTEMPORARY PUNISHMENTS AND MODERN SENSIBILITIES

I want to conclude this chapter by discussing some of the issues raised by corporal and capital punishments in the late twentieth century, since these, more clearly than anything else, illustrate how modern sensibilities operate to structure the practices of contemporary penal systems. One might begin with the simple question: why aren't corporal punishments used today? Lest the answer to this should appear too self-evident, it is worth pointing to some of the forceful penological arguments that might be used in favour of such methods. Put simply, if legal sanctions are designed to inflict hard treatment upon the offender in accordance with their just deserts—and in the 1970s and 1980s this aim has largely come to displace concerns about treatment and rehabilitation —then corporal punishment would appear to be an obvious means to this end. Moreover, if deterrence or retribution is what is wanted, then the direct infliction of pain upon the body has a number of important penological advantages over competing methods. Unlike imprisonment (which is very expensive, difficult to manage, and which creates its own problems by bringing together large numbers of offenders under the same roof) and unlike the fine (which varies in effect according to the offender's means, and which frequently results in imprisonment for those who cannot pay) corporal punishments can be inexpensive, they can be precisely calibrated, their side-effects can be minimized, and they can be delivered reasonably efficiently and uniformly. In these terms, at least, there are strong reasons to consider corporal punishments as a policy option within modern penal strategies. And yet penologists, by and large, do not even mention this possibility. It is not an option on the modern agenda. Instead, corporal punishments are a fact of history, occasionally reinvoked for dramatic effect by reactionary politicians, but more usually cited as evidence that the penal systems of earlier times were less civilized than our own.[68]

Why is this? The answer of course is that our modern sensibilities—or at least those of the sectors of society which are influential in policy-making— have been attuned to abhor physical violence and bodily suffering. Gross violence, deliberate brutality, the infliction of physical pain and suffering, all these are felt by many people to be intolerably offensive in themselves and to

are to be found in literary accounts such as Faller's *Turned to Account*. For a comparative study of the social psychology of punishing which stresses the role of what Nietzsche called 'ressentiment' see S. Ranulf, *Moral Indignation and Middle Class Psychology* (New York, 1964).

[68] Graeme Newman recently shocked the criminological world by suggesting the reintroduction of corporal punishments in his book *Just and Painful: A Case for the Corporal Punishment of Criminals* (New York, 1985). Newman was careful to present this suggestion in ways which tried to square it with modern sensibilities and 'civilized' ideas: the method used would be electric shocks which could be precisely calibrated, medically administered, given without long-term injury, etc. Most reviewers expressed outrage. A more analytical review by Jonathan Simon argued that the suggestion was anachronistic, being out of step with modern social practices (and what I would term modern sensibilities). J. Simon, 'Back to the Future: Newman on Corporal Punishment', *American Bar Foundation Research Journal* (1985), 927 ff.

have no legitimate place within the public policy and legal institutions of a civilized nation. During the last 100 years, most legal systems have abolished the last traces of such corporal methods, abandoning the use of flogging in the army and in prison discipline, and eventually the use of whipping or 'birching' in the punishment of juvenile offenders. The same sensibilities have led to recent policies which outlaw the use of even mild corporal punishments in schools, and to proposals that parents should be prohibited from using physical forms of chastisement in disciplining their children. Clearly then, the open infliction of physical pain and suffering strikes many of us as distasteful and is increasingly excluded from public policy.

But it needs to be emphasized that this ban upon violence and the infliction of pain is *not* a general one. On the contrary, an understanding of the human impact of some contemporary punishments makes it clear that government policy still permits the infliction of pain and public opinion still tolerates it—so long as it takes a particular form. It is well known to those with experience of imprisonment, for example, that incarceration, particularly for long periods of time, can produce acute mental and psychological suffering. It can also bring about physical deterioration and the erosion of cognitive and social skills, and it frequently results in serious emotional and economic distress for the prisoner's family.[69] The social degradation of having to share a tiny cell with strangers—which in Britain involves not only a lack of privacy and personal security but often the necessity of having to perform one's bodily functions in front of others, and then 'slopping out' excrement—is, in modern civilized society, a brutalizing and dehumanizing punishment in itself. But because these pains are mental and emotional rather than physical, because they are corrosive over an extended period rather than immediate, because they are removed from public view, and because they are legally disguised as a simple 'loss of liberty', they do not greatly offend our sensibilities and they are permitted to form a part of public policy. In keeping with the demands of a 'civilized' society, the experience of pain is ushered 'behind the scenes'— whether this is behind the walls of a prison, or behind the 'front' with which prisoners conceal their emotional distress.

Norval Morris once remarked that he might consider corporal punishment as a possible penal method if it could be made 'unemotive'—that is, if it could be robbed of its aggressive and sexual overtones, depersonalized, bureaucratized. In his view this was impossible, so the issue did not arise and he rejected corporal punishment completely. But, in doing so, he touched upon an important point.[70] Unlike our other penal methods—the prison, the fine, supervision, etc.—which have been rendered unemotive in precisely these

___

[69] See S. Cohen and L. Taylor, *Psychological Survival: The Experience of Long-Term Imprisonment* (Harmondsworth, 1972); L. S. Sheleff, *Ultimate Penalties: Capital Punishment, Life Imprisonment, Physical Torture* (Columbus, Ohio, 1987); Sykes, *The Society of Captives*, ch. 4 on 'The Pains of Imprisonment'.
[70] Professor Morris's informal remarks were made in the context of a seminar on 'Sanctions' at the School of Law, New York University, 8 Nov. 1984.

ways, the problem with bodily punishments is that their violence cannot be denied. In the delivery of pain to a human being—whether by crude methods such as whipping, or by more sophisticated forms such as the electric shock—one always sees the immediate evidence of suffering, and the brutality involved is inescapable. The wince of pain or the scream of agony announce the fact of violence and render it visible, whereas the mental anguish and gradual deterioration of an incarcerated inmate is much more difficult to observe and much easier to overlook. The crucial difference between corporal punishments which are banned, and other punishments—such as imprisonment—which are routinely used, is not a matter of the intrinsic levels of pain and brutality involved. It is a matter of the *form* which that violence takes, and the extent to which it impinges upon public sensibilities. Modern sensibilities display a definite selectivity. They are highly attuned to perceive and recoil from certain forms of violence, but at the same time they have particular blind spots, or sympathetic limitations, so that other forms are less clearly registered and experienced. Consequently, routine violence and suffering can be tolerated on condition that it is discreet, disguised, or somehow removed from view.

Such areas of insensitivity are well known to campaigners who have to struggle to overcome public indifference and make people aware of famine abroad or poverty at home when the tendency is to ignore any forms of suffering which are not immediately visible, or to do with 'people like us'. They are also pointed up by Keith Thomas in his work on changing attitudes towards cruelty to animals, where he shows that sensibilities have always been highly selective and differentiated in their concerns. Instead of extending sympathy to all animals equally, it has tended to be those animals which scream and whimper when in pain, or which seemed most 'human' in appearance or behaviour, which win our concern and protection, while other species (such as fish or reptiles or insects) tend not to elicit human warmth or concern. Precisely the same selectivity seems to operate in the realm of punishment, which is nowadays organized in ways which routinely disguise the massive violence which is still employed. Because the public does not hear the anguish of prisoners and their families, because the discourses of the press and of popular criminology present offenders as 'different', and less than fully human, and because penal violence is generally sanitized, situational, and of low visibility, the conflict between our civilized sensibilities and the often brutal routines of punishment is minimized and made more tolerable. Modern penality is thus institutionally ordered and discursively represented in ways which deny the violence which continues to inhere in its practices.

One vivid illustration of this characteristic, which shows both the continued investment in penal violence, and the limitations of public sensibilities, is the history of modern attempts to find an 'acceptable' method of capital punishment. This history begins with the French Revolution and its introduction of the guillotine as a method of performing the execution, since the guillotine was designed as a humanitarian (and 'democratic') machine which could terminate life without inflicting any unnecessary pain upon the offender. Ever since then, governments and states have sought to discover new methods which might perform this ultimate act of violence while simultaneously concealing its brutal and painful aspects. At first the concern was to develop a means of ensuring that death would be instantaneous and would not depend upon the skill of an individual executioner—hence the trapdoor gallows, the firing squad, and the guillotine itself. Later, in the late nineteenth and twentieth centuries, the movement was towards elaborate technical devices—such as the electric chair and the gas chamber—which had the effect of distancing and dehumanizing the fatal act; rendering it as a technical, scientific operation rather than one human being deliberately killing another. In effect, the moral question whether it was right to kill or not came to be translated into a question of aesthetics: could judicial killing be undertaken tastefully, in a manner which disguised its brutal aspects? One can see this in the language of official bodies such as the British Royal Commission on Capital Punishment, or various state legislatures and commissions in the USA, which stresses the need for 'seemly', 'humane', and 'decent' methods which avoid the 'degrading' and 'barbarous' associations of older. methods.[71]

Given the gravity of a decision to kill another human being it may well seem perverse and absurd to agonize over questions of decorum and presentation, but it is a fact of political life that these cosmetic aspects of penality have been crucial in making judicial killing acceptable to modern public opinion. Perhaps the highpoint in this search for a method which can kill without offending public sensibilities is the development of the 'lethal injection' which is now used in several US states. This technique of killing involves the injection of a lethal dose of 'an ultra-fast-acting barbiturate' in combination with a paralytic agent into the veins of the offender. According to its proponents, this method is virtually painless and offers 'an alternative, pleasanter, method of execution'.[72] It is represented as a quasi-medical procedure, to be undertaken not by executioners but by medical personnel, and of course in its form it imitates a routine, curative practice of modern health care.[73] As the British Royal Commission expressed it, such a method 'might facilitate the provision of executioners' because 'what was needed of them could be represented rather as an act of mercy than as an execution'.[74]

This attempt to represent judicial killing as a form of euthanasia has been taken up by more than a dozen US states during the last 10 years. In practice, the distancing of the executioners from their victims has been further facilitated

---

[71] The quotations are taken from F. E. Zimring and G. Hawkins, *Capital Punishment and the American Agenda* (Cambridge, 1986). Much of the material in this section is drawn from Zimring and Hawkins' study.

[72] The phrase is from the British Royal Commission Report on Capital Punishment, 1949–53, quoted in Zimring and Hawkins, *Capital Punishment and the American Agenda*, p. 112.

[73] In fact the American Medical Association eventually adopted the position that physicians should not be participants in an execution (ibid. 114–15).

[74] Ibid. 113.

at the scene of the execution by the erection of a brick wall which separates the condemned from the technicians, and permits the fatal dose to be administered through a tiny opening in the wall. The offender, who is strapped upon a stretcher-trolley like a patient awaiting an operation, is put to death anonymously, under the guise of a medical procedure, by technicians who do not immediately witness the effects of their actions.[75] This strange, and actually rather horrifying scene encapsulates many of the important characteristics of modern punishment —its privatization, its sanitization, the careful denial of its own violence—and it shows the formal properties which modern sensibilities require of punitive action.

Interestingly, Zimring and Hawkins show that the states which have adopted this method have tended to be those which, in the late 1970s or 1980s, reintroduced capital punishment after a long period of disuse or abolition. The problem which these states faced was that, for many people, the electric chair and the gas chamber had come to seem anachronistic, and out of keeping with modern sensibilities. 'Two decades of disuse . . . had rendered chambers and chairs the stuff of wax museum exhibits rather than instruments of public policy. Thus to maintain an active execution policy required a means of killing less obviously discordant with today's institutions and values.'[76] The use of 'therapeutic' drugs and medicalized procedures is thus an attempt to generate an acceptably 'modern' mode of execution—but, as Zimring and Hawkins argue, this has failed on a number of counts. The actual deployment of this method has revealed the impossibility of painless, sterile executions, and has shown lethal injections to be just as gruesome as the other contemporary methods of putting offenders to death. Moreover, the continued existence of capital punishment in the USA—in whatever form it is embodied—increasingly strikes many Americans as simply uncivilized, since virtually every other developed, democratic society has long since ceased to rely upon this practice.

Zimring and Hawkins argue that it has been the peculiarities of US politics which have allowed the death penalty to be retained into the 1980s rather than any peculiar backwardness of that country's moral sensibilities. At one level, retention of the death penalty has been a symbolic, reactive response by a number of state legislatures which deeply resented federal government and supreme court interference in having declared this method 'unconstitutional' in the Furman decision of 1972; by legislating new capital statutes these states were asserting the claims of local independence. At another and more funda-mental level, however, the death penalty has become a potent symbol of hardline campaigns against crime, which, in their turn, encapsulate many of the social fears and the racial and class tensions of US society. It has thus been retained more as the symbol of a particular politics than as an instrumental aspect of penal policy—a point which is largely confirmed by the massive

[75] For a description, see Amnesty International, *United States of America: The Death Penalty* (London, 1987), pp. 114–25.
[76] Zimring and Hawkins, *Capital Punishment and the American Agenda*, p. 122.

number of offenders who have been sentenced to death without actually being executed. That the death penalty appears to have massive popular support in the USA does not differentiate that nation from others, since virtually every other country has exhibited this kind of public opinion so long as the capital sanction is in place and usually for many years afterwards. Once governments have proceeded to abolish the death penalty—and abolition has always occurred in the face of majority popular opposition—then public opinion tends slowly to change accordingly, and to learn to regard other sanctions as the 'ultimate' measures available in civilized society.[77] However, changing public opinion requires more than just the legal abolition of capital punishment: it also requires sustained public education and moral leadership. In many abolitionist countries, the death penalty lives on as a powerful symbol to be evoked whenever it appears politically useful.

This last point serves to show the extent to which sensibilities—which have a force and reality of their own—can none the less be shaped and influenced by political process and social forces. In the same way that social institutions can provide a sentimental education for a population, bringing about a refinement of feeling and a growing sensitivity to the rights or the sufferings of others, other, more reactionary policies can begin to undo this civilizing process, and to unleash aggressions, hostilities, and selfishness in the sphere of public life. Cultural and political forces thus struggle to create sensibilities and ways of feeling among the social groups which they address. In much the same way, the penal sensibilities of a society can be gradually heightened or else eroded by means of governmental example and political persuasion.

One important way in which critics and reformers have attempted to work on the sensibilities of the public (or at least upon the governing élite) is to try to make visible the brutality and suffering which is hidden in penal institutions—to bring violence out from behind the scenes, thus allowing it to impinge upon public consciousness and disturb the public conscience. Progressive and reforming movements typically proceed in this way—as has been seen recently in areas such as domestic violence and child abuse—and it has been the traditional role of the penal reformer to do precisely this. John Howard deliberately shocked the sensibilities of his contemporaries by showing the unseen violence, squalor, and suffering of the prisons and by emphasizing the humanity of those prisoners and debtors who endured it. In the same way prison reform in the twentieth century has often followed upon an event which has brought home to middle-class opinion the true character of punishments

---

[77] Zimring and Hawkins, *Capital Punishment and the American Agenda*, pp. 14–22. It is perhaps important to add that, on a world scale, countries which have abolished the death penalty are still a distinct minority. The recent Amnesty International report, *When the State Kills: The Death Penalty v. Human Rights* (London, 1989) lists 35 countries that have abolished the death penalty for all crimes, 18 which have done so for all 'ordinary' crimes (i.e. excluding military offences, treason, etc.) and a further 27 countries which can be considered de facto abolitionists in that they have not carried out executions for the past 10 years or more. Together, these abolitionist countries constitute only 44% of all countries in the world.

and the fact that prisoners are sometimes 'people like them'—as when suffragettes or conscientious objectors or political dissidents experienced imprisonment for themselves and communicated their experience to their peers.

If sensibilities do influence the forms which punishments take—and it seems clear that they do, though never directly or exclusively—then two consequences should follow. The first is the theoretical consequence that any analysis of penal forms or penal history must take these issues into account. We ought never to dismiss evidence of sensibilities as 'mere ideology' in the way that Rusche and Kirchheimer and even Foucault tend to do. The second is a practical point, namely, that cultural struggle, exposé journalism, and moral criticism—the traditional tools of the penal reformer—do have some measure of effectiveness in bringing about penal change. Penal forms are embedded within objective social structures *and* cultural frameworks. Political initiative, moral argument, the cultivation of sensibilities, and cultural education all play a part in shaping the details and regimes of society's penal institutions. Even if we cannot see the immediate possibility of changing society's infrastructure of class relations or its exclusory institutions, its administrative rationality, and its moral pluralism, we can still look to the influence of moral and cultural struggles in the penal realm. Social institutions may be more flexible than structuralist sociology allows.

11

Punishment as a Cultural Agent
Penality's Role in the Creation of Culture

1. Punishment and the Production of Culture

In my discussion of punishment and culture up to this point I have stressed the ways in which penal practices and discourses have been shaped by changing forms of mentality and sensibility. My concern has been to show how society's cultural patterns come to be imprinted upon its penal institutions, so that punishment becomes a practical embodiment of some of the symbolic themes, constellations of meaning, and particular ways of feeling which constitute the wider culture. Much of my argument has been cast in historical terms, seeking to show that the sources of penal change and the determinants of penal form are to be located not just in penological reasoning, or economic interest, or strategies of power, but also in the configurations of value, meaning, and emotion which we call 'culture'. In other words, and with due consideration to the interplay of variables and the multiplicity of determinants, the concern of the last two chapters has been to show 'culture' as a 'determinant' of punishment.

At a time when certain sociological theories and historical interpretations threaten to reduce the phenomenon of punishment to a matter of power-plays or stripped-down strategies of control, there is some value in stressing the causal formulation implied above, even if it does seem hopelessly self-evident when pronounced in general terms. (Would anyone really deny that culture helps shape punishment?) But as a description of the relations which hold between 'punishment' and 'culture' this formulation tells only half of the story—and perhaps the less interesting half at that. In truth, the broad patterns of cultural meaning undoubtedly influence the forms of punishment. But it is also the case that punishments and penal institutions help shape the overarching culture and contribute to the generation and regeneration of its terms. It is a two-way process—an interactive relationship—and if one is to think in terms of cause and effect or vectors of determination, then the arrows must run in both directions simultaneously (though they need not be of equal magnitude nor drawn on the same plane). Like any major social institution, punishment is shaped by broad cultural patterns which have their origins elsewhere, but it also generates its own local meanings, values, and sensibilities which contribute—in a small but significant way—to the *bricolage* of the dominant culture. Penal institutions are thus 'cause' as well as 'effect' with regard to culture.

This two-way relationship—which seems to confound the mechanical notions of causality which still sometimes prevail in social science—is nothing other than the constitutive interplay between the general and the particular: in this case, the local culture of penality and the generic cultural patterns of society. Foucault has captured something of the sense of this when he insists that penal relations are not just an expression of governmental power but are also a positive enactment and extension of it. In much the same way, I wish to argue that penal institutions positively construct and extend cultural meanings as well as repeating or 'reaffirming' them. Instead of thinking of punishment as a passive 'expression' or 'reflection' of cultural patterns established elsewhere, we must strive to think of it as an active generator of cultural relations and sensibilities. The aim of the present chapter, then, is to indicate just how penal practices contribute to the making of the larger culture, and to suggest the nature and significance of that contribution.

Like all social practices, punishment can be viewed from the point of view of social action or of cultural signification. It can be approached in cause-and-effect terms as an institution which 'does things' or in interpretative what-does-it-mean terms as an institution which 'says things'. (The distinction which this implies is undoubtedly analytical rather than real, and may obscure more than it reveals, but it does describe different modes of analysis which currently exist.) To a large extent, penologists have tended to analyse punishment in terms of social action and have been concerned to trace the impact of its practices in terms of its direct effects upon those immediately affected by its activities. Punishment is viewed as a set of practices which incarcerate, supervise, deprive of resources, or otherwise regulate and control offenders, and the task of the penologist is to measure the direct effects of these actions, tracing the reformative, deterrent, or incapacitative consequences of penal measures upon the population of offenders who have undergone sanctions. Penological research is thus typically the measurement and assessment of punishment conceived as a form of direct social action.

Even within conventional penology, however, it is recognized that punishment is also intended to address a wider population—to speak to potential offenders and to the public at large—and that in this respect it operates not by behavioural methods or physical action but instead by means of symbols, signs, declarations, and rhetorical devices. A few penologists have set about tracing these wider effects of penality, looking for evidence of 'general deterrence' or for indications that sentencing decisions affect levels of public satisfaction or insecurity but, on the whole, penologists have been unhappy with the unavoidable imprecision involved in research of this kind. The difficulties of accurate measurement, the lack of reliable data, and the impossibility of isolating penal variables from other attitude-forming forces, have led most penologists and criminologists to limit their research to more immediate—and more tangible—penological effects.

Given the concerns of conventional penology, and the practical tasks which that discipline sets itself, this reluctance to become embroiled with the wider social and cultural effects of punishment is perhaps understandable. Establishing hard penological information is sufficiently difficult in itself and sufficiently important in its consequences to justify a specialist form of endeavour operating within fairly narrow limits. However, for a sociology of punishment which seeks to understand penality's general role in society—as distinct from its direct effect upon offenders—any such reluctance would be misplaced and self-defeating. We have already seen that much of the literature which makes up the sociology of punishment is an attempt to trace the wider consequences of penality, asking how penal measures have reached beyond the offender population to influence social relations more generally. Sometimes this work has been undertaken in cause-and-effect terms, seeing punishment as a form of social action with a measurable impact upon other spheres (for example, quantitative research on the relationship between penal sanctions and the labour market). More often, though, it has combined a version of this approach with a more interpretative style of analysis, as, for example, where punishment is seen as an ideological mechanism (as in the writings of Hay or Pashukanis) or as a moral communication (as with Durkheim and Mead). And in adopting this more interpretative approach, the sociology of punishment has often exchanged the precision of detailed, grounded analysis for the suggestiveness and insight of more speculative and impressionistic interpretation —sometimes to good effect, sometimes not.

In seeking to analyse penal practice as an agent of cultural production or as a form of social signification, I am aware that I will be making interpretative statements which are backed by illustrative example rather than by solid evidence, and that my theoretical arguments will outrun the available data. To the extent that this calls for excuse or apology—and if it does then so does much of modern social theory—my defence plea is one of necessity, for it seems that the nature of the phenomena I am pursuing makes such methods inevitable, at least at this stage of the game.

2. PENALITY COMMUNICATES MEANING

The suggestion that will be pursued in this chapter is that penal practices, discourses, and institutions play an active part in the generative process through which shared meaning, value, and—ultimately—culture are produced and reproduced in society. Punishment, among other things, is a communicative and didactic institution. Through the media of its practices and declarations it puts into effect—and into cultural circulation—some of the categories and distinctions through which we give meaning to our world.

Values, conceptions, sensibilities, and social meanings—culture, in short— do not just exist in the form of a natural atmosphere which envelopes social action and makes it meaningful. Rather, they are actively created and recreated by our social practices and institutions—and punishment plays its part in this generative and regenerative process. Punishment is one of the many institutions which helps construct and support the social world by producing the shared categories and authoritative classifications through which individuals understand each other and themselves. In its own way, penal practice provides an organizing cultural framework whose declarations and actions serve as an interpretative grid through which people evaluate conduct and make moral sense of their experience. Penality thus acts as a regulatory social mechanism in two distinct respects: it regulates conduct directly through the physical medium of social action, but it also regulates meaning, thought, attitude—and hence conduct—through the rather different medium of signification.

In the course of its routine activities, punishment teaches, clarifies, dramatizes, and authoritatively enacts some of the basic moral–political categories and distinctions which help form our symbolic universe. It routinely interprets events, defines conduct, classifies action, and evaluates worth, and, having done so, it sanctions these judgments with the authority of law, forcefully projecting them on to offenders and the public audience alike. To some extent, this expressive, symbolizing function of penal practice is already recognized and understood—not just in the thinking of philosophers like Joel Feinberg but also in the practice of judges and penal practitioners, who are acutely aware that their statements and actions reach out to a wide audience and have a symbolic significance for many.[1] But when this expressive quality of penality is discussed, even in Feinberg's work, attention is usually focused upon the obvious signs of reprobation, condemnation, and stigma which penal sanctions clearly and self-consciously convey. What remains unexplored is the way in which penality is involved in the production of wider and more fundamental social meanings, which go beyond the immediacies of condemnation and speak of other subjects and other symbols.

The suggestion which I wish to make here, and to explore in the pages that follow, is that penality communicates meaning not just about crime and punishment but also about power, authority, legitimacy, normality, morality, personhood, social relations, and a host of other tangential matters. Penal signs and symbols are one part of an authoritative, institutional discourse which seeks to organize our moral and political understanding and to educate our sentiments and sensibilities. They provide a continuous, repetitive set of instructions as to how we should think about good and evil, normal and pathological, legitimate and illegitimate, order and disorder. Through their judgments, condemnations, and classifications they teach us (and persuade us) how to judge, what to condemn, and how to classify, and they supply a set of languages, idioms, and vocabularies with which to do so. These signifying practices also tell us where to locate social authority, how to preserve order and community, where to look for social dangers, and how to feel about these matters, while the evocative effect of penal symbols sets off chains of reference and association in our minds, linking the business of punishment into questions of politics, morality, and social order. In short, the practices, institutions, and

[1] Feinberg, *Doing and Deserving*.

discourses of penality all *signify*, and the meanings which are conveyed thereby tend to outrun the immediacies of crime and punishment and 'speak of' broader and more extended issues. Penality is thus a cultural text—or perhaps better, a cultural performance—which communicates with a variety of social audiences and conveys an extended range of meanings. No doubt it is 'read' and understood in very different ways by different social groups—and the data we have on this crucial issue of 'reception' (as the literary critics call it) are woefully inadequate.[2] But if we are to understand the social effects of punishment then we are obliged to trace this positive capacity to produce meaning and create 'normality' as well as its more negative capacity to suppress and silence deviance.

I am conscious that in pursuing this line of enquiry I am retracing ground that has, to some extent, been covered in earlier chapters of this book. My previous discussions of Marxism, of Elias, and especially of Durkheim have already suggested that penal rituals and practices can and do affect social attitudes by shaping the understandings and sensibilities of their social audience. In some sense or other, concepts such as 'ideology' and 'collective representation' are intended to imply the cultural constitution of subjectivity, community, and social relations, and to the extent that punishment is seen as having an ideological aspect (cf. Hay, Pashukanis, Hall *et al.*) or a moral function (cf. Durkheim, Erikson, Garfinkel) these other analyses address the point that I wish to make here. However, these Marxist and Durkheimian discussions have been circumscribed, in ways that I have already indicated, by the theoretical frameworks within which they exist. The Marxist concept of ideology has been used to reveal class domination in the realm of culture or ideas, but it has revealed little else, while the Durkheimian conception of penal signs is at once too 'collective', in so far as it lacks a sense of social division, and too much a 'representation' in that penal signs are merely a repetition of what already exists elsewhere, in the *conscience collective.* One account lacks any sense of penality's independent rhetorical qualities, while the other conceives it as a rhetoric which must always be an expression of class interests.

At certain points, Foucault's work begins to present a more positive and expansive discussion of penality's rhetorical qualities, especially when he discusses 'the meaning of the scaffold' in the early modern period, and later, the 'semiotic' style of punishment suggested by certain reformers in the eighteenth century. But in his discussion of modern penality, the analysis of signs gives way to the analysis of discourses—such as scientific criminology or rehabilitative penology—which are dealt with primarily as instrumental forms of power–knowledge, functioning in a disciplinary process. Consequently the wider, symbolic significance of penal practices and statements is left largely unexplored.

---

[2] For a discussion of some of the problems, see N. Walker, *Sentencing: Theory, Law and Practice* (London, 1985), pp. 101–4.

In order to deal with these important issues clearly and without unnecessary restriction, I have chosen to take up this question of penal signification and deal with it explicitly, using concepts which are appropriate to the problem at hand. And rather than assume—as do the functionalist accounts of Durkheim and certain Marxists—that one already knows how penality communicates and with what effects, I will be addressing the issues in a way which is appropriate to the state of our knowledge, which is to say by means of some very basic enquiries. To that end, I will raise the following simple questions: how, and by what means, do penal practices signify and communicate meaning? What are punishment's social audiences? What kinds of meanings and categories do penal practices convey? How have these meanings varied over time? And finally why, if the foregoing is true, is punishment such a resonant and expressive social institution?

3. How does penality signify?

When we inspect the varied activities which make up the penal complex with a view to investigating its communicative or signifying aspects, our attention is immediately drawn to the more public and declaratory practices of the institution. In the past, these would have included all those sanctions which were executed in public, before a watching crowd—such as the pillory, the whipping cart, the stocks, the scaffold, or the various kinds of public works and public humiliations. Included too would be the rituals of public confession and the semi-official printed broadsheets which were sold to the public, both of which articulated in more explicit terms the moral message which these public punishments sought to convey. Nowadays, of course, penal sanctions are rarely executed in public, but there are still elements of penal practice which are deliberately designed for public consumption and which are communicated to a social audience. One thinks particularly of the judicial declaration of sentence, and any remarks which the judge chooses to append to this crucial speech-act: a declaration or performative statement which is directed not just at the offender but also—via the press and the public gallery—to victims, to potential offenders, and to the public at large. In the late twentieth century, as in the eighteenth, the moment of sentencing is understood as 'an occasion for addressing the multitude' and there is seldom a newspaper which appears without carrying an account of some judge's remarks and the circumstances which prompted them.

There are also other occasions and other ways in which our penal institutions set about addressing a wide audience. Government policy statements are written to describe and justify penal practice to the public. The same is true of all the annual reports produced by the many agencies involved in the criminal justice process, and of the reports of commissions of enquiry set up to investigate specific scandals or to provide a basis for new reforms. An equally prolific, though less authoritative, form of penological representation derives from the work of penal reformers, critics, and, nowadays, academics, whose accounts of the penal system, its philosophical basis, or its inherent problems and need for change often reach a wide audience, and occasionally attain a semi-official status—especially if the authorities choose to accept their findings or their recommendations for reform. These documents, and others, provide a public representation of penal practice, in an orthodox textual form, often composed in equal part of factual description, persuasive rhetoric, and institutional propaganda. And to the extent that historians and sociologists have examined the signifying (or 'ideological') aspects of punishment, it is usually to these texts that they have first turned.

However, to confine our analysis to the speech-acts, performances, and publications which are officially intended for public consumption would be to ignore some of the most important signifying aspects of penality. In particular, it would neglect all those practices and discourses which function as instrumental, operative elements of the sanctioning process but which also perform a crucial rhetorical or representational role at the same time. If we wish to understand the cultural messages conveyed by punishment we need to study not just the grandiloquent public statements which are occasionally made but also the pragmatic repetitive routines of daily practice, for these routines contain within them distinctive patterns of meaning and symbolic forms which are enacted and expressed every time a particular procedure is adopted, a technical language used, or a specific sanction imposed. Despite the attention given to policy documents, commission reports, and philosophical statements, it is the daily routine of sanctioning and institutional practice which does most to create a particular framework of meaning (Foucault would say a 'regime of truth') in the penal realm, and it is to these practical routines that we should look first of all to discover the values, meanings, and conceptions which are embodied and expressed in penality.

It would seem, then, that the conventional distinctions drawn between instrumental activities and symbolic activities, or between 'social action' and 'cultural meaning' are of little use here. For these analytical divisions imply a separation which in reality does not exist—as we have seen, in penality the instrumental *is* symbolic and the social act of punishment, however mundane, is at the same time an expression of cultural meaning. Perhaps a better set of terms to use in this context would be the notion of a 'signifying practice' (which can be discursive or non-discursive) and of a 'practical rhetoric'—both of which have the advantage of traversing the artificial divide between language and action, the mental and the physical, the ideal and the real. In any case, the important thing to realize is that *all* practices, of whatever kind, are potentially signifying practices. Whatever else it does, even the most mundane form of conduct in the social world is also a possible source of expression, of symbolization, and of meaningful communication—every action is also a gesture. And as I shall argue in a moment, official penal practice is particularly laden with social and cultural significance.

The presence of symbolic meaning within the everyday forms of pragmatic penal action is most easily observed if we consider the practice of sentencing. In 'passing sentence' the sentencer performs a routine, instrumental action which has the effect of activating a subsequent legal process. He or she performs a speech-act—'I sentence you to three years imprisonment'—which has the practical effect of authorizing and setting in motion a procedure of incarceration. The activity of sentencing is thus an operative element in an instrumental process of dealing with offenders. But the declaration of sentence also conveys a symbolic statement which may be read and understood by a wide audience (or audiences) beyond the court-room.

At the minimum, the sentence may be repeating a message which is already well known—for example, that the legal system condemns acts of criminal violence, and will punish them severely. In such cases, the sanction of 'three years imprisonment' signals a particular level of social censure, and fixes the meaning of that censure in a way that will be conventionally understood. Thus 'imprisonment' signifies the stigma or infamy of true criminality; 'three years' further qualifies the message, showing the censure to be of medium severity, pitched somewhere between the maximum and minimum available. If this kind of sentence is the standard tariff for the offence in question, then the symbolic statement which it contains is likely to occur without comment or analysis on the part of the public, and so the significance of the message will be merely reaffirmative. But the importance of the communication is dramatically heightened if the symbolic message which it contains is unexpected or in some way controversial. So, for example, if the three years imprisonment was imposed for a particularly heinous rape, its comparative leniency might be taken to symbolize a denigration of women's rights, or a demeaning of the particular victim involved, and might seem to imply (or 'symbolize') a particular understanding of the relations between men and women, and their relative worth, which resonates with patriarchal attitudes and traditions. On the other hand, if the same sentence was given to a drunk driver or someone found guilty of insider trading on the stock market, then a very different political and social message would be implied which would, in present circumstances, disturb the taken-for-granted evaluations of such conduct and the state's attitude towards it.

It seems clear from this example that as well as being a cog in an instrumental process, sentencing is a signifying practice of some importance. The various sanctions available to the court are not merely a repertoire of techniques for handling offenders, they are also a system of signs which are used to convey specific meanings in terms which are generally understood by the social audience.[3] Each specific sanction has attached to it a recognizable symbolism, so that, in any particular context, imprisonment means one thing, a fine another, probation something else, and so on. Thus whenever a sentence

---

[3] See on this P. Q. Hirst, 'The Concept of Punishment' in his *Law, Socialism and Democracy*, and also Feinberg, *Doing and Deserving*.

is passed, the sentencer knowingly deploys a conventional device for the expression of meaning, and engages in a symbolic communication of greater or lesser significance.

Another means by which penality signifies is through the discourses and penological knowledges which are used in its practices. As Foucault showed in *Discipline and Punish*, and as I sought to demonstrate in *Punishment and Welfare*, specific discourses—such as 'criminology', 'eugenics', or 'social work'—are put to work in penal institutions and help organize the practices of classification, assessment, reform, or incapacitation which different regimes adopt. Much of this is internal to the institutions, and is articulated in technical documents and expert decisions, so it might well be considered to be of limited rhetorical significance—to be primarily a method of doing things rather than of saying things. But, once again, these technical discourses and the practices which they make possible are not merely a silent, functioning machinery. They are also, as Kenneth Burke insists, a kind of 'oratory' even though they often pass for sheer 'information', 'knowledge', or 'science'.[4]

When the penal system adopts a particular conception of criminals and criminality, or a specific way of classifying prisoners, or a particular psychology of motivation and reform; or when it begins to use a particular vocabulary to describe offenders and to characterize their conduct, such conceptions and vocabularies are never confined to the in-house activities of expert practitioners. Instead they feed back into the wider society, and frequently enter into conventional wisdom and general circulation. Terms such as 'degenerate', 'feeble-minded', 'imbecile', 'delinquent', 'kleptomaniac', 'psychopath', and 'career criminal' quickly became common currency after only a few years of official use, as did the associated vocabularies of 'treatment' and 'rehabilitation'. Nor are these merely disembodied words, used without meaningful consequence, for their adoption in common use brings with it a whole way of thinking which slowly changes social attitudes, or at least makes available new vocabularies of motive and new explanatory languages with which to think about crime and human conduct. Moreover, as we will see, to represent the business of punishment in quasi-scientific terms, and to organize penal practices accordingly, promotes a particular image of the state and of its authority, and of its relationship to offenders and other citizens. Indeed, it has been argued with some force that the official adoption of scientific languages and rehabilitative forms in modern penal institutions has sometimes had more to do with the cultural symbolism involved than with the desire fully to implement the practices that they imply.[5] As anyone who has compared official rhetoric to the actualities of institutions will know, many 'policies' exist more at the level of public representation than of operational practice.

So penal practices and discourses, however workaday or instrumental they may seem, tend simultaneously to signify in ways which connect with the

[4] K. Burke, *A Rhetoric of Motives* (Berkeley, 1969).
[5] See e.g. Smith and Fried, *The Uses of the American Prison*.

wider culture. Indeed, what information we have about the formulation of penal policy and the management of institutional regimes strongly suggests that penal functionaries are conscious of this symbolic resonance and take pains to control the way in which their practices will be interpreted. A crucial intermediary here is, however, the various media which relay and represent penal events to the public. And since these media have their own dynamics and commercial concerns, it is generally the case that news values and editorial interests restrict and select the penal messages that are effectively conveyed to a wide public audience.[6]

A further source of public representation and cultural symbolism to be found in the penal realm is the actual fabric of penal institutions and the appearance of penal functionaries. As Pat Carlen has shown in some detail, the structural, spatial, and temporal arrangements deployed in court-rooms, and their positioning of the parties involved in the proceedings, convey definite symbolic meanings which are of some importance in the conduct of a trial.[7] Similarly, the fact that prison officers wear uniforms and probation officers do not, conveys an important and much discussed difference in image and social meaning as well as having certain implications for the wearer's self-conception.[8] In much the same way, the furnishings and arrangements of a juvenile court or children's hearing are designed to differentiate it symbolically from a regular court of law.

One of the most important instances of this symbolism of physical appearance, at least in modern penal systems, is contained in the external imagery of the prison, and in the iconography of institutional architecture. This, after all, is the physical aspect of modern punishment which is most directly visible to the public eye, and prison architects and designers have usually taken care to control the imagery thus projected and to use it to good effect. Recent studies of penitentiary architecture by Robin Evans and John Bender have shown how design conventions and vocabularies of representation have changed over time, producing major alterations in the style and decoration used in prison façades, portals, and entrance lodges.[9] Thus the kind of *tableau vivant* appearance which the Newgate prison displayed to the public in the eighteenth century, with its conventional city-gate architecture enlivened by the visible appearance

---

[6] On the role of the media with respect to criminal justice, see Ericson *et al.*, *Negotiating Control: A Study of News Sources*; id., *Visualizing Deviance: A Study of News Organization* (Toronto, 1987); and S. Cohen and J. Young (eds.), *The Manufacture of News: Deviance, Social Problems and the Mass Media* (London, 1981).

[7] Carlen, *Magistrates' Justice*.

[8] On the social significance of uniforms, see A. Giddens, *The Nation State and Violence* (Oxford, 1985), p. 114.

[9] Evans, *The Fabrication of Virtue*, and Bender, *Imagining the Penitentiary*. Other useful studies include P. Q. Hirst, 'Power/Knowledge: Constructed Space and the Subject', in R. Fardon (ed.), *Power and Knowledge: Anthropological and Sociological Approaches* (Edinburgh, 1985); N. Johnstone, *The Human Cage: A Brief History of Prison Architecture* (New York, 1973); P. Dickens, S. McConville, and L. Fairweather (eds.), *Penal Policy and Prison Architecture* (Chichester, 1978); and the United Nations Social Defence Research Institute, *Prison Architecture* (London, 1975).

of prisoners at the begging gate and at the open windows, later gave way to the very different imagery of *architecture terrible*, which was explicitly designed to project a visual representation of the meaning of imprisonment. This representational form physically conveyed a fearful, deterrent image of incarceration by means of horrific façades covered with decorative details such as spikes, draped chains, and statues of convicts, or else by adopting an enclosed, mausoleum-like appearance which bespoke the symbolism of entombment and the living death which incarceration might involve.

It is of particular interest in the present context that, as Evans points out, the deterrent façades which were designed for many nineteenth-century prisons actually belied the reality of what went on inside. While, internally, the penitentiaries enacted a reformed and comparatively humane regime, the exterior walls still implied a gothic image of dungeons, chains, and abandonment. As Evans puts it: 'the persistence of castle and fetter as the principal emblems of imprisonment bore no relation to the realities of contemporary discipline, nor were they meant to. They were employed as a consciously deceptive deterrent, keeping old fears alive by reflecting a popular, melodramatic picture of the prison back towards the public.'[10] Subsequently, the symbolically explicit architecture—or *architecture parlante*—of the reformed prisons (some of which can still be seen, for example, at the old entrance of the state penitentiary at Trenton, New Jersey, or at the gateway of the Amsterdam house of correction) gave way to what one might call the *architecture faisante* of Pentonville and after. This was an architecture which eschewed emblematics or iconography in favour of a 'purely functional' design, adapted to the disciplinary and reformative logic of the internal prison regime and to the individual cell-and-inspection principles which formed the basis of that system.[11] Henceforth, prisons were designed—often by penal administrators rather than architects— as instrumental devices, built upon 'causal' principles rather than as symbolic monuments concerned with external display. However, as I have already suggested, signification tends to occur, whether intended or not, and even the blank architecture of the new prisons soon became a potent symbol of confinement. As Evans points out: '. . . Jebb's radial cell blocks, which henceforth would form the skyline of every new [British] prison, became a direct and powerful evocation in their own right, though he had not regarded their appearance as a matter of any importance in designing them.'[12] Indeed, as Nicholas Taylor argues, the massive prisons of the Victorian age are a prime example of what Edmund Burke described as the 'Sublime'—an aesthetic which combines qualities of Terror, Obscurity, Vastness, and Silence to produce a powerful effect of awe upon the beholder.[13]

[10] Evans, *The Fabrication of Virtue*, pp. 225–6.
[11] For an interesting discussion of architecture's role in the construction of subjectivity, see Hirst, 'Power/Knowledge: Constructed Space and the Subject'.
[12] Evans, *The Fabrication of Virtue*, p. 4.
[13] N. Taylor, 'The Awful Sublimity of the Victorian City: Its Aesthetic and Cultural Origins', in H. J. Dyos and M. Wolff (eds.), *The Victorian City: Images and Realities*, ii (London, 1973).

Today we still build prisons according to the functional logic which emerged in the course of the nineteenth century, and their exteriors are generally designed to serve the ends of security, containment, and anonymity, rather than deliberate or carefully construed representation. But these muted, functional buildings nevertheless project an eloquent and well-understood symbolism, which speaks of unshakeable authority, of stored-up power, and of a silent, brooding capacity to control intransigence. Indeed it is precisely because it subverts this calm imagery of institutional power and order that the sight of protesting inmates on a prison roof is so disturbing to the public and authorities alike.

One might add that it is in the realm of literature, drama, and phantasy that the traces of the prison's symbolic power are most graphically and pervasively encountered, though such effects generally elude the measuring tools of social science. For having lived in the presence of these secretive yet evocative buildings for more than 200 years, their imagery and the complex of emotions and meanings which they suggest have by now become embedded in our culture. So much so, that nowadays 'the prison' is as much a basic metaphor of our cultural imagination as it is a feature of our penal policy.[14]

4. The question of audience

If, as I have been arguing, penal practice must also be regarded as a signifying practice and if that signifying aspect is sometimes controlled and put to official use as a form of rhetoric, then the question of intended audience becomes important. Rhetoric, in whatever form, is always an attempt to persuade, to produce identifications, to move its recipients to attitude and to action.[15] Consequently, it is generally formulated with a specific audience in mind, seeking to adopt a form of address which will engage people of a particular kind, in a particular situation. In order to succeed, any rhetoric must first create recognition on the part of its audience—its audience must recognize its concerns, be familiar with its language, feel themselves to be specifically addressed by the speaker, and so on. So even though a rhetoric sets out to transform an audience in some way or other, the envisaged audience and its characteristics may be crucial in shaping the general form which the signifying practice will adopt.

In the penal sphere, there are, as we have seen, a variety of situations in which signifying practices occur and a variety of audiences to which they are addressed. The most immediate recipients of the messages conveyed by penal measures are, of course, the population of convicted offenders. It is they who are first in line to be 'taught a lesson' by punishment, both in the court-room

[14] In *Imagining the Penitentiary* John Bender describes how 'the removal of penal confinement from the realm of direct experience' eventually prompted 'the projection of punishment into imagination', p. 231.
[15] See Burke, *A Rhetoric of Motives*, p. 41.

where they are sentenced and subsequently in undergoing their sanction. The judge's homily and the terse, 'plain speaking' words of condemnation which often accompany the passing of sentence are the mode by which this message is first conveyed, and, as we have seen, the sentence itself communicates a definite meaning which is clearly signalled to the individual offender. Once inside a custodial institution (or even in a probation office, or some other penal situation), the offender becomes part of a different and larger audience—the audience of inmates. This audience may be addressed in a whole variety of ways—as 'clients', as 'patients', as 'prisoners', or 'residents'—and more or less effort may be made on the part of the authorities to enter into a communicative relationship with the inmates.

In the original vision of penitentiary reformers such as Howard, prisoners were to be continually addressed by moral exhortations, lectures, and sermons until they were convinced of the sinfulness of their actions and the righteousness of their punishment. Similarly, the advocates of rehabilitation in the twentieth century urged that the offender be made a participant in a therapeutic encounter, through which he or she would come to learn a set of norms and attitudes better adapted to normal social life. In practice, most modern institutions—and many non-custodial measures—have failed to implement these developed forms of persuasion, and have singularly lacked the moral rhetoric and communicative relations which reformers envisaged. Indeed, in comparison with the institution's original intentions, or with the public's lingering beliefs in the prison's moral efficacy, the internal regimes of most modern prisons are remarkably deficient in 'moral tone' and rarely adopt any serious attempt to instil virtue or morality beyond the basic demands of obedience and discipline.[16]

Nevertheless, these institutions do inevitably address a specific rhetoric to their inmate audiences, even if it is only the amoral and dehumanizing rhetoric of a regime which treats prisoners primarily as bodies to be counted and objects to be administered. For the daily practices of an institution, no matter how mundane, tend to take on a definite meaning for those who are subjected to them. And whatever meanings the judge, or the public, or the penitentiary reformers meant to convey by sending offenders to prison, it is the day-to-day actualities of the internal regime which do most to fix the meaning of imprisonment for those inside.[17] If this regime is just, fairly administered,

---

[16] In 19th-cent. prisons moral lectures and uplifting talks were commonplace, as were the visits of chaplains, religious sermons, and Bible-readings. Even in the 20th cent., places such as Borstals and juvenile reformatories laid great stress upon the communication of moral and religious truths. In most modern prisons this has largely disappeared and television and films have replaced moral exhortations as a form of diversion.

[17] In the atmosphere of confinement and deprivation which imprisonment creates, even the most petty or trivial aspects of life can take on a heavy weight of significance. The quality of prison food, the distribution of minor privileges, the tone of voice of staff, the idiosyncratic habits of other inmates, personal belongings of little financial value, can all become the focus of intense emotion and the cause of serious conflicts. Similarly, the lay-out and furnishings of a prison cell, the

caring, and humane, it is possible that its recipients will learn some of the lessons of citizenship, though prison inmates usually form a formidably sceptical audience. However, if, as is more usual, the prison regime belies its good intentions, and in the name of administrative convenience, allows a measure of injustice, or arbitrariness, or indifference, or brutality, then it is likely to inspire nothing but resentment and opposition from this particular audience. Any moral message which the authorities may wish to hold out will be spoiled by the signs of hypocrisy, by self-contradiction, or simply by the extent to which inmates are already alienated from the legal system and all that it stands for.

If convicted offenders form the most immediate audience for the practical rhetoric of punishment, being directly implicated within its practices and being the ostensible target of its persuasive attempts, there is also another, distinctive audience which experiences punishment up close. This is the audience of penal professionals—of all those functionaries who staff the penal system, and make it work. Perhaps surprisingly, those sociological accounts of punishment which deal with the symbolic or ideological effects of penality tend to ignore this group, preferring to think instead of offenders, the working class, or 'the public' as the target groups addressed by penal representations. But it is undoubtedly the case that in modern penal politics the professionals who run the system form the largest single interest group, and are perhaps the most attentive and influential audience in respect of penal policy and institutional practice. Like the offenders whom they administer, penal functionaries are caught up in the details of penal practices and are affected by the forms which these practices adopt.

Professional 'punishers' are defined by penal forms and penal relations in the same way as those whom they punish, so that the symbolism and rhetorical content of specific sanctions is of crucial importance to the administrators and staff of these institutions. Thus a penal measure which is couched in the language of welfare or correctionalism identifies the penal agent as one of the 'helping professions' and implies a status, a public image, and a career which accord with this role—which is one reason why the rehabilitative ethos was so widely supported by the penal agents of most countries. Alternatively, a more punitive rhetoric can seek to redefine a measure such as probation or parole, emphasizing its role as a form of community punishment and supervision, and, in so doing, it can threaten to transform 'experts' in social work counselling into mere supervisors and police agents.[18]

The predominant idiom in which punishment is phrased will thus tend to

availability of radios, televisions, and telephones, the prison's sanitary arrangements, the conduct of family visits, and so on, may take on a significance for inmates which is hard to appreciate for those who have never been 'inside'.

[18] This has already occurred, to some extent, in the USA. The 1988 Home Office Green Paper *Punishment, Custody and the Community* (Cmnd. 424), if implemented, would bring about similar changes in England and Wales.

identify not just the nature of those punished, but also the character of those who are employed in the penal process. A religious idiom will impart a certain evangelical quality to the work of penal agents, a therapeutic idiom will cast them as correctional agents, while an administrative style will define those involved as managers, administrators, and bureaucratic functionaries. (Though within each of these frameworks there is room for a division of labour: in a prison it may only be the governors, chaplains, and 'professionals' who perform a religious or reformative role, while the officers are mere turnkeys or security guards.) Of course the definition of an occupational role is not merely a matter of rhetoric or vocabulary—qualifications, training, salary, function, and status are all involved. But many of the occupational groups involved in the penal system are still poorly established, are of uncertain status, and have experienced rapidly changing work regimes: in such circumstances, penal functionaries have a large stake in the ways in which penal measures are expressed and defined.

Of course this professional audience is not exactly a unified one, and will often be divided by the factional interests and the diverging self-conceptions of the various groups involved. As Jacobs showed in his account of the Stateville penitentiary, a rhetoric which favours correctional experts and a therapeutic conception of penality may be experienced by rank and file prison guards as a threat to their status. Similarly, an action which symbolizes arbitrariness or injustice to the prisoners may be undertaken because it signifies something quite different—such as power and leadership—to the audience of prison guards.[19] But whatever its internal differences and complications, there can be no doubt that penal professionals form a crucial audience for penal representations and rhetoric. Whenever policy documents are drafted, or new institutional regimes devised, one of the major considerations taken into account is the way in which these developments will be received by penal agents—in terms of both their practical consequence *and* their symbolic significance. Great care is taken to ensure that suitable terms are used, that the language is appropriate and acceptable to interested parties, and that the imagery projected by the document or practice does not negatively affect the morale or self-conception of the groups most directly involved. As sociologists have occasionally noted in other contexts, one of the major functions of 'ideology' in the penal realm is to maintain the support and morale of those who staff penal institutions. And the more penal practice becomes professionalized, technical, and privatized (in the ways discussed earlier), the more it generates documents and rhetorics which have as their primary audience, the functionaries of the system.[20]

---

[19] Jacobs, *Stateville.*

[20] Another well-informed and increasingly influential audience is composed of the various reform groups which exist on the fringes of the penal system, together with academic criminologists and researchers. The modern policy-making process often involves a degree of consultation with such groups, and official statements may be phrased in terms which connect with the ideologies of the more forceful lobbyists. See M. Ryan, *The Acceptable Pressure Group: A Case-Study of the Howard League and R.A.P.* (Farnborough, 1978), and P. Rock, *A View from the Shadows* (Oxford, 1986).

The third major audience to which penal rhetoric is directed is usually termed 'the general public'. This, in a sense, is the ultimate audience for all penal symbolism, particularly in open, democratic societies, because all juridical punishments are state activities and potentially subject to public review.[21] It is also an audience which is at a distance from events, and is often reached through intermediaries (especially the press, and 'common knowledge'), which tends to make it impressionable rather than informed, and more susceptible to broad imagery than to fine detail. Sometimes this wide audience is directly addressed, as where policy announcements are made in public form, or where prison walls and court practices are made visible for all to see. More often the communication is mediated, and indirect—thus an institutional regime or a technical policy directive will have a more immediate audience, to which it is chiefly directed, but, because it may be subsequently relayed to a wider public, care is usually taken to give it an appropriate symbolic form. Where this proves to be too difficult, the tendency of modern penal institutions is to seek control over the dissemination of information and representations, for example by limiting press and public access, censoring prisoners' mail, or by ensuring that official accounts are the only authorized source of information available.

Within routine penal practice, specific public audiences are frequently identified and directly addressed. Thus, for example, judges frequently address themselves to what they think of as 'the criminal fraternity' and seek to convey a definite message to that group—invariably a deterrent message expressed through the device of 'exemplary' sentencing. Similarly government ministers and officials sometimes address declarations of intent towards specific groups of offenders or potential offenders such as terrorists, drunk drivers, drug-dealers, police-killers, and so on. On their surface, these declarations are straightforward threats of a deterrent type, aimed at a specific audience, and as such they may occasionally be effective. But they are also, and quite deliberately, an oblique communication with a different and larger audience— 'the general public'—to whom they are intended to express not a threat but a reassurance.

Public statements—whether verbal or practical—which convey particular attitudes towards crime, also communicate a range of associated meanings to the onlooking public. Governments, officials, and the judiciary are, of course, well aware of this and routinely employ this oblique mode of public address in order to represent themselves and their policies to a broad audience. Given the social differentiation which exists in modern society, 'the general public' is frequently a very divided audience and its various sectors will differ in their receptivity to particular forms of rhetoric. Particular policies, styles of repre-

---

[21] Even where penal institutions are owned and managed by private agencies or corporations they are, in modern society, carrying out legally imposed penal sanctions with the delegated authority of the state. In this sense, juridical punishment remains a 'state activity' even when its administration is delegated to others.

sentation, and languages of punishment will appeal to different sectors of the audience, and modern politicians are skilled at manipulating the symbolism of 'law and order' in order to connect with the fears, insecurities, and prejudices of their intended audience. Thus a penal representation which is publicly made may be 'received' by the public as a whole, as, for example, in the context of a general election, where maximum publicity is given to such statements. But it may well have the effect of further dividing that audience, and exacerbating the polarities of race, class, and ideology.

5. WHAT KIND OF MEANINGS DO PENAL PRACTICES CONVEY?

We have already seen that the fact of legal punishment carries with it a clearly understood internal meaning; indeed one might argue that part of punishment's definition is that it conveys a symbolism of censure, condemnation, and reprobation. But here I want to point to some of the other meanings which punishment broadcasts to its social audience.

In the process of punishing, penal institutions demonstrate (and give authority to) specific practices of blaming, holding accountable, and fixing responsibility. These institutions tacitly hold out their own practices as models or exemplars, showing how conduct and persons are to be held to account, by whom, and on which terms. Potentially at least, there are as many ways of doing this as there are competing moralities, but the established institutions of punishment give their authority to a particular form of accountability, and in doing so they sanction a particular form of moral ordering and a specific conception of morality. Nor is this a marginal or specialist activity—a justice only for criminals. It is literally the Law, the authoritative voice of society, using force and authority publicly to enact its basic terms and relationships and to impress them, like a template, upon the conduct of social life.

Implicit within every penal relation and every exercise of penal power there is a conception of social authority, of the (criminal) person, and of the nature of the community or social order that punishment protects and tries to re-create. Whenever an offender is held to account, a sentence passed, or a sanction imposed, these figures of authority, personhood, and community are represented (symbolically) and enacted (materially) by the words and actions involved. Punishment is thus a concrete and practical demonstration of the official verities. It is a dramatic, performative representation of the way things officially are and ought to be, whatever else the deviant would make of them. And by means of its example, its repetition, and its practical enactments, punishment helps construct a social regime in which these forms of authority, personhood, and community are in fact the established ones.

As I have already stressed, penality does not create this 'regime of truth', this socially constructed world, all by itself. Other structures, practices, and symbolic forms (of an economic, political, or cultural kind) are also and more centrally involved in what is, after all, a complex, aggregative process of world-making. But nor does punishment simply echo what is already established: the law and its sanctioning practices play an independently constructive role in the creation of a cultural order. As a distinctive institution, punishment imparts a specific framework of meaning which co-ordinates with other social representations but is not reducible to them. We can perhaps see this more clearly if we examine these embodied conceptions in more detail.

5.1 *The depiction of social authority*

Take, first of all, the way in which social authority is figured or represented in punishment. In the acts and institutions of punishment, the state—or ruling élite of whatever kind—self-consciously constructs its own public image and, in part, its own reality. The forms which punishments take, the symbols through which they claim legitimacy, the discourses in which they represent their meaning, the organizational forms and resources which they employ, all tend to depict a particular style of authority—a definite characterization of the power which punishes.

Both Foucault and Durkheim have shown how the absolutist state represents and re-creates itself as 'absolute' in the act of punishment by means of a terrifying display of military might, together with an invocation of divine right and authority. In this political context, the exercise of punishment is one of many ceremonies in which the distance between sovereign and subjects is measured and the ascendancy of authority revealed. The public execution takes the form of a theatrical spectacle in which the sheer force of the sovereign's power is publicly displayed upon the body of the condemned. At the same time, the vital connection between the sovereign and God is reinforced, not just by the display of the sovereign's power over life and death, but also by the religious language and symbolism (of the publicly announced sentence, the offender's ritualized confession, and the cleric's prayers and benediction) which tie the law of the sovereign to the will of God and the natural order of things. In this form of punishment, authority is construed as absolute, divinely inspired, and socially ascendant.

Social authority is figured differently in the penal practice of the nineteenth-century liberal state. Here the overarching motif is not one of Power or of Faith but of Law. In the language of nineteenth-century punishment, the state is represented as the embodiment of the social contract, the socially authorized upholder of rights and enforcer of duties under the law. Within this framework, punishment is not so much a sovereign act as a contractual duty which the state performs in accordance with the law, observing strict adherence to its terms. Punishments cease to be personalistic, bearing the stamp of the sovereign will. The authority they suggest is institutional, rather than individual—the rule of law not the rule of a prince. The preferred sanctions of this penal style—sanctions such as the prison or the fine—are non-violent, regulated, uniform, and are dispensed in a controlled and lawful manner. The power which they symbolize, though still awesome in its way, is circumspect, clearly defined, and precisely limited. It has the authority of duly enacted law.[22]

To take a final example, the penal-welfare or 'correctionalist' practices and discourses of twentieth-century penality project a rather different image and style of governing authority. Their emphasis upon normalization and rehabilitation instead of punishment, upon individualized treatment instead of strict uniformity, and upon expertise and science rather than law and legal categories, all tend to redefine the state and its authority in welfarist rather than legal terms. The rhetorical representation here is of a state which cares for its citizens, has the resources to improve life, and takes extensive responsibility for the regulation of individual and social conduct. In the practice of probation, in social work with offenders, in the therapeutic counselling of prisoners—and in all the policy statements which promote this rehabilitative concept of punishment—we see a state which relates to its subjects not in the limited terms defined by law and contract but in a more expansive, supportive, and even therapeutic role. Within the symbolism of this signifying system, social authority is characterized in terms which suggest the professional ascendency of the doctor or the administrator. It projects an image of the social state which is defined by its ability and its willingness to assist, to care for, and, where necessary, to exert control over its subjects on the basis of a superior expertise and rationality.[23]

The forms through which punishment is exercised thus lead and persuade us to think about governmental power and social authority in a particular way. Spectators at an eighteenth-century public execution, visitors to a nineteenth-century penitentiary, observers at a twentieth-century correctional facility, will all tend to construe the meaning of the power to punish, and of state authority, in rather different ways. They will read different rhetorics, encounter different symbolic forms, and experience different ways of organizing and legitimizing the act of punishment—and their engagement with these signs and symbols will help shape the specific meaning which 'authority' has for them and for their particular society.

5.2 *The depiction of individual subjects*

Sociologists and historians have recently begun to explore the ways in which penal institutions symbolize and partially constitute the specific forms of power and social authority which are established in societies. Rather less well investigated, however, is the way in which penality, through its signifying and rhetorical practices, helps construct individual subjectivities. There has, of course, been much analysis of the ways in which penal institutions seek to reconstruct and reform—or indeed destroy—the offenders with whom they deal, and much of the best historiography in this area is taken up with describing the idealized visions of humanity which penal institutions have

---

[22] See Garland, *Punishment and Welfare*, chs. 1 and 2.
[23] Ibid., chs. 1 and 8.

projected on to their reluctant inmates. But it is important to realize that the involvement of penality in the construction of subjects goes further than this, and affects a wider population. Penal practices, discourses, and institutions hold out specific conceptions of subjectivity and they authorize specific forms of individual identity. In its routine practices—as well as in its more philosophical pronouncements—penality projects definite notions of what it is to be a person, what kinds of persons there are, and how such persons and their subjectivities are to be understood. Through its procedures for holding individuals acountable, penality defines the nature of normal subjectivity and the relationship which is generally assumed to hold between individual agents and their personal conduct. Thus, for example, modern courts will insist that individuals generally direct their own actions, have choice, will, intention, rationality, freedom, and so on, and judges will usually proceed to treat the offender in these terms. Similarly, the institutions of penality dictate the recognized ways in which this subjectivity and the individual control of conduct are prone to break down, for instance through insanity, diminished responsibility, provocation, passion, or whatever, so that an offender who is not normal according to the court's definition must then become deviant in ways which the court can recognize. In the social space of the court-room, no other identities are officially available.

In the course of its routine practices, penality spells out its assumptions about persons and gives these assumptions an institutional reality.[24] Individuals who appear before the courts are addressed, examined, and understood according to the law's implicit conception of a normal person and normal attributes. No matter what the reality of that individual is, the law insists upon seeing him or her in a particular, predefined way, and dispensing judgment accordingly. Institutions such as prisons, reformatories, and probation do the same thing, taking for granted specific conceptions of the person and projecting these on to the actual inmates or clients they encounter. Penality thus sets up the various subjects which appear before it in an authoritative and influential way. Its conception (or conceptions) of normal identity, being the one which is entrenched in law and legal proceedings, has a major cultural importance. It is the one which is expected of people, being socially and legally sanctioned and routinely enforced. Penality, in this respect, acts as an authoritative Other which helps to define the individual selves which stand in relation to it. It provides a basic model for our understanding of other people and for our understanding of ourselves.[25]

---

[24] Cf. Goffman, *Asylums*, p. 164: 'Built right into the social arrangements of an organization . . . is a thoroughly embracing conception of the member—and not merely a conception of him *qua* member, but behind this a conception of him *qua* human being.'

[25] Thus the reason why feminists have been so critical of the 'irrational' images of women sometimes mobilized in criminal justice has less to do with the discriminatory penal treatment that these might entail, than with the wider cultural identities which they help to reproduce for women in general. See Allen, *Justice Unbalanced*.

Again, we can see this more clearly if we consider how this works in concrete historical cases. Thomas Zeman describes how the Puritan punishments of seventeenth-century Massachusetts characterized the accused (and the 'normal subject') according to the terms of Protestant theology. Such persons were understood as free moral agents, able to choose good and evil and charged with responsibility for the state of their souls. Within this understanding of the human subject, spiritual attitude was the primary determinant of conduct, while material circumstances were a minor and subordinate force. The criminal who had chosen to defy God and Law was thus a sinner (which was indeed the fate of all men and women to some degree) and was punishable accordingly. However, even in the act of punishment, the offender's soul continued to be an object of concern and penal rituals were designed to encourage individual acts of atonement and redemption. Moreover, as we saw earlier, the sinful subjectivity of the offender was clearly represented as being akin to that of the onlooking members of the public. The penal authorities strove to produce a 'true sight of sin' on the part of the accused and the watching community, thereby revealing the truth of the human condition and the flawed nature of human subjectivity.[26]

Towards the end of the eighteenth century, and following in the wake of the Enlightenment, the new codes of law and penal practice which sprang up in Europe and America took up a rather more secular conception of the internal dynamics and characteristics of human persons. This Enlightenment subject of law was construed in various ways—as a Lockian creature of habit, shaped by experience as well as Reason, as a utilitarian calculator, rationally manœuvring between pleasure and pain, or as a moral agent guided by the faculty of moral sense—and the details of penitentiaries and reformative regimes were carefully adapted to suit these different conceptions. So for instance the model penitentiary regimes of the USA in the 1830s would begin by subjecting new prisoners to an extended period of silent, solitary confinement which amounted to a kind of prolonged sensory deprivation. But this treatment was originally designed not just to discipline individuals but literally to strip them of all the evil impressions and bad associations which had brought them to crime, and thus re-create a kind of Lockian *tabula rasa*. This reconstituted subject could then be exposed to a completely controlled environment in which only authorized and positive impressions (such as work, education, moral instruction) would be experienced, all negative impressions (such as idleness, other prisoners, the outside world) having been strenuously effaced.[27]

---

[26] Zeman, 'Order, Crime and Punishment: The American Criminological Tradition'. P. Q. Hirst notes that the medieval Inquisition made individuals fully accountable for their (heretical) private thoughts, thereby promoting a particular conception of subjectivity, its depths, and its responsibilities. Hirst, *Law, Socialism and Democracy*, p. 156.

[27] The Revd John Clay, an ardent supporter of the separate system, recorded how 'a few months in the solitary cell renders a prisoner strangely impressible. The chaplain can thus make the brawny navvy cry like a child; he can work on his feelings in almost any way he pleases; he can,

Other prison regimes, such as those designed by Howard, Bentham, or the Pennsylvania Quakers, based themselves upon—and in turn projected—slightly different conceptions of how subjects are normally made, and how, in the course of penal practice, they might be remade. But despite these variations, the central category of the reformed legal codes was the idea of the subject as free, rational, responsible, and self-directed. Throughout most of the nineteenth century, individuals who appeared before the courts—however feckless, incompetent, or socially disadvantaged—were addressed as if they were Enlightenment subjects, the only alternative category in law being the deranged, mad, non-subject.[28] And, as we have already seen, this constantly reiterated proposition—that individuals are free subjects and responsible for what they do—is a cultural message of immense power, and one which remains in place today.

Towards the end of the nineteenth century, and at various points during the twentieth, this classical subject-in-law was joined by alternative figures of subjectivity and personhood. Alongside the free subject, the criminal law came to recognize (and help establish) other categories of persons, often with diminished responsibility and less than full control over their personal conduct. Thus penal institutions have witnessed the creation of categories such as 'the degenerate', 'the feeble-minded', 'the inebriate', 'the habitual offender', 'the moral imbecile', 'the psychopath', and have adopted the specific procedures of recognition and treatment deemed appropriate to them. Occasionally, though perhaps not often, they become the basis for an authentic identity, as where an offender says 'I'm a habitual offender (or an inebriate or a psychopath)—I can't help myself' or, in the style of Jean Genet: 'So I'm a thief am I? Well so be it!' More often they become prescriptions to be evaded or subverted by those to whom they are applied. More importantly, though, and quite beyond the institutions, such categories provide the elements for a convenient cultural framework through which normal subjects can think about abnormality and the conditions which produce it.

Categories such as these allow us to identify and make sense of the marginal and the troublesome in our society—and to do so in ways which accord with our institutionalized practices and commitments. Moreover, by defining an extended range of deviant or pathological subjectivities, these new categories subtly modify our conception of the norm from which they deviate. These images of the defective self which are now projected by penal practice (as well as by psychiatry, social work, educational institutions, etc.) have contributed to the modern tendency to view the self as a machinery to be maintained and

so to speak, photograph his thoughts, wishes and opinions on the patient's mind and fill his mouth with his own phrases and language.' Quoted in C. Emsley, *Crime and Society in England 1750–1900* (London, 1987).

[28] On the legal subject and madness in the 19th cent., see R. Smith, *Trial by Medicine* (Edinburgh, 1981). Foucault's *Madness and Civilization* discusses the relation between the Age of Reason, concepts of the person, and conceptions of madness.

repaired by specialists and to rethink what was once known as 'evil' in terms of pathology rather than moral choice.

Subjectivity, personhood, personal identity—all these are socially and culturally constructed, and there is now an impressive historical and anthropological literature which describes how this construction takes place.[29] They are shaped by a whole range of social institutions, symbols, categories, and practices which teach, impose, and cultivate particular ways of being in the world. Penality takes a part in this process of 'making up people'. It helps form subjectivities, selves, and identities and the mental frameworks which we use to understand them. As I have stressed, these subjectivity-creating practices affect a public that is much wider than that of offenders or inmates, for, in constituting deviant identities, penality also holds out an image of what it is to be 'normal'—of what a standard subjectivity should be. We all 'appear before' the courts and penal institutions in the important sense that these institutions form a basic landmark in our social lives. It is not just 'the criminal' who is interpellated by the symbols of penality—the identity of the 'law-abiding citizen' derives in part from the same symbolic frame.[30]

5.3 *The depiction of social relations*

As a final example of the symbolic forms rendered in the course of penal practice one might point to the way in which penality expresses and projects a definite conception of social relations, holding out an imagery of the ways in which individuals relate—or ought to relate—to one another in society.

Of course one way in which penality helps form social relations is by specifying the behavioural standards to which social relations must conform. Through its regulations and prohibitions the criminal law sets legal limits to the kinds of individual conduct and social relations which will be tolerated, thus defining the boundaries within which permissible behaviour can take place. But penality does more than just police the boundaries in which social relations take place: it also helps define the nature and quality of these relations themselves. Through its practices and its symbolic forms, penal practice helps give meaning and definition—as well as a certain tone and colouring—to the bonds which link individuals to each other and to society's central institutions.

One can see this quite clearly in the way in which penal practice symbolizes a definite relationship between the offender and 'society' or between the

[29] See e.g. M. Mauss, 'A Category of the Human Mind: The Notion of the Person, the Notion of Self', in id., *Sociology and Psychology* (London, 1979); M. Carrithers, S. Collins, and S. Lukes (eds.), *Concept of the Person: Anthropology, Philosophy, History* (Cambridge, 1986); Hirst and Woolley, *Social Relations and Human Attributes*, ch. 6 and Heller *et al.* (eds.), *Reconstructing Individualism: Autonomy, Individuality and the Self in Western Thought.*

[30] The examples I have given here merely outline the ways in which this process occurs. In practice, the figures of subjectivity which are expressed in penality are nuanced, multiple, and varied. Different institutions, different sanctions, different procedures all hold out slightly different images of the person: the fine, probation, reformatories, maximum security regimes, psychiatric orders, etc., can each suggest slightly different kinds of subjectivity.

offender and the state. In the act of punishing, this key relationship—and its terms—are spelled out in what amounts to a practical lesson in political obligation. As we have seen, this bond between punisher and punished has been variously represented as a relationship between a sovereign power and a disloyal subject, between a legal state and a citizen in violation of the social contract, or between a welfare state and an individual in need of care and reform. But however it is figured, one sees in punishment a characterization of this basic social relationship, the mutual obligations which it implies, and the terms and symbols through which it should be understood.

At another level of signification, the practices of penality also suggest the relations which hold between offenders and victims, and indeed between offenders and the other members of the community. Thus, for example, the community may be invoked (and rhetorically described) as bearing responsibility for the offender—as having a continuing relationship with its deviant members which must be recognized and lived up to. Community relations and obligations of this kind are explicitly evoked in certain religious communities and even today are suggested by certain forms of 'community corrections'. Alternatively, the criminal may be characterized as a being apart, as an outlaw or a 'criminal type' who is less than fully human, in which case it is a relationship (or perhaps a non-relationship) of difference and exclusion which is implied.

Similarly, the relation between the offender and the victim in any particular case can be construed as involving an essential social link between two members of a community—a link which, however flawed, is worth repairing if possible. Just such a relationship is implied and projected by some of the mediation and reconciliation schemes which are developing on the margins of modern penal systems and by those reform programmes which urge the settlement of disputes by civil rather than criminal means.[31] Alternatively, and more commonly, this relationship can be depicted as a meeting of strangers, a contingent encounter between two separate and unrelated individuals which calls for compensation and punishment rather than reconciliation. In such circumstances the individuals' relations are shown to be with the state rather than with each other, and the law depicts itself as a set of rules to regulate strangers rather than an expression of community life.

Through the methods which it adopts to deal with crime and criminals, and through the idioms in which it frames its own practices, penality also teaches us how we should understand the breakdown of social relations. The criminological conceptions which are embodied in its practices identify the roots of social evil—as sin, greed, faulty conditioning, individual pathology, or whatever—and they describe the shapes which this evil can take. Moreover, these same penal methods and conceptions help suggest the proper emotional attitudes which we should adopt in the face of deviant behaviour, whether it be anger, or righteous indignation, compassion or indifference. As we saw earlier, penal

[31] See Christie, *Limits to Pain*, ch. 11 and also the essays in M. Wright and B. Galaway (eds.), *Mediation and Criminal Justice: Victims, Offenders and Community* (London, 1989).

forms are fashioned out of the prevailing (or emergent) codes of thought and feeling; they are a practical embodiment of specific mentalities and sensibilities. In the routines of penal practice, penalty projects these sensibilities back on to society, thus helping to generate and maintain the attitudes which it was designed to express.

In these ways, penality expresses a definite sense of how social relations are (and should be) constituted in that particular society. It points to society's sources of order and its sources of danger, to the principles which hold it together and those which threaten to pull it apart. If the authorized view is that law, faith, and morality are what bind society together, then these bonds will be emphasized in the penal process. If socialization is seen as a matter of family life, or education, or market relations, or work and industry, then these forms too will be symbolized and displayed in the language and practice of punishing. In this respect, penality projects a sense of what 'society' actually is, and helps construct social life in these terms.

5.4 *Other representations*

The sketchy account of penality's symbolic rhetoric set out here is not intended as an exhaustive or detailed description. All I have done is to point to some of the meanings which penality routinely denotes and some of the ways in which it denotes them. In the nature of things—which is a brief way of saying 'given the polysemic possibilities of virtually any social practice'—penal symbols can be made to speak of other things. Specific sanctions or institutions can take on new associations and extended connotations. Depending on their context of use—or even upon accidental association—they can become metaphors and symbols for conveying meanings of the most varied and contingent kinds, in much the way that the Bastille became a symbol not just of social oppression but also of revolution, and the cross used in the Roman penal system came to stand for Christ's relationship to the human race.

Only detailed case-studies can trace the ways in which specific penal policies come to 'speak of' specific other things. And although the writings of historians such as Robert Nye or sociologists such as Stuart Hall have begun to explicate in detail some of these chains of reference and symbolic association, much more needs to be done before we can chart the rhetorical range and significance of punishment and its role as a cultural institution. Nevertheless, there can be little doubt that historically, and also in the present, penality has been rich in symbolic meaning and capable of sustaining extended rhetorical use.

6. THE SIGNIFICANCE OF PUNISHMENT

Why is this? Why is punishment apparently capable of such symbolic resonance and force? What makes it an area of social life to which people attend and from which they draw meaning?

Sociologists such as Georges Gurvitch or Mary Douglas might attribute this symbolizing power to punishment's status as an arena of social tension and social conflict.[32] It is, after all, the site at which law and deviance are brought most visibly together, where social anomalies and contradictions are directly addressed, the point at which purity and danger dramatically intersect. Penal institutions deal with human and moral problems of a profound and intractable kind—with the fragility of social relations, the limits of socialization, the persistence of human evil, and the insecurity of social life. And as anthropologists have shown, the intractable problems of social and human existence provide a rich soil for the development of myths, rites, and symbols as cultures strive to control and make sense of these difficult areas of experience. Punishment—as an archetypal feature of human existence—figures prominently in some of the most important cultural artefacts of Western society, including classical drama, traditional cosmologies, religions such as Christianity, and heresies such as psychoanalysis. The practical business of punishing offenders thus takes place within a cultural space which is already laden with meaning and which lends itself easily to symbolic use.

Moreover, as earlier chapters of this book have shown, the institutions of punishment connect directly into other major social realms and institutions, linking up with the circuits of power, exchange, morality, and sensibility which hold society together. In this sense punishment has some of the qualities of what Marcel Mauss described as a 'total social fact'. It is an area of social life which spills over into other areas and which takes its social meaning as much from these connections as from itself, thus accumulating a symbolic depth and richness which go beyond its immediate functioning.[33]

Punishment also seems to fit the description of what Shils has called a societal 'center', which is to say it forms a key point in the social universe, a strategic location where power is expressed, identities created, social relations forged, and life or death decisions made.[34] As we saw earlier, the nature of such 'centers'—their intrinsic importance as foundations for social order—makes them charismatic. They attract the attention and the imagination of members of society by virtue of their key place in the order of things and their capacity to make things happen in an authoritative way. Thus it is something more than mere entertainment that draws attention to the process of punishing—much of which is routine in the extreme. Rather it is the perceived importance of the institution and its ability to draw upon the drama of large events. One might even use this explanation to help account for the 'anti-charisma' of certain notorious criminals, whose personal encounters with these forces of social

[32] Douglas, *Purity and Danger*, and G. Gurvitch, 'Social Control', in id. and W. Moore (eds.), *Twentieth Century Sociology* (New York, 1945).

[33] Mauss outlines his conception of a 'total social fact' in *The Gift: Forms and Functions of Exchange in Archaic Societies* (New York, 1967).

[34] Shils, *The Constitution of Society*. See also Geertz, 'Centers, Kings and Charisma: Reflections on the Symbolics of Power'.

order seem to lend their lives a fascination which they would otherwise entirely lack.

No doubt,too, there is a psychological dimension to this phenomenon. As I have already suggested, the socialized members of a society have usually experienced an emotional training in punishment and the threat of punishment which leaves them with a lasting emotional investment in the matter. The drama of crime and punishment acts out 'for real' a psychic conflict between instinctive drives and their repression which most adults experience to some degree. This being the case, the symbols of penality seem to resonate with the personal memories and associations of individuals in particular ways, producing attitudes and involvements which would not otherwise arise. As politicians have frequently discovered, penal rhetoric can be 'good for persuading with' precisely because it touches upon some of the deep-seated anxieties and ambivalences which individuals commonly experience.

The meanings projected by penality today—or indeed at any time—are many and varied. Its rhetorics and signifying practices combine to form a dense cacophony of sounds and images rather than a carefully orchestrated message, although here and there clear patterns emerge and dominant themes are sounded. Even the basic representations which I have discussed are often, in practice, confusingly mixed up together. At various points in the penal realm one sees the imagery of 'moral man', 'economic man' and 'psychological man', fleetingly appear as different procedures or agencies reflect disparate conceptions of human nature and its workings. In one court-room a social-contract state may be punishing while in another the welfare state is dispensing help. Penal rhetoric, like penality itself, is the living embodiment of a long historical tradition within which arguments have occurred and differences remain. Its multiplicity of meaning is thus a reflection of its historical development, in which one strategy, vocabulary, or conception has been laid upon another, without expunging all traces of the earlier style. The result is a kind of mosaic or palimpsest in which the archaic and the contemporary are able to coexist.

But the diversity of meaning which is conveyed by contemporary penality is not just a historical product, ill-adapted to modern society. On the contrary—the symbolic diversity of penal practice, its utilization of different idioms, and its tendency to project contradictory and ambivalent messages has a contemporary basis. This is the case because contemporary penality exists within societies which are themselves marked by pluralism and moral diversity, competing interests and conflicting ideologies. In such a context, and with the need to appeal to a range of different audiences at one and the same time, it is no surprise to find that penality displays a range of rhetorical identifications and a mosaic of symbolic forms.

In discussing here the many ways in which penal institutions signify and project meaning, I have focused upon the question of signification rather than the issue of reception and response. No real assessment has been offered of penal rhetoric's ability to move its audience to attitude and action for the simple reason that no reliable data currently exist on this matter. If and when the question is researched we will no doubt find that the effectivity of penal rhetoric varies with audience, context, chain of association, frequency of repetitions and so on.

Nor have I discussed the issue of penal policy-makers' ability to control the way in which their projected images are read—a question of no little importance since there are many examples in penal history of rhetorical appeals which failed and punishments which 'created the wrong impression'. But I am willing nevertheless to suggest that such practices do have an effect, that their meanings can be to some degree controlled, and that the social results are not insignificant. In short, I venture to believe that the ways in which we punish, and the ways in which we represent that action to ourselves, makes a difference to the way we are. Now to say this is not to suggest that punishment is the primary or foremost institution in the process of cultural formation—families, schools, the workplace, the media, are generally more important in this respect. But culture and subjectivities are composite creations, built up out of countless encounters and experiences and in that process of composition the institutions of criminal law and punishment do play an important part.

If this is indeed the case, then it should alter the way we think about punishment and penal institutions. In designing penal policy we are not simply deciding how to deal with a group of people on the margins of society— whether to deter, reform, or incapacitate them and if so how. Nor are we simply deploying power or economic resources for penological ends. We are also and at the same time defining ourselves and our society in ways which may be quite central to our cultural and political identity. An important part of a society's penal rhetoric is taken up with the suggestion of a social vision. This vision may be Utopian or pessimistic, redemptive or abandoning, and it may picture accurately or inaccurately the nature of the society it depicts. But whatever its tone and its proximity to the truth, it will be a rhetoric of some considerable importance.

The representations projected by penal practice are not just threats aimed at criminals: they are also positive symbols which help produce subjectivities, forms of authority, and social relations. To paraphrase Michel Foucault, punishment does not just restrain or discipline 'society'—punishment helps create it.

12

Punishment as a Social Institution

1. THE NEED FOR THEORY

In the opening pages of this book I drew a distinction between studies of punishment which are 'penological' in a narrow sense, and a wider, more sociological approach which is concerned to stand back and reflect upon penal institutions, trying to figure out what exactly 'punishment' involves, how it works, what it means, and where it fits in the social scheme of things. As will be all too clear by now, the stance I have adopted is the latter one and the result has been not a work of penology or even penal philosophy, but instead a work of social theory centred upon the institutions of punishment.

In an area of social life as hard and practical as punishment, this pursuit of 'theory' may seem a little misplaced. What need can there be for theorizing when the point of punishment is obvious and when penal systems are plagued by problems of the most mundane kind? Why resort to interpretation when punishment's purposes—and its practical defects—are obvious to anyone? One answer to this would be that it is precisely the 'obviousness' of these everyday problems of punishment—and the dismaying fact that they stubbornly refuse to go away—which prompts an enquiry of a more fundamental kind. In the face of punishment's intractable problems one is led to ask how are we to understand an institution so riven with contradiction, with failure, and with self-defeating policies? What are the forces and the counterforces which keep this institution—and its problems—in place? How can an institution be both relatively stable and deeply problematic at one and the same time?

Another response, equally forceful in my view, is to insist that 'theory' is not some kind of flight from reality. Properly pursued, theoretical argument enables us to think about that real world of practice with a clarity and a breadth of perspective often unavailable to the hard-pressed practitioner. It allows us a chance to escape the well-worn thought routines and 'common-sense' perceptions which penality—like any other institution—builds up around itself like a protective shell. Theory enables us to develop analytical tools and ways of thinking which question these established habits of thought and action, and seek alternatives to them.

Theoretical work seeks to change the way we think about an issue and ultimately to change the practical ways we deal with it. It is, in its own way, a form of rhetoric, seeking to move people to action by means of persuasion, that persuasion being achieved by force of analysis, argument, and evidence.[1]

---

[1] This is the ideal of rational argument: the scientific ideal. It would, however, be naïve to suppose that the persuasive power of 'good scholarship' depends only upon reasoning and evidence. On the role of rhetoric in the social sciences, see H. White, *Tropics of Discourse: Essays in Cultural Criticism* (Baltimore, 1978), and id., *Metahistory: The Historical Imagination in Nineteenth Century Europe* (Baltimore, 1973); C. Geertz, *Works and Lives: The Anthropologist as Author* (Stanford, 1988); J. Clifford and G. E. Marcus (eds.), *Writing Culture: The Poetics and Politics of Ethnography*

Theorizing is also, therefore, a form of action—one might even say of 'practice'—though its medium is that of symbols and its effect will depend upon whether this symbolic action ultimately affects the way people and institutions actually conduct themselves.[2] When theory does succeed as a form of action, it does so first of all by changing how people perceive things and the attitudes they adopt towards them. What I want to do in this concluding chapter is to show how the theoretical work which has been undertaken here might make us think differently about punishment—first of all as analysts, who seek to understand this institution in all its complexity, and then, importantly, as citizens, who might wish to think more seriously and more deeply about an institution for which we are at least partly responsible.

With respect to the sociology of punishment, the present study does not aim to set out a specific thesis or pursue a single line of interpretation. Instead, it explores penality from a number of different angles in an effort to construct a composite picture of the phenomenon, superimposing different perspectives to suggest a fuller, more three-dimensional image than is usually perceived. This analysis has been organized around the arguments of a number of theoretical traditions, each of which presents a particular interpretation of punishment couched within a broader theory of society or social institutions. However my approach to these theories has been determined by my project, rather than by theirs. I have sought to use these theories not as conceptual frameworks for thinking about 'society' but instead as a source of specific interpretations of penality—interpretations whose validity can stand independently of the general theories which produced them. For my purposes here, the theories of Durkheim, Foucault, the Marxists, and so on have become sources of insight about punishment's social role and significance and producers of facts about its operation and effects—resources to be drawn upon selectively rather than inviolable world-views which can only be swallowed whole.

Proceeding from one explanatory perspective to another I have tried to show how each one asks slightly different questions about the phenomenon, each pursues a different aspect, reveals a different determinant, outlines a different connection. Sometimes, of course, different theorists do address the same issue, only to interpret it in different ways—as when Marxists and Durkheimians disagree about the role of the state or of popular sentiment in the formation of penal policy. In such cases I have tried to argue out this disagreement and resolve it in favour of the best explanation—or to develop an alternative one of my own. At other times one theorist lays emphasis upon a

---

(Berkeley, 1986); and J. Gusfield, *The Culture of Public Problems: Drinking-Driving and the Symbolic Order* (Chicago, 1981). On rhetoric in criminology, see D. Garland, 'Politics and Policy in Criminological Discourse: A Study of Tendentious Reasoning and Rhetoric', *International Journal of the Sociology of Law*, 13 (1985), 1–33.

[2] Louis Althusser coined the term 'theoretical practice' to avoid the idea of an absolute division between 'theory' and 'practice' and capture the sense of theorizing as a form of action. See also K. Burke on *Language as Symbolic Action: Essays on Life, Literature and Method* (Berkeley, 1966).

particular aspect of a complex phenomenon—for instance Foucault's stress on the instrumentalized, rationalized character of modern penal systems—while another stresses a different aspect, as Durkheim does when he points to the persistence of expressive, emotional, and non-rational elements. In these instances I have tried to show how each interpretation might be modified by the other to take account of the dialectical interplay of the various forces which structure modern penality. In other cases it may be that a particular theorist successfully identifies an element of penality which seems to escape the scrutiny of other theoretical accounts—as with Foucault on power–knowledge techniques, Durkheim on the role of the onlooker, Rusche and Kirchheimer on the role of the labour market, or else Spierenburg on changing sensibilities. In response to this I have tried to suggest how different elements and aspects of penality may fit together to form a complex, internally differentiated whole, and to point to some of the ways in which these different elements are structurally arranged and interrelated.

Throughout the work I have tried to show how we might play different interpretations off against each other—and against the factual evidence which we possess—and thus overlay them, build them up, and use each one to correct and refine the others. What others have seen as rival approaches which are mutually exclusive I have tried to turn into 'reciprocal commentaries, mutually deepening'.[3] In effect I have been building upon the fragments of social and historical theory as they currently exist to suggest the outlines of a wide-ranging and reasonably comprehensive sociology of punishment.

The danger of such an undertaking, of course, is that it may all too easily collapse into an arbitrary eclecticism. In drawing upon arguments made by different theorists about 'punishment and society' one can too readily assume an identity of concerns where none in fact exists, and end up in an intellectual tangle of incompatible premises, ambiguous concepts, and shifting objects of study. Trying to say everything at once, one can wind up saying nothing with any clarity or conviction. But, conscious of these risks, I have tried to suggest the explanatory power of pluralism without falling into the logical absurdities of eclecticism. I have not sought to add together global theories of 'society' which are theoretically and ideologically incompatible. Nor have I tried to pursue at once the very different theoretical projects that each of these traditions marks out. Instead, I have tried to harness these works for a project which none of their authors envisaged, but to which all can be made to contribute—namely, the construction of a rounded sociological account of penality.

As a centre-piece for this project I have set out a number of simple questions concerning the social foundations, functions, and effects of punishment: questions which each approach in some way addresses. And throughout the investigation I have tried to keep these questions steadfastly in view while

---

[3] Geertz, *Local Knowledge*, p. 234.

drawing upon the various theories and historical accounts for suggestions as to how they might be answered. Moving, on this basis, back and forth between interpretations has allowed a complex picture of penality to emerge, drawing upon the insights of all these theories without being tied to the global framework of any one of them.

2. THE OVERDETERMINATION OF PENAL EVENTS AND INSTITUTIONS

The implicit argument which runs throughout this enterprise has been that a pluralistic, multidimensional approach is needed if we are to understand the historical development and present-day operation of penality. If there is to be a sociology of punishment—and by that I mean a set of general parameters from which specific studies can take their theoretical bearings—then it should be the kind of sociology advocated by Marcel Mauss when he talked about the need for a synthesis and consolidation of perspectives. It should be a sociology which strives to present a rounded, completed image; a recomposition of the fragmentary views developed by more narrowly focused studies.[4]

One can rephrase this argument as being a warning against reductionism in the analysis of punishment—by which I mean the tendency to explain penality in terms of any single causal principle or functional purpose, be it 'morals' or 'economics', 'state control' or 'crime control'. Instead of searching for a single explanatory principle, we need to grasp the facts of multiple causality, multiple effects, and multiple meaning. We need to realize that in the penal realm—as in all social experience—specific events or developments usually have a plurality of causes which interact to shape their final form, a plurality of effects which may be seen as functional or non-functional depending upon one's criteria, and a plurality of meanings which will vary with the actors and audiences involved—though some meanings (or, for that matter, causes and effects) may be more powerful than others. The aim of analysis should always be to capture that variety of causes, effects, and meanings and trace their interaction, rather than to reduce them all to a single currency.

In this connection, the concept of 'overdetermination'—first developed by Freud and subsequently taken up by historians, political scientists, and sociologists—is particularly useful, because it embodies this understanding and captures it in a single theoretical term. As Peter Gay explains, ' "overdetermination" is in fact nothing more than the sensible recognition that a variety of causes—a variety, not infinity—enters into the making of all historical events, and that each ingredient in historical experience can be counted on to have a variety—not infinity—of functions'.[5] This concept of overdetermination—along with related ones such as 'condensation' (the

---

[4] Mauss, *The Gift*, p. 78: 'Whereas formerly sociologists were obliged to analyse and abstract rather too much, they should now force themselves to reconstitute the whole.'

[5] P. Gay, *Freud for Historians* (New York, 1985), p. 187.

fusion of several forces and meanings in the same object) and 'polysemy' (the capacity of an object to support multiple meanings and interpretations)—have been used in this work to move the sociology of punishment from a series of more or less singular interpretations towards a more multidimensional framework in the belief that this will improve analysis and deepen understanding.

For the historian, the injunction to 'seek complexity . . . and tame it' has always been central to scholarly practice, and in many histories of punishment one sees this principle acted out to good effect.[6] As John Beattie has put it, summing up his magisterial study of penal change in early modern England:

. . . changes in punishment are almost certain not to arise from a simple, one-dimensional effect. The forms of punishment employed by a society at any one moment are shaped by a variety of interests and intentions. They arise in response to what must often be antagonistic considerations, including the framework of law, what is technologically possible, what seems desirable or necessary in the light of the apparent problem of crime, what society is willing to accept and pay for. Why one method of punishment loses favour over time and gives way to another is a complex question because penal methods evolve within a larger social and cultural context that in imperceptible ways alters the limits of what is acceptable and what is not.[7]

Sociologists forget this at their peril, but they do sometimes forget it—as occasionally do historians—usually in an effort to develop a more general social theory, to drive home a critical point, or simply to domesticate the chaos of experience by reference to some clear explanatory principle. When this occurs, and when singular interpretations emerge, it is important that these be identified as specific contributions to be placed alongside others, rather than as comprehensive accounts that can stand by themselves.

3. PUNISHMENT AS A SOCIAL INSTITUTION

In order to ground this approach to the study of punishment, we need more than just methodological imperatives. We also need an appropriate conceptual image of the phenomenon—a theoretical depiction or representation of the object of study which will itself suggest the kind of complexity I have been stressing and the kind of analysis which this requires. At present there are a number of conceptions which are frequently used to ground our understanding of penality. Punishment can be viewed as a kind of technical apparatus which forms an instrumental means to an end, and this seems to be the way in which the penology of crime control chooses to imagine it. It can be seen as a coercive relationship between the state and the offender, which is the central image underlying many critical studies of penality. It can also be represented as a legal procedure, a form of power, an instrument of class domination, an expression of collective feeling, a moral action, a ritual event, or an embodiment of a certain sensibility. And as we have seen in our discussions, each of these images captures a certain aspect of the phenomenon, a certain truth about its

---

[6] Ibid.   [7] Beattie, *Crime and the Courts*, p. 470.

character which one would wish to retain, but does so in a fragmentary way, leaving out of focus as much as it brings in.

As an alternative to these fragmentary images—or rather as a background and framing device in which to set them—I suggest we use the concept of a social institution as a means of thinking about punishment. Penality should be seen not as a singular kind of event or relationship but rather as a social institution which, by definition, entails the kind of complexity of structure and density of meaning which we have come across again and again. Such an image is admittedly a little abstract, and already very 'sociological'. One can only see things in this way on the basis of a developed understanding and an appreciation of the distinctive characteristics of 'social institutions'. But then this is true to some degree of all the conceptual images which are already in use. We can only imagine something as 'a means to an end' because we have already learned to think in these terms, and, having become acquainted with this way of thinking, we use its imagery and its metaphors as lenses with which to view the world. Learning to think of punishment as a social institution, and to picture it primarily in these terms, gives us a way of depicting the complexity and multifaceted character of this phenomenon in a single master image. It enables us to locate the other images of punishment within this overall framework while also suggesting the need to see penality as being tied into wider networks of social action and cultural meaning.

Social institutions—which include the family, the law, education, government, the market, the military and religion, among others—are highly patterned and organized sets of social practices. They are society's settled means of dealing with certain needs, relationships, conflicts, and problems which repeatedly recur and must be managed in an orderly and normative way if social relations are to be reasonably stabilized and differentiated. Each institution is organized around a specific area of social life and provides a regulatory and normative framework for human conduct in that area. Typically, such institutions evolve slowly, over a long period of time, so that their present character is often shaped by history and tradition as much as by the contemporary functions which they perform. Developed social institutions are, in effect, established frameworks for the satisfaction of needs, the resolution of disputes and the regulation of life in a particular social sphere. Having developed as a means of managing tensions, arbitrating between conflicting forces, and getting certain necessary things done, social institutions typically contain within themselves traces of the contradictions and pluralities of interest which they seek to regulate. As John Anderson puts it, institutions are the scenes of particular conflicts as well as being means to a variety of ends, so it is no surprise to find that each particular institution combines a number of often incompatible objectives, and organizes the relations of often antagonistic interest groups.[8]

[8] See J. Anderson, *Studies in Empirical Philosophy* (Sydney, 1962) and the introduction by J. E. Passmore. Note that this conception avoids an overly functional view of social institutions. They are products of history and the scenes of continuing conflict, not just functional mechanisms.

Being directed towards a particular aspect of social life, and a specific set of needs and problems, each institution has its own intrinsic rationality and its own way of doing things—what one might term its own institutional culture— built up around the accumulated store of knowledge, techniques, normative rules, and working procedures which it has developed. Members or personnel of the institution are generally guided by this institutional logic whenever they function within it, and they are obliged to frame any problem or issue in the terms dictated by the institutional framework. Thus to deal with an issue as a legal problem, or a moral issue, as a family matter or a question of market forces—or, indeed, to approach it as a penal problem—is to subject it to very different ways of thinking and acting, each one with its characteristic languages, norms, and principles. In a sense, each institutional site gives rise to a distinctive world of its own with its own characters and roles, statuses and rule-governed relationships—as anyone who moves from one setting (or jurisdiction) to the other will readily experience.

But these institutional worlds are only partly self-contained. They open up on to other worlds and connect into a social network which extends well beyond their particular domain. Each institution occupies a particular place in the wider social field and routinely relates to its social environment, affecting and being affected by the social forces which surround it. Institutions link up with other institutions and with the world outside. They are affected by the forces of economics, politics, culture, and technology. For all their apparent autonomy, each one is situated within an ensemble of social forces and is structured by the values and social arrangements which form its effective environment. Social institutions thus live a complex life of their own, but they are also constitutive elements within a larger social structure. Each one forms a kind of junction-point in the social field upon which a range of forces converge, as well as being a setting for its own particular norms and practices.

To understand a phenomenon of this kind—and, more specifically, to understand penality—we need to think in terms of complexity, of multiple objectives, and of overdetermination. We need to think of it as a historical emergent which is also a functioning system; as a distinctive form of life which is also dependent upon other forms and other social relations. Somehow or other we must learn to view it both in its integrity, as an *institution*, and in its relatedness, as a *social* institution. Such a way of thinking may involve a degree of difficulty, and it certainly lacks the spare elegance of some of the more reductionist approaches. But forms of thought are useful only if they are appropriate to their object, and a sociology of punishment which is to come to terms with the complexity of penality must develop concepts and images which are adequate to it.

4. THE LIMITS OF THEORY

To say that punishment is a social institution in the sense described, that it is conditioned by an ensemble of social and historical forces, that it has an institutional framework of its own and that it supports a set of regulatory and significatory practices which produce a range of penal and social effects— which is, in short, what this study has been saying—does not amount to a general theory of punishment. To produce such a theory, it would be necessary to do more than show, as I have shown, the ways in which moral, political, economic, cultural, legal, administrative, and penological conditions converge upon the penal realm and shape the forms of penality; or how, in turn, penal measures serve to enforce laws, regulate populations, realize political authority, express sentiments, enhance solidarities, emphasize divisions, and convey cultural meanings. One would have to go rather further than this and construct a model of these interacting forces which specified the precise pattern of their interaction, identified regular causal sequences, and revealed principles of determination and structuration which are reasonably constant over time.

Such models are still to be found in the social science literature—most notably in the Marxist tradition—but they appear less and less convincing as ways of conceiving social process and historical outcome. They are a legacy of the nineteenth-century scientism which viewed society as a closed, mechanical system, and left little room for agency, contingency, and accident in the historical process. In contemporary social thought these global theories and rigid models have been giving way to more open-ended, pragmatic theorizing which seeks to interpret the varieties of social and historical experience rather than search for iron laws and structural necessities.

It seems to me that the sociology of punishment has no need for a general theory of this kind, and that any attempt to build a single theoretical model of the causes, forms, and consequences of penality would be misconceived. One reason for this is that 'penality' exists as a single, unified entity only in the restricted sense that it is a bounded institutional realm, established in law with jurisdiction to administer penal sanctions. At any one time the boundaries of that realm are more or less set and identifiable, which allows us to talk sensibly about its composition, its functions, its relationship with non-penal institutions, and so on. (It also allows governments to develop penal policies which have a measure of unity and impart some coherence in this complicated array of practices and procedures.) However, in most other respects, 'penality' must be seen as a generic term which covers a multitude of different elements which happen to form part of an institutional complex. 'Penal systems' are composed of specific agencies, offices, apparatuses, rules, procedures and beliefs, strategies, rhetorics, and representations, each of which will have its own history, its own determinants, and its own specific effects. The specific conditions which produce the prison are not those which gave rise to the probation service, any more than the electronic tag can be explained in the same way as the electric chair. And the impact of external pressures (for instance, the rise of a punitive, law-and-order politics) may cause very different effects in different areas of penality (thus prisons may expand while social work sanctions decline). Penal policy—which is itself constantly changing in response to a variety of forces, internal and external—makes use of all these different agencies, institutions, and sanctions but requires an explanation in its own terms, to do with policy formulation and the processes of decision-making involved.

Of course there are broad, structuring patterns which help shape penality over time—as we saw when we discussed secularization, rationalization, civilization, the development of commodity production, the rise of the state, and so on. But a theoretical model of punishment couched in these terms is likely to be so unspecific as to be banal. Large-scale historical forces do not fit together in a stable interplay that can be duplicated in theory, any more than they 'work themselves out' in predetermined historical outcomes. In fact grand forces such as 'rationalization' or 'civilization' do not exist as such outside of historical interpretations. Rather it is historians and sociologists who study the vast myriad of events, large and small, and seek to understand and characterize them by means of these analytical tools. Consequently, it is only in combination with specific histories, empirical studies, and concrete analyses that any theoretical 'model' can be of much use in this field.

The fact that we have been able—through empirical research and theoretical reflection—to discern the kinds of determinants and functional requirements which tend to shape punishment, does not mean that we can predict, in any particular instance, how penal developments will turn out. 'Overdetermination' does not imply a range of forces which flow smoothly together in the same direction, intent on the same result. It implies constant conflict, tension, and compromise and suggests outcomes which are unique in their particularity rather than uniformly shaped by a pre-cut mould. Penal history is thus made up of 'historical individuals', as Weber would put it. In the shaping of any penal event—whether it be a sentencing decision, the formation of a regime, or the legislative enactment of a penal policy—a large number of conflicting forces are at work. Broad ideological ambitions may run up against immediate financial constraints, political expediency may conflict with established sensibilities, the perceived requirements of security may differ from those of morality, the professional interests of one group may be in tension with those of another, and the pursuit of any one value will generally involve the violation of several others. These swarming circumstances are only ever resolved into particular outcomes by means of the struggles, negotiations, actions, and decisions which are undertaken by those involved in the making and the implementation of policy, and can only be traced by detailed historical work. There is no settled hierarchy of purposes or causal priorities which prevails at every point allowing us to describe, once and for all, the sequence of forces and considerations which 'determine' the specific forms which penality displays.

Theoretical work of the type I have been discussing alerts us to the kinds of constraints and structures within which penal policy is developed. It points to the interconnections which link penality to other spheres of social life and the functional role which it occupies in the network of social institutions. It can reveal institutional dynamics, characteristics, and effects which might otherwise go unacknowledged and of which policy-makers themselves may be unaware. But only empirical research can determine how these conditioning circumstances come together at a particular moment to shape a course of action or define a particular event. Theory should be a set of interpretative tools for guiding and analysing empirical enquiry—not a substitute for it.

What I have tried to do in this study is to demonstrate how the theoretical tools of sociology can be used to help us think about punishment in its various aspects. As we have seen, each of the different traditions of social theory provides a specific set of tools in the form of a specially adapted conceptual vocabulary, designed to explicate a particular aspect or dimension of social life. And, as we have also seen, each of these interpretative vocabularies has its uses in understanding punishment, and becomes more or less useful depending upon the questions asked and the characteristics being explained. Thus in some circumstances, and for some people (e.g. those groups for whom the law is merely superior force, coercively imposed) punishment is an exercise of raw power, best understood in vocabularies such as those supplied by Foucault or Marx. Yet at other points, and for other people—perhaps in the same society and the same penal system—punishment may be an expression of moral community and collective sensibility, in which penal sanctions are an authorized response to shared values individually violated. In these circumstances, the vocabularies of power and ideology need to be tempered by the rather different concerns articulated by Elias and Durkheim. The purpose of my study is not to create a grand synthesis of these traditions, nor to construct some kind of overarching theoretical model, for the reasons I have stated above. Rather, it tries to suggest how we might handle the range of perspectives and vocabularies through which punishment can be variously understood, and outlines a conception of penality which can ground this multiplicity of interpretations and show how they interrelate.

For those who like their social theory cut and dried, or who believe that a single vocabulary can be evolved that answers all the questions, this style of analysis may seem to leave too much undone. It might seem necessary to go one step further and to gather up all these intertwining interpretations in a single narrative, insisting that punishment is 'above all' (or else 'at base') a story about, say, 'power' or about 'control'. Indeed one can see how such an approach might characterize all the causes, effects, and operations of punishment in terms of power over bodies, power over meanings, economic power, technical power, repressive power, constitutive power, and so on. Such an analysis undoubtedly achieves a rhetorical force and a radical tone, and can form the basis for some formidable polemics against the institutions concerned. But in analytical terms—as we saw in our discussion of Foucault—such a move is distinctly unhelpful, tending to skate over the importance of such things as moral authority, sensibilities, and culture, and to blur the different social conditions which ground penal power and make it possible.[9]

5. SOME CONSEQUENCES OF THIS CONCEPTION

The burden of my argument, then, is that underlying any study of penality should be a determination to think of punishment as a complex social institution. What I have in mind—and it may not be fully conveyed by the terms I have used—is something akin to Mauss's idea of a 'total social fact', which on its surface appears to be self-contained, but which in fact intrudes into many of the basic spheres of social life.[10] Like the institutions of gift exchange which Mauss described, punishment is a distinctive social institution which, in its routine practices, somehow contrives to condense a whole web of social relations and cultural meanings.

Punishment is, on the face of things, an apparatus for dealing with criminals —a circumscribed, discrete, legal–administrative entity. But it is also, as we have seen, an expression of state power, a statement of collective morality, a vehicle for emotional expression, an economically conditioned social policy, an embodiment of current sensibilities, and a set of symbols which display a cultural ethos and help create a social identity. At once an element of social organization, an aspect of social relations, and an ingredient of individual psychology, penality runs like a connecting thread through all the layers of social structure, connecting the general with the particular, the centre with its boundaries. What appears on its surface to be merely a means of dealing with offenders so that the rest of us can lead our lives untroubled by them, is in fact a social institution which helps define the nature of our society, the kinds of relationships which compose it, and the kinds of lives that it is possible and desirable to lead there.

---

[9] Ironically, this 'radical' move may even be unhelpful in political terms, since its failure to separate out different dimensions of punishment, or even to identify the different social forces that support it, provides little guidance for the siting of oppositional struggles and little indication of the different strategies that they might employ. Strategies for contesting state power are likely to be very different from strategies for changing popular culture or remoulding sensibilities.

[10] As Evans-Pritchard says in his introduction to *The Gift*, Mauss's notion of understanding is to see social phenomena in their totality: ' "Total" is the key word of the Essay, the exchanges of archaic societies which he examines are total movements or activities. They are at the same time economic, juridical, moral, aesthetic, religious, mythological and socio-morphological phenomena. Their meaning can only be grasped if they are viewed as a complex concrete reality, and if for convenience we make abstractions in studying some institution we must in the end replace what we have taken away if we are to understand it' (pp. vii–viii). Unfortunately the connotations of the word 'total'—which suggests the complete, functional interconnection of *all* aspects of society— and of 'social fact'—which is altogether too positivistic— makes Mauss's term more problematic than the overused but still useful idea of a 'social institution'. It is also worth emphasizing that Mauss's idea of a 'total social fact' seeks to capture the significance of such an institution within pre-modern societies which are not extensively differentiated and where consciousness is not fragmentary. In such circumstances, social actors experience 'the gift' in the 'total' way which he describes. In modern, functionally differentiated societies, however, the crucial point is that 'total social facts' may not be experienced as such.

This developed conception of penality has, I think, important implications for the way we think about punishment and penal policy. By making the social dimensions of punishment explicit, and by showing the kinds of internal conflicts and social consequences which penal institutions entail, the sociology of punishment provides a more adequate empirical basis for policy evaluation, philosophical reflection, or political judgment in this area. As things stand at present, the evaluation of punishment is too readily cast in the narrow terms of instrumental utility. We are too prone to think of punishment as a simple means to a simple end—usually that of crime control—and to treat all other aspects of the institution as minor considerations. So, for instance, imprisonment, or probation, or rehabilitative policies, or even capital punishment, are all too frequently approached as if the major question to be answered concerned their technical efficacy as instruments of crime control. Their evaluation thus turns primarily upon measurements of recidivism, of deterrence, and of correlative crime rates rather than upon judgments of their total worth as social practices. But, as I have argued throughout this work, we can hardly begin to understand penal institutions if we insist upon treating them as instrumentalities, geared to a single penological purpose, so the tendency to evaluate them in these terms seems misguided and unproductive.

Thus to recall and extend an important example, we might take the case of the prison in modern society. As every critical report reminds us, this institution signally fails to achieve the ends of crime control which, it is assumed, form its basic *raison d'être*. Most prisoners are not reformed, new generations of criminals go undeterred, national crime rates are not forced into decline, so that by all these criteria the prison is deemed an inefficient instrument (though, it should be noted, not much more inefficient than most of its alternatives). This margin of failure—it is not suggested that prison has *no* success—is such that the prison presents a serious puzzle for social commentators and penal reformers alike. Theorists such as Foucault assume that the prison's failures must, in some covert political sense, be 'useful for power'. Historians such as Stone assume it is a 'vestigial institution' which has somehow outlived its usefulness. Criminologists throw up their hands in despair at the 'irrationality' of policy and urge governments to pay heed to their own research findings and the failures which they imply. But, in an important sense, this argument is misconceived, and the 'puzzle' of imprisonment arises only because of the misconceived starting-points from which these analyses begin.

Neither the prison, nor any other penal institution, rests solely upon its ability to achieve such instrumental ends. Despite recurring Utopian hopes and the exaggerated claims of some reformers, the simple fact is that no method of punishment has ever achieved high rates of reform or of crime control—and no method ever will. All punishments regularly 'fail' in this respect because, as I have already pointed out, it is only the mainstream processes of socialization (internalized morality and the sense of duty, the informal inducements and rewards of conformity, the practical and cultural networks of mutual expectation and interdependence, etc.) which are able to promote proper conduct on a consistent and regular basis. Punishment, so far as 'control' is concerned, is merely a coercive back-up to these more reliable social mechanisms, a back-up which is often unable to do anything more than manage those who slip through these networks of normal control and integration. Punishment is fated never to 'succeed' to any great degree because the conditions which do most to induce conformity—or to promote crime and deviance—lie outside the jurisdiction of penal institutions.

It will always be open to critics of the prison to point to its failures of crime control and use these as an argument for reform. But it seems altogether inappropriate for a sociologist or a historian to take these same arguments and draw from them the conclusion that the prison is a penological failure which owes its existence to some covert political strategy or else to the dead hand of history. Like all complex institutions, the prison simultaneously pursues a number of objectives and is kept in place by a range of forces. Crime control—in the sense of reforming offenders and reducing crime rates—is certainly one of these objectives but by no means the only one. As we have seen, the prison also serves as an effective means of incapacitation, securely excluding offenders from society, sometimes for very long periods, and containing those individuals who prove too troublesome for other institutions or communities. Unlike lesser penalties, it does not require much in the way of co-operation from the offender, so can deal with recalcitrant individuals, by force if necessary. In the absence of the generalized use of capital punishment, forced exile, or transportation, the prison thus forms the ultimate penalty for most modern penal systems, providing a compelling and forceful sanction of last resort. Most importantly, the prison provides a way of punishing people—of subjecting them to hard treatment, inflicting pain, doing them harm—which is largely compatible with modern sensibilities and conventional restraints upon open, physical violence. In an era when corporal punishment has become uncivilized, and open violence unconscionable, the prison supplies a subtle, situational form of violence against the person which enables retribution to be inflicted in a way which is sufficiently discreet and 'deniable' to be culturally acceptable to most of the population. Despite occasional suggestions that imprisonment is becoming too lenient—a view which is rarely shared by informed sources—it is widely accepted that the prison succeeds very well in imposing real hardship, serious deprivation, and personal suffering upon most offenders who are sent there.

In terms of penological objectives then, the prison supports a range of them, and is 'functional' or 'successful' with respect to some, less so with respect to others. Nor is there any need to argue that the prison's 'failures' are somehow 'useful'—as Foucault and others do. The fact that prison frequently reinforces criminality and helps produce recidivists is not a 'useful' consequence desired by the authorities, or part of some covert 'strategy'. It is a tolerated cost of pursuing other objectives such as retribution, incapacitation, and exclusion, and is accepted in the same reluctant way that governments absorb the high financial costs entailed in the frequent use of imprisonment. So long as such costs appear to the authorities—and to the public—to be outweighed by the desirability of imprisoning offenders (and this desire has become an established element within public beliefs, institutional frameworks, and social traditions) then the prison remains a 'functional' institution—and neither a puzzle nor an anachronism.

Consequently—and this is my point—if one wishes to understand and evaluate the prison as an institution—and the same arguments apply to the fine, probation, community service, and the rest—it does little good to do so on a single plane or in relation to a single value. Instead one must think of it as a complex institution and evaluate it accordingly, recognizing the range of its penal and social functions and the nature of its social support. Nor does this mean that one must abandon a critical approach because the prison is less irrational than it at first seems. One can challenge the institution by showing that the control of troublesome individuals can be undertaken in more humane and positive settings, that exclusion is anyway an unacceptable goal in a caring society, or that many prisoners are no real danger to the public and could, under certain conditions, be tolerated in the community. One could endeavour to expose the real psychological violence which exists behind the scenes of even the best prisons and argue that such violence is as retrograde and uncivilized in its way as the corporal and capital punishments which the prison replaced. Equally one could challenge the cost of prison as a means of expressing punitive sentiments and exacting retribution against offenders and show ways in which funds and resources could be put to better use—for instance in compensating victims, in crime-prevention schemes, or in basic educational and social provision. In effect, the more one's understanding of an institution begins to capture its nuances and complexities—and its positive effects together with its negative ones—the more thoroughgoing, informed, and incisive will be the critique that one can mount.

Thinking of punishment as a social institution should change not only our mode of understanding penality but also our normative thinking about it. It should lead us to judge punishment according to a wider range of criteria and to bring to bear the kinds of demands and expectations which we customarily apply to social institutions. To say this is not to suggest that there is some universal normative approach which we always adopt towards social institutions —different institutions have distinctive functions and characteristics and give rise to diverse forms of evaluation. But, nevertheless, when we think of 'the family' or 'the law', 'the government' or 'the economy', and subject them to normative judgment, we do so in ways which are considerably more complex than our thinking about punishment tends to be. In none of these cases do we think it proper to judge these institutions according to purely instrumental criteria, nor do we suppose that they should serve a single end, or affect only a particular sector of the population. Instead, they are all commonly viewed as if they were 'total social facts', the character of which is in some way constitutive of society's identity and character.

Perhaps the best example of this is the kind of thinking which emerges whenever a democratic society deliberately undertakes to reform its major social institutions by means of a written constitution. People do not ask of such a constitution merely that it should 'work' with some degree of efficiency—although that is itself crucial. They also demand that its moral, political, economic, and cultural significance be considered, and that these wider ramifications be made to conform, as far as is possible, to deeply held conceptions of what kind of people they are, how they wish to be governed, and what kind of society they wish to create. The implication of my arguments is that punishment should be considered in the same kind of way and in the same kind of depth as other social institutions. In other words, we need an enriched form of penological thinking which considers penality as an institution through which society defines and expresses itself at the same time and through the same means that it exercises power over deviants.

To think of punishment in this way is to question the narrow, instrumental self-description that modern penal institutions generally adopt (and which technical penology tends to repeat) and instead to suggest a more socially conscious and morally charged perception of penal affairs. By demonstrating the deeply social nature of legal punishment, and revealing the values and commitments which are embodied within its practices, the sociology of punishment tends to undermine any attempt to compartmentalize 'the penal question' or to deal with it in a purely administrative way. By showing how penal issues pull together many diverse currents of political and cultural life, such an approach helps to reconstitute a more comprehensive social awareness and to counter the tendency of modern institutions to fragment consciousness and narrow perception. It gives a sense of the sociality of punishment—of the extended significance and depth of stored-up meanings which exist beneath the surface of this specialist legal institution.

It is unlikely that this perception, however widely shared, could lead to any willingness or capacity on the part of the public to become more involved in the administration of punishment, or to take more responsibility for its forms (though community action groups which seek to promote such aims are in fact emerging in Britain and North America). Punishment may be a social institution but the power to punish offenders is presently monopolized by the state and directed by state-employed professionals. But nevertheless it is possible that such a vision may arm the critics of state policies and aid them in their efforts to reform state practices and institutional procedures. In particular it could give strength to an argument (which is occasionally heard but rarely taken seriously) to the effect that the institutions of punishment should be seen—and should see themselves—as institutions for the expression of social values, sensibility, and morality, rather than as instrumental means to a penological end. An awareness of penality's wider significance makes it easier to argue that the pursuit of values such as justice, tolerance, decency, humanity, and civility should be part of any penal institution's self-consciousness—an intrinsic and constitutive aspect of its role—rather than a diversion from its 'real' goals or an inhibition on its capacity to be 'effective'.

Given a measure of rethinking and reorganization along these lines, modern societies might begin to expect less in the way of 'results' from penal policy. Indeed, they might be encouraged to treat it instead as a form of social policy which should, where possible, be minimized. For despite the utilitarian myth of the Enlightenment that punishment can be made to produce positive and useful results—a myth which was taken up and renewed by the rehabilitative ideologies of the twentieth century—punishment is better viewed in terms of tragedy than of comedy. It is, as we have seen, an institution which has a last-resort necessity in any society—authority must in the end be sanctioned if it is to be authoritative, and offenders who are sufficiently dangerous or recalcitrant must be dealt with forcibly in some degree. But however necessary it sometimes is, and however useful in certain respects, punishment is always beset by irresolvable tensions. However well it is organized, and however humanely administered, punishment is inescapably marked by moral contradiction and unwanted irony—as when it seeks to uphold freedom by means of its deprivation, or condemns private violence using a violence which is publicly authorized. Despite the claims of reforming enthusiasts, the interests of state, society, victim, and offender can never be 'harmonized', whether by rehabilitation or anything else. The infliction of punishment by a state upon its citizens bears the character of a civil war in miniature—it depicts a society engaged in a struggle with itself. And though this may sometimes be necessary, it is never anything other than a necessary evil.

This tragic quality of punishment, it seems to me, is made more apparent when we approach the issue in a broader, sociological way. Instead of appearing to glorify punishment as a functionally important social institution, the sociology of punishment may be taken to suggest its limitations and point to alternative ways of organizing its tasks. Above all, it teaches that a policy which intends to promote disciplined conduct and social control will concentrate not upon punishing offenders but upon socializing and integrating young citizens—a work of social justice and moral education rather than penal policy. And to the extent that punishment is deemed unavoidable, it should be viewed as a morally expressive undertaking rather than a purely instrumental one.

Bibliography

ADAMSON, C., 'Punishment After Slavery: Southern State Penal Systems, 1865–1890', *Social Problems*, 30 (1983), 555–69.

—— 'Toward a Marxian Penology: Captive Criminal Populations as Economic Threats and Resources', *Social Problems*, 31 (1984), 435–58.

ALEXANDER, F., and STAUB, J., *The Criminal, the Judge and the Public: A Psychological Analysis* (London, 1931).

ALLEN, F., *The Decline of the Rehabilitative Ideal* (New Haven, 1981).

ALLEN, H., *Justice Imbalanced: Gender, Psychiatry and Judicial Decisions* (Milton Keynes, 1987).

American Friends Service Committee, *Struggle for Justice* (Philadelphia, 1971).

Amnesty International, *United States of America: The Death Penalty* (London, 1987).

—— *When the State Kills: The Death Penalty v. Human Rights* (London, 1989).

ANDERSON, J., *Studies in Empirical Philosophy* (Sydney, 1962).

ARIES, P., *Centuries of Childhood: A Social History of Family Life* (New York, 1965).

AYERS, E. L., *Vengeance and Justice: Crime and Punishment in the Nineteenth Century American South* (New York, 1984).

BARNES, H. E., *The Evolution of Penology in Pennsylvania* (Montclair, NJ, 1968).

BARTHES, R., *Mythologies* (London, 1973).

BEAN, P., *Punishment* (Oxford, 1981).

BEATTIE, J. M., *Crime and the Courts in England, 1660–1800* (Princeton, 1986).

—— 'Violence and Society in Early Modern England', in A. Doob and E. Greenspan (eds.), *Perspectives in Criminal Law* (Aurora, 1984).

BEAUMONT, G. DE, and TOCQUEVILLE, A. DE, *On the Penitentiary System in the United States* (Carbondale, 1964; orig. pub. Philadelphia, 1833).

BEIER, A. L., *Masterless Men: The Vagrancy Problem in Britain, 1560–1640* (London, 1985).

BENDER, J., *Imagining the Penitentiary: Fiction and the Architecture of Mind in Eighteenth Century England* (Chicago, 1987).

BENTHAM, J., *An Introduction to the Principles of Morals and Legislation*, ed. by H. L. A. Hart and J. H. Burns (London, 1970; orig. pub. London, 1789).

BERKSON, L. C., *The Concept of Cruel and Unusual Punishment* (Lexington, Mass., 1975).

BEYLEVELD, D., *A Bibliography on General Deterrence Research* (Westmead, 1980).

BIANCHI, H., and VAN SWAANINGEN, R. (eds.), *Abolitionism: Towards a Non-Repressive Approach to Crime* (Amsterdam, 1986).

BLUMBERG, A., *Criminal Justice* (Chicago, 1967).

BOTTOMS, A. E., 'Neglected Features of Contemporary Penal Systems' in D. Garland and P. Young (eds.), *The Power to Punish* (London, 1983).

—— and MCWILLIAMS, W., 'A Non-Treatment Paradigm for Probation Practice', *British Journal of Social Work*, 9 (1979), 159–202.

—— and PRESTON, R. H. (eds.), *The Coming Penal Crisis* (Edinburgh, 1980).

BOURDIEU, P., *Distinction: A Social Critique of the Judgement of Taste* (London, 1985).

Box, S., *Recession, Crime and Punishment* (London, 1987).

BREWER, J. and STYLES, J. (eds.), *An Ungovernable People: The English and their Law in the Seventeenth and Eighteenth Centuries* (New Brunswick, NJ, 1980).

BRODY, S. R., 'The Effectiveness of Sentencing', *Home Office Research Unit Study*, 35 (London, 1976).

BROWN, R., 'The Idea of Imprisonment', *The Times Literary Supplement* (16 June 1978).

BURKE, K., *A Rhetoric of Motives* (Berkeley, 1969).

——— *Language as Symbolic Action: Essays on Life, Literature and Method* (Berkeley, 1966).

CAIN, M., and HUNT, A. (eds.), *Marx and Engels on Law* (London, 1979).

CANETTI, E., *Crowds and Power* (Harmondsworth, 1973).

CARLEN, P., *Magistrates' Justice* (Oxford, 1976).

——— *Women's Imprisonment: A Study in Social Control* (London, 1983).

——— and WORRALL, A. (eds.), *Gender, Crime and Justice* (Milton Keynes, 1987).

CARRITHERS, M., COLLINS, S., and LUKES, S. (eds.), *Concept of the Person: Anthropology, Philosophy, History* (Cambridge, 1986).

CASTEL, F., CASTEL, R., and LOVELL, A., *The Psychiatric Society* (New York, 1982).

CASTEL, R., *The Regulation of Madness: The Origins of Incarceration in France* (Berkeley, 1988).

CHAMBLISS, W. J., 'Functional and Conflict Theories of Crime: The Heritage of Émile Durkheim and Karl Marx', in id. and M. Mankoff (eds.), *Whose Law? What Order?* (New York, 1976).

——— and MANKOFF, M. (eds.), *Whose Law? What Order?* (New York, 1976).

CHRISTIE, N., 'Conflicts as Property', *The British Journal of Criminology*, 17 (1977), 1–15.

——— *Limits to Pain* (Oxford, 1982).

CLEMMER, D., *The Prison Community* (New York, 1940).

CLIFFORD, J. and MARCUS, G. E. (eds.), *Writing Culture: The Poetics and Politics of Ethnography* (Berkeley, 1986).

CLOWARD, R., *et al.*, *Theoretical Studies in Social Organization of the Prison* (New York, 1960).

COHEN, G. A., *Karl Marx's Theory of History: A Defence* (Princeton, 1978).

COHEN, S., 'The Punitive City: Notes on the Dispersal of Social Control', *Contemporary Crises*, 3 (1979), 339–63.

——— *Visions of Social Control: Crime, Punishment and Classification* (Cambridge, 1985).

——— and SCULL, A. (eds.), *Social Control and the State* (Oxford, 1983).

——— and TAYLOR, L., *Psychological Survival: The Experience of Long-Term Imprisonment* (Harmondsworth, 1972).

——— and YOUNG, J. (eds.), *The Manufacture of News: Deviance, Social Problems and the Media* (London, 1981).

CONLEY, J., 'Prisons, Production and Profit: Reconsidering the Importance of Prison Industries', *The Journal of Social History*, 14 (1981), 257–75.

CRESSEY, D. R., 'Hypotheses in the Sociology of Punishment', *Sociology and Social Research*, 39 (1955), 394–400.

CULLEN, F. T., and GILBERT, K. E., *Re-affirming Rehabilitation* (Cincinatti, 1982).

CURRIE, E., *Confronting Crime: An American Challenge* (New York, 1985).

DAHRENDORF, R., *Law and Order* (London, 1985).

DAVIS, J., 'The London Garotting Panic of 1862: A Moral Panic and the Creation of a Criminal Class in Mid-Victorian England', in V. A. C. Gatrell *et al.* (eds.), *Crime and the Law* (London, 1980).

DE FOLTER, R., 'On the Methodological Foundation of the Abolitionist Approach to the Criminal Justice System. A Comparison of the Ideas of Hulsman, Mathiesen and Foucault', *Contemporary Crises*, 10 (1986), 39–62.

DELEUZE, G., and GUATTARI, F., *Anti-Oedipus: Capitalism and Schizophrenia* (New York, 1977).

DICKENS, P., McCONVILLE, S., and FAIRWEATHER, L. (eds.), *Penal Policy and Prison Architecture* (Chichester, 1978).

DIIULIO, J. J., *Governing Prisons: A Comparative Study of Correctional Management* (New York, 1987).

DONZELOT, J., *The Policing of Families: Welfare Versus the State* (London, 1980).

DOSTOEVSKY, F. M., *The House of the Dead* (Harmondsworth, 1985; orig. pub. 1860).

DOUGLAS, M., *How Institutions Think* (Syracuse, New York, 1986).

——*Natural Symbols: Explorations in Cosmology* (Harmondsworth, 1973).

——*Purity and Danger: An Analysis of the Concepts of Pollution and Taboo* (London, 1966).

DOWNES, D., 'Abolition: Possibilities and Pitfalls', in A. E. Bottoms and R. H. Preston (eds.), *The Coming Penal Crisis* (Edinburgh, 1980).

——*Contrasts in Tolerance: Post-War Penal Policy in The Netherlands and England and Wales* (Oxford, 1988).

DREYFUS, H. L., and RABINOW, P., *Michel Foucault: Beyond Structuralism and Hermeneutics* (2nd edn., Chicago, 1983).

DUFF, A., *Trials and Punishments* (Cambridge, 1986).

DUMM, T. L., *Democracy and Punishment: Disciplinary Origins of the United States* (Madison, 1987).

DURKHEIM, É., *L'Éducation morale* (Paris, 1925).

——*Moral Education* (New York, 1973).

——*The Division of Labor in Society*, trans. G. Simpson (New York, 1933).

——*The Division of Labour in Society*, trans. W. D. Halls (London, 1984).

——'The Dualism of Human Nature and its Social Conditions', in K. H. Wolff (ed.), *Essays on Sociology and Philosophy* (New York, 1964).

——*The Elementary Forms of the Religious Life* (London, 1976).

——*The Rules of Sociological Method* (New York, 1938).

——'Two Laws of Penal Evolution', orig. appeared in *Année sociologique*, 4 (1902) 65–95. Repr. as ch. 4, 'The Evolution of Punishment', in S. Lukes and A. Scull (eds.), *Durkheim and the Law* (Oxford, 1983).

——and MAUSS, M., *Primitive Classifications* (Chicago, 1963).

EHRENZWEIG, A. A., *Psychoanalytic Jurisprudence: On Ethics, Aesthetics and 'Law'* (Leiden, 1971).

EKIRCH, A. R., *Bound for America: The Transportation of British Convicts to the Colonies, 1718–1775* (Oxford, 1987).

ELIAS, N., *The Civilizing Process, i. The History of Manners* (Oxford, 1978; orig. pub. 1939).

——*The Civilizing Process, ii. State Formation and Civilization* (Oxford, 1982; orig. pub. 1939). (Published in the USA under the title *Power and Civility*.)

EMSLEY, C., *Crime and Society in England 1750–1900* (London, 1987).

ERICSON, R. V., and BARANEK, P. M., *The Ordering of Justice* (Toronto, 1982).

————and CHAN, J. B. L., *Negotiating Control: A Study of News Sources* (Toronto, 1989).

————and —— *Visualizing Deviance: A Study of News Organisation* (Toronto, 1987).

ERIKSON, K., *Wayward Puritans: A Study in the Sociology of Deviance* (New York, 1966).

EVANS, R., *The Fabrication of Virtue: English Prison Architecture, 1750–1840* (Cambridge, 1982).

FALLER, L., *Turned to Account: The Forms and Functions of Criminal Biography in Late Seventeenth and Early Eighteenth Century England* (Cambridge, 1987).

FEELEY, M., *The Process is the Punishment* (Beverly Hills, 1979).

FEINBERG, J., *Doing and Deserving* (Princeton, 1970).

—— and GROSS, H., *Philosophy of Law* (Enrico, Calif., 1975).

FINE, B., KINSEY, R., LEA, J., PICCIOTTO, S., and Young, J. (eds.), *Capitalism and the Rule of Law: From Deviancy Theory to Marxism* (London, 1979).

FOUCAULT, M., *Discipline and Punish: The Birth of the Prison* (London, 1977).

—— *Madness and Civilization: A History of Insanity in the Age of Reason* (New York, 1965).

—— 'On Attica: An Interview', *Telos*, 19 (1974), 154–61.

—— *Power/Knowledge: Selected Interviews and Other Writings 1972–1977*, ed. C. Gordon (New York, 1980).

—— *The Archaeology of Knowledge* (London, 1972).

—— *The Birth of the Clinic: An Archaeology of Medical Perception* (London, 1973).

—— *The History of Sexuality, i. An Introduction* (New York, 1978).

—— *The History of Sexuality, ii. The Use of Pleasure* (New York, 1986).

—— *The Order of Things: An Archaeology of the Human Sciences* (London, 1970).

—— 'The Subject and Power' in H. L. Dreyfus and P. Rabinow, *Michel Foucault: Beyond Structuralism and Hermeneutics* (Chicago, 1983), 208–26.

FREEDMAN, E., *Their Sisters' Keepers: Women's Prison Reform in America, 1830–1930* (Ann Arbor, 1981).

FREIBERG, A., 'Reconceptualizing Sanctions', *Criminology*, 25 (1987), 223–55.

FREUD, S., *Civilization and Its Discontents* (New York, 1962; orig. pub. London, 1930).

—— 'Criminality from a Sense of Guilt', in 'Some Character-Types Met with in Psycho-Analytical Work' in id., *Collected Papers*, iv, ed. by J. Riviere (New York, 1959; 1st pub. in *Imago*, 4 (1915–16)).

—— 'The Economic Problem of Masochism' in id., *On Metapsychology*, vol. xi of the Pelican Freud Library (Harmondsworth, 1984).

GARDNER, G., 'The Emergence of the New York State Prison System: A Critique of the Rusche and Kirchheimer Model', *Crime and Social Justice*, 29 (1987), 88–109.

GARFINKEL, H., 'Conditions of Successful Degradation Ceremonies', *The American Journal of Sociology*, 61 (1956), 420–4.

GARLAND, D., 'British Criminology Before 1935', *The British Journal of Criminology*, 28 (1988), 131–47.

—— 'Durkheim's Theory of Punishment: A Critique', in id. and P. Young (eds.), *The Power to Punish* (London, 1983).

—— 'Philosophical Argument and Ideological Effect', *Contemporary Crises*, 7 (1983), 79–85.

—— 'Politics and Policy in Criminological Discourse: A Study of Tendentious Reasoning and Rhetoric', *International Journal of the Sociology of Law*, 13 (1985), 1–33.

—— *Punishment and Welfare: A History of Penal Strategies* (Aldershot, 1985).

—— 'The Criminal and His Science: A Critical Account of the Formation of Criminology at the End of the Nineteenth Century', *The British Journal of Criminology*, 25 (1985), 109–37.

—— 'The Punitive Mentality: Its Socio-Historical Development and Decline', *Contemporary Crises*, 10 (1986), 305–20.

—— and YOUNG, P. (eds.), *The Power to Punish: Contemporary Penality and Social Analysis* (London, 1983).

—— and YOUNG, P., 'Towards a Social Analysis of Penality', in id. (eds.), *The Power to Punish* (London, 1983).

GASS, W., 'Painting as an Art', *New York Review of Books*, 35: 15 (13 Oct. 1988).

GATRELL, V. A. C., 'Crime, Authority and the Policeman-State, 1750–1950', in F. M. L. Thompson (ed.), *The Cambridge Social History of Britain, 1750–1950*, 3 vols. (Cambridge, forthcoming).

—— 'The Decline of Theft and Violence in Victorian and Edwardian England', in id. *et al.* (eds.), *Crime and the Law* (London, 1980).

—— LENMAN, B., and PARKER, G., *Crime and the Law: The Social History of Crime in Western Europe since 1500* (London, 1980).

GAY, P., *Freud for Historians* (New York, 1985).

GEERTZ, C., 'Centers, Kings and Charisma: Reflections on the Symbolics of Power', in id., *Local Knowledge: Further Essays in Interpretive Anthropology* (New York, 1983).

—— 'Deep Play: Notes on the Balinese Cockfight', *The Interpretation of Cultures* (New York, 1973).

—— *Local Knowledge: Further Essays in Interpretive Anthropology* (New York, 1983).

—— *Negara: The Theatre State in Nineteenth Century Bali* (Princeton, 1980).

—— 'Stir Crazy', *The New York Review of Books* (26 Jan. 1978).

—— 'The Growth of Culture and the Evolution of Mind', in id., *The Interpretation of Cultures* (New York, 1973).

—— 'The Impact of the Concept of Culture on the Concept of Man', in id., *The Interpretation of Cultures* (New York, 1973).

—— *The Interpretation of Cultures* (New York, 1973).

—— 'Thick Description: Toward an Interpretive Theory of Culture', in id., *The Interpretation of Cultures* (New York, 1973).

—— *Works and Lives: The Anthropologist as Author* (Stanford, 1988).

GERTH, H. H., and MILLS, C. WRIGHT (eds.), *From Max Weber* (London, 1948).

GIDDENS, A., *Durkheim* (Hassocks, Sussex, 1978).

—— *The Constitution of Society* (Oxford, 1984).

—— *The Nation State and Violence*, vol. ii of *A Contemporary Critique of Historical Materialism* (Oxford, 1985).

GILLIS, J., *Youth and History: Tradition and Change in European Age Relations* (New York, 1974).

GOFFMAN, E., *Asylums: Essays on the Social Situation of Mental Patients and Other Inmates* (Garden City, NY, 1961).

GRABOWSKY, P. N., 'Theory and Research on Variations in Penal Severity', *British Journal of Law and Society*, 5 (1978), 103–14.

GREEN, T. A., *Verdict According to Conscience: Perspectives on the English Criminal Trial Jury, 1200–1800* (Chicago, 1985).

GREENWOOD, P., *Selective Incapacitation* (Santa Monica, 1982).

GURR, T. R., 'Historical Trends in Violent Crime: A Critical Review of the Evidence', in N. Tonry and N. Morris (eds.), *Crime and Justice*, iii (Chicago, 1981), 295–353.

GURVITCH, G., 'Social Control', in id. and W. Moore (eds.), *Twentieth Century Sociology* (New York, 1945).

GUSFIELD, J., *The Culture of Public Problems: Drinking Driving and the Symbolic Order* (Chicago, 1981).

Home Office, *Punishment, Custody and the Community*, Cmnd. 424 (London, 1988).

HACKING, I., 'Making Up People', in T. C. Heller *et al.* (eds.), *Reconstructing Individualism* (Stanford, 1986).

HALL, S., CRITCHER, C., JEFFERSON, T., CLARKE, J., and ROBERTS, B., *Policing the Crisis: Mugging, the State, and Law and Order* (London, 1978).

HARDING, C., and IRELAND, R. W., *Punishment: Rhetoric, Rule and Practice* (London, 1989).

HARRÈ, R. (ed.), *The Social Construction of Emotions* (Oxford, 1986).

HASKELL, T. L., 'Capitalism and the Origins of Humanitarian Sensibility', *The American Historical Review*, 90 (1985), 339–61, 547–66.

HAWKINS, G., and ZIMRING, F., *Deterrence: The Legal Threat in Crime Control* (Chicago, 1973).

HAY, D., 'Property, Authority and the Criminal Law', in id. *et al.*, *Albion's Fatal Tree* (Harmondsworth, 1975).

—— LINEBAUGH, P., RULE, J. G., THOMPSON, E. P., and WINSLOW, C., *Albion's Fatal Tree: Crime and Society in Eighteenth Century England* (Harmondsworth, 1975).

HELLER, T. C., SOSNA, M., and WELLBERG, D. E. (eds.), *Reconstructing Individualism: Autonomy, Individuality, and the Self in Western Thought* (Stanford, 1986).

HERRUP, C., 'Law and Morality in Seventeenth Century England', *Past and Present*, 106 (1985), 102–23.

HIMMELFARB, G., 'The Haunted House of Jeremy Bentham', in id., *Victorian Minds* (New York, 1968).

HIRSCH, A. VON, *Doing Justice: The Choice of Punishments* (New York, 1976).

HIRST, P. Q., *Law, Socialism and Democracy* (London, 1986).

—— *On Law and Ideology* (London, 1979).

—— 'Power/Knowledge: Constructed Space and the Subject'. in R. Fardon (ed.), *Power and Knowledge: Anthropological and Sociological Approaches* (Edinburgh, 1985).

—— and WOOLLEY, P., *Social Relations and Human Attributes* (London, 1982).

HOUGH, M., and LEWIS, H., 'Penal Hawks and Penal Doves: Attitudes to Punishment in the British Crime Survey', in Home Office Research and Planning Unit, *Research Bulletin*, 21 (1986).

HOWARD, J., *An Account of the Principal Lazarettos of Europe* (Montclair, NJ, 1973; orig. pub. Warrington, 1789).

—— *The State of the Prisons in England and Wales* (Montclair, NJ, 1973; orig. pub. Warrington, 1777).

HUGHES, R., *The Fatal Shore: A History of the Transportation of Convicts to Australia, 1787–1868* (London, 1987).

HULSMAN, L., 'Critical Criminology and the Concept of Crime', *Contemporary Crises*, 10 (1986), 63–80.

—— and BERNAT DE CELIS, J., *Peines perdues: le système pénal en question* (Paris, 1982).

IGNATIEFF, M., *A Just Measure of Pain: The Penitentiary in the Industrial Revolution* (London, 1978).

—— 'Class Interests and the Penitentiary: A Reply to Rothman', *The Canadian Criminology Forum*, 5 (1982), p. 66.

—— 'State, Civil Society and Total Institutions: A Critique of Recent Histories of Punishment', in S. Cohen and A. Scull (eds.), *Social Control and the State* (Oxford, 1983).

INNES, J., 'Prisons for the Poor: English Bridewells, 1550–1800', in F. Snyder and D. Hay (eds.), *Labour, Law and Crime: An Historical Perspective* (London, 1987).

IRELAND, R. W., 'Theory and Practice within the Medieval English Prison', *The American Journal of Legal History*, 31 (1987), 56–67.

JACOBS, J. B., *New Perspectives on Prisons and Imprisonment* (Ithaca, NY, 1983).

—— *Stateville: The Penitentiary in Mass Society* (Chicago, 1977).

JACOBY, S., *Wild Justice: The Evolution of Revenge* (London, 1985).

JAY, M., *The Dialectical Imagination* (London, 1973).

JOHNSTONE, N., *The Human Cage: A Brief History of Prison Architecture* (New York, 1973).

JONES, G. STEDMAN, *Languages of Class* (Cambridge, 1982).

KADISH, S. (ed.), *Encyclopedia of Crime and Justice*, 4 vols. (New York, 1983).

KAFKA, F., *In the Penal Settlement* (London, 1973).

KENNEDY, M., 'Beyond Incrimination: Some Neglected Aspects of the Theory of Punishment', in W. J. Chambliss and M. Mankoff (eds.), *Whose Law? What Order?* (New York, 1976).

KING, P. J. R., 'Decision-Makers and Decision-Making in the English Criminal Law, 1750–1800', *Historical Journal*, 27 (1984), 25–58.

KING, R., and MORGAN, R., *The Future of the Prison System* (Aldershot, 1980).

KITTRIE, N., *The Right to be Different* (Baltimore, 1972).

KRIEKEN, R. VAN, 'Violence, Self-Discipline and Modernity: Beyond the Civilizing Process', *The Sociological Review*, 37 (1989), 193–218.

LACEY, N., *State Punishment: Political Principles and Community Values* (London, 1988).

LANGBEIN, J., 'Albion's Fatal Flaws', *Past and Present*, 98 (1983), 96–120.

—— *Torture and the Law of Proof* (Chicago, 1976).

LASCH, C., 'Historical Sociology and the Myth of Maturity: Norbert Elias' Very Simple Formula', *Theory and Society*, 14 (1985), 705–20.

LEA, J., and YOUNG, J., *What is to be Done About Law and Order?* (Harmondsworth, 1984).

LENMAN, B., and PARKER, G., 'The State, the Community, and the Criminal Law in Early Modern Europe', in V. A. C. Gatrell *et al.*, *Crime and the Law* (London, 1980).

LEWIS, O. F., *The Development of American Prisons and Prison Customs, 1776–1845* (Albany, 1922).

LEWIS, W. D., *From Newgate to Dannemora: The Rise of the Penitentiary in New York, 1796–1848* (Ithaca, NY, 1965).

LOFLAND, J., 'The Dramaturgy of State Executions', in H. Bleakley and J. Lofland, *State Executions Viewed Historically and Sociologically* (Montclair, NJ, 1977).

LOWMAN, J., MENZIES, R. J., and PALYS, T. S. (eds.), *Transcarceration: Essays in the Sociology of Social Control* (Aldershot, 1987).

LUCAS, J. R., *On Justice* (Oxford, 1980).

LUKES, S., *Émile Durkheim: His Life and Work* (London, 1973).

—— and SCULL, A. (eds.), *Durkheim and the Law* (Oxford, 1983).

MCCONVILLE, S., *A History of English Prison Administration, i. 1750–1877* (London, 1981).

MACFARLANE, A., *The Justice and the Mare's Ale: Law and Disorder in Seventeenth Century England* (Cambridge, 1981).

MCGOWAN, R., 'The Image of Justice and Reform of the Criminal Law in Early Nineteenth Century England', *The Buffalo Law Review*, 32 (1983), 89–125.

MACINTYRE, A., *After Virtue* (Notre Dame, Indiana, 1981).

MCKELVEY, B., *American Prisons: A History of Good Intentions* (Montclair, NJ, 1977).

MCMANNERS, J., *Death and the Enlightenment: Changing Attitudes to Death among Christians and Unbelievers in Eighteenth Century France* (Oxford, 1981).

MALCOLMSON, R. W., *Popular Recreations in English Society, 1700–1850* (Cambridge, 1973).

MALINOWSKI, B., *Argonauts of the Western Pacific* (London, 1922).
—— *Crime and Custom in Savage Society* (Totowa, NJ, 1966; orig. pub. London, 1926).
MANNHEIM, H., *The Dilemma of Penal Reform* (London, 1939).
MARTINSON, R., 'What Works?—Questions and Answers about Prison Reform', *The Public Interest*, 35 (1974), 22–54.
MARX, K., *Capital*, i (London, 1976; orig. German edn. pub. 1867).
MASUR, L., *Rites of Execution: Capital Punishment and the Transformation of American Culture, 1776–1865* (New York, 1989).
MATHIESEN, T., 'The Future of Control Systems—The Case of Norway', in D. Garland and P. Young (eds.), *The Power to Punish* (London, 1983).
—— *The Politics of Abolition* (London, 1974).
MATZA, D., *Delinquency and Drift* (New York, 1964).
MAUSS, M., 'A Category of the Human Mind: The Notion of the Person, the Notion of Self', in id., *Sociology and Psychology* (London, 1979; orig. pub. London, 1938).
—— *The Gift: Forms and Functions of Exchange in Archaic Societies* (New York, 1967; orig. French edn., 1925).
MEAD, G. H., 'The Psychology of Punitive Justice', *American Journal of Sociology*, 23 (1918), 577–602.
MELOSSI, D., 'The Penal Question in *Capital*', *Crime and Social Justice*, 5 (1976). Repr. in T. Platt and P. Takagi (eds.), *Punishment and Penal Discipline* (Berkeley, Ca., 1980).
—— and PAVARINI, M., *The Prison and the Factory: The Origins of the Penitentiary System* (London, 1981).
MENNINGER, K., *The Crime of Punishment* (New York, 1968).
MESSINGER, S. L., BERECOCHEA, J. E., RAUMA, D., and BERK, R. A., 'The Foundations of Parole in California', in *Law and Society Review*, 19 (1985), 69–106.
MILLER, P., and ROSE, N. (eds.), *The Power of Psychiatry* (Cambridge, 1986).
MINSON, J., *The Genealogy of Morals: Nietzsche, Foucault, Donzelot and the Eccentricity of Ethics* (London, 1985).
MONTESQUIEU, BARON DE, *The Spirit of the Laws* (Edinburgh, 1762; orig. pub. 1748).
MORRIS, A. M., *Women, Crime and Criminal Justice* (Oxford, 1987).
MORRIS, M., and PATTON, P., *Michel Foucault: Power, Truth, Strategy* (Sydney, 1979).
MORRIS, N., *The Future of Imprisonment* (Chicago, 1974).
MORRIS, T., and MORRIS, P., *Pentonville* (London, 1963).
NEWMAN, G., *Just and Painful: A Case for the Corporal Punishment of Criminals* (New York, 1985).
NIETZSCHE, F., *The Genealogy of Morals* (in *The Birth of Tragedy and the Genealogy of Morals*) (New York, 1956; orig. German edn., 1887).
NYE, R. A., *Crime, Madness and Politics in Modern France: The Medical Concept of National Decline* (Princeton, 1984).
O'BRIEN, P., *The Promise of Punishment: Prisons in Nineteenth Century France* (Princeton, 1982).
PASHUKANIS, E. B., *Law and Marxism: A General Theory*, ed. C. Arthur (London, 1978; orig. Russian edn., 1924).
PATTON, P., 'Of Power and Prisons', in M. Morris and P. Patton, *Michel Foucault: Power, Truth, Strategy* (Sydney, 1979).
PERROT, M. (ed.), *L'Impossible Prison* (Paris, 1980).
PLATT, A. M., *The Child Savers: The Invention of Delinquency* (Chicago, 1977).
PLATT, T., and TAKAGI, P. (eds.), *Punishment and Penal Discipline* (Berkeley, Ca., 1980).

—— and —— 'Perspective and Overview' in id. (eds.), *Punishment and Penal Discipline* (Berkeley, Ca., 1980).

PLUMB, J. H., 'The New World of Children in Eighteenth Century England', *Past and Present*, 67 (1975).

POULANTZAS, N., *State, Power, Socialism* (London, 1978).

PUGH, R. B., *Imprisonment in Medieval England* (Cambridge, 1970).

RADZINOWICZ, L., *A History of English Criminal Law and its Administration from 1750* (London, 1948–86), 5 vols. (vol. v with R. Hood).

RANULF, S., *Moral Indignation and Middle Class Psychology* (New York, 1964).

RIEFF, P., *The Triumph of the Therapeutic: Uses of Faith After Freud* (Chicago, 1966).

ROCK, P., *A View from the Shadows: The Ministry of the Solicitor General of Canada and the Making of the Justice for Victims of Crime Initiative* (Oxford, 1986).

ROSE, N., *The Psychological Complex: Psychology, Politics and Society in England 1869–1939* (London, 1985).

ROTHMAN, D., *Conscience and Convenience: The Asylum and its Alternatives in Progressive America* (Boston, 1980).

—— 'Prisons: The Failure Model', *Nation*, 21 December 1974.

——*The Discovery of the Asylum: Social Order and Disorder in the New Republic* (Boston, 1971).

RUSCHE, G., 'Labor Market and Penal Sanction: Thoughts on the Sociology of Punishment' (orig. pub. 1933), translated and repr. in T. Platt and P. Takagi (eds.), *Punishment and Penal Discipline* (Berkeley, Ca., 1980).

—— and KIRCHHEIMER, O., *Punishment and Social Structure* (New York, 1968; orig. pub. New York, 1939).

RYAN, M., *The Acceptable Pressure Group: A Case-Study of the Howard League and R.A.P.* (Farnborough, 1978).

—— *The Politics of Penal Reform* (London, 1983).

SALEILLES, R., *The Individualization of Punishment* (London, 1913).

SARTRE, J.-P., *Saint Genet: Actor and Martyr* (London, 1988).

SCHAMA, S., *The Embarrassment of Riches: An Interpretation of Dutch Culture in the Golden Age* (London, 1987).

SCHATTENBURG, G., 'Social Control Functions of Mass Media Depictions of Crime', *Sociological Inquiry*, 51 (1981), 71–7.

SCHWARTZ, R. D., and MILLER, J. C., 'Legal Evolution and Societal Complexity', *American Journal of Sociology*, 70 (1964), 159–69.

SCULL, A., *Decarceration: Community Treatment and the Deviant—A Radical View* (Englewood Cliffs, NJ, 1977).

SELLIN, T., *Slavery and the Penal System* (New York, 1976).

SELZNICK, P., *The Moral Commonwealth*, unpub. MS (Feb. 1988).

SENNETT, R., and COBB, J., *The Hidden Injuries of Class* (New York, 1972).

SHARPE, J., *Crime in Early Modern England, 1550–1750* (London, 1984).

SHEARING, C., and STENNING, P., 'From the Panopticon to Disney World: The Development of Discipline', in A. Doob and E. Greenspan (eds.), *Perspectives in Criminal Law* (Aurora, 1984).

SHELEFF, L. S., 'From Restitutive Law to Repressive Law: Durkheim's *The Division of Labor in Society* Revisited', *Archives européenes de sociologie* (*European Journal of Sociology*), 16 (1975), 16–45.

—— *Ultimate Penalties: Capital Punishment, Life Imprisonment, Physical Torture* (Columbus, Ohio., 1987).

SHILS, E., *The Constitution of Society* (Chicago, 1982).

SIMON, J., 'Back to the Future: Newman on Corporal Punishment', *American Bar Foundation Research Journal* (1985), 927 ff.

SKOLNICK, J., *Justice Without Trial* (New York, 1966).

SMART, B., *Foucault, Marxism and Critique* (London, 1983).

SMART, C., *Women, Crime and Criminology* (London, 1976).

SMITH, A., *The Theory of Moral Sentiments* (Oxford, 1976; orig. pub. 1759).

SMITH, D., 'Norbert Elias—Established or Outsider', *Sociological Review*, 32 (1984), 367–89.

SMITH, J., and FRIED, S., *The Uses of the American Prison* (Lexington, Mass., 1974).

SMITH, R., *Trial by Medicine* (Edinburgh, 1981).

SOROKIN, P. A., *Sociocultural Dynamics*, ii (New York, 1937).

SPARKS, R. F., 'The Enforcement of Fines: The Process from Sentence to Committal', *The British Journal of Criminology*, 13 (1973), 92–107.

SPERBER, D., *Rethinking Symbolism* (Cambridge, 1975).

SPIERENBURG, P., 'From Amsterdam to Auburn: An Explanation for the Rise of the Prison in Seventeenth Century Holland and Nineteenth Century America', *The Journal of Social History*, 4 (1987).

—— (ed.), *The Emergence of Carceral Institutions: Prisons, Galleys and Lunatic Asylums, 1550–1900* (Rotterdam, 1984).

—— 'The Sociogenesis of Confinement and its Development in Early Modern Europe', in id. (ed.), *The Emergence of Carceral Institutions* (Rotterdam, 1984).

—— *The Spectacle of Suffering: Executions and the Evolution of Repression* (Cambridge, 1984).

SPITZER, S., 'Notes Toward a Theory of Punishment and Social Change', *Research in Law and Sociology*, 2 (1979), 207–29.

—— 'Punishment and Social Organisation: A Study of Durkheim's Theory of Evolution', *Law and Society Review*, 9 (1975), 613–37.

—— 'The Rationalization of Crime Control in Capitalist Society', in S. Cohen and A. Scull (eds.), *Social Control and the State* (Oxford, 1983).

—— and SCULL, A., 'Social Control in Historical Perspective' in D. Greenberg (ed.), *Corrections and Punishments* (Beverly Hills, Ca., 1977).

STONE, L., *The Family, Sex and Marriage in England, 1500–1800* (Harmondsworth, 1979).

—— *The Past and the Present Revisited* (London, 1987).

SUTHERLAND, E. H., *White Collar Crime* (New York, 1949).

—— and CRESSEY, D. R., *Criminology* (Philadelphia, 1970).

SUTTON, J., *Stubborn Children: Controlling Delinquency in the USA, 1640–1981* (Berkeley, 1989).

SYKES, G., *The Society of Captives* (Princeton, 1958).

TAYLOR, I., *Law and Order: Arguments for Socialism* (London, 1981).

—— WALTON, P. and YOUNG, J., *The New Criminology: For a Social Theory of Deviance* (London, 1975).

TAYLOR, N., 'The Awful Sublimity of the Victorian City: Its Aesthetic and Cultural Origins', in H. J. Dyos and M. Wolff (eds.), *The Victorian City: Images and Realities*, ii (London, 1973).

THOMAS, K., *Man and the Natural World: Changing Attitudes in England 1500–1800* (Harmondsworth, 1984).

—— *Religion and the Decline of Magic* (London, 1971).

THOMPSON, E. P., 'Time, Work Discipline and Industrial Capitalism', *Past and Present*, 38 (1967), 56–97.

—— *Whigs and Hunters: The Origins of the Black Act* (Harmondsworth, 1975).

TOMBS, R., 'Crime and the Security of the State: The "Dangerous Classes" and Insurrection in Nineteenth Century Paris', in V. A. C. Gatrell *et al.* (eds.), *Crime and the Law* (London, 1980).

TURNER, V., *The Ritual Process* (Ithaca, NY, 1977).

United Nations Social Defence Research Institute, *Prison Architecture* (London, 1975).

VEBLEN, T., *The Theory of the Leisure Class* (London, 1971; orig. pub. 1899).

WALKER, N., *Sentencing: Theory, Law and Practice* (London, 1985).

—— and HOUGH, M. (eds.), *Public Attitudes to Sentencing: Surveys from Five Countries* (Aldershot, 1988).

WALTERS, R. H., CHEYNE, J. A., and BANKS, R. K. (eds.), *Punishment* (Harmondsworth, 1972).

WEBB, R., and HARRIS, D., *Welfare, Power and Juvenile Justice* (London, 1987).

WEBB, S., and WEBB, B., *English Prisons Under Local Government* (London, 1922).

WEBER, M., *Economy and Society*, eds. G. Roth and C. Wittich, 2 vols. (Berkeley, Ca., 1978; orig. pub. 1920).

—— *The Protestant Ethic and the Spirit of Capitalism* (London, 1985; orig. German edn., 1905).

WHITE, H., *Metahistory: The Historical Imagination in Nineteenth Century Europe* (Baltimore, 1973).

—— *Tropics of Discourse: Essays in Cultural Criticism* (Baltimore, 1978).

WIENER, M. (ed.), *Humanitarianism or Control? A Symposium on Aspects of Nineteenth Century Social Reform in Britain and America*, *Rice University Studies*, 67 (1981), 1.

—— 'The March of Penal Progress?', *The Journal of British Studies*, 26 (1987), 83–96.

WILSON, J. Q., and KELLING, G., 'Broken Windows', *Atlantic Monthly* (Mar. 1982), 29–38.

WRIGHT, G., *Between the Guillotine and Liberty: Two Centuries of the Crime Problem in France* (New York, 1983).

WRIGHT, M., and GALAWAY, B. (eds.), *Mediation and Criminal Justice: Victims, Offenders and Community* (London, 1989).

YOUNG, P. J., *Punishment, Money and Legal Order* (Edinburgh, forthcoming).

YOUNG, W., 'Influences Upon the Use of Imprisonment: A Review of the Literature', *The Howard Journal*, 25 (1986), 125–36.

ZEMAN, T., 'Order, Crime and Punishment: The American Criminological Tradition', Ph.D. diss., University of California (Santa Cruz, June 1981).

ZILBOORG, G., *The Psychology of the Criminal Act and Punishment* (London, 1955).

ZIMRING, F. E., and HAWKINS, G., *Capital Punishment and the American Agenda* (Cambridge, 1986).

ZYSBERG, A., 'Galley and Hard Labor Convicts in France (1550–1800)', in P. Spierenburg (ed.), *The Emergence of Carceral Institutions* (Rotterdam, 1984).

Index